SKI & SNOWBOARD
AMERICA™

Pacific Northwest & British Columbia

Contact

Dear Readers:

Every effort was made to make this the most accurate, informative, and easy-to-use guidebook on the planet. Any comments, suggestions, and corrections regarding this guide are welcome and should be sent to:

Outside America™
c/o Editorial Dept.
300 West Main St., Ste. A
Charlottesville, VA 22903
editorial@outside-america.com
www.outside-america.com

We'd love to hear from you so we can make future editions and future guides even better.

Thanks and happy trails!

SKI & SNOWBOARD AMERICA™

Pacific Northwest & British Columbia

The Complete Guide to Downhill Skiing, Snowboarding, Heli-skiing, Cat-skiing, and the Greatest Winter Sports throughout British Columbia and the Pacific Northwest

by Santo Criscuolo

The Globe Pequot Press

Guilford, Connecticut

Published by
The Globe Pequot Press
P.O. Box 480
Guilford, CT 06437
www.globe-pequot.com

Produced by
Beachway Press Publishing, Inc.
300 West Main St., Ste A
Charlottesville, VA 22903
www.beachway.com

Editorial Assistance given by Sarah Torrey, Hee Jong Oh,
David Sarratt, Byrd Leavell III, Morgan Guyton, Meredith
Bosler, Lisa Gschwandtner

Cover Design by Beachway Press

Maps designed and produced by Beachway Press

Find Outside America™ at **www.outside-america.com**

*Cover Photo: Big air off the deep-powdered trails of Kimberley
Ski Resort in British Columbia. Photo by Karl Weatherly*

**Library of Congress Cataloguing-in-Publication Data
is available.**

ISBN: 0-7627-0844-1

Printed in the United States of America
First Edition/First Printing

Foreword

I've skied most of the resorts and many of the runs that Santo Criscuolo writes about. It's obvious to me that he has gathered all of this valuable information for you by personally skiing or boarding every run at every resort he writes about.

Choose your destination wisely by comparing what Santo has to say about each one of them. Then after you make your reservations, take this guide with you and follow his advice when you choose which runs to take. If you follow Santo's guide and all of the advice that he has to offer in this book, you will be guaranteed to get a lot more enjoyment out of your resort and lift ticket dollar.

I'm Warren Miller and as I've been saying for years, "If you don't visit one or more of these resorts this winter, you'll be one year older when you do."

Warren Miller

Acknowledgments

I love sports analogies and this one is my favorite: Michael Jordan is considered to be the greatest basketball player to ever lace up a pair of high-tops. He is smart, quick, graceful, and creative. Without a doubt he had all the right moves. But his peers and the experts all say that what made him better than anyone ever to play the game was how he affected his teammates. He inspired them to reach inside and be better basketball players. Though I don't play basketball, I have been lucky enough to be surrounded by several Michael Jordan's who have inspired me to be a better skier, writer, and human being.

My mother and stepfather deserve most of the credit for being patient enough to teach me how to ski. It is a gift that has shaped my life. Kristin Hamilton for her constant support and friendship. Teresa Navotny was the first person to believe I could be a writer. Sara Kim typed my first articles from my sloppy penmanship before I learned to type. (To this day she is the best copy editor I have ever had.) Andy Walker and Jim Steenburgh deserve special thanks for driving me to and from The Summit for ski school lessons every weekend for years while I slept in the car. And for following me under the ropes and into closed areas. Mike Walker provided almost as many rides and great deals on gear. Eric Carleson at Smith Sport Optics stuck with me through injury after injury. Ron Aikens taught me how to ski the bumps. Karl Weatherly made me look like a star in his photos. Ivan Agerton exceeded the speed limit to make sure we caught our flight home from Sun Valley. Thanks for risking a ticket and your neck to make the flight. Amy and Mark Poffenbarger contributed greatly on Silver Mountain, 49° North, and Mount Spokane. Brian Towey's insight into Mount Hood and Hood River, OR, was fabulous. Erin Hatvany at MindSpring saved my computer and two year's worth of work from a virus. Geoff Straight and Mike Watling of TLH Heliskiing hooked me up with four days of some of the best turns of my life. And without Scott Adams and his Beachway Press team, none of this would have been possible.

The following also deserve recognition for their assistance: John Gifford at Stevens Pass; Kelly Graham at Crystal Mountain Resort; Kathy and Richard Sharp from the Tatoosh Motel; Theolene Bakken at 49° North; Gene Landsmann at Mt. Ashland; Pat Nowack at Silver Mountain; Christopher Nicholson at Sun Peaks Resort; Mary Naylor at Ski Brundage; The Whistler

Resort Association; The Summit Lodge at Whistler Resort; Tiia Sumera at Mt. Bachelor; Cheryl van Wamelen at Grouse Mountain; Brian Lyall at Panorama Mountain; Blair Ireland at Big White Ski Resort; Muriel MacLeod at Fernie Alpine Resort; Matt Moesteller at Ski Louise LTD; Allison Girard at Mission Ridge; Gord Vizzutti at Silver Star Mountain; Anne Pigeon at Whitewater Ski and Winter Resort; Mandy Elvy at Mount Washington; Bill Mullane at Schweitzer Mountain Resort; Gwen Howat at Mt. Baker; Gretchen Anderson at Bogus Basin; Rick Hotus at The Summit; John Tullis at Timberline Lodge; Jack Sibbach at Sun Valley; Kim Muller, Suzanne Hickey, and Susan Darch at Whistler Resort; Connie Rabold, Laura Street, and Jill Greenwood at The Whistler Resort Association; Debbie Peebles at the Best Western Vernon Lodge; Randy Rogers at Willamette Pass; Jim Greene at Red Mountain; Kathlene Goyette at White Pass; Dean Cooper at Lookout Pass; and Andy Lovell at Kelly Canyon. I apologize if I have left anyone off the list.

Table of

Contents

Alpine Resorts: Washington

Alpine Resorts: Oregon

Alpine Resorts: Idaho

Heli-Skiing & Cat-Skiing

Heli-Skiing

Cat-Skiing Operations

Appendix

Preface

L et's get something out of the way right up front: I am completely un-
objective when it comes to snowriding in the Pacific Northwest.
And completely selfish. Which is why this book was so difficult for
me to complete. Let me explain why.

I have carved turns on over 60 different mountain ranges in Europe,
South America, Canada, and the United States. I have laid tracks with
some of the best free skiers and snowboarders in the world. I have bagged
fresh lines on active volcanoes, from helicopters, snowcats, behind snowmobiles, by the light of the moon, and down sand dunes (we were really
desperate for turns that summer!). While I haven't been everywhere or seen
everything, I have been lucky enough to ski more than most. And the con-
clusion I have come to after nearly 30 years of searching for the perfect line
is that there is no place on earth like the Pacific Northwest. Hear me out
and I think you'll agree.

First, the best resort in the Western Hemisphere, *Whistler-Blackcomb*, is
located in the Northwest. I once said this to an ex-pro racer from California
whom I met while skiing in Argentina. He didn't believe me and told me I
was full of BS. I dared him to meet me at Whistler and tell me I was wrong.
He did. And at the end of the first day, what did he have to say? "I hate to
admit it, but you're right."

Second, British Columbia is the heli-ski capital of the world. Over 30
heli-ski and cat-skiing operations attract skiers and snowboarders from
Japan, Europe, Australia, and North America. Nowhere else are there as
many operations in such a small geographic region. Nowhere.

Third, I am extremely proud to call myself a Northwest snowrider when
so many of the world's best have come from this region. There are the
Olympic medalists Nancy Green, Ross Rebagliatti, Steve and Phil Marhe,
Picabo Street, and Bill Johnson. There is the five-time World Pro Mogul

Champion Scott Kauf, extreme skier Mike Hattrup, and snowboarder Craig Kelly. Even the Austrians can't claim this many famous snowriders. Fourth, and fifth, Northwest snowriders coined the term "steep and deep." They must have because it is truer here than anywhere else on the continent. With the exception of the Chugach Mountains in Alaska, which you can only ski from a helicopter or snowcat, Northwest mountain ranges are steeper than any other in North America. Ask ski filmmakers Warren Miller and Greg Stump and they'll tell you that one of the reasons they like to film in the Northwest is because the terrain is so nasty. And what about deep? Mount Rainier in Washington held the world's record for the most snowfall in a single season for years until Mount Baker, also located in Washington, broke the record in 1999.

Speaking of snow, it is true that Northwest flakes can be a bit heavy. That may be why the Northwest isn't as popular as Colorado or Utah. But I am even biased about this. If you learn to ski here you're equipped to ski anywhere in the world. I can't tell you how many times I have sat on a chairlift in some place like Utah listening to locals complain about poor snow conditions. I rarely say anything, but in my mind I am shaking my head and thinking: "You have got to be kidding! The snow is awesome." Because I'm used to riding less than ideal conditions, the snow they whine and snivel about feels like heaven, as it does to other Northwest snowriders. And when they come up here to ski or board, most of them can't hack it.

So, back to why the book was so difficult to complete. While I have ample evidence to back up my claims, I think it's fairly clear that I am a bit of a fanatic when it comes to snowriding in the Northwest. I found myself constantly trying to keep my fanaticism in check—no easy task, mind you.

As for being selfish, this may have been the most difficult obstacle to overcome when writing the book. I don't really want the rest of the world to know just how good the snowriding is here in the Northwest. I'd prefer to keep it all for myself.

Why write the book at all then? Over the years, skiing has been a significant part of my life. I want to give back to the sport that has given so much to me. Skiing has taken me all over the world, introduced me to new cultures, established lifelong friendships, created good times, and helped me through bad times. I owe the sport, and I hope my book will help you get even just a little bit of what I got, and still get, out of skiing. Good luck, and may your edges be sharp, your turns smooth, and the snow at your feet fresh, light, and deep.

Santo Criscuolo

Introduc

A note from the folks behind this endeavor...

We at Outside America look at guidebook publishing a little differently. There's just no reason that a guidebook has to look like it was published out of your Uncle Ernie's woodshed. We feel that guidebooks need to be both easy to use and nice to look at, and that takes an innovative approach to design. You see, we want you to spend less time fumbling through your guidebook and more time enjoying the adventure at hand. At any rate, we hope you like what you see and enjoy the places we lead you. And most of all, we'd like to thank you for taking an adventure with us.

Happy Trails!

Introduction

Inside the Pacific Northwest and British Columbia

Despite offering up two of the world's most famous ski resorts, *Whistler-Blackcomb* and *Sun Valley*, and holding the title "Heli-ski Capital of the World," the Pacific Northwest is somehow better known for coffee shops, microbrews, grunge bands, and Microsoft®. The reasons for this oversight are simple. First off, the Pacific Northwest gets a bad rap for its snow quality, which in the Cascades region can be heavy and damp—hence, the sarcastic nickname "Cascade concrete." Secondly, because many Washington and Oregon ski areas are situated in national forests, building extensive resort villages is simply out of the question. Consequently, these areas can't bill themselves as destination resorts. Finally, though many Idaho and British Columbia (BC) resorts are blessed with light, dry snow, they simply lack the funds with which to become destination resorts—largely due to their inaccessibility and distance from major urban centers.

All this keeps many Northwest ski areas under the North American ski community radar—which, if you ask a Northwest resident, is just fine. Local snowriders know just how good the skiing is here. Marked by stunning beauty, challenging terrain, and snow levels measured in feet not inches, the Northwest might be one of the best places in the world for a snowrider to live.

From any of the major cities, skiers and snowboarders can reach internationally known areas like BC's *Whistler-Blackcomb*, Oregon's *Mount Bachelor*, and Idaho's *Sun Valley*. There are over 70 resorts and ski areas from which to choose, all offering snow adventures unique to their mountains, surrounding landscape, and communities. At Oregon's *Mount Ashland*, snowriders learn about Shakespeare while carving turns. At Idaho's *Schweitzer Resort*, snowriders enjoy sunshine and dusty, dry snow. Skiers and boarders at Washington's *Crystal Mountain* are treated to awesome terrain with up-close and personal views of Mount Rainier. *Mount Baker*, also located in Washington, is snowboarder's paradise. BC's *Fernie*, *Kimberley*, and *White Water* serve up cold bowls of powder snow on a regular basis. And the list goes on. With 70 resorts and ski areas on the menu, not to mention 30-plus heli-ski and snowcat skiing operations, the Pacific Northwest is a virtual smorgasbord of ski adventures.

And here's more good news. Many Northwest ski areas are currently undergoing major upgrades. Even areas on national forest land are building new day lodges. BC's *Sun Peaks* resort recently added an entire new village. No matter where snowriders travel in the Northwest, they're greeted with improvements and expansion. While

1

local residents are enjoying these long-awaited upgrades, it's just a matter of time before resort developers turn their focus to marketing their new and improved resorts to the rest of the country. It won't be long before all of North America knows what locals in the Northwest have known for years. The skiing out here is out of this world!

Why the Term *Snowriding*?

Nobody knows exactly how the term *snowriding* originated. Warren Miller made it popular in 1996 with his film *Snowriders*. He used it again in the sequel, *Snowriders 2: The Journey Continues*, in 1997. Miller refused to make a distinction between snowboarders and skiers. And why should he? Skiers and snowboarders are cut from the same cloth. Both love steep lines; smooth, silky corduroy; deep powder; fresh mountain air; and beautiful scenery. Thus, the terms *skiing, snowboarding, riding,* and *snowriding* are used interchangeably, with just a few exceptions. For example, most snowboarders dislike riding moguls. When moguls are mentioned in the book, they are in the context of traditional skiing. And while skiers can have a blast in halfpipes and terrain parks, manmade obstacles are outlined in the context of snowboarding. In any case, the term *snowriding* is here to stay.

Besides skiers and snowboarders being obsessed with riding the snow, ski technology has also brought the two sports closer together. Shape skis now allow skiers to ride the snow more like snowboarders do. Skiers' turns have opened up and are more similar to the huge sweeping arcs that make snowboarders look so graceful. Skiers are finding their way into halfpipes and terrain parks as well.

It's ironic that snowboarding, which seemed on its way to taking over the skiing industry, is in large part responsible for the shaped ski, and therefore the revitalization of the ski industry. In the late 1980s snowboarding exploded onto the scene and soon became a hip new sport with its own industry and culture. In fact, until the introduction of the shape ski, snowboarding was the fastest-growing segment of the winter sports world. It was growing so fast and gathering so much attention that many snowboarders declared skiing a dying sport. In reality, even at its peak, snowboarding only accounted for roughly 15 percent of annual skier visits nationwide. In recent years, snowboarding's growth, though strong, has leveled off. But its affect on skiing is undeniable.

Prior to snowboarding, skiers tended to hit the slopes with hundreds and hundreds of short radius turns, unless they were downhillers or giant slalom skiers. Nowhere is this more evident than in Greg Stump's 1989 film *Licensed to Thrill*, in which the first well-known extreme skiers—Glen Plake, Scott Schmit, and Mike Hattrup—defined extreme skiing. Plake, Schmit, and Hattrup charged down sick lines that were so steep they barely held snow. They negotiated the dangerous pitches with quick, hard, aggressive, powerful hop turns. This style of skiing, while efficient for dangerous slopes, was not exactly graceful. Moreover, it took tremendous strength and ability.

During this time, snowboarders pushed the extreme edge even further. They rode the same slopes as skiers but did it faster and with far fewer turns. With a shorter, wider surface area—but nearly as much edge length—on which to ride the snow, snowboarders were able carve wide-open, rocket-fast arcs on nasty terrain. Skiers couldn't believe it, but they made a mental note and took it back to their R & D departments.

On the ski slopes, a similar scenario played itself out. Resorts began building terrain parks and halfpipes for snowboarders. At first, skiers wanted nothing to do with the halfpipes and terrain parks since traditional slalom skis weren't equipped for such terrain. The long, stiff boards were simply too difficult to maneuver in a halfpipe.

K2 was the first to act. In 1995, the company introduced the K2 Four with the notion of making skiing easier for novice skiers while providing advanced skiers the ability to ride the snow more like snowboarders. Soon, extreme skiers like Seth Morrison and Doug Combs began carving giant arcs on burly terrain just as snowboarders did. Additionally, negotiating a pair of shaped skis, which are much shorter than traditional slalom skis, through halfpipes and terrain parks became much easier. Skiers started flashing killer tricks on "snowboard-specific" terrain. Moreover, they took these tricks out onto the rest of the slopes. Look no further than the 1998 Olympics. Johnny Mosely brought home the gold medal in the mogul competition, thanks to the sweet trick he pulled while copping a huge piece of air.

Snowriding: Past to Present
Origins

Skiing, as we know it, began as cross-country (or Nordic) skiing and was developed thousands of years ago in Scandinavia. Exactly how long ago, no one is sure. Several 3,000-year-old models with leather bindings have been uncovered in Scandinavia, and skis dating as far back as 2500 BC have been unearthed in Siberia. More recently, archaeologists in Sweden have discovered what appears to be a short, wide ski, which carbon dating revealed to be roughly 4,500 years old.

Over 1,500 years ago, inhabitants of Scandinavia, Northern Russia, and Central Asia required an efficient means of transport during their long, snow-filled winters. Further evolution of the ski occurred in Scandinavian regions during the 13th and 17th centuries when skies were employed by the military to aid in winter troop and supply movement. In Norway, the first ski troopers began operating in 1747, using long, wooden ski boards and a pole for basic transportation through snow-covered mountains. From centuries of practical applications, skiing as sport was born.

Skiing was brought to North America by Scandinavians in the early 1800s. It is believed to have taken hold when gold miners in California's Sierra Nevada mountains strapped on 12-foot skis made of solid oak—one long ski and one short—with a heavy pole used for push-off. Farther north in the Rockies, Idaho's *Sun Valley* holds the distinction of being the continent's first ski area, opening in 1936 and having been inspired by Union Pacific Railroad president W. Averell Harriman. For all practical purposes skiing as a sport was born in North America.

Since then, many Pacific Northwest residents have been responsible for helping develop the sports of skiing and snowboarding. Some of the best skiers in history have grown up in the Northwest. The Mahre Brothers, who won Olympic gold and silver medals in the 1970s, spent their childhood at White Pass, Washington. Nancy Green, the first North American women to win an Olympic gold medal in the downhill, learned to ski at Red Mountain, BC. And Ross Rebagliatti, the first-ever snowboarder to win an Olympic Gold medal, calls Whistler, BC, his home.

Besides world famous athletes, major manufacturers call the Northwest home as well. K2, Ride Snowboards, Columbia Sportswear, Helly Hansen, Smith, Scott, and others are all located in the Northwest. All of them share in making snowriding a healthy, growing industry—in the Northwest and throughout North America.

3

Cross-Country Skiing

With the emergence of alpine skiing as a popular sport, Nordic skiing had become nearly a forgotten pastime from its humble Scandinavian origins. But lately its re-emergence is growing beyond its faithful coterie of followers. The physical benefits that cross-country offers far outweigh those of alpine skiing, requiring considerable stamina and strength over longer distances. The sport combines a full cardiovascular workout with a discovery of the great outdoors. When a strong natural snow base develops in their areas, Nordic skiers traverse woodland trails at designated touring centers, state parks and forests, and national recreation areas. Here they can encounter rugged topography, varied wildlife, and scenic vistas. But perhaps the most appealing aspect of Nordic skiing is that Nordic skiers can roam on just about any open surface with enough of a powder base. In fact, many skiers simply use parking lots, campgrounds, road shoulders, golf courses, or open fields.

As far as equipment is concerned, the difference between an alpine and Nordic ski is size and width. Nordic skis are thinner and usually longer than alpine skis. And Nordic boots are attached to the skis only at the toe, allowing the heel to lift off, similar to a person's walking motion. A sticky wax coats the ski's base so that skiers can push off the ski and turn—a stark contrast from the secured bindings found on alpine skis.

Telemark Skiing

While alpine skis have themselves undergone serious changes in design, Nordic skis also have some interesting variations. Over a decade ago, ski skating was developed—a faster technique that involves using steps similar to ice-skating. In addition, Telemark skiing—its name derived from the Telemark district of Norway—is a variation of downhill skiing, but on Nordic skis. The "tele" turn is its distinguishing component: The outside ski is advanced ahead of the other, then turned inward at a continually widening angle through the carve. To facilitate this propulsive motion, Telemarkers use specially designed skis that are usually lighter and thinner than alpine skis. The sport's hybrid nature allows Telemark skiers to hit both backcountry trails and commercial downhill slopes. This versatility has brought a wider range of skiers out to test their mettle on the slopes of Pacific Northwest resorts—all of which permit Telemarking—though you're not likely to spot an abundance of Tele skiers on any alpine mountain.

Snowboarding

The American-bred sport was created in the 1960s by inventor Sherman Poppen, whose "Snurfer" was a popular toy-store item that sold over one million sets. Snurfers were made of wood, and steered by a rope attached to the front tip. The modern snowboard would be pioneered in the late 1970s when surfer Jake Burton teamed with champion skateboarders Tom Sims and Chuck Barfoot to design a single, metal-edged board that would run faster than skis and be able to carve mountains with ease. Burton picked up the idea when he jokingly participated in a ski resort Snurfer event, and later realized that a foot-retention device would allow more stability on the wooded board. He took his concept to Vermont's *Stratton Mountain*, incorporating into his designs steel edges and high-back foot bindings more familiar to skiers.

It took awhile for the U.S. ski industry to accept the alternative snowboard to the tradition-laced sport. As recently as 1985, only seven percent of ski areas in the country permitted snowboards on their trail networks. Today just a small number of resorts still restrict boarding, and they're hard-pressed to ignore its economic potential. Like skis, modern snowboards come in varying sizes and weights, but differ depending on the style of rider, offering varying shapes and flex patterns. Boards are generally broken down into four classifications: race, alpine, freeriding, and freestyle; and nearly all are made of a wood core, fiberglass, and p-tex. Not surprisingly, the world's largest manufacturer and seller of snowboards is Jake Burton.

Snowboarding's growth is finally starting to level off but continues to be strong and healthy. It's estimated that more than 12 percent of the country's lift tickets sold during the 1996-97 season were by snowboarders. Boarders can either shred downhill slopes, cutting giant-slalom turns, or roam "freestyle" in designated snowboard parks filled with man-made obstacles—or just about any "hits" the ski area will allow. Since ski areas generally prohibit dangerous jumping on their trails, snowboard parks allow freestylers the opportunity to catch air on obstacles such as gap jumps, spines, tabletops, slides, quarterpipes, ramps, rollerz, and whales. While snowboard parks are more prevalent and easier to maintain, many Northwest resorts construct cylindrical trenches of hard-packed snow known as halfpipes—an idea taken from skateboard parks and ramps. Halfpipes are difficult to maintain, requiring an expensive grooming apparatus or the constant work of employees to keep them operating. Many of the Northwest ski areas have invested in the equipment. However, natural conditions still often determine the availability and quality of pipes.

How to Use This Book

The beauty of Outside America's *Ski & Snowboard America*™ series is its ease of use. Each resort/ski area lists its information in similar fashion, incorporating visual icons and titles to find the information you're looking for quickly. You'll also find a detailed section on heli-skiing and cat-skiing in the Pacific Northwest *(see page 308)*.

Because of the large distinction between destination resorts and day ski areas, Idaho, Oregon, Washington, and British Columbia are broken down into two classifications: Resorts and Ski Areas. Each contains the following sections:

Resort Information

Listed at the beginning of each ski area is its relevant resource information, including address, phone numbers, websites, accepted credit cards, operating hours, and typical length of season. Phone numbers include any toll-free and direct ski reports, and numbers for information, lodging, or reservations. Credit cards accepted at the ski area are typically used for lift tickets, rentals, instruction, dining, and ski shop items. Website and e-mail addresses are provided by participating resorts. Skiers may use a resort's Internet address to find up-to-the-hour snow reports, number of operating slopes and lifts, and other basic information regarding the ski area. Also provided are the normal open and close dates during its ski seasons. Since weather patterns vary dramatically, open and close dates are based on the resort's average season.

Background

This section provides an overview of the ski area, detailing its history as well as its plans for the future.

Mountain Stats

The Mountain Stats offer readers a glimpse at each resort's vital statistics. These include: elevation, vertical drop, primary slope direction, annual snowfall, skiable days, skiable terrain, number of runs, longest run, lifts, lift capacity, terrain classification, night skiing, snowmaking, and annual visits. Each item in Mountain Stats is defined in the book's Glossary.

Getting There

This section displays full directions by car from regional metropolitan centers. Highway and state route maps are also given for each ski area. Directions and key information for travel by air, train, boat, and bus are featured when applicable.

Trail Profiles

Here, skiers and snowboarders are expertly guided through each area's skiable terrain. Relative to each ski area, readers can expect expert tips and guidance, such as hidden snow stashes known only to locals, advice on how to avoid the crowds, pointers on efficiently navigating the mountain, and the best places to go after a long day of skiing or boarding. Novice, intermediate, and advanced terrain are afforded equal attention, and particular focus is placed on each area's natural conditions and mountain topography.

Snowboarding Highlights

This section explores each resort's snowboard scene, featuring detailed descriptions of terrain parks, halfpipes, and snowboard-worthy slopes and trails. Boarders will find the number and types of hits and obstacles for terrain parks and halfpipes. Also offered are expert tips and advice on particular aspects of each area's snowboard-specific terrain.

Other Winter Sports

All other winter sports activities are listed here, including information on cross-country skiing, Telemarking, backcountry touring adventures, snowtubing, and much more. The type, length, location, and availability of Nordic trails are generally listed for cross-country ski trails.

Snowrider Services

This section includes guest services available at each ski area. All prices are based on the 2000–2001 ski season, unless otherwise noted. Lift Tickets features prices and times of all tickets. Rentals includes prices and types of ski and snowboard rentals. Nordic Trail Passes details all relevant cross-country ski information, when applicable. Services includes ski school information and rates for skiing, snowboarding, and cross-country skiing (when applicable), and also lists childcare information.

Room & Board

This category identifies lodging and dining opportunities—both on-site and nearby—for each of the ski areas. Descriptions, prices, locations, and phone numbers are given for each lodging and dining option, while establishments of particular interest are highlighted in special sidebars.

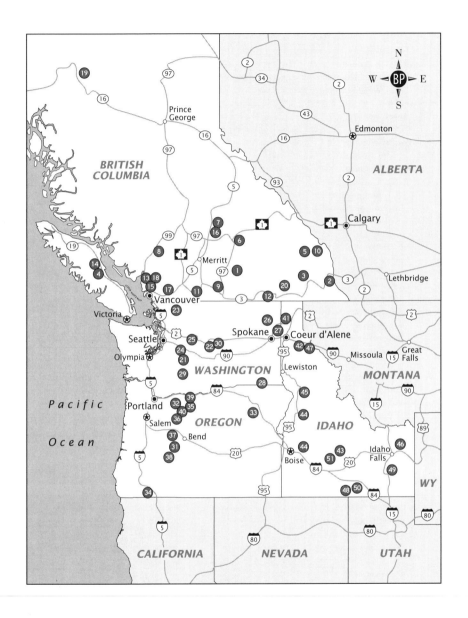

Pacific Northwest & British Columbia

	Base Elevation	Summit Elevation	Vertical Drop	Slope Direction	Annual Snowfall	Skiable Days	Skiable Terrain	Number of Runs	Longest Run	Number of Lifts	Lift Capacity
Big White Ski	4,950 ft	7,606 ft	2,550 ft	South	294"	150	2,075 ac	100	4.5 mi	8	17,800
Fernie Alpine Resort	3,500ft	6,316 ft	2,811 ft	Northeast	345"	150	2,500 ac	97	3 mi	9	12,300
Kimberley Ski	4,035 ft	6,500 ft	2,465 ft	Northeast	144"	120	2,000 ac	68	4 mi	9	8,000
Mt Washinton	3,558 ft	5,215 ft	1,657 ft	Northwest	324"	138	1,500 ac	50	1.2 mi	8	10,400
Panorama Mtn Village	3,800 ft	7,800 ft	4,000 ft	Northwest	145 "	130	2,000 ac	100+	2.1 mi	10	7,602
Silver Star Mtn	3,780 ft	6,280 ft	2,500 ft	South/NE	225"	180	1,440 ac	84	5 mi	8	12,100
Sun Peaks	3,933 ft	6,824 ft	6,824 ft	South/NE	220"	150	1,096 ac	80+	5 mi	6	7,263
Whistler/Blackcomb	2,214 ft	7,494 ft	5,280 ft	360°	318"	210	3,414 ac	100+	7 mi	16	29,895
Apex Resort	5,197 ft	7,187 ft	2,000 ft	North	200+"	125-140	550 ac	60	3 mi	5	4,029
Fairmont Hot Springs	4,200 ft	5,200 ft	1,000 ft	Southwest	150"	100	300 ac	13	1 mi	2	3,200
Maning Park	4,339 ft	5,868 ft	1,417 ft	Northeast	228"	100	183 ac	24	1.9 mi	4	4,171
Red Mtn	3,888 ft	6,699 ft	2,900 ft	360°	300"	130	1200 ac	83	5 mi	5	6,150
Cypress Mtn	3,000 ft	4,750 ft	1,750 ft	West/East	236	120	205 ac	25	2.2 mi	5	5,800
Forbidden Platea	2,300 ft	3,450 ft	1,150 ft	Southeast	130"	150	340 ac	22	1.3 mi	4	3,400
Grouse Mtn	900 ft	4,100 ft	1,210 ft	East	315"	120	202 ac	22	1 mi	10	5,500
Harper Mtn	3,600 ft	5,000 ft	1,400 ft	North	150"	100	400 ac	15	2.5 mi	3	3,600
Hemlock Valley	3,300 ft	4,500 ft	1,200 ft	N/A	180"	N/A	300 ac	34	7,460 ft	4	4,000
Mount Seymour	3,300 ft	4,600 ft	1,300 ft	Southwest	120"	120	60 ac	21	1.5 mi	4	3,700
Ski Smithers	3,700 ft	5,500 ft	1,750 ft	South/NE	72"	118	285 ac	34	2 mi	4	2,900
White Water	5,400 ft	6,700 ft	1,300 ft	N/A	360+"	130	600 ac	34	5,280 ft	2	3,400
Crystal Mtn	4,400 ft	7,012 ft	3,100ft	Various	340"	140	2,300 ac	50	3.5 mi	10	17,310
Mission Ridge	4,570 ft	6,770 ft	2,200 ft	East	200"	130	2,200 ac	35	2.2 mi	6	4,300
Mount Baker	3,500 ft	5,050ft	1,550 ft	NW/NE	645"	150	1,000 ac	38	1.8 mi	10	11,000
Stevens Pass	4,061 ft	5,845 ft	1,800 ft	360°	450"	150	1,125 ac	37	1 mi	11	15,800
Summit	3,000 ft	N/A	N/A	North	400"	150	2,666 ac	65	N/A	22	33,890
49° North	3,956 ft	5,774 ft	1,852 ft	North	300"	120	1,100 ac	42	2.5 mi	5	4,200
Mount Spokane	3,818 ft	5,883 ft	2,065 ft	N/A	180"	N/A	2,500 ac	38	8,000 ft	5	5,000
Ski Bluewood	4,450 ft	5,650 ft	1,200 ft	North	300"	150	430 ac	24	2 mi	4	3,950
White Pass	4,500 ft	6,000 ft	1,500 ft	North	350"	150	635 ac	32	2.5 mi	6	6,225
Badger Mtn	3,000 ft	3,800 ft	800 ft	North	100"	50	20 ac	4	1,700 ft	3	1,800
Mt Bachelor	5,700 ft	9,065 ft	3,365 ft	360°	300"	220	3,686 ac	70	2 mi	13	21,000
Timberline	6,000 ft	8,540 ft	3,590 ft	South	400"	335	1,430 ac	32	3 mi	6	8,961
Anthony Lakes	7,100 ft	8,000 ft	900 ft	North	300"	136	300 ac	21	1.5 mi	2	1,500
Mount Ashland	6,350 ft	7,500 ft	1,150 ft	North	300"	120	200 ac	23	1 mi	4	5,350
Mt Hood Meadows	4,523 ft	7,300 ft	2,777 ft	East	430"	160	2,150 ac	86	3 mi	12	16,145
Mt Hood Ski Bowl	3,600 ft	5,056 ft	1,500 ft	North	300"	150	960 ac	65	3+ mi	9	4,600
Hoodoo Ski Area	4,668 ft	5,703 ft	1,035 ft	North	180"	120	806 ac	24	1 mi	5	5,280
Willamette Ski Area	5,120 ft	6,683 ft	1,563 ft	360°	300"	120	550 ac	29	2.1 mi	6	8,400
Cooper Spur	4,500 ft	5,000 ft	500 ft	Northeast	120"	100	150 ac	7	1,500 ft	4	1,000
Summit	3,900 ft	4,300 ft	400 ft	Southeast	150"	60	52 ac	6	2,640 ft	1	1,200
Schweitzer Mtn	4,700 ft	6,400 ft	2,400 ft	N/S	300"	130	2,350 ac	58	2.7 mi	6	7,092
Silver Mtn	4,000 ft	6,300 ft	2,200 ft	North	300"	140	1,500 ac	51	2.5 mi	7	8,100
Sun Valley	5,750 ft	9,150 ft	3,400 ft	Various	200"	150	2,054 ac	77	3 mi	19	28,180
Bogus Basin	5,800 ft	7,600 ft	1,800 ft	North	250"	140	2,600 ac	51	1.5 mi	8	8,200
Brundage Mtn	5,840 ft	7,640 ft	1,800 ft	West	300"	140	1,300 ac	38	2+ mi	5	5,135
Kelly Canyon	5,600 ft	6,600 ft	1,000 ft	North	120"	120	740 ac	26	6,900 ft	5	3,750
Lookout Pass	4,800 ft	5,650 ft	850 ft	North	350"	80	140 ac	14	1.6 mi	2	1,150
Magic Mtn	6,410 ft	7,200 ft	790 ft	East	120"	40	380 ac	11	1 mi	3	5,000
Soldier Mtn	6,970 ft	9,570 ft	2,600 ft	N/A	160"	N/A	2,300 ac	36	6,600 ft	4	3,080
Pebble Creek	6,300 ft	8,300 ft	2,000 ft	Northwest	250"	120	1,100 ac	45	6,000 ft	3	3,300
Pomerelle	8,000 ft	9,000 ft	1,000 ft	North	500"	120	200 ac	24	2 mi	3	5,500

Regions (left margin): BRITISH COLUMBIA · WASHINGTON · OREGON · IDAHO

Ski Resorts

Resorts at a Glance

Night Skiing	Snowmaking	Annual Visits	Ski Rentals	Snowboard Rentals	Nordic Ski Rentals	Telemark Rentals	Snowshoe Rentals	Ski Schools	Childcare	On-site Lodging	On-site Restaurant	On-site Lounge/Pub
✓	✗	525,000	✓	✓	✓	✗	✗	✓	✓	✓	✓	✓
✗	✓	250,000	✓	✓	✓	✓	✓	✓	✓	✓	✗	✗
✓	✓	130,000	✓	✓	✓	✗	✗	✓	✓	✓	✓	✓
✗	✗	250,000	✓	✓	✓	✗	✓	✓	✓	✓	✓	✓
✓	✓	165,000	✓	✓	✓	✗	✓	✓	✗	✓	✓	✓
✓	✗	250,000	✓	✓	N/A	✗	✗	✓	✓	✓	✓	✓
✗	✓	210,000	✓	✓	✓	✗	✗	✓	✓	✓	✓	✓
✗	✓	2.14 mil	✓	✓	✗	✗	✗	✓	✓	✓	✓	✓
✓	✓	100,000	✓	✓	✗	✗	✗	✓	✓	✓	✓	✓
✓	✓	22,000	✓	✓	✗	✗	✗	✓	✓	✗	✓	✓
✗	✗	60,000	✓	✓	✓	✓	✓	✓	✓	✓	✓	✓
✗	✗	130,000	✓	✓	✗	✓	✗	✓	✓	✓	✓	✓
✓	✗	200,000	✓	✓	✗	✓	✓	✓	✓	✗	✓	✓
✓	✗	12,500	✓	✓	✗	✗	✗	✓	✓	✗	✓	✓
✓	✓	355,000	✓	✓	✓	✗	✓	✓	✗	✗	✓	✓
✓	✓	30,000	✓	✓	✗	✗	✗	✗	✗	✗	✓	✗
✓	✗	N/A	✗	✗	✗	✗	✗	✓	✗	✓	✓	✓
✓	✗	N/A	✓	✓	✗	✗	✓	✓	✗	✗	✓	✓
✗	✗	45,000	✓	✓	✗	✗	✗	✓	✓	✓	✗	✗
✗	✗	70,000	✓	✓	✗	✓	✗	✓	✗	✗	✓	✓
✓	✓	320,000	✓	✓	✗	✓	✗	✓	✓	✓	✓	✓
✗	✗	100,000	✓	✓	✗	✗	✗	✓	✗	✗	✓	✓
✗	✗	175,000	✓	✓	✗	✗	✓	✓	✓	✗	✗	✗
✓	✗	380,000	✓	✓	✗	✗	✗	✓	✗	✗	✗	✓
✓	?	400,000	✓	✓	✓	✗	✓	✓	✓	✗	✗	✗
✗	✗	60,000	✓	✓	✗	✗	✗	✓	✓	✗	✗	✗
✓	?	100,000	✓	✓	✗	✗	✗	✓	✗	✗	✗	✗
✗	✗	54,000	✓	✓	✗	✗	✗	✓	✗	✗	✗	✗
✓	✓	100,000	✓	✓	✓	✗	✗	✓	✓	✓	✗	✗
✗	✗	4,000	✗	✗	✗	✗	✗	✓	✗	✗	✗	✗
✗	✗	570,000	✓	✓	✓	✓	✗	✓	✓	✗	✓	✓
✓	?	280,000	✓	✓	✗	✗	✗	✓	✓	✓	✓	✓
✗	✗	24,000	✓	✓	✓	✗	✓	✓	✗	✗	✓	✗
✓	✗	86,000	✓	✓	✗	✗	✗	✓	✗	✗	✗	✗
✓	✗	350,000	✓	✓	✓	✗	✗	✓	✗	✗	✗	✗
✓	✓	140,000	✓	✓	✗	✗	✗	✓	✗	✗	✗	✗
✓	✗	40,000	✓	✓	✓	✓	✗	✓	✗	✗	✗	✗
✓	✗	N/A	✓	✓	✓	✗	✓	✓	✓	✗	✗	✗
✓	✗	10,000	✓	✓	✗	✗	✗	✓	✗	✓	✗	✗
✗	✗	3,000	✓	✓	✗	✗	✗	✓	✗	✗	✗	✗
✓	✓	135,000	✓	✓	✓	✗	✗	✓	✓	✓	✓	✓
✓	✓	N/A	✓	✓	✗	✗	✗	✓	✓	✓	✓	✓
✗	✓	400,000	✓	✓	✗	✗	✗	✓	✓	✓	✓	✓
✓	✓	300,000	✓	✓	✗	✗	✗	✓	✓	✓	✓	✓
✗	✓	108,000	✓	✓	✗	✗	✗	✓	✓	✗	✓	✗
✓	✓	50,000	✓	✓	✗	✗	✗	✓	✗	✗	✓	✗
✗	✗	25,000	✓	✓	✓	✗	✗	✓	✗	✗	✓	✓
✗	✗	6,000	✓	✗	✗	✗	✗	✓	✗	✗	✗	✗
✗	✓	N/A	✗	✗	✗	✗	✗	✗	✗	✗	✓	✗
✓	✓	45,000	✓	✓	✗	✗	✗	✓	✗	✗	✓	✗
✓	✓	60,000	✓	✓	✗	✗	✗	✓	✗	✗	✓	✓

9

Major Alpine Resorts
1. Big White Ski Resort
2. Fernie Alpine Resort
3. Kimberley Alpine Resort
4. Mount Washington Alpine Village
5. Panorama Mountain Village
6. Silver Star Mountain Resort
7. Sun Peaks Resort at Tod Mountain
8. Whistler–Blackcomb Resort

Other Alpine Resorts
9. Apex Resort
10. Fairmont Hot Springs Resort
11. Manning Park Resort
12. Red Mountain

ALPINE RESORTS:
BRITISH COLUMBIA

Day Ski Areas
13. Cypress Mountain
14. Forbidden Plateau
15. Grouse Mountain
16. Harper Mountain
17. Hemlock Valley Resort
18. Mount Seymour
19. Ski Smithers
20. Whitewater Ski & Winter Resort

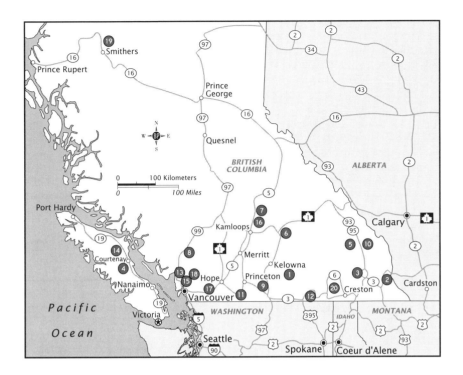

The province is simply one of the most beautiful places on the planet. Ripe with natural beauty, British Columbia has over 10 major mountain ranges and at least 30 snow-capped peaks rising 9,000 feet or higher. Within its boundaries are the source of the mighty Columbia River; gigantic glaciers; permanent snowfields; glacier-fed lakes, rivers and streams; and thousands of nooks, crannies, cracks, crevices, fissures, fingers, inlets, islands, straits, sea-side cliffs, and hidden beaches riddling the coast—all within a day's drive of Canada's largest West Coast city, Vancouver.

This incredible landscape transforms British Columbia into a moisture-manufacturing plant. Drop several inches of precipitation on any of the peaks over 3,500 feet in the middle of winter and the entire province could be a destination ski resort. Snowriders will find over 30 ski areas and just as many heli-ski and snowcat skiing operations to choose from. It's no wonder British Columbia is considered the heli-ski capital of the world. Nowhere else will snowriders find as many backcountry operations located so close together.

As if carving turns after being dropped from a helicopter weren't already the ultimate powder adventure, British Columbia also boasts North America's biggest and baddest ski area, Whistler-Blackcomb Resort. Whistler's dueling peaks provide more terrain and vertical than any other mountain in the Western Hemisphere—and its Whistler's on-slope accommodations and aprés-ski activities will compete with any mountain resort in the world.

But the story doesn't end with Whistler. Among British Columbia's other mentionables are the legendary powder of Whitewater, the family-friendly Big White, rowdy Red Mountain, the sensational skiing and multicolored village of Silver Star Mountain, the steeps of Sun Peaks, and the rapidly growing resorts of Fernie and Kimberley.

For non-Canadian residents, a trip to British Columbia is even more enticing considering the strength of the America dollar, Japanese yen, and German deutsche mark. Ski and snowboard adventures cost roughly 60 percent of what they would cost in the United States. Japanese and German tourists already know it's cheaper to pull off a ski trip in Canada than it is to vacation in their own backyards. So it's no surprise that British Columbia's larger resorts are packed with an international clientele.

In addition to low-cost lifts and lodging, Canadians are well known for welcoming guests with open arms. Few areas in the world come close to providing as high a level of customer service as British Columbia. Canadian resorts are in the business of producing smiles, and they always make the extra effort to do so.

When it comes to snow quality, British Columbia can range from cold smoke powder in the East to the damp, heavy cottage cheese found in the Coast Mountains. The changing conditions from mountain to mountain, and sometimes day to day, help Canada produce some of the best snowriders in the world. Nancy Green, North America's first Olympic ski medalist, grew up at Red Mountain; and Ross Rebagliatti, the first man ever to win a gold medal in Olympic snowboard competition, calls Whistler home.

Getting Around British Columbia

◐ AREA CODES

The area code for the Greater Vancouver area is **604**, and for the rest of the province and Vancouver Island it's **250**.

▬ ROADS

For winter road conditions call 1–800–567–4977. The website for the British Columbia Department of Transportation is *www.th.gov.bc.ca/bchighways*.

✈ BY AIR

Many of BC's ski areas are serviced by small airports with connecting flights to major hubs. The resort/ski area or a travel agent can best advise you on the least expensive and/or most direct way to connect from wherever you're departing.

BC has two international airports, **Vancouver International Airport** (YVR) at *www.yvr.ca* and **Victoria International Airport** (YYJ) at *www.cyyj.ca*, but many BC resorts can also be accessed by Washington's Spokane International Airport (GEG), Bellingham International Airport (BLI), and Seattle's Sea-Tac International Airport (SEA), as well as Alberta's Calgary International (YYC).

To book reservations on-line, visit your favorite airline's website or search one of the following travel sites for the best price: *www.cheaptickets.com*, *www.expedia.com*, *www.previewtravel.com*, *www.priceline.com*, *http://travel.yahoo.com*, *www.travelocity.com*, *www.trip.com*—just to name a few. Many of these sites can connect you with a shuttle or rental service to get you from the airport to the ski area.

▣ BY BUS

Greyhound Canada (*www.greyhound.ca* or 1–800–661–8747) services all of the major cities in BC and connects with Greyhound in the U.S. Greyhound Canada's website has timetables for most scheduled intercity bus services throughout BC. The website also includes schedules for **Pacific Coach Lines** (*www.pacificcoach.com* or 604–662–8074), which offers service between Vancouver and Victoria; and **Maverick Coach Lines** (604–662–8051), which services Squamish, Whistler, Pemberton, and Nanaimo.

☒ BY TRAIN

Via Rail services Vancouver Island and the mainland. For more information and schedules, visit *www.viarail.ca* or 1–800–561–8630 (in BC). **Amtrak** offers daily service to Vancouver from Seattle, WA, with connections with the Amtrak network in the U.S. For more information and schedules, visit *www.amtrak.com* or call 1–800–872–7245.

BC Rail offers daily service between Whistler, Lillooet, and North Vancouver Station (1311 W. 1st Street). The schedule allows daytrips to Whistler from North Vancouver with a 7 A.M. departure and an 11 P.M. return. A shuttlebus connects this train with the Sea Bus ferry to downtown Vancouver. For more information visit *www.bcrail.com/bcrpass/bcrpsca.htm* or call 1–800–339–8752 (in BC) or 1–800–663–8238 (outside of BC).

☒ BY FERRY

BC Ferries connects Vancouver Island with the mainland. For more information and schedules, visit *www.bcferries.bc.ca* or call 1–888–223–3779 (in BC) or (250) 386–3431 (in Victoria).

The **Victoria Clipper** provides service between Seattle, WA, and Victoria. The Victoria Clipper also offers packages to Whistler. For more information and schedules, visit *www.victoriaclipper.com* or call (206) 448–5000 (in Seattle, WA), (250) 382–8100 (in Victoria), or 1–800–888–2535 (outside of Seattle and Victoria only).

❷ VISITOR INFORMATION

For visitor information or a travel brochure, call the British Columbia Tourism Bureau at 1–800–663–6000 or visit their website at *www.discoverbc.com*.

☒ CONVERSIONS

American's traveling in BC will need to know a few basic conversions. The speed limit on most major freeways is 50 to 60 mph (80 to 100 kph) and 30 mph (50 kph) in most cities and towns. Most speedometers are equipped with both miles-per-hour and kilometers-per-hour. Gasoline is sold in liters, with one gallon equaling 3.78 liters. (For a complete metric conversion chart, see the last page of this book—see page 354.)

Americans traveling to Canada can expect strong currency exchange rates in their favor—as can Germans and Japanese. At the time of printing, the exchange rate was: 1 U.S. dollar equals 1.477 Canadian dollars. For up-to-the-minute exchange rates, visit *www.xe.net/ucc*.

☒ SALES TAXES

All prices under British Columbia resorts and ski areas are quoted in Canadian dollars. They may or may not include GST (Goods and Services Tax), currently seven percent.

MAJOR ALPINE RESORTS: BRITISH COLUMBIA

Big White Ski Resort

Courtesy Big White Ski Resort

Big White Ski Resort
Box 2039, St. R
Kelowna, British Columbia, Canada V1X 4K5

Ski Report: (250) 765–7669
Information: 1–800–663–2772;
   (250) 765–3101
E-mail: *bigwhite@silk.net*
Website: *www.bigwhite.com*
Credit Cards: VISA, MasterCard, & American
   Express

Operating Hours: 8:30 A.M.–3:30 P.M. daily.
Night Skiing: 3:30 P.M.–9 P.M. Tuesday–
Saturday (December 20–March 30)

Season: Mid November to mid April

Background

Sometimes a name says it all. Big White Ski and Snowboard Resort is a perfect example. Located deep in the interior of British Columbia, Big White is the Province's third largest ski resort. Only the Whistler-Blackcomb combo and Fernie Alpine Resort offer more terrain. The resort has over 100 named runs, 2,000-plus acres of skiable terrain, over 24 feet of annual snowfall, 10 lifts (including four high-speed quads), and a fleet of groomers—in short, Big White provides "Big" skiing for snowriders of almost all abilities. Snowriders will find powder fields, acres of gladed tree skiing, miles of long rolling cruisers, and giant slopes of gentle terrain perfect for learning the finer points of snowriding.

Despite being rewarded by some of Canada's most bountiful snow conditions (24 feet of light, dry powder annually) the resort has its share of natural drawbacks. Because much of the skiing is well above treeline, the area is often shrouded in fog and clouds. Dubbed "Big White Out" by many locals, the resort's lack of contrasting scenery under cloudy, gray conditions can cause skiers and snowboarders difficulty in finding their lines.

Originally opened in 1963, Big White was a local favorite for many years before turning into a destination ski resort in 1985, when the Schumann family purchased the area. They have been injecting money into the resort ever since—to the tune of $100 million. The upgrades have included the installation of high-speed quads, a new warming hut, a 32,000-square-foot Village Center Mall, and possibly the best daycare facility in the entire Northwest. Superb skiing, two snowboard parks, seven different restaurants and bars, a café, deli, mountain store, medical center, gift shop, a youth activity center, and three day lodges—Big White has it all. And as long as the U.S. dollar remains strong, Big White is an excellent value.

Getting There

- **From Portland, OR:** Take I-5 north to Seattle. *[Follow Seattle directions below.]*
- **From Seattle, WA:** Take I-5 north to WA 539. Take WA 539 north to WA 546. Take WA 546 east to Sumas, WA. Enter Canada and turn right on Trans Canada Highway 1 (TCH 1) and go east to Hope. *[Follow Vancouver directions below.]*
- **From Vancouver, BC:** Take TCH 1 east to Hope. From Hope, go north on Provincial Highway 5 (PH 5)—also known as the Couquahalla Toll Highway. Please note that a toll is required to travel on portions of PH 5A. Take PH 5 to Merritt, BC. From Merritt take PH 97C south and then PH 97C east to Kelowna. Drive through Kelowna and turn right on PH 33. Follow signs to the resort from here.

- **From Boise, ID:** Take I-84 north to U.S. 95. Go north on U.S. 95 to Lewiston, Idaho. From Lewiston, go west on U.S. 12 to U.S. 195. Head north on U.S. 195 to Spokane. *[Follow Spokane directions below.]*
- **From Spokane, WA:** Take U.S. 395 north to the Canadian border. Take PH 3 West to Osoyoos and head north on PH 3A/97 to Kelowna. Drive through Kelowna and turn right on PH 33. Follow signs to the resort from here.

🛬 **Airport Services:** For guests traveling from outside of the Northwest, the closest regional airport is Kelowna Airport (YLW). Guests flying from Seattle, Portland, or Spokane, should check with Horizon Air (1–800–547–9308) for special ski packages. In the past, prices have been under $100 per person per day for three days of skiing, lodging, and air and ground transportation. Shuttle transportation to and from the airport is available and can be arranged through Big White's central reservation office at 1–800–663–2772.

Mountain Stats

Westridge Base Elevation: 4,950 feet *(1,509 m)*
Village Center Elevation: 5,706 feet *(1,755 m)*
Summit Elevation: 7,606 feet *(2,319 m)*
Vertical Drop: 2,550 feet *(777 m)*
Primary Slope Direction: South
Annual Snowfall: 294 inches *(747 cm)*
Skiable Days: 150
Skiable Terrain: 2,075 acres patrolled *(840 ha)*; 750 groomed acres *(304 ha)* 1,325 acres *(537 ha)* alpine and glades

Runs: 100
Longest Run: 4.5 miles *(7.2 km)*
Lifts: 4 high-speed quads, 1 fixed grip quad, 1 triple, 1 double, 1 T-bar
Lift Capacity: 17,800 skiers per hour
Terrain Classification: 18% novice; 30% intermediate; 26% expert; 26% extreme
Night Skiing: 38 acres *(15 ha)*; Night vertical drop is 1,624 feet *(495 m)*
Snowmaking: None
Annual Visits: 525,000

Trail Profiles

Big White is a novice and intermediate snowrider's paradise. In addition to receiving relentless dumps of light, dry snow, Big White is blessed with acres and acres of gentle rolling terrain. Even from the top of the mountain, snowriders will find blue and green trails leading back to the Village, allowing nearly all abilities to explore the entire area.

Big White welcomes young snowriders with open arms. The Plaza chair is dedicated to kids and starts below the lodge, via a tunnel that kids love to ski through. The terrain is gentle and set aside for children only, prohibiting aggressive skiers from shooting down its slopes. The two runs accessed from the Plaza chair, *Hummingbird* and *Woodcutter*, are also close to the daycare center and easy for parents to find.

Strong intermediate snowriders will enjoy the *Sun Rype Bowl*. The bowl is essentially a big powder field that funnels into *Black Bear Glades*. It can be reached by hanging a left off the top of the Gem Lake Express to *Kalina's Rainbow*. Then, drop into its 700 feet of vertical and 1,000-foot width. A bit of advice: ski the bowl early in the morning if it's been snowing the night before. Aside from the bowl never being groomed, this side of the mountain is more exposed, and the wind tends to deposit snow in the bowl. Riding early means fresh tracks.

Near the bottom of the *Sun Rype Bowl*, the run funnels into the *Black Bear Glades*. Advanced snowriders will have a blast exploring the trees. Intermediates should stick to their right, which will deposit them into *Blue Ribbon*. *Blue Ribbon* was designed with a major downhill race in mind for the future. It may be the best cruiser on the mountain. It's like an amusement park ride with stomach-dropping steeps, rollerz, and an S-turn that's fun to rocket through.

Courtesy Big White Ski Resort

When Old Man Winter pounds the area, the result is a cold, angry wind and poor visibility. On stormy days, the best plan is to head over to the Black Forest. Located lower on the hill and accessed from the Black Forest Express, the terrain here is sheltered from the weather and groomed each day. Big White dedicates a significant portion of its staff to laying down near-perfect corduroy from the time the lifts shut down to the next day's opening. *Cougar Alley*, *Whiskey Jack*, and *Bear's Paw* are just three of the several super-buffed trails that Big White has to offer. Even more is available off the Bullet Express and the Ridge Rocket Express. *Paradise*, *Perfection*, and the *Spruce Trail* are all coast-to-coast looooong, buttery smoooooth sexy turns on ego snow.

Advanced skiers usually head straight for *The Cliff*, *Pegasus*, *Camel's Back*, and *Parachute Bowl*—each is accessible from the Alpine T-bar. These runs—the only legitimate steeps at Big White—are relatively short but intense nonetheless. Looking over the edge of *The Cliff* has made many a snowrider queasy. This area is for expert skiers only, and it's highly recommended to stay high on the right near the bottom to reach the *Cliff Ski Out Trail*. The alternative is making a long walk across the frozen Rhonda Lake.

Marked terrain aside, a few more unmapped steeps can be found to the left in the trees, above *Sundance* and *Easter Gully*, while looking down the hill from the top of Bullet Express. The *Easter Chutes*, as they are referred to by the locals, consist of steep, short, and narrow corridors through the forest. Even more tree skiing abounds off the Powder and Falcon chairs. The *Thunder*, *Black & Blue*, *Sapphire*, *Corkscrew*, *Flagpole*, and *Blackout Glades* provide days and days worth of new lines and routes to explore through the forest. The lines in here are tight and steep, requiring quick and controlled turns.

Snowboarding Highlights

What a difference a decade makes. In 1983, snowboarding wasn't even permitted at Big White. Boarders had to hike up the mountain in order to ride the area's bountiful terrain. Now that snowboarding is a permanent part of the resort equation, one-plankers from all over Canada are trekking to Big White in increasing numbers. Certain sections of Big White can now best be described as winter skate parks. The resort offers an advanced park and a novice park, totaling eight acres dedicated exclusively to snowboarding. In addition, Big White boasts a 450-foot advanced halfpipe—with four to six-foot trannies and 10- to 12-foot high walls—and a novice quarterpipe. Both pipes were built and are groomed by a Pipe Grinder. The pipes are constructed and maintained under the supervision of Flynn Seddon—retired World Cup Slalom and halfpipe competitor and president of the BC Snowboard Association. The advanced halfpipe lies between the Bullet Express and Black Forest Express lifts in the terrain park, and includes parts of *Sundance*, *Freeway*, and *Wood Pecker*. Featured in the November 1997 issue of *Snowboarder Magazine*, the park is loaded with monster jumps, spines of varying sizes, tabletops, diamonds, and an assortment of changing hits. An old double-decker English bus, serving as a hangout zone, tops off the park.

Courtesy Big White Ski Resort

The quarterpipe is situated in the Plaza Park and serves as the novice/intermediate pipe. Plaza is located on *Speculation* off of the Ridge Rocket Express. Though smaller than the advanced park, it contains many of the same features.

More Fun in the Flakes

Skinny ski snowriders enjoy the 16 miles (25 km) of marked **cross-country trails**, 8 miles (13 km) of which are groomed. If you're interested in **ice skating** at the Village Center, rentals are available from the Rental Shop in the Village Centre Mall. For a faster paced snowriding adventure, try a **snowmobile tour**. Information and bookings are available from Big White Central Reservations or by calling (250) 765–8888. Call Aerial Sensations at (250) 765–2FLY if you'd like to try your hand at **tandem paragliding**. Rentals are available for **snowshoeing** from the Rental Shop in the Village Center Mall. Information on and bookings for **horse-drawn wagon rides** are available from Big White Central Reservations.

Skier Services

💲 Lift Tickets

Ages 19–64: $45/day, $35/afternoon, $16/night • **Ages 13–18:** $38/day, $29/afternoon, $16/night • **Ages 6–12:** $24/day, $18/afternoon, $13/night • **Ages 65–69:** $31/day, $24/afternoon, $13/night • **Age 5 & younger and 70+:** Free • *Prices based on the 2000–2001 ski season using Canadian currency (not including GST). See page 354 for conversion information.*

Courtesy Big White Ski Resort

Nordic Trail Passes

$10 for the day • *Prices based on the 2000–2001 ski season using Canadian currency (not including GST). See page 354 for conversion information.*

Rentals

Ski Rentals: $25/adults and youths for full-day; $17/junior for full-day; 800 sets. Type of Gear: Dynastar, Elan, Rossignol, and Salomon • **Snowboard Rentals:** $35/adults and youths; $26/kids; 300 sets. Type of Gear: Burton, Rossi, Original Sin, Salomon, Morrow, and Forum • **Nordic Ski Rentals:** $25/all ages • *Prices based on the 2000–2001 ski season using Canadian currency (not including GST). See page 354 for conversion information.*

Services

Ski School: Private lessons $46/hour; Group lessons $30/hour; Learn to Ski Program $41 (includes rentals, beginner lift, and a two-hour lesson) • **Snowboard School:** Private lessons $46/hour; Group lessons $30/hour; Learn to Board Program $60 (includes rentals, beginner lift, and a two-hour lesson) • **Childcare:** Licensed from 18 months to 3 years; Kid's Club for ages 3–12. 1–800–663–2772 • *Prices based on the 2000–2001 ski season using Canadian currency (not including GST). See page 354 for conversion information.*

Room & Board

🛏 Lodging

After improving the on-snow experience and the day-lodge facilities, the Schumanns went to work improving the on-slope accommodations. A luxurious hotel was constructed while the existing structure, the White Crystal Inn, received a major facelift. As a result, Ski Canada readers voted the Inn as Canada's "Best New Skier's" hotel. Big White increased their on-hill lodging capacity even more by building condos and chalets at the base of the mountain. The result of the construction and renovation is a cozy mountain village at the base of a terrific ski area that puts special emphasis on the family ski experience. For reservations call 1–800–663–2772 or (250) 765–8888.

More than just kid-friendly

The Big White Kid's Center was voted "Best in Canada" by Ski Canada Magazine in 1997–98. Why? Any kid who has visited Big White will tell you. The Center was designed with one word in mind...Fun. The Center's design is wavy and crooked, like a cartoon come to life. Giant rabbit ears grow from a wonky television set. The rooms are big and bright. The colors are playful, and the atmosphere is reassuring. If kids are not in the daycare playing or having a snooze in the Sleepy Time Room, they're out on the slopes taking lessons from skilled pros who love teaching children to ski. The facility is fully licensed and can take children 18 months to six years old. Reservations are highly recommended.

The favorite kids' attraction at Big White is the Enchanted Forest, accessible from the Falcon and Powder chairs. The name is derived from its resident "snow ghosts"—small trees cocooned in a thick blanket of snow and ice. The snow ghosts come in all shapes and sizes and leave the imagination wondering if there is more than trees beneath the snow. The Enchanted Forest is a must-see and must-ski for kids as well as adults.

On-site **The White Crystal Inn** offers 50 units with ski lockers, sauna, and central location in resort; rates start at $125/night. 1–800–663–2772 • **The Coast Resort** at Big White offers queen beds, fireplace, galley kitchen, outdoor pool, hot tub, ski lockers, and health club; rates start at $125/night. 1–800–663–2772 • **The Eagles Resort** offers three-bedroom condos holding up to 12 persons, queen beds, fireplace, dishwasher, laundry, games, ski and snowboard lockers, sauna, and spa; rates start at $175/night. (604) 521–0886 • **Graystokes Inn** offers one- and two-bedroom condos with outdoor hot tub, sauna, ski and snowboard locker room, and laundry; rates start at $95/night. 1–800–663–2772 • **The Whitefoot Lodge** offers budget, kitchenette, one-bedroom, and two-bedroom condos with kitchen (not in budget), and access to hot tub, sauna, ski and snowboard locker room, laundry, and Mountain Mart Grocery Store; rates start at $52/night. 1–800–663–2772 • **Samesun Travel Hostel** is a 45 bed hostel with ski-in ski-out convenience to one of Big White's famous powder runs, outdoor hot tubs, a kitchen, vending machines, jukebox, payphone, T.V./V.C.R., laundry, Internet access, and a restaurant and bar upstairs; rates start at $15/night. (250) 765–7050.

Kelowna–33 miles (*55km*) away

There are numerous choices for accommodations in Kelowna. Below is one interesting and affordable alternative. For a more complete listing call Kelowna's Visitor Bureau. 1–800–663–4345 or see *www.kelownachamber.org*
• **The Siesta Motor Inn** offers 94 units with kitchen, barbecue grill, outdoor/indoor pool, Jacuzzi, and sauna; rates start at $245/week. 1–800–663–4347

Courtesy Big White Ski Resort

⊕ Dining

On-site

Beano's Coffee Parlor serves big, fresh sandwiches and made-from-scratch hot chocolate with whipped cream. (250) 765–3101 • **The Cliff's Bar & Grill** is located in Coast Resort, offers a warm, comfortable environment for breakfast, lunch, and dinner. (250) 491–0221 •
Coltino's Ristorante is located in Das Hoftbraunhaus, features Italian and North American cuisine with a full breakfast buffet served daily from 8 A.M. to 10 A.M. (250) 765–5611 • **Grizzly Bear Lounge & Restaurant** is located in the White Crystal Inn, with a big-screen TV and tasty helpings. (250) 765–4611 • **Raakel's Pub** is located in Das Hoftbraunhaus offers food, fun, and nightly entertainment, with pizza delivery in the evening. (250) 765–5611 • **Ridge Day Lodge** is a cafeteria-style lodge with big, crackling fireplace, located at base of Ridge Rocket Express, perfect for quick food and beverages, or barbecue from the Sizzlers Barbecue on the patio. (250) 765–3101 • **Snowshoe Sam's** is located next to the Whitefoot Lodge and offers a bar downstairs, and restaurant upstairs with superb food and a big stone fireplace. (250) 765–1516.

Kelowna–33 miles (*55km*) away

There are many more choices of restaurants in Kelowna so it is difficult to recommend only a few. For an idea of the many available choices see *www.kelownachamber.org*.

Fernie Alpine Resort

Fernie Alpine Resort
Ski Area Road
Fernie, BC
Canada V0B 1M1

Ski Report: 24 hour (250) 423–3555
  In Calgary: (403) 244–6665
  In Spokane: (509) 747–7495
  In BC: 1–900–451–4997
  In Alberta: (403) 246–5853
Information: (250) 423–4655
E-mail: *info@skifernie.com*
Website: *www.skifernie.com*
Credit cards: Visa & MasterCard

Operating Hours: 9 A.M.–4 P.M. daily
Season: Late November to mid April

Don Weixl

Background

The late 1990s ushered in an era of consolidation and renovation in the ski resort industry. British Columbia's Fernie Alpine Resort was no exception. Purchased by Skiing Louise Ltd. in 1997, Fernie received an infusion of capital, making possible a tremendous growth spurt that doubled the resort's size. Lifts were installed that added more than 1,500 acres of skiable terrain to the resort. And with 2,500 total skiable acres, Fernie has become one of BC's largest resorts. The expansion opened up three new bowls and increased Fernie's vertical by 400 feet.

Located in BC's southeast corner, Fernie encompasses five big bowls of Canadian Rockies-style frosted flakes. This means the snow is usually deep—29 feet per year on average—and light… feather light. We're talking cold-smoke champagne powder. Flake for flake the snow is consistently drier at Fernie than most areas in the Northwest. Every year the snow gods bury the area's fields, fences, and most importantly, the ski slopes. This beautiful resort towers over the town of Fernie, which is an easy five-minute drive from the lifts and surrounding Elk Valley. From the upper lifts the view draws into its frame the sleepy valley community, ancient old growth forests, and the wandering Elk River. In the opposite direction, big country skies and the trails of Fernie cut into a massive ridge of mountains that includes three peaks, all nearly 7,000 feet high—Elephant Head, 6,709 feet; Polar Peak, 6,841 feet; and Grizzly, 6,900 feet. Fernie's lifts climb 6,316 feet into the bowls, to the base of the cliffs that form the gigantic ridge.

Mountain Stats

Base Elevation: 3,500 feet *(1,067 m)*
Summit Elevation: 6,316 feet *(1,926 m)*
Vertical Drop: 2,811 feet *(857 m)*
Primary Slope Direction: Northeast
Annual Snowfall: 345 inches *(875 cm)*
Skiable Days: 150
Skiable Terrain: 2,500-plus acres *(1,013 ha)*
Runs: 97
Longest Run: Nearly 3 miles *(5 km)*

Lifts: 1 high-speed quad, 2 fixed-grip quads, 2 triples, 2 T-bars, 1 poma, 1 handle tow
Lift Capacity: 12,300 skiers per hour
Terrain Classification: 30% novice; 40% intermediate; 30% advanced
Night Skiing: None
Snowmaking: 1% at base only
Annual Visits: 250,000

Getting There

- **From Seattle, WA:** Take I-90 east to Coeur d'Alene, ID. From there, take U.S. 95 north to the Canadian border. U.S. 95 becomes Provincial Highway 95/3 (PH 95/3). Continue on PH 95/3 to Cranbrook. Just past Cranbrook, head east on PH 3. Follow PH 3 to Fernie and follow the signs to the ski area.

- **From Vancouver, BC:** Head east on Trans-Canada Highway 1 (TCH 1) to Hope, BC. At Hope, head east on PH 3 to Fernie. Follow the signs to the ski area.

Airport Services: The closest international airport is Calgary International Airport (YYC)—a 3.5-hour drive from Fernie. From Seattle or Portland, a good plan is to fly into Glacier Park International Airport (FCA) in Kalispell, MT, and make the two-hour drive. Or even better, fly into Cranbrook Airport (YXC) in Cranbrook, BC, and the drive is only one hour and 15 minutes (but expect to change planes in Calgary or Vancouver). Airport shuttles can be arranged through Fernie Alpine Resort at (250) 423-4655.

Trail Profiles

With 97 trails, five alpine bowls, one new express quad, and one new fixed-grip quad, Fernie has something to offer snowriders of all abilities. The Timber Bowl Express and White Pass fixed-grip quad were installed in the summer of 1998, opening up another 1,500 acres of terrain in the *Siberia*, *Timber*, and *Currie* bowls. All three bowls are located on the area's south end, which benefits skiers by allowing more runs for all abilities right from the top. Plus, the additional terrain means more elbow room for skiers and boarders.

Novice riders can take *Falling Star* from the top of the White Pass quad—which is incidentally Fernie's highest point. Located just to the skier's right off the lift, this gentle rolling run explores terrain in *Timber Bowl* and *Siberia Bowl* as it loops around the boundary of the ski area. On the other side of the lift, *Currie Powder* and *Gilmar Trail* take beginners through *Currie Bowl*. The White Pass quad follows the ridge between *Currie* and *Timber* bowls. Taking *Falling Star* and *Gilmar Trail* via *Currie Powder* requires going all the way to the base of the Timber Bowl Express. Novice skiers also flock to *Meadow Run*—a short, wide-open slope with a gentle grade. Accessing *Meadow Run* via the Deer triple chair makes for a short turnaround time, allowing snowriders to log several runs per day on this lift.

Snowboarding Highlights

The lower half of *Deer Run* is the site of Fernie's Kokanee Terrain Park , which drops 700 vertical feet and covers just over two acres of terrain. Boarders make laps on the Deer chairlift and can hit roughly eight to 10 terrain obstacles, including tabletops, a jump box, spines, berms, and rollerz. The park is built each year by trail crewmembers with input from local riders. The riding conditions in the park and halfpipe are snow dependent, so check the daily snow report for updates, especially early in the season.

The halfpipe is located on *Bambi's Run* near the base of the mountain. It's constructed with a Pipe Dragon that Fernie shares with the Kimberley Alpine Resort (also owned by the Ski Louise group). The pipe is 300 feet long and 25 feet wide, with 10 to 12-foot verts and 4 to 6-foot trannies. But most boarders prefer to cut lines though Fernie's deep, light snow. All five bowls offer fresh powder on a consistent basis.

Intermediates will also enjoy the terrain accessible from the new chairs. There are more than 10 new intermediate runs between *Currie*, *Timber*, and *Siberia* bowls, all of which are accessible from the new lifts. Try *Pillow Talk* and *Highline* for mellow gladed tree skiing in *Timber Bowl*. In *Currie Bowl*, *123's* connects with the *Gilmar Trail* for a long distance cruiser. On the north end of the area, in the *Lizard Bowl* and *Cedar Bowl*, there are another 12 to 16 designated blue runs. *Cascade*, *Bow*, and *Weasel* are all straight shots from the top of *Lizard Bowl* to the base of the Bear T-bar. Just be sure to keep riding to the left of the bowl to avoid the black diamond runs at the bottom. In *Cedar Bowl*, try *Cruiser* for a long, wide, rolling run—ideal for practicing carving techniques and sweeping fast turns. To reach the top of *Lizard* and *Cedar*, take the Elk quad to the Bear T-bar and then to the Face Lift handle tow. All of the runs in *Lizard* funnel back to the base of the area while snowriding in *Cedar* requires a T-bar ride on *Haul Back*.

For advanced and expert snowriders, Fernie is a virtual smorgasbord of challenging terrain. *Big Bang*, off the right of the Timber Bowl Express, features lines that are packed tight and steep through the trees. From the top of the White Pass lift, ride the ridge between the *Currie* and *Timber* bowls. *Diamond Back* is a narrow cut through the trees with a steep fall line. *Shaky's Acres* is a designated blue run that would qualify as black diamond elsewhere. Located on the other side of the lift in *Timber Bowl*, *Shaky's Acres* offers a succession of steep fall-away pitches.

Mogul mongers will want to check out *Boomerang*, located off the Boomerang triple chair. For 1,600 vertical feet the big bumps bang away at skiers down an off-camber fall line.

More Fun in the Flakes

Access to the nine miles (15 km) of groomed and trackset **cross-country trails** in the forest adjacent to the resort is free of charge. Maps are available in the guest service office. Rentals and tours are available at the Mountain Edge shop.

Those interested in **snowmobiling** can call East Kootney Snowmobile Rentals at (250) 423-3700; Fernie Wilderness Adventures at (250) 423-6704; or Quad Miester at (250) 423-3696. **Horse-drawn sleigh rides, dogsled rides, snowshoe tours**, and **night snowmobile tours** are available at the resort by calling (250) 423-4655.

If you want to try your hand at **cat-skiing**, give Island Lake Lodge a call at (250) 423-3700 (*see page 326*) or Sno-Much-Fun at (250) 426-5303.

Skier Services

🅂 Lift Tickets

Ages 18–64 (non-student): $46/full-day; $38/half-day • Ages 6–12: $15/full-day; $15/half-day; **Ages 5 & younger:** Free • **Ages 13–17, Ages 65+, and Ages 18–24 (with student ID):** $38/full-day; $32/half-day • *Prices based on the 2000–2001 ski season using Canadian currency. See page 354 for conversion information.*

🅁 Rentals

Ski Rentals: $22–$46/adults; $16–$23/children; 600 sets. Type of Gear: Rossignol, Elan, Salomon, Volant, and Volkl (skis); Salomon and Technica (boots)• **Snowboard Rentals:** $29/adults; $23/children; 300 sets. Type of Gear: Rossignol and Limited Salomon • **Nordic Ski Rentals:** $18/adults; $14/children; 20 sets. Type of Gear: Madsuss • **Telemark Rentals:** $29/adults; 15 sets. Type of Gear: Salomon, Volkl, and Volant • **Snowshoe Rentals:** $18/adults; $14/children; 20 sets. Type of Gear: Atlas • *Prices based on the 2000–2001 ski season using Canadian currency. See page 354 for conversion information*

🅂 Services

Ski & Snowboard School: 60 ski instructors and 60 snowboard instructors; Private lessons $50/hour; Group lessons: $27/half-day; Beginner's package $42 (includes beginner's lift, lesson, and rentals) • **Telemarking School:** Beginner's Package $42 (includes beginner's lift lesson and rentals)

Childcare: Available throughout the season with reservations strongly recommended. A licensed facility for children newborn to school age. Open 9 A.M.–4 P.M. daily. Call (250) 423–4655 • *Prices based on the 2000–2001 ski season using Canadian currency. See page 354 for conversion information.*

Room & Board

■ Lodging

Fernie Alpine Resort has many new options available for ski-in ski-out lodging. Most are condominiums with kitchen facilities. The condos are a perfect way to save money because guests can bring groceries and eat in instead of dining out in restaurants every night. For those who want more nightlife and more options, the town of Fernie is only five minutes away. There are several B&Bs, hotels, shopping, and restaurants to choose from. For general reservations, call 1–800–258–7669 or 1–888–SKI–REAL or (250) 754–7325.

On-site

Cornerstone Lodge offers 26 one- and two-bedroom suites plus condominium/hotel units for sale and rent; rates $176–$250. 1–800–258–7669 • **Fernie Mountain Properties** features great accommodations for families and groups with three- and six-bedroom chalets; rates vary. (250) 423–9286 • **Wolf's Den Mountain Lodge** features a family atmosphere with hot tubs, a game room, and convenient access to skiing; rates $69–$129. (250) 423–9202 • **Griz Inn Sport Hotel/Condominiums**, offers standard hotel rooms, one- two- and three-bedroom condos, loft condos, hot tub, sauna, indoor pool, and close proximity to slopes; rates $85–$310/night. 1–800–661–0118 or (250) 423–9221 • **Lizard Creek Lodge** is a ski-in ski-out luxury hotel/condominium featuring fine dining, spa, pool, and Jacuzzi; rates vary. 1–800–258–7669 • **Timberline Village** offers units with full kitchen, dishwasher, microwave, fireplace, cable TV, and private balconies, with whirlpool, laundry, grills, and games in the common areas; rates start at $135/night. 1–800–667–9911 or (250) 423–8334 or *www.fernieproperties.com* • **Polar Peak Lodges** offers three-bedroom vacation homes with fully equipped kitchen, laundry, and fireplace; rates start at $285/night. 1–800–667–9911 or (250) 423–6878 or *www.fernieproperties.com* • **Kerrin Lee-Gartiner's Snowcreek Lodge** offers ski-in, ski-down convenience, deck or balcony, fully equipped kitchen, gas fireplace, cable, Internet access, and shared heated pool, underground parking, office workstations, and fitness center; rates start at $143/night. 1–888–558–6878 or (250) 423–6878 or *www.fernieproperties.com.*

Fernie–5 miles (3 km) away

Raging Elk Hostel offers dorm beds, private single and double rooms, kitchen facilities, and Internet access; rates start at $16/night. (250) 423–6811 • **Cedar Lodge** offers queen beds, pool, whirlpool, sauna, and lounge; rates $59–$89/night. 1–800–977–2977 or (250) 423–4622 • *Call the **Fernie Chamber of Commerce** for more options (250) 423–6868, or visit them on-line at www.city.fernie.bc.ca.*

⑪ Dining

Fernie–5 miles *(3 km)* away

Elk Valley Pizza offers homemade crusts and sauces, salads, wings, and bread. (250) 423–0007 • **JV's Pantry & Family Restaurant** is known for delicious prime rib dishes and pasta and features different nightly specials all week long. (250) 423–3848 • **Rip & Richard's Eatery** specializes in Southwestern cuisine and features a French wood-burning oven for breads, pizzas and calzones. (250) 423–3002 • **The Old Elevator Restaurant** was originally built in 1908 as a grain feed store with the original elevator and loft still intact, offers generous portions. (250) 423–7115 • *Call the* **Fernie Chamber of Commerce** *for more options (250) 423–6868, or visit them on-line at www.city.fernie.bc.ca.*

The Curse of William Fernie

In 1897 William Fernie encountered a tribe of Native Americans during a prospecting trip. At once he spotted the Chief's daughter wearing a necklace of shining black stones. Realizing the stones were coal, Fernie inquired of their source. The Chief agreed to show him in return for marrying his daughter. Fernie agreed. But after learning the location of the coal deposit, he reneged. Angered by this, the Chief laid a curse on the valley, vowing it would meet with fire, flood, and famine. Fernie ignored the curse and founded the town that today still bears his name and the Crows Nest Pass Coal Company.

True to the chief's warning, a terrible fire destroyed a large portion of the town's business district in 1904. The worst disaster, though, occurred in August 1908 when a forest fire wiped out nearly the entire town. Fernie was rebuilt, only to be flooded in 1916 when the Elk River ran over its banks, swamping most of West Fernie. During the Great Depression, near-famine conditions made the townspeople believe the curse might never end.

In 1964, members of the Kootenai Tribes, headed by Chief Ambrose Gravelle (Chief Red Eagle), assembled in Fernie for the ceremonial lifting of the curse. Mayor James White made amends with the Chief by smoking the "Pipe of Peace." As a reminder of the curse, the Ghost of Mount Hosmer can be seen each sunny summer evening on a rock face high above the city. The "ghost" is a spectacular shadow in the form of a rider on horseback.

Kimberley Alpine Resort

Kimberley Alpine Resort

Box 40
Kimberley, BC
Canada, V1A 2Y5

Ski Report & Information: (250) 427–4881
Reservations: 1–800–667–0871
Email: *kimbvac@rockies.net*
Website: *www.skikimberley.com*
Credit Cards: Visa & MasterCard

Operating Hours: 9 A.M.–4 P.M. Sunday and Monday; 9 A.M.–9:30 P.M. Tuesday–Saturday.
Night Skiing: 5 P.M.–9:30 P.M. Tuesday–Saturday (Christmas through March)

Season: Early December to mid April

Background

Visiting British Columbia's Kimberley is a be-*yodel*-ful experience. The old mining town is home to the world's largest cuckoo clock—a life-size "Happy Hans" figure that emerges every hour from his shuttered room and yodels his welcome to Kimberley's guests. The yodeling is just the beginning of a distinctly Bavarian winter adventure. The town, which sits just minutes from the ski lifts, is decorated and constructed like a high-mountain European village. In a pedestrian mall known as the Platzl, visitors meet servers adorned in dirndls and lederhosen while discovering hand-painted fire hydrants, hanging flower baskets, water fountains, brightly colored footbridges, and a wandering minstrel.

While the town has much to offer, the resort is best known for its awesome snowriding. Located on Northstar Mountain in the Purcell Mountain Range, Kimberley is blanketed with an average of 12 feet (3.7 m) of dry, fluffy snow each year. Snow conditions are so consistent the area guarantees satisfaction. If the snow is not up to fluff, simply return the ticket within one hour and receive a pass good for another day. Bear in mind that in early spring, warm temperatures can lead to hard pack and the occasional rain. The premium snow falls between January and early March.

Like many of its neighboring resorts (Fernie, Panorama, and Red Mountain), Kimberley has recently undergone a growth spurt. In 1997, the resort received approval from BC Lands for a major trail expansion that allowed Kimberley to increase its terrain by 35 percent.

Kimberley now boasts nearly 2,000 acres of skiable terrain, including 15 new runs and 3 new lifts. The recently built Tamarack double, on the ridge between the Buckhorn double and the Easter triple chair, increased the vertical on the backside by roughly 400 feet and opened up another 500 acres of terrain. Nearly all of the new trails are cut on advanced slopes.

The new North Star Express is located between Buckhorn chair and the Maverick T-bar. Kimberley's third chair and first express quad begins in the new village, located 300 feet below the original base area. The new village will include hotels, a new day lodge, restaurants, a new learning area, and access to Trickle Creek Golf Resort.

Mountain Stats

Base Elevation: 4,035 feet *(1,231 m)*
Summit Elevation: 6,500 feet *(1,982 m)*
Vertical Drop: 2,465 feet *(751 m)*
Primary Slope Direction: Northeast
Annual Snowfall: 144 inches *(366 cm)*
Skiable Days: 120
Skiable Terrain: Nearly 2,000 acres *(810 ha)*
Runs: 63
Longest Run: 4 miles *(6.5 km)*

Lifts: 1 high-speed quad, 2 triples, 2 doubles, 1 T-bar, 3 surface
Lift Capacity: 8,000 skiers per hour
Terrain Classification: 20% novice; 45% intermediate; 35% advanced
Night Skiing: 2 runs—*The Main* and the Beginner handle tow area
Snowmaking: 10%
Annual Visits: 130,000

Getting There

- **From Portland, OR:** Take I-5 north to Seattle. Then take I-90 east and follow the Seattle directions below.
- **From Seattle, WA:** Take I-90 east to Coeur d'Alene, ID. From here take U.S. 95 north to Canadian border. At Cranbrook, continue on Provincial Highway 95A (PH 95A) north to Kimberley. Follow signs to the ski area.
- **From Spokane, WA:** Take I-90 east to Coeur d'Alene, ID. From here take U.S. 95 north to the Canadian border. Continue going north on PH 95A. Follow PH 95A north to Kimberley. Follow signs to the ski area.
- **From Vancouver, BC:** Take Provincial Highway 3 east to Cranbrook. At Cranbrook, take PH 95A north to Kimberley. Follow signs to the ski area.

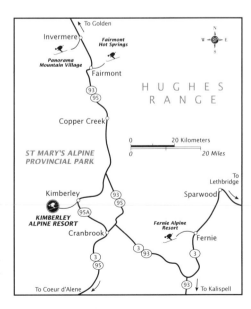

✈ **Airport Services:** For guests traveling from outside of the Northwest, the Calgary International (YYC) and Vancouver International (YVR) airports are serviced by most major carriers. Most travelers will fly into Calgary, Alberta or Vancouver, BC, before changing to Air BC or Air Canada and continuing on to Cranbrook Airport (YXC)—a 15-minute drive to Kimberley.

🚌 **Bus Service:** From Calgary, Alberta, the bus arrives in Kimberley daily at 12:15 A.M. and leaves for Calgary at 6:15 P.M. From Vancouver, BC, the bus arrives in Kimberley Tuesday–Saturday at 10:15 A.M.

Trail Profiles

Kimberly's trails and lifts have been designed so snowriders can take advantage of the region's large expanse of terrain—not to mention the 12 feet of annual snowfall. The front side of North Star Mountain is loaded with wide-open blue and green cruising runs—all named after mining claims once staked on the mountain.

Novice snowriders flock to *The Main*, the mountain's signature run. Located on the front side, *The Main* is a wide-open, fall-line cruiser with rolling slopes that change to an intermediate pitch as it approaches the bottom. To avoid this steeper pitch, take the *Easy Way Out* to the right. Slightly narrower than *The Main*, but just as gently pitched, is *The Mambo*. It connects with *The Main* to make for a long, full run of confidence-building turns. From this junction, *The Buckhorn* leads to the base over additional intermediate terrain.

Boundary and *Rosa* are solid intermediate cruising trails that twist and turn while frequently changing widths. Also for intermediates, *The Dean* offers three choices: a steep pitch with small moguls, a wider cruising trail, or sometimes, a natural halfpipe. Covered with moguls, *School House* is a fantastic run for learning the fine art of bump skiing.

The advanced action is on Kimberley's backside, where black diamond trails abound. The entire area is accessible from any of the three front-side chairs. Without question, *Easter* is one of Canada's most challenging mogul runs. Hot bump skiers hit this run to show off for the captured crowds overhead on the Easter lift. The trail begins with an aggressive pitch full of moguls and throws a double angle at skiers, as well as a few jumps at the bottom.

Locals are especially fond of the steepness of *Flush*, which has a 50 to 55-degree angle. Falling on this run means being FLUSHed out at the bottom. Once at the bottom, ride back to the top via the Easter Triple chair. Heading back to the lodge is easy. Take the four-mile *Ridgeway* trail back to the base.

Kimberley's only drawback is its chairlift circuit. Covering 2,300 feet of vertical in the slightly outdated chairs can eat up precious ski time (recent lift upgrades should alleviate much of this down time). On the other hand, the slower chairs can provide a much-needed rest for tired knees. Plus, the higher a lift's skier capacity the faster the area's snow is skied out. New snow quickly becomes chewed up and packed down.

Snowboarding **Highlights**

Snowboarding is a big focus at Kimberley. The resort sports a terrain park between *Rosa* and *Dreadnought* and a halfpipe on *The Main*. The pipe is constructed with a Pipe Dragon that Kimberley shares with other resorts owned by the Ski Louise group. The pipe is 25 feet wide and 300 feet long, with 10 to 12-foot verts and four to six-foot trannies.

The park drops 700 vertical feet and covers just over two acres of terrain. The Maverick T-bar gives boarders quick access to the park's eight to 10 obstacles, including table tops, a jump box, spines, berms, and rollerz. The park is built each year by crew members with input from local riders. Thanks to its location on *The Main*, the park is also lit for night riding.

More Fun in the Flakes

The Kimberley Nordic Club **cross-country ski** trail network consists of a variety of double trackset trails with center skating lanes. In addition to three loops of 2, 3, and 4 miles (3, 5, and 7 km), there are also a variety of single trackset secondary trails and a 2-mile (3.3-km) loop lit for night skiing. Be sure to try the new 0.6-mile (1-k) *Cardiac Arrest* trail. It climbs almost 200 feet (60 meters) to an open ridgeline with views in every direction before swooping down to the *Snowbird* trail. The trails are accessed adjacent to the Kimberley Ski & Summer Resort. Turn left to the Kirkwood Inn, and the trailhead is located at the end of the parking lot.

The Mountain Recreation Center offers racquetball, squash, volleyball, and a weight room. **Ice-skating** is offered at the Kimberley Civic Center. Call (250) 427-3622 for more information.

Skier Services

⑤ Lift Tickets

Ages 18–64: $43/day, $35/half-day • **Students:** $35/day, $30/half-day • **Ages 13–17:** $35/day, $30/half-day • **Ages 6–12:** $15 • **Ages 65+:** $35/day, $30/half-day • **Ages 5 & younger:** Free • *Prices based on the 2000–2001 ski season using Canadian currency (GST included). See page 354 for conversion information.*

🎿 Nordic Trail Passes

$3 per person per day with a family maximum of $10 • *Prices based on the 2000–2001 ski season using Canadian currency (GST included). See page 354 for conversion information.*

🎿 Rentals

Ski Rentals: $20–$37/adults; $12–$17/kids, $5/preschool kids; 600 sets. Type of Gear: Rossignol, Salomon, K2, Elan, and Volant • **Snowboard Rentals:** $30; 200 sets. Type of Gear: Rossignol • **Nordic Skis:** $15/adults; $9 kids • *Prices based on the 2000–2001 ski season using Canadian currency (GST included). See page 354 for conversion information.*

31

🛅 Services

Ski School: 50 instructors; Private lessons $35–$40/hour, $55–$65/two hours; Group lessons $20–$25/hour; Beginner's package $29–$39 (includes rentals, lift ticket, and lesson) • **Snowboard School:** 50 instructors; Private lesson $35–$40/hour; Group lessons $19–$24/hours; Beginner's package $30–$40 (includes lift ticket, lesson, and rentals) • **Childcare:** $5/hour, daily maximum $30; 8:30 A.M.– 4:30 P.M. daily; 18 months to six years; reservations strongly recommended; (250) 427–4881 • *Prices based on the 2000–2001 ski season using Canadian currency (GST included). See page 354 for conversion information.*

Room & Board

🛏 Lodging

On-site

Kimberley Vacations Reservations can book the following locations, or you can call direct using the numbers for each selection; 1–800–667–0871 or (250) 427–4877 • **Trickle Creek Residence Inn by Marriott** is located at the base of the resort near the new chair lift; 1–877–282–1200 • **Inn West Condominiums** features one- and two-bedroom condos with kitchen, fireplaces, private balconies, indoor hot tub, an outdoor heated pool, and daily housekeeping, children 12 & under stay free; rates $67–$100/night; 1–800–663–4755 or (250) 427–7616 • **Kirkwood Inn Condominiums** offers hotels and one- and two-bedroom condos, queen size beds, private bathrooms, and fireplaces and Jacuzzis in the condos, children 12 & under stay free; rates $49–$112/night; 1–800–663–4755 • **Mountain Edge Resort Inn** offers one-bedroom suites and condos with fireplace, kitchen, private balcony, covered parking, laundry, and three dry saunas, children 14 & under stay free; rates $56–$104/night; 1–800–525–6622 • **Silver Birch Chalets** is a hotel with double beds, a small fridge, private bathroom, and a living area, children 14 & under stay free; rates $51–$65/night; 1–800–525–6622 • **Mountain Chalets** offers hotel rooms and condos with queen beds, pull out couch, fireplace, private balcony, and free shuttle service to the downtown area; rates $48–$85/night; 1–800–905–8338 • *Call Resort's reservation line for more information at 1–800–667–0871 or (250) 427–4877.*

Kimberley– 3 miles (5km) away

SameSun Travel Hostel is a Bavarian-style building located in the German "Platzl" area of downtown, above a 125-seat pub; rates start at $15/night for dorm bed; (877) 562–2783 • **Mountain Recreation Center** is an RV center, located near the Kimberley Alpine Resort, with indoor tennis, squash, racquetball, and fitness room; rates start at $16/night; (250)

427–2622 • *Call Kimberley Vacations at 1–800–667–0871 or visit their website at www.kimberleyvacations.bc.ca.*

⊕ Dining

On-site

Kelsey's Restaurant is located in the Marriott at the Resort Village • **Kootenay Haus** is the resort's mountain top eatery, with access available from the top of the Rosa Chair • **Mozart's House Inn & Restaurant** serves European specialties (250) 427–7671 • **North Star Centre** offers various family dining locations, such as the Mingles Grill and Krug Stube • **The Snowdrift Cafe** serves natural cuisine. Great coffees and desserts (250) 427–2001.

Kimberley–3 miles (5km) away

Golden Inn Restaurant features great Chinese dining; (250) 427–5513 • **The Old Baurenhaus** serves freshly prepared Bavarian specialties; (250) 427–5133 • **Grubstake Diner** features homemade burgers and delicious pizza; (250) 427–5227 • **Kimberley Sub Shack** serves soups, sandwiches, and Mexican food; (250) 427–5010

The Old Baurenhaus Restaurant

In 1989 Tony Schwarzenberger, a German cabinetmaker and restaurateur, relocated to Kimberley. With him came four gigantic containers. Two held his tools, equipment, and personal belongings, while the other two occupied the carefully packed pieces of his house—yes, his house—a 350-year-old wooden structure that he painstakingly reassembled at the base of the North Star Mountain, just two minutes from the base of the mountain. Originally built to house the servants of a castle, the Old Baurenhaus is now a dining establishment that serves Bavarian-style cuisine. Tony lives on the top floor, the restaurant sits on ground level, and his workshop is in the basement. For more information (250) 427–5133.

Mount Washington

Mount Washington Alpine Resort
Box 3069
Courtenay, BC
Canada V9N 5N3

Ski Report: (250) 338–1515
Information: (250) 338–1386
  From Vancouver: (604) 619–0550
  From Victoria: (250) 213–3375
E-mail: *ski@mtwashington.bc.ca*
Website: *www.mtwashington.bc.ca*
Credit Cards: Visa & MasterCard

Operating Hours: 9 A.M.–3:30 P.M. daily
Snowtubing: 1 P.M.–9:00 P.M. daily

Season: December to April

Randy Lincks/Mt. Washington Alpine Resort

Backdrop

Mount Washington is one of four ski areas on Vancouver Island. While it may be charming to see water in every direction from the top of the mountain, it also makes reaching the resort a bit of a challenge—and it adds to the adventure. The necessary ferry ride to Vancouver Island is absolutely breathtaking. Mount Washington's scenery and superior skiing add up to one of the best-kept secrets in the world.

The resort's 5,215-foot summit is one of the highest points on the island. Views of the Georgia Strait and the snow-capped crags and ice-blue glaciers of the BC Coast Range are unbelievable. As for snow, Mount Washington is truly blessed. The area receives an incredible 32 feet per year on average. Because the resort is surrounded by water, though, snow conditions can vary to the extremes. On any given run, on any given day, snowriders might lay tracks in anything from water-soaked cottage cheese to dusty, dry, cold-smoke powder. But one thing is for sure: The odds of gouging the bases of skis or snowboards are virtually nil.

Mount Washington is currently in the middle of a five-year, $18 million expansion plan. Already completed upgrades include the new Deer Lodge Condominium Hotel, the Ozone Snowtubing Park, and the bottom-to-top high-speed quad Eagle Express. Deer Lodge is a 59-room hotel and is the first portion of the much-anticipated Mount Washington Village Center. The Village borders Strathcona Park, a stunning alpine setting offering ski-in ski-out accommodations in a variety of lodges, chalets, and condos. Ozone Park is a lift-accessed and lighted snowtubing area. And the Eagle Express replaces the old Blue chair, shortening the ride to the peak to only six minutes.

The resort has undergone major re-constructive surgery in other areas as well. The Alpine Lodge is completely refurbished and includes the new Fireweeds Restaurant and Fat Teddy's Bar & Grill. Fireweeds boasts delicious cuisine and is under the careful direction of Chef Hans Zilmann. Fat Teddy's is a 250-seat lounge, complete with a river-rock fireplace, stage, dance floor, game area, and outdoor deck.

Mountain Stats

Base Elevation: 3,558 feet *(1,085 m)*
Summit Elevation: 5215 feet *(1,590 m)*
Vertical Drop: 1,657 feet *(505 m)*
Primary Slope Direction: Northwest
Annual Snowfall: 324 inches *(975 cm)*
Skiable Days: 138
Skiable Terrain: 1,500 acres *(608 ha)*
Runs: 50
Longest Run: 1.2 miles *(1.9 km)*

Lifts: 1 high-speed quad, 1 fixed grip quad, 2 triples, 1 double, 1 poma lift, 1 handle tow, 1 tubing surface lift
Lift Capacity: 10,400 skiers per hour
Terrain Classification: 25% novice: 40% intermediate: 35% advanced
Night Skiing: Friday and Saturday nights
Snowmaking: None
Annual Visits: 300,000

Getting There

- **From Seattle, WA and Portland, OR:** Take I-5 north to U.S./Canada border. *[Directions continued below.]*
- **From Spokane, WA:** Take I-90 west to I-405. Go north on I-405 to I-5. Take I-5 north to U.S./Canada border. *[Directions continued below.]*
- **From Boise, ID:** Take I-84 north to I-82. Continue on I-82 north until I-90. Then take I-90 west to I-405. Go north on I-405 to I-5. Take I-5 north to U.S./Canada border. *[Directions continued below.]*

[Continued.] Once across the border, take Provincial Highway 15 (PH 15) north. Stay on PH 15 until the Trans-Canada Highway 1 (TCH 1). Follow TCH 1 through **Vancouver, BC.** TCH 1 ends near Whytecliff, but PH 99 continues. Follow PH 99 (also known as the Sea to Sky Highway) to the Nanaimo Ferry Terminal. Ferry signs are very visible. From Nanaimo take PH 19 north to Courtenay and follow signs to Mount Washington.

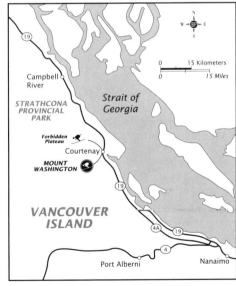

📧 **Ferry Service:** Call British Columbia Ferries for a schedule: 1–888–223–3779

✈ **Airport Services:** For guests traveling from outside the Northwest the closest major airport is in Victoria. Most travelers will fly into Vancouver, BC, before changing to Air BC or Air Canada and continuing on to either Courtenay (YQQ) or Campbell River (YBL) airports.

🚌 **Bus Services:** These companies offer daily scheduled service to the resort. Call for details. Mount Washington Ski Shuttle: (250) 338–1386; Mount Washington Ski Bus: (250) 475–3339; Forest Bus Tours: (250) 754–3464; and Smith Transportation: (250) 756–2544

Trail Profiles

Mount Washington's 50 trails and 1,500 acres of skiable terrain are never crowded, mainly because getting there is a bit of a trek. Unlike some other BC resorts, the slopes of Mt. Washington will never resemble a giant anthill from the base. While the snowriding at Mount Washington is fantastic, the resort could stand to benefit from enhancing the trail system for novice skiers. Unfortunately, no easy trails are available from top to bottom. Beginners are relegated to the lower half of the resort and are unable to take in the magical views from the mountain's peak.

Beginners will, however, enjoy the long, gentle trails accessed by the Red chair. *Jack's Run* and *Westerly* are wide-open groomed slopes that deposit snowriders near the cross-country lodge. To reach the main lodge, take the Green chair up and ski *Home Run* or *Easy Out*. Both offer mild terrain right to the base area. Novice skiers and boarders will also appreciate *Green Acres*. The popular family run is extra wide, moderately pitched, groomed daily, and easily accessed from the rope tow, Discovery Platter, or Green chair.

Intermediates will find several trails to choose from around the mountain. From the top of the Eagle Express try *Linton's Loop, Retirement, Whiskey Jack* or *Coaster*. All three begin above the treeline and take you all the way to the base area. Expect great powder runs on fresh-snow days and moguls and groomed corduroy on others. *Invitation, The Gully* and

![Snowboarding icon] **Snowboarding Highlights**

No longer does Mount Washington lend itself just to skiers. In recent years, the resort jumped on the snowboarding bandwagon, and the investment has paid off. Each season, crewmembers construct two highly rated terrain parks and a halfpipe.

The advanced Central Park covers the entire *Retirement* trail and is accessed from the top of the Eagle Express quad. *Retirement's* 800 feet (244 m) of vertical includes rolls, banked turns, pyramids, pro jumps, spines, and tabletops. A 300-foot halfpipe with 10- to 12-foot walls is sculpted daily with a Pipe Dragon.

The Red Park, found off the Red chair, is designed with novice boarders in mind. Covering the lower half of *Red Run*, the park has fewer—and much tamer—features than Central Park. Keep in mind, though, the top of *Red Run* is a black diamond. Novice riders desiring an easier entrance into the park can hang a left off the top of the lift and shred down the first run, *Tyee*. Stay on the left side of *Tyee* to cross over to the bottom of Red.

Fantastic can be accessed off the Sun Rise quad. None of these runs climb above the tree-line, but sleek cruising is just about guaranteed.

Advanced and expert snowriders will find challenging terrain on the west side of the mountain. The new Eagle Express quad offers visitors access to *Boundary, Far Out,* and *Raven.* Wide but usually saturated with moguls, the trails have steep lines that begin above the trees and drop quickly into cut trails. Even steeper and bumpier are *Schum's Delight, Fletcher's Challenge,* and *Sunrise Face*—the steepest trails at Mount Washington. *Powder Face* is a wide-open run of face shots and thigh-deep powder on major snow days.

For stashes and caches of untracked snow, try the gladed areas off the Sunrise quad, between *Fletcher's Challenge* and *Schum's Delight.* Also, check out the northwest side of the Eagle Express Area for even more tree skiing.

More Fun in the Flakes

Mount Washington is a paradise for **cross-country skiing**. Over 25 miles (40 km) of trackset and skating trails of varying skill levels spread out west form the resort area. Groomed and patrolled regularly, the trails are lift serviced and partially located in BC's oldest provincial park, Strathcona.

After the sunsets be sure to take a **Lantern Light Cross-country Tour**, held Saturday nights beginning in December. The tour includes dinner, hot chocolate, a bonfire, and a magical night of skiing or snowshoeing by lanterns. Reservations are required. The resort offers guided **snowshoeing tours** that take you into the surrounding backcountry. Rentals are available, as are tips on snowshoeing techniques. For details on either activity, contact the lodge at (250) 338–1386.

Ozone Park is a lift-accessed and night-lit **snowtubing** recreation area. The park is over a half-mile long (875 m) and consists of three tubing chutes. There is a $15 fee for unlimited usage.

Skier Services

💲 Lift Tickets

Adult: $44/day • **Youth/Senior:** $36/day • **Child:** $23/day • *Prices based on the 2000–2001 ski season using Canadian currency. See page 354 for conversion information.*

🎿 Nordic Trail Passes

Adult: $16 • **Youth/Senior::** $12 • *Prices based on the 2000–2001 ski season using Canadian currency. See page 354 for conversion information.*

🎿 Snowtubing Park Tickets

$10/3 hour pass • $15/day • *Prices based on the 2000–2001 ski season using Canadian currency. See page 354 for conversion information.*

⛷ Rentals

Ski Rentals: $22/adults; $15/kids; 2000 sets. Type of Gear: Rossignol, Elan, and Head • **Snowboard Rentals:** $36/adults; $28/kids; 400 sets. Type of Gear: Rossignol • **Nordic Ski Rentals:** $16/adults; $12/kids • **Snowshoe Rentals:** $9/adults; $6/kids • *Prices based on the 2000–2001 ski season using Canadian currency. See page 354 for conversion information.*

👥 Services

Ski School: 60 instructors, Private lessons $30–$38/hour and $10–$15 more for each additional hour; Group lessons $11/hour with a minimum of 20 skiers; Beginner's package $46 (includes lift ticket, rentals, and lesson) • **Snowboard School:** 60 instructors, Private lessons $30–$38/hour and $10–$15 more for each additional hour; Group lessons $11/hour with a minimum of 20 skiers; Beginner's package $67 (includes lift ticket, rentals, and lesson) • **Nordic Ski School:** Beginner's package $33 (includes rentals, lesson, and trail pass) • **Childcare:** For children ages five and younger. Licensed, limited space, advanced registration is required: (250) 344–1386 • *Prices based on the 2000–2001 ski season using Canadian currency. See page 354 for conversion information.*

Room & Board

Mount Washington Ski Resort is currently in the middle of major upgrades and is remodeling many of the slope-side accommodations. Guests' choices are growing each year between chalets, hotels, and condominiums. Deer Lodge opened recently, providing visitors with a comfortable luxurious place to rest after a hard day on the slopes. Alpine Lodge has been completely remodeled and welcomes visitors as well. In addition, there are several B&Bs to choose from as well as hotels in nearby Courtenay. *Call Central Reservations for information about packages or to make reservations; 1–888–231–1499.*

🛏 Lodging

On-site

Deer Lodge is a 59-room slope-side hotel with fireplaces, jetted tubs, whirlpool, and balconies; rates $110–$190/night; 1–888–686–4663 • **Paradise Ridge Accommodations** offers two- and three-bedroom condos and three-bedroom townhouses, all with fully equipped kitchen, gas fireplace, pool, hot tub, and sauna; rates $135–$275/night; 1–877–287–9491 or *www.paradiseridge.bc.ca* • **Cat's Meow B&B** offers two cozy guest bedrooms in a slope-side chalet with ski in/ski out ability, fireplace, breakfast, and view; rates $65–$90/night; (250) 897–1871 or (250) 658–0087.

Courtenay–14 miles (23km) away

Coast Westerly Hotel offers 108 deluxe rooms, cold beer and wine store, indoor pool, saunas, exercise room, ski waxing room, and locking ski racks; rates $95–$104/night; 1–800–668–7797 or (250) 338–7741 • **Crown Isle Villas** offers deluxe suites, and one- and two-bedroom condos with kitchens, Jacuzzi baths, fireplaces and decks, fitness center, and

Randy Lincks/Mt. Washington Alpine Resort

ski packages available; rates $178–$320/night; 1–888–388–VIEW or (250) 338–7777 or *www.crownisle.com* • **Kingfisher Oceanside Resort & Spa, Quality Inn & Suites** offers14 beachfront suites with fireplaces, whirlpools, and kitchens; 28 rooms with spa, outdoor hot tub, heated pool, fitness room, steam cave, sauna, and ski shuttle; rates $80–$225/night; 1–800–663–7999 or (250) 338–1323 or *www.kingfisher-resort-spa.com* • **Saratoga Beach Resort** offers a quiet, relaxing ocean side retreat with cottages, cable TV, some fireplaces, and RV sites; rates $16–$70/night; (250) 337–5511 • *Call the Comox Valley Chamber of Commerce for more options: (250) 334–3234 or www.tourism-comox-valley.bc.ca.*

Dining

On-site

Fireweed's Restaurant offers fine dining with a view of the ski runs • **Fat Teddy's Bar & Grill** serves great pub food with true atmosphere on the main level of the Alpine Lodge • **Alpine Cafeteria** is located on the top floor of the Alpine Lodge • **The Hungry Marmot** is located on the Marmots level of the Alpine Lodge • **Nordic Café** is located in the Nordic Lodge and accessed from the cross country trails or from the base of the Red chair.

Courtenay–14 miles (23km) away

Atlas Café serves Mexican, Italian, Japanese, Indian, and Mediterranean dishes for break-fast, lunch, and dinner; (250) 338–9838 • **Kingfisher Oceanside Restaurant** offers water-front dining with a view of the coast mountains, nearby islands, and marine life, serving fresh seafood, authentic German schnitzels, Sunday brunch, and a seafood buffet; (250) 334–9600 • **The Old House Restaurant** serves hearty, homemade West Coast cuisine in a cozy atmosphere with four stone fireplaces, and rough hewn timbers; (250) 338–5406 • **Union Street Grill** is a pub-style restaurant open for all meals, features a large selection of dishes, kids' menu and great blues and jazz; (250) 897–0081.

Panorama Mtn Village

Panorama Mountain Village
Toby Creek Road
Panorama, British Columbia
Canada V0A 1T0

Ski Report: (250) 342–6941
Information: 1–800–663–2929;
  (250) 342–6941
E-mail: *paninfo@intrawest.com*
Website: *www.panoramaresort.com*
Credit Cards: Visa & MasterCard

Operating Hours: 9 A.M.–4 P.M. daily
Night Skiing: Open daily, 4 P.M.–9 P.M.

Season: Mid December to mid April

Background

Winter outdoor enthusiasts who know southeast British Columbia's Panorama might agree it's the most underrated ski resort in the Northwest. Panorama boasts the second highest vertical drop (4,000 feet) of any Canadian ski resort, and ski rags routinely ignore the area's plush grooming, long-distance runs, and bone-dry snow. Then there are the majestic Canadian Rockies. To properly take them in, *View of 1,000 Peaks* is a must for any snowrider.

As a member of the Purcell Range, Panorama is a natural vista from which to view the main spine of the Canadian Rockies. In every direction, literally thousands of peaks are jammed together like fraternity boys in a phone booth. The closest crags are Mount Nelson and Monument Peak. Mount Assiniboine, which sits just south of Banff, Alberta, at 11,800 feet, is the region's largest mountain and is visible to the east on clear days. Add an intimate ski-in ski-out mountain village and one of the largest heli-ski zones in the world and Panorama is a gold rush of snowriding waiting to happen. Fact is, the resort should be more popular. On the other hand, not being part of the "in-crowd" has its advantages. Lengthy lift lines and on-slope anthill-like congestion simply don't exist at Panorama. But this reprieve from development could be short-lived.

Panorama was recently purchased by Intrawest—the same industry giant responsible for making Whistler-Blackcomb one of the world's biggest and most successful resorts. As of yet, the massive expansion seen at Whistler hasn't exploded on Panorama. And it's likely that it won't, as the village, by design, is not a resort like Whistler. While area management readies for the growth spurt, now is a good time to experience Panorama, before the rush begins.

Mountain Stats

Base Elevation: 3,800 feet *(1,160 m)*
Summit Elevation: 7,800 feet *(2,380 m)*
Vertical Drop: 4,000 feet *(1,220 m)*
Primary Slope Direction: Northwest
Annual Snowfall: 145 inches *(347cm)*
Skiable Days: 130
Skiable Terrain: 2,700 acres *(810 ha)*
Runs: 110
Longest Run: 2.1 miles *(3.4 km)*

Lifts: 5 surface lifts, 2 doubles, 1 triple, 1 high-speed quad, 1 village gondola
Lift Capacity: 7,602 skier per hour
Terrain Classification: 20% novice: 25% intermediate: 30% advanced: 25% expert
Night Skiing: 4 runs, snowboard park, and halfpipe
Snowmaking: 50% allowance
Annual Visits: 170,000+

Getting There

- **From Portland, OR:** Take I-5 north to Seattle. *[Follow Seattle directions below.]*
- **From Seattle, WA:** Take I-90 to Spokane. *[Follow Spokane directions below.]*
- **From Spokane, WA:** Take I-90 east to Coeur d'Alene, ID. From Coeur d'Alene, take US 95 north to the town of Invermere, BC. At the Canadian border, US 95 changes to Provincial Highway 3/95/93 (PH 3/95/93). Take the Invermere exit and proceed into town. Follow Panorama Ski Resort signs to the ski area.
- **From Vancouver, BC:** Take Provincial Highway 3 (PH 3) east to PH 3/95/93. Follow this road north to the town of Invermere. Take the Invermere exit and proceed into town. Follow Panorama Ski Village signs to the ski area.

Airport Services: For guests traveling from outside the Northwest, the Calgary International Airport (YYC) is the closest major gateway airport. Most travelers will fly into Calgary.

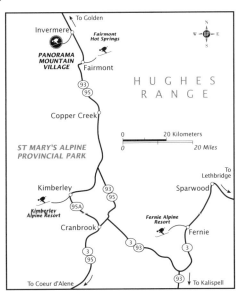

Trail Profiles

Located on the warm side of the Rockies, Panorama offers 2,000 acres of skiable terrain. Snowmaking covers 50 percent of the named runs up to the first 3,200 feet of vertical. This almost guarantees an early season-opener (November) for race training camps, but Panorama is not open to the general public until December. The snowmaking also allows top-to-bottom skiing in late spring. Ten lifts, including one high-speed detachable-quad, provide access to 100-plus trails. The resort's one flaw is its lift circuit. Five of the 10 lifts are surface lifts. Riding two surface lifts to the summit can be tough on the legs. Moreover, surface lifts are typically slow. But the slower pace keeps the snow from being skied out too fast; not to mention it keeps lift ticket prices in check.

A visit to Panorama in the past has always meant thigh-burning top-to-bottom super-G turn-'til-you-can't-see-straight better-bring-the-big-sleds snowriding. As exhilarating as this was (and still is), the resort offered little in the way of variety. Until now. Although Intrawest hasn't yet overhauled the chairlift circuit, it has opened 1,000 acres of new terrain, making Panorama a more well-rounded resort. A fifth of the new acreage is aptly named the *Extreme Dream Zone*.

Located on the north side of the summit, the *Zone* is a "Dream" because Old Man Winter deposits more snow in this area than anywhere else on the mountain. And it's good quality snow at that. Because it's in a high alpine basin, the *Zone* catches extremely light snow, and conditions remain relatively consistent. Freshies abound in the *Zone* days after big storms. Because of the steep and ungroomed fall-line snowriding, it's fair to call the *Zone* "Extreme." The *Zone* is filled with cliff bands, gladed tree skiing, and constricting throats like *Gunbarrel* and *Zone 2*. The *Lower Zone* is a basin filled with large lateral and terminal moraines left by the glacier that carved the basin ages ago. *Dunes* and *Fat Chance* follow the wacky and challenging terrain. The moguls carved by skiers can be monstrous but are well shaped, since the skiers who choose these runs tend to make consistent fall-line turns. *Last Chance* skirts the north side of the *Zone* and is probably Panorama's best bump run.

Snowboarding Highlights

Panorama recently built a new terrain park and a new halfpipe accessible from the Toby chair. The *Show Zone* covers three runs—*Newtimer, Hoggs Flats,* and *Eagle Glide*—and is lit for night riding. The park is a hit with the riders and boarders from all over Canada. In 1999 Panorama hosted the Western Canadian Boarder Cross and Halfpipe Championships. Competition was fierce as riders ripped through the park, which is filled with rollerz, kickers, banked turns, quarterpipes, and tabletops. Plus, Panorama constructs a FIS regulation halfpipe in the park. At the top of the pipe, riders (mostly kids) hang out in The Love Shack—parents need not worry; this funky cabin is a spot for boarders to congregate, listen to music, and grab a hot chocolate and snacks. The park is built by area crewmembers with input from local riders.

Though Panorama is catering more to the freestyle crowd, the most popular form of riding here is carving. The huge amount of smoothly groomed vertical is ideal for hard-boot riding and laying down gigantic turns.

It should be noted that the large elevation difference and massive amount of terrain lead to substantial variations in snow conditions. The *Sun Bowl* faces south while the *Zone* faces north. Spring conditions can offer powder and corn on the same day. From top to bottom, the snow changes from soft, forgiving powder that blows up in your face to damper heavier snow near the bottom.

Stronger intermediate snowriders can take in the stunning *View of 1,000 Peaks* around the *Upper Zone*, then drop in on *Elmo* to nibble on bits of the *Zone* without terrifying themselves in the *Gunbarrel*. For less extreme but still adventurous terrain, intermediates can explore *Sun Bowl*. Located on the other side of the mountain, *Sun Bowl* provides an opportunity for less-aggressive snowriders to experience tree skiing, bumps, and powder minus the steepness of the *Zone*.

Scott Rowed,/Panorama Mountain Village

The mountain's lower and middle sections feature boulevard sized runs ideal for cruising. *Skyline, Roller Coaster*, and *Fritz's* drop 3,000 vertical feet in just 1.2 miles (2 k). At 2.2 miles (3.5 k) long, *Schober's Dream* is the ultimate cruiser when it's groomed—or thigh-burning hell if it's bumpy. Fortunately, it's groomed once a week. When combined with *Roy's* run from the summit, *Schober's* is about 3 miles (5 k) long.

Novice terrain includes the secluded beginners-only Silver Platter lift at the base, *Eagle Glide* on the Toby chair, *Horseshoe* on the Quad chair, and *Outrider* on the Sunbird chair. This is mostly green terrain that's always immaculately groomed. There are a few pitches that are accessible from the Quad and Sunbird lifts that may appear intimidating to a first-time skier or boarder. The good news is that the runs are wide, and there are escape routes around the steeper lines.

More Fun in the Flakes

Explore the new Beckie Scott Nordic Center which offers 10.5 miles (17 k) of groomed and classic **cross-country skiing** trails. Ski rentals, change rooms, lockers, showers, and snacks are all available at the center.

For **snowmobiling**, adventures call 1–800–663–2929. **Heli-skiing** is available through R.K. Heli-Ski Panorama Inc. at (250) 342–3889 *(see page 317)*.

Enjoy Panorama's new 6,000-square-foot heated **Slope Side Hot Pools** Guests will find heated outdoor swimming pools, landscaped water slides, and hot tubs. The cost is included for guests of Panorama. The waterpark is located in upper village.

Skier Services

🅢 Lift Tickets

Ages 19 and older: $49/day, $38/half day • **Ages 13–18:** $39/day, $32/half day • **Ages 65 and older:** $39/day, $32/half day • **Ages 7–12:** $27/day, $20/half day • **Ages 6 and younger:** $9/day, $6.50/half day • **Ages 19–25 (Student):** $43/day, $34/half day • *Prices based on the 2000–2001 ski season using Canadian currency (excluding GST). See page 354 for conversion information.*

🅐 Nordic Trail Passes

Adult: $5 • **Child:** $4 • *Prices based on the 2000–2001 ski season using Canadian currency (excluding GST). See page 354 for conversion information.*

🅡 Rentals

Ski Rentals: $20/adults; $15/children; 500 sets. Type of Gear: Rossignol, Salomon, Atomic, Kastle, Volant, and Nordica • **Snowboard Rentals:** $35/adults; 100 sets. Type of Gear: Rossignol, Burton, and Salomon • **Nordic Ski Rentals:** $15/adults; $10/children • Snowshoe Rentals: $15/day • **Snowblade Rentals:** $25/day; $6/hour • *Prices based on the 2000–2001 ski season using Canadian currency (excluding GST). See page 354 for conversion information.*

🅢 Services

Ski School: 20 instructors; Private lessons $59/hour; Group lessons $39/hour, Beginner's package $79 (includes lift tickets, lessons, and rentals) • **Snowboard School:** 10 instructors; Private lessons $59/hour; Group lessons $39/hours; Beginner's package $79 (includes lift tickets, lessons, and rentals) • For **reservations** or more information see *www.skischool.com*, email *mariah@rockies.net*, or call 1–800–505–7799 • *Prices based on the 2000–2001 ski season using Canadian currency (excluding GST). See page 354 for conversion information.*

Room & Board

🅛 Lodging

Panorama already offers several options for ski-in ski-out lodging. Accommodations range from traditional hotel rooms (105 in all) to 355 condominium and townhouse units, many of which have been constructed or upgraded recently. While the resort maintains a low-key village atmosphere, guests will find a full range of services offered to ensure a relaxing vacation. Panorama recently introduced its 6,000-square-foot heated waterpark, which features heated outdoor swimming pools, landscaped water slides, and hot tubs. The park, located in the upper village, is free to guests staying at the resort.

On-site

The Hearthstone Townhomes offer one of the best locations on the mountain. Designer one- two- or three-bedroom townhomes located at the base of the ski slopes feature major appliances, laundry, fireplace, TV, king beds, pull out sofa beds, and a private parking area • **Panorama Springs at Ski Tip & Tamarack Lodge** offer a designer studio and one- and two-bedroom suites with full kitchen, dishwasher, double sofa bed, fireplace, balcony, and direct access to the Mile 1 high-speed quad chair. Family Style Condominiums in Toby Creek or Horsethief Lodges offer family style studios, one- and two-bedroom units, or three-bedroom units (Horsethief only), with kitchen, dishwasher, fireplace, TV, balcony, and underground parking • **The Pine Inn Hotel** is located at the base of Mile 1 high-speed quad chair, adjacent to Ski Tip Lodge, and offers ski-in ski-out standard rooms with full bath, TV, phone, hot tub, sauna, lounge and restaurants • *For reservations or information on the following contact Panorama at 1–800–663–2929 or www.panoramaresort.com. Each is available with a variety of lift/lodging package deals; rates $79–$500/night, depending on season and occupancy.*

Nearby

See **Fairmont Hot Springs Resort** *(page 81)* for additional lodging and dining options.

Ⓓ Dining

On-site

Kicking Horse Bar and Grill is a sports saloon with hearty meals, great burgers, and live entertainment on weekends, ages 19 and above • **Jackpine Pub** is a traditional Alpine pub with darts, pool, beer, and a simple menu; ages 19 and older • **Starbird Steakhouse** is a family style steakhouse serving breakfast, lunch, and dinner with fish, pasta, chicken, and vegetarian dishes • **The Great Hall Daylodge** offers family dining with salad bar, pizza, sandwiches, baked goods, and burgers for people on the slopes • **Toby Creek Dining Room** offers a truly Canadian menu with wild game, "hot rocks," fondues, unique house-made desserts, and an extensive wine list in a formal dining setting • **The Clubhouse at Greywolf** serves steak sandwiches, pastas, and pizzas • *For reservations or information on the following contact Panorama at 1–800–663–2929 or www.panoramaresort.com.*

Silver Star Mtn Resort

Silver Star Mountain Resort

P.O. Box 3002
Silver Star Mountain, British Columbia
Canada, V1B 3M1

Ski Report: (250) 542–1745
Information: (250) 542–0224
E-mail: *star@silverstarmtn.com*
Website: *www.silverstarmtn.com*
Credit Cards: VISA, MasterCard, & AMEX

Operating Hours: 8:30 A.M.–3:30 P.M. daily.
Night Skiing: Tuesday–Saturday 3:30
P.M.–9:00 P.M.
Season: Mid November to mid April

Don Weixl/Silver Star Mtn Resort

Background

Few of British Columbia's ski areas can hang their tuques (hats) on as many awards as Silver Star Mountain. *Ski Canada* magazine awarded Silver Star number one rankings in the categories for "Best Family Skiing," "Best Grooming," "Best Back Bowl Skiing," and "Best Base Village." *enRoute* magazine rated Silver Star "one of Western North America's top ten resorts." And *Skiing* magazine referred to Silver Star as "one of the best places you've never skied." All of the awards are well deserved. Located just minutes away from Vernon, BC, Silver Star offers skiers and snowboarders a complete winter adventure, including a multi-colored Victorian base village, luxurious amenities, family entertainment, and best of all, awesome snowriding.

Silver Star is a two-faced mountain, with Vance Creek on the south side and Putnam Creek on the north. Both sides already offer great terrain for boarders and skiers of all levels, but the future looks even brighter. The BC Ministry of Environment, Lands, and Parks approved a 10-year master plan to more than double the area's total acreage from 2,200 to 5,000. This will ultimately translate into more trails for carving, turning, gliding, sliding, jumping, tree banging, exploring, ripping, shredding, cruising, etc. The plan will also increase the resort's guest accommodations.

Children and the young at heart have benefited most from the first phase of expansion, which took place in the late 1990s with the development of the Knoll, a delightful winter playground for children of all ages. Located on the west side of the resort and accessed by

the Silver Queen chair, the Knoll includes Brewer's Skating Pond, a novice ski hill, a miniature snowmobile course through the trees, and the fabulously popular Tube Town. The ski
hill provides a gentle pitch and is safely tucked away from more aggressive snowriders, which
makes novice skiers and boarders feel more comfortable. The trail leading back to the main
village winds its way through several of the Victorian homes built in the forest. Due to strict
design codes, every building, commercial or residential, must include at least five colors on
its exterior and must be in the Victorian style of architecture. Exploring the terrain amidst
the houses, hotels, and condos is like skiing in a world colored by a giant box of Crayola
Crayons. Kids love it.

Mountain Stats

Base Elevation: 3,780 feet *(1,152 m)*
Summit Elevation: 6,280 feet *(1,915 m)*
Village: 5,280 feet *(1,610 m)*
Vertical Drop: 2,500 feet *(760 m)*
Primary Slope Direction: South on the
Vance Creek side and Northeast on the
Putnam side.
Annual Snowfall: 23 feet *(701 cm)*
Skiable Days: 180
Skiable Terrain: 3,065 acres
Runs: 107 marked downhill trails
Longest Run: 5 miles *(8.1 km)*

Lifts: 2 detachable quads, 1 fixed grip
quad, 2 doubles, 2 T-bars, 1 handle-tow
Lift Capacity: 13,800 skiers per hour
Terrain Classification: 20% novice; 50%
intermediate; 20% advanced; 10%
expert
Night Skiing: 3:30 P.M.–9:00 P.M.
Tuesday–Saturday; 2 lifts open
Snowmaking: None needed
Annual Visits: 342,000

Tube Town consists of three groomed runs designed specifically for intertubing. Silver
Star provides hi-tech tubes and a Dopplemeyer lift designed to take tubers back to the top
of the slope. Each run looks like a short but wide frozen-water slide. At the bottom there's
a run out area—where several employees keep everything under control. Tube Town is a fantastic day or night activity for the entire family or a great way to take a break from skiing.
(Tickets for Tube Town are separate from the cost of a lift ticket.) Next to Tube Town is the
Mini Z Park, where real miniature snowmobiles take kids 14 and younger through a twisting trail in the forest. Each lap is roughly $3.

Phase two of the resort's master plan focuses on the already picturesque Victorian Village.
The expansion of the village and the surrounding area will increase the number of beds from
2,400 to 7,100. Completed in late 1997, the Silver Creek Hotel was the first of the new
hotels to open. The exterior features cultured stone, cedar accents, and a mansard style roof.
Inside guests will find imported Italian tile, custom designed furniture, and spacious suites
(each boasting a completely self-sufficient kitchenette). These special touches provide visitors with a warm atmosphere to round out their mountain experience.

Phase three will concentrate on the development of two additional high-speed quads.
The first new lift planned for installation is the Silver Woods high-speed quad. Its top tower
will be located at the top of the Knoll residential area, and drop 1,500 feet below the loading area of the Vance Creek high-speed quad. This will open up approximately 200 acres of
mostly intermediate terrain.

Next, on the Putnam Creek side, Silver Star will install the Valhalla high-speed quad. Three runs are already cut and open for skiing. Skiers and boarders who are willing to hike 20 minutes will find fresh turns almost every time. The new chair will provide access to 400 acres of new snowriding, most of which is advance to expert terrain.

Lastly, Silver Star will install the Trinity Bowl Express. This will open up 300 acres of terrain between the Putnam and Vance Creek sides of the mountain, which will solve Silver Star's only real drawback. The resort is near perfect right now except for the fact that there is a long traverse out to the Putnam Creek side of the mountain. When the Trinity Bowl Express is installed, the long traverse will be eliminated. Ninety percent of the terrain in *Trinity Bowl* will be intermediate to advanced.

With all this expansion, it's easy to assume that the cost of visiting Silver Star will increase dramatically. Not likely. The resort seems dedicated to providing a quality winter vacation to families at an affordable price. Every year there are specially priced packages that include lifts and lodging. Prices are so good, they're sometimes hard to believe. Moreover, dining at Silver Star is another great value. The resort is too close to the town of Vernon to charge unreasonable prices. And as long as the U.S. dollar remains stronger than the Canadian dollar, Silver Star will be an exceptional value.

Getting There

- **From Portland, OR:** Go North on I-5. *[Follow Seattle direction below.]*
- **From Seattle, WA:** Take I-5 north to WA 542 (Exit 255). WA 542 is also named East Sunset Drive and the Mount Baker Highway. Take WA 542 to WA 9. Head north on WA 9 to the town of Sumas. Cross into Canada and take TCH 1 east toward Hope. *[Follow Vancouver direction below.]*
- **From Vancouver, BC:** Take Trans-Canada Highway 1 (TCH 1) east to Hope. Take Provincial Highway 5 (PH 5) north to Merritt. Please note that a toll is required to travel on portions of PH 5. At Merritt, take PH 5A south to Aspen Grove. At Aspen Grove, follow PH 97C east until it ends at PH 97. Take PH 97 north to Vernon, BC. Drive through Vernon and turn right at 48th Avenue, which becomes Silver Star Road. Follow Silver Star Road to the resort.
- **From Spokane, WA:** Head north on U.S. 395 to the US-Canadian border. Once in Canada, take PH 3 west to Rock Creek. At Rock Creek, take PH 33 north toward Kelowna. At Kelowna, follow PH 97 north to Vernon.

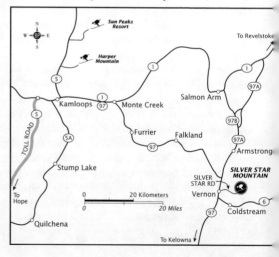

Drive through Vernon and take a right onto 48th Ave., which becomes Silver Star Road. Follow Silver Star to the resort.

✈ **Airport Services:** For guests traveling from outside of the Northwest, the closest regional airport is Kelowna Airport (YLW). Guest flying from Seattle or Portland, check with Horizon Air (1–800–547–9308) for special ski packages. In the past, prices have been under $100 per person per day for three days of skiing, lodging, and air and ground transportation. Once arriving in Kelowna, a pre-registered shuttle is available to the ski area. Call Central Reservations at 1–800–663–4431 if you need shuttle transportation.

Trail Profiles

Silver Star's 107 trails are all accessible from the Vance Creek Express, which is located on the front side (the Vance Creek side) of the mountain. To reach the back side (the Putnam Creek side), snowriders must skate out *Bergerstrasse*, a long flat green trail, to Paradise Camp and then make yet another traverse out to the runs on either side of the Putnam Creek Express. Paradise Camp serves as small mid-mountain restaurant and the mid-station for the Putnam Creek Express, which transports skiers and boarders up and down the back side. The traverse may be long, but the snowriding is some of the best in the Northwest.

For an advanced skier warm-up and a challenging intermediate run, hang a right at Paradise Camp and head out to the *Gypsy Queen*, a long, plush, rolling cruiser with a super consistent fall line. The pitch is just steep enough to provide enough speed to rip long, fast giant slalom turns. Feel free to hang it all out as traffic is virtually non-existent on this superbly manicured slope.

On the other side of the chair, try *Sunny Ridge* for another long blue cruiser. *Sunny Ridge* is another run that advanced and intermediate snowriders will love. Advanced snowriders can rip mach five turns down its face, while intermediates can go at their own pace on the velvety corduroy. Intermediates will only find a couple more blues runs on the back side. In fact, of the 30-plus in the Putnam Creek area, less than 10 are blue or green runs. Hence, Putnam Creek is the local favorite for aggressive snowriders.

From *Sunny Ridge* drop into *Holy Smoke* or *Bon Diablo*. Both are single black diamond runs. They offer steep pitches but nothing completely insane. They are packed with natural hits and small drops that roll over and down on to the lower sections of the trail. Both develop small bumps late in the day but any advanced snowrider should be able to handle both runs. It's on the other side of the Putnam Creek Express where skiers and boarders find wicked terrain.

3 Wise Men is the first trail down the *Bergerstrasse*, to the skier's left of the mid-station. (There is no reason to go all the way to the top of the Putnam Creek Express until heading back to the village. Simply unload at the mid-station to explore this area.) There is nothing intelligent about *3 Wise Men*. The fall line is steep and riddled with several small, unavoidable hits on the top half. While descending, the trail narrows into a gully that's similar to a giant halfpipe, but the trannies in this halfpipe are littered with bumps, stumps and jumps. Plus, the bottom of the backside is roughly 1,000 feet lower than on the village side, which often results in heavy snow. This can mean snow conditions change in the middle of the run. In any case, there's enough to worry about as *3 Wise Men* remains steep and turns thin near the bottom.

The Headwall and *Chute 5* are a little farther down the *Bergerstrasse*, and both offer steep bump-riddled terrain. They are as steep as *3 Wise Men* but wider from top to bottom, and longer.

On the Vance Creek side, advanced boarders and skiers will love the trails in the Attridge area. Take the Summit chair to the top and hang a left on the *Attridge Access Trail*. Another long traverse, the trail delivers snowriders to the land of pow pow. Because the runs are short in this area and the Putnam side attracts most of the advanced powder skiers, runs like *Out Back*, *Fast Back* and *Bus Back* usually provide fresh tracks even late in the day. Not many skiers visit this area any more.

The rest of the Vance Creek side of the mountain is dedicated to intermediate snowriders. The best plan is to head straight to the top of the Vance Creek Express and take in the spectacular views of the Monashee and the Pinnacle mountains. Even the tip of Big White Ski Resort is visible on a clear day. Closer to Silver Star, look for the sparkling blue waters of Lake Kalamalka and Lake Okanagan. From there, carve turns down any one of immaculately groomed runs like *Over the Hill*, *Sundance*, *Whiskey Jack*, and *Little Dipper*. All offer consistent fall line turns on football field wide intermediate trails. While all are groomed to perfection every day, *Whiskey Jack* is the favorite among locals. The *Jack* offers the steepest pitch and slightly undulating terrain. Its popularity, however, can cause the *Jack* to be congested at times.

Novice and lower intermediate snowriders should stick to *Deer Park*, *Far Out*, and the *BX Corral*. The *Corral* is a short run accessed by the Town T-bar and is the perfect area to work on basic snowriding skills. *Deer Park* and *Far Out* allow every one to explore the top of the mountain. Both are long and extremely gentle green trails that start at the top of the mountain and return to the village.

More Fun in the Flakes

Silver Star offers 28 miles (45 km) of groomed and trackset **cross-country skiing tails**, 2.5 miles (4 km) of lit track for **night skiing**, and 31 miles (50 km) of track trails at the adjacent Sovereign Lake area.

Skating is found on Brewers Pond, which is open daily until 9 P.M. Skating is included with the purchase of any lift ticket. Skate rentals are available at Silver Queen Day Lodge.

Adjacent to the pond in Tube Town. Newly built, Tube Town provides the fun of **tubing** in a safe and controlled environment.

Silver Star Snowmobile Adventures provides daily guided **snowmobile tours** of the extensive snowmobile area within Silver Star Provincial Park. The office is located adjacent to the village in parking lot D, next to Brewer's Skating Pond. Call 1–800–416–5794 or (250) 558–5575 for more information. For kids ages six to 14, Mini Z Park has miniature snowmobiles.

Sleigh rides are available Tuesday, Wednesday, and Saturday from 4:30 P.M. to 9 P.M. Free of charge to all on-mountain hotel guests. Departs from the village. Call (250) 545–4956 for more information. **Dogsled rides** are offered around Brewers Pond or in the sub-alpine with an experienced musher and his team of huskies. Call (250) 545–3901 for details. For **guided snowshoe tours,** both scenic and historical, call (250) 558–6023.

Snowboarding Highlights

Boarders will find acres and acres of terrain to choose at Silver Star, but most riders congregate in one of the two halfpipes and the terrain park. The park is located under the Yellow chair and runs roughly from the *Main Street* green trail down to near the bottom of the Vance Creek Express. Riders will find several natural and manmade obstacles like spines, tabletops, diamonds, and jumps—not to mention the halfpipe which is built and maintained by trail crewmembers and their Pipe Grinder. The pipe trannies are four to six feet high and the verts are six to eight feet high, making for big air and serious tricks. Vertical drop is 850 feet (259 m) while the length is 1,200 feet (366 m). The newest pipe is located on the *Start Gate* trail. It covers 450 to 475 feet (137–145 m) and is built with the ISF standards in mind—it's an Olympic competition halfpipe. Snowboarders are also drawn to the Attridge area mentioned above. *Attridge* is somewhat of an unofficial freestyle zone where hits can be built without the burden of skiers and patrollers.

Skier Services

Lift Tickets

Ages 19–64: $47/day • **Ages 13–18:** $40/day • **Ages 6–12:** $25/day • **Ages 65–69:** $33/day • **Ages 70 and older:** free • **Ages 5 and younger:** free • *Prices based on the 2000–2001 ski season using Canadian currency. See page 354 for conversion information.*

Rentals

Ski Rentals: $35/adults; $14/ages 6–12; $11/ages 3–5; 500 sets. Type of Gear: Rossignol, Olin, Salomon, Volant, K2, and Volkl; shaped skis only available • **Snowboard Rentals:** $37/adults; $30/ages 6–12; 200 sets. Type of Gear: Burton, K2 • *Prices based on the 2000–2001 ski season using Canadian currency. See page 354 for conversion information.*

Services

Ski School: 85 instructors; Private lessons $42/hour; Group lessons $23–$32/hour; Beginner's package $35 (includes lift ticket, lesson, and rentals)—For reservations call (250) 558–6065 • **Snowboard School:** 85 instructors; Private lessons $42/hour; Group lessons $23–$32/hour; Beginner's package $60 (includes lift ticket, lesson, and rentals)—For reservations call (250) 558–6065 • **Nordic Ski School:** Beginner's package $35 (includes rentals, lift ticket, and track pass) • **Fitness Center:** The center is located in the National

Altitude Training Center, adjacent to Putnam Station Hotel. On-mountain hotel guests may use the facilities at no charge. The center includes a fitness room, an indoor swimming pool, and massage therapy. Call for information and appointments: (250) 558–6017 • **Childcare:** Licensed resort care facility. Reservations required. Call the Children's Center at (250) 558–6028. Open 8 A.M.–4 P.M. daily • *Prices based on the 2000–2001 ski season using Canadian currency. See page 354 for conversion information.*

Room & Board

🛏 Lodging

Silver Star guests have several lodging choices when staying on the hill. In addition to practically brand new and recently renovated hotels there is a small community of winter vacation homes available to rent—all with ski-in and ski-out access. The Victorian village looks like an old western town colored with Crayola Crayons. Prices are reasonable, as there are ski and lodging packages available for well under $100 per day per person. For more information, call Central Reservations at 1–800–663–4431 or e-mail them at *reserv@junction.net.*

On-site

Silver Star Club Resort offers a variety of rooms and the facilities offer an aquatic center, fitness center, restaurant, and lounge; rates $119–$272; 1–800–610–0805 or *www.deltasilverstar.com* • **Putnam Station Inn** rooms have queen-sized beds, coffeemaker, and refrigerator, a hot tub and dining room are located in the hotel, and a pool across the street special rates and benefits available for couples; rates $109–$259/night; 1–800–489–0599 • **Lord Aberdeen Hotel** offers one- and two-bedroom apartments with full kitchens, queen, and twin beds available, ideal for families; rates $130–$180/night; 1–800–553–5885 or *www.lordaberdeen.com* • **Silver Lode Inn** offers comfortable rooms with TVs and telephones, rooms available with fireplaces and Jacuzzi tubs, public indoor hot tub, and a Swiss-style restaurant are on the premises; rates $99–$164/night; 1–800–554–4881 or *www.silverlode.com* • **The Pinnacles Suite Hotel** suites can accommodate 8–17 people, rooms are furnished with queen-sized beds, bunk-beds, and futons, full kitchen and bath; larger units have hot tub and barbecue, living area, and dining area; rates $150–$455/night; 1–800–551–7466 or *www.pinnacles.com* • **The Kickwillie Inn** features six suites with equipped kitchens, fireplaces, rooftop hot tub, and TV room; rates $150–$180/night depending on the room and season; 1–800–551–7466

Vernon–11 miles *(18 km)* away

The Best Western Vernon Lodge rooms have one or two queen-sized beds and cable TV, some have kitchenette and refrigerator, other facilities available to guests include a restaurant, indoor pool, and hot tub; rates $73–$95/night; 1–800–528–1234 • **Down in the Valley Bed & Breakfast Retreat** is minutes from the Silver Star Mountain Resort, offers breathtaking views of Swan Lake, screened outdoor spa, and veranda; rates $65/night; (250) 545–0873 or *www.silk.net/bandb/top_ok1.htm* • *Call Vernon Tourism at 1–800–665–0795 or visit them at www.vernontourism.com for more options.*

⏷ Dining

Visitors find plenty of reasonably priced dining options in the village. The town of Vernon is just too close for the resort to hold its guests hostage with high prices. Thanks to the reasonable prices, most guests arrive at Silver Star and don't leave until it is time to go home.

On-site

Silver Lode Dining Room serves haute cuisine by internationally acclaimed chef Isidore Borgeard with an extensive wine list • **Clementine's Dining Room** offers a full menu, weekly specials, and children's menu • **Bugaboos** is a Euro-style café with coffee, liqueurs, and fresh Dutch pastries • **Italian Garden** serves pizza, pasta, and cappuccino • **Charly's Bar** offers a small intimate lounge with a huge stone fireplace • **Vance Creek Saloon** serves light meals, snacks, pool table, and entertainment • **Craigellachie Dining Room** offers a full menu selection, weekly specials, and award-winning children's menu • **Cellar Lounge** is a unique wine bar with rustic charm and light meals • **Lord Aberdeen Deli** serves deli foods and exotic healthy take out • **Town Hall** offers self serve home cooking and vegetarian choices • **Paradise Camp** is a mini day lodge located at the mid-station of Putnam Creek Express with a section of hot and cold food, and large outdoor sundeck with barbecue.

Sun Peaks Resort at Tod Mountain

Sun Peaks Resort at Tod Mountain
#50-3150 Creekside Way
Sun Peaks, BC
Canada V0E 1Z1

Ski Report:
  Kamloops (250) 578–7232
  Vancouver (604) 290–0754
Information: 1–800–807–3257;
  (250) 578–7842
E-mail: *info@sunpeaksresort.com*
Website: *www.sunpeaksresort.com*
Credit cards: All major

Don Weixl/Sun Peaks Resort

Operating Hours: 8:30 A.M.–3:30 P.M. daily

Season: Mid November to mid April

Backdrop

When Sun Peaks opened in 1961 it was simply known as Tod Mountain. As the area grew it began to enjoy a reputation for being a skier's mountain, catering to locals and hardcore experts. It was short on amenities and big on rowdy terrain. In 1992, in stepped Nippon Cable Company. Nippon Cable acquired the area and set out to transform the modest ski area into the finest destination resort in the interior of British Columbia. The first step was to officially rename the mountain Sun Peaks—a fitting description considering the area receives over 2,000 hours of sunlight a year. Next, Nippon Cable assembled a development team, many of whom were responsible for transforming Whistler-Blackcomb into North America's number-one-ranked mountain resort.

In just four short years, Sun Peaks has constructed a luxurious alpine village, an efficient lift circuit, and one of the best winter playgrounds in the Northwest. Covering two mountains—Top of the World (6,824 feet) and Sundance (5,676 feet)—the resort boasts 80 marked trails, 6 gladed areas, and nearly 3,000 vertical feet of skiing. But the real prize here is the snow. An average temperature of 22 degrees Fahrenheit (-6 degrees Celsius) virtually guarantees that the 18.5 feet of annual snowfall is light and dry.

Sun Peaks Village is tucked away at the end of a tranquil valley that gradually widens from west to east to embrace the clear blue waters of McGillvray Lake. The alpine setting is

Mountain Stats

Village Base Elevation:
4,117 feet *(1,255 m)*
Burfield Base Elevation:
3,933 feet *(1,199m)*
Burfield Summit Elevation:
6,824 feet *(2,080 m)*
Vertical Drop: 2,891 feet *(881m)*
Primary Slope Direction: Northeast and south
Annual Snowfall: 220 inches *(559 cm)*
Skiable Days: 150

Skiable Terrain: 1,151 acres *(466 ha)*
Runs: 80+
Longest Run: 5 miles *(8 km)*
Lifts: 4 surface lifts, 1 triple, 1 fixed grip quad, 2 high-speed quads (1 with bubble cover)
Lift Capacity: 8,030 skiers per hour
Terrain Classification: 22% novice; 56% intermediate; 22% advanced
Snowmaking: 80 acres or 7% allowance
Annual Visits: 225,000

home to over 3,000 beds and a variety of shops, restaurants, pubs, and hotels. Most are ski-in/ski-out facilities.

Ecosign Mountain Resort Planners—a leading mountain resort design and environmental planning firm—manages the development of Sun Peaks. Nippon Cable is one of two major shareholders in Whistler-Blackcomb Resort as well as one of the world's chief manufacturers of mountain-lift technology. Over the next five years Nippon will facilitate a $250 million investment to help Sun Peaks become one of North America's best alpine resorts. And they are well on their way to accomplishing their goal. The Best of Canada Skiing Awards recognized Sun Peaks for its variety of terrain, grooming, kids' facility, hotel service, and skier-to-lift ratio. *Ski Canada* also ranked Sun Peaks "Number One for Best Weather" in 1997, while *Mountain Sports and Living*, formerly *Snow Country* magazine, awarded Sun Peaks with the "Best Mountain Trails and Slope Design" in 1995 and then the "Best Mountain Design" award in 1998.

Getting There

- **From Portland, OR:** Take I-5 to Seattle, WA. *[Follow Seattle directions below.]*
- **From Seattle, WA:** Take I-5 north to WA 542 (Exit 255). Take WA 542 (also named East Sunset Drive and the Mount Baker Highway) to WA 9. Head north on WA 9 to the town of Sumas. Cross into Canada and take TCH 1 east toward Hope. *[Follow Vancouver directions below.]*
- **From Vancouver, BC:** Take Trans-Canada Highway 1 (TCH 1) east to Hope. Take Provincial Highway 5 (PH 5) north toward Kamloops, BC. Please note that a toll is

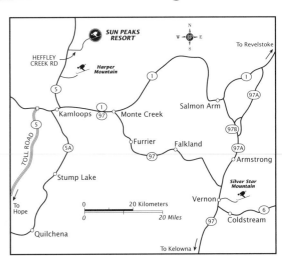

55

required to travel on portions of PH 5. From Kamloops, take PH 5 (Yellow Head Highway) north to Heffley Creek Road. Turn right and then make a quick left at the Heffley Creek Store. Follow this road to the resort.

✈ **Airport Services:** For guests traveling from outside the Northwest, the closest regional airport is Fulton Field Airport (YKA) in Kamloops, BC. Most travelers will fly into Calgary, Alberta, or Vancouver, BC, before changing to Canadian Airlines or Air Canada and continuing on to Kamloops. For shuttle service from the Fulton Field Airport or the Bus Depot to Sun Peaks, call Sun Star Shuttle at (250) 319–3539.

Trail Profiles

Sun Peaks still offers all the roughneck black diamond terrain that earned it its reputation, but now it has slopes for all abilities. The addition of new intermediate terrain on *Sundance Ridge*, combined with new high-speed quads, short lift lines, and buttery smooth grooming, make the area a must-ski. With 80 runs covering over a 1,000 acres, Sun Peaks has plenty of terrain to tackle for snowriders of all abilities.

First-timers and young children usually start with the Platter lift. Its base is at the village and it services the novice runs *Sunbeam, Cowabunga,* and *Gentle Giant.* The trails are short, wide, gently pitched, and groomed velvety smooth nightly. The kids' area also includes two "carpet lifts." Just stand on the carpet and up and away you go.

The Sundance Express is a natural next step for novices. The low-lying terrain here is sheltered from wind, as well as from more advanced skiers and snowboarders. Trails are wide and gentle, including an easy run called *Homesteader* and a faster cruiser known as *Sundance. Sundance* also provides access to the Sun Peaks Terrain Park, which was designed for snowboarders but is open to skiers as well. There are two huge halfpipes, burly kickers, and great launch pads for awesome airplane turns and aerial manuevers.

Novice skiers and lower intermediates will also be able to explore most of the mountain. Located at the top of the Sunburst Express quad, *Cahilty* is a plush, gentle green trail that

connects with *5 Mile,* which can be accessed from the top of the Crystal chair and the Burfield quad. Much of *5 Mile* is equivalent to a 10-lane super highway. Though its width is enormous, it also tends to be congested. Many trails on the mountain's Sunburst side funnel into *5 Mile,* leading snowriders back to the village.

Advanced and strong intermediates have a plethora of cruising runs off the top of the Sunburst Express. Hang a left and then drop down *Exhibition,* right next to the upper section of the lift, or try *Cruiser.* Both are wide-open trails with consistent fall lines and super-fast corduroy—but not so challenging that an intermediate skier won't enjoy the run. These are signature trails for Sun Peaks—perfect grooming on fall lines cut straight downhill. Best of all, skiers and boarders can ride as fast as their abilities will allow. So long as snowriders are in control and not endangering others, the ski patrol isn't inclined to hassle them.

Don Weixl/Sun Peaks Resort

Also from the top of the Sunburst are steeper runs like *Cariboo, Bluff, Sting, Intimidator,* and *5th Avenue.* The latter two are big-bump runs. Head right off Sunburst and hang one left after another as they all drop off the ridge and connect with 5 *Mile.* All are single black diamond runs, providing soft pillows of snow to blast down. Between each trail there are bands of gladed trees. The terrain here is challenging and the turns are tight. For a little less claustrophobic tree skiing, take a right from the top of Sunburst and enter the *Cahilty Glades.* The pitches are less steep and the trees not as tight.

Real pros should head to the Crystal chair from Sunburst. An easy right follows to *Spillway*—one of a select few of totally steep and groomed black diamond runs in the Northwest. While it is smooth, *Spillway* just may be the steepest groomed run in British Columbia.

Indeed, Sun Peaks is a powder paradise. Stashes of snow can be found even days after big dumps. Try taking the Burfield quad to the top and skiing down *Juniper Ridge.* Head toward the trees at *Mid Mountain* and look for the hiking trail up a small slope. Make the five to 10-minute trek over to the other side of *Mid Mountain* and the trees open up into a slope covered in untracked snow. At the cat track (*Roundabout*), hang a left. *Roundabout* is a bit flat so it may require poling out to the Burfield mid-station.

Another stash of "pow pow" (powder) is on *Gil Hill.* From the top of the Burfield, hang an easy right and follow the hiking path for 10 to 20 minutes. Then hang another right for fresh tracks. As the lines get cut up, just keep hiking farther out. The first line is *Inner Gils,* then *Main Face* and *Executioner.* In between are numerous unnamed and unmapped lines that are ripe for the picking. Be aware, however, this area is out-of-bounds, unpatrolled, and quite risky. The farther out you get, the steeper the runs get—and avalanche danger increases. The best bet is to connect with a local who really knows the area. On the bright side, most of the runs connect back into 5 *Mile,* including some that first hook into a flat access road. However, skiers and boarders lacking speed end up skating and walking out to 5 *Mile.*

The West Bowl T-bar provides access to excellent intermediate snowriding. Most locals will ride the quad chair and Crystal chair in the morning before moving on to *Mid Mountain, The Gils,* or *Upper Challenger. Upper Challenger* is accessed from the top of the Burfield lift via the *Chief.* The *Chief* is to the skiers' left off *Juniper Ridge* and offers intermediates a safe and controlled powder-skiing experience. Advanced snowriders often prefer to blast through *Chief* and then take the soft left toward *Challenger* before reaching the flats above the Burfield mid-station. For the freshest tracks stay to the right or left edges (of the trail) on *Upper Challenger.* Once into the trees the run begins to tighten up. Hit the narrow trails through the forest that head to *Lower Challenger. Lower Challenger* is steep and loaded with small trees and brush. Not much summer grooming goes on in this area. Moreover, *Lower Challenger* is relatively low on the mountain, resulting in lower snow depths. Cutting lines through *Lower Challenger* requires taking chances with stumps and tough turns through the sticks and brush. Still, it's often worth the effort. *Lower Challenger* deposits skiers to the bottom of the Burfield mid-station and the original Tod Mountain lodge.

In the spring, it's highly recommended to try the area below *Harry's Run* and *Long Draw* off of the West Bowl T-bar. A bowl full of corn snow and a slew of turns will create lots of smiles. Follow *Roundabout* back to the Burfield mid-station. Another option, though not recommended, is the *7 Mile Road.* This route is long and relatively flat. The old ungroomed fire road leads all the way to the bottom of the mountain.

Snowboarding Highlights

Sun Peaks offers snowboarders what is arguably the best terrain park in the Northwest. The park is accessible from the top of the Sundance Express quad and covers most of the *Sunrise Trail*. The park is 2,500 feet (763 m) long, with almost 800 feet (244 m) of vertical. There are two halfpipes: the larger one at the top offers 6-foot trannies and 9-foot verts; the smaller one at the bottom has 3-foot trannies and 6-foot verts. The pipes are both excavated into the ground rather than just built up with snow. These pipes open early every season with consistent sizes and shapes, whether or not Sun Peaks has banner snow years.

In the middle, riders will find a world-class bordercross that is also excavated into the ground. It contains seven banked turns, a tabletop, a spine, and several other big bad and burly hits. Boarders can cop air straight off the kickers or from an angle with big sweeping airplane turns. To maximize the fun factor, exit the Sundance chair and head into the *Sunrise Glades*. These are just to skiers' left of the run. After snaking through the trees and bagging all the natural hits, then enter the terrain park.

There's also great freeriding in the *Cahilty Glades* off of the Sunburst chair. Natural hits and drops abound here on runs like the *Head Walls* and *Sacred Line* (off the Crystal chair). *Sacred* isn't on a map but you can find it just to the skiers' left of *Head Walls* and between *The Chute*. *Sacred* is usually steep and powdery.

Racer-heads prefer long cruising runs like *Exhibition* and *Cruiser*. These long groomed trails allow them to practice their carving techniques. Lastly, try *Roller Coaster*, located on the lower section of Burfield. There is a huge lifter in the middle of it. Boarders are usually copping sick air off the jump.

More Fun in the Flakes

Sun Peaks Resort offers many activities other than downhill skiing and snowboarding, many of which are free. **Cross-country skiing** can be enjoyed on 12.4 miles (20 km) of marked wilderness trails and 12.4 miles (20 km) of groomed and trackset. And it can be enjoyed for free. Other tours are available through the resort: **snowshoe tours** (rentals available) and **snowmobile tours**. Maybe you'd like to try something new, perhaps **paragliding** or **dogsledding**. Step back in time by cruising around Sun Peaks the old fashioned way with guided **horse-drawn sleigh rides**. The resort's Sports Center is a good stop for those looking to do a little **drop-in hockey** (rentals are available). The center also has two **outdoor skating** rinks, and outdoor swimming pool, a hot tub, and much more.

For more information or to book an activity, call the Activities and Information Center at (250) 578-5542.

Skier Services

⑤ Lift Tickets

Ages 18–65: $46/day • **Ages 13–18:** $41/day • **Ages 6–12:** $26/day • **Ages 65+:** $32 •
Prices based on the 2000–2001 ski season using Canadian currency (not including GST). See page 354 for conversion information.

🎿 Rentals

Ski Rentals: Ages 13–64: $27–$38; Ages 6–12 and 64+: $18–$22; Ages 5 and younger: $10; 1,000 sets. Type of gear: Rossignol, Elan, and Head • **Snowboard Rentals:** Ages 13–64: $37; Ages 6–12 and 64+: $27; 300 sets. Type of gear: Burton, Rossignol, and Elan • **Nordic Ski Rentals:** Ages 13–64: $17; Ages 6–12 and 64+: $13 • *Prices based on the 2000–2001 ski season using Canadian currency. See page 354 for conversion information.*

🏂 Services

Ski & Snowboard School: 80 ski instructors, 20 snowboard instructors; Private lessons $79 for 1.5 hours; Group lessons $29 for 2 hours; Discover Skiing and Snowboarding class $50–$60 dollars (includes, beginner lift rentals and lessons) • **Childcare:** Licensed. (250) 578-5484 • *Prices based on the 2000–2001 ski season using Canadian currency. See page 354 for conversion information.*

Room & Board

🛏 Lodging

On-site

Nancy Green's Cahilty Lodge is operated by Olympic medalist Nancy Green, offers ski-in/ski-out convenience, full service rooms, ski room, laundry, and covered parking; rates $80–90/night; 1–800–244–8424 or (250) 578–7454 or *www.cahiltylodge.com* • **Sun Peaks Lodge and Heffley Inn** includes private bathrooms, whirlpool, spa, and a masseuse on-call; rates $105–200; 1–800–333–9112 or (250) 578–7878 or *www.sunpeakslodge.com* • **Sundance Lodge** offers full-service studios, lofts, and suites with ski-in/ski-out convenience; rates $110–$350/night; 1–800–483–2888 or (250) 578–0200 or *www.sundancelodge.com* • **Woodlands Fireside Lodge & Hearthstone Lodge at Sun Peaks** offers guests suites with kitchenettes, health club, restaurant, lounge, and ski packages; rates $95–395; 1–888–659–2211 or (250) 578–8588 • *Call Central Reservations at 1–800–807–3257 for more options.*

Kamloops–31 miles *(53 km)* away

See the Harper Mountain chapter *(see page 112)* for lodging in Kamloops • *Call Kamloops Visitor Info Center at 1–800–662–1994 or visit them at www.city.kamloops.bc.ca for more options.*

🍽 Dining

On–site

Bento's Day Lodge is located at the base and offers cafeteria-style dining • **Sunburst Lodge** is located at Mid Mountain and opens daily for lunch and twice a week for dinner and torchlight ski (Wednesdays and Thursdays) • **Masa's Bar & Grill** is in the Village Day Lodge and offers a pub-style environment and nighttime entertainment with a great variety of activities as well • **Mackers on the Mountain,** located in Nancy Greene's Cahilty Lodge offers traditional West Coast cuisine in a lively atmosphere • **Bottom's Restaurant** located in the Sundance Lodge features a fun-filled atmosphere with great food. Also visit the **European Style Bolacco Caffé • Heffley Steakhouse** located in the Heffley Inn features Canadian beef in fine dining, high country style • **Stumboeck's Val Senales Dining Restaurant** offers a fine dining experience with great attention to detail. Also visit the **European Style Kaffé Stubé • Stellar's Restaurant,** located in the Radisson Hearthstone Lodge, provides fine European cuisine and delightful decor both indoors and out • **Mountain High Pizza,** located in the Radisson Hearthstone Lodge, offers classic or specialty pizzas to eat in or take out • **Ingrid's Village Café** offers healthy home cooking for the mountain appetite • **Powder Hounds,** located in the Radisson Fireside Lodge, is an entertaining spot to mingle.

Kamploops–31 miles *(53 km)* away
Rock-n-Firken Bar and Grill offers the best pub food and assortment of libations in Kamloops; (250) 376–6121 • *Call Kamloops Visitor Info Center at 1–800–662–1994 or visit them at www.city.kamloops.bc.ca for more options.*

Whistler–Blackcomb

Whistler-Blackcomb Resort
4545 Blackcomb Way
Whistler, BC
Canada V0N IB4

Ski Report: (604) 932–4211
Information: (604) 932–3141
Email: *info@whistler-resort.com*
Website:
  www.whistler-resort.com
  www.whistler-blackcomb.com
Credit Cards: All major

Operating Hours: 8:30 A.M.–5 P.M.
Season:
  Blackcomb: Late November to late April. Re-opens on the Horstman Glacier from mid June to early August.
  Whistler: Late November to mid June.

Background

Whistler-Blackcomb is the Michael Jordan, Wayne Gretzky, and Babe Ruth of snowriding all rolled into one. It is the undisputed king of North American ski resorts. Blackcomb or Whistler mountain, alone, is reason enough for snowriders to trek clear across the world to vacation here. But combine the "Two Peaks" and Whistler-Blackcomb stands without a peer as the biggest and best resort on the continent—probably in the Western Hemisphere.

Whistler-Blackcomb is the largest ski area in North America with over 7,000 acres of skiable terrain, 200 marked trails, 12 bowls, and three glaciers. Even separately, the two mountains can boast the greatest vertical rise of any mountain in North America. Blackcomb mountain climbs 5,280 feet above its base to 7,494 feet, beating out its partnering peak by a mere few hundred feet.

Due to the incredible expanse of terrain available, the resort has built an unbelievably efficient high-speed lift system featuring 15 express lifts (three gondolas and 12 high-speed quads) in a total system of 33 lifts. The circuit of lifts is designed to ensure easy access from each of the resort's six bases (all within five to ten minutes walking distance of each other and all with high-speed lifts) and decrease time spent waiting in lines. Such efficiency is vitally important to an area that generated a total of 2.14 million skier visits in 1998/1999.

Mountain Stats

Blackcomb

Base Elevation: 2,214 feet *(675 m)*
Summit Elevation: 7,494 feet *(2,288 m)*
Vertical Drop: 5,280 feet *(1,609 m)*
Primary Slope Direction: 360 degrees
Annual Snowfall: 318 inches *(808 cm)*
Skiable Days: 210
Skiable Terrain: 3,414 acres *(1,383 ha)*
Runs: 100 marked trails plus unlimited options in five bowls, two of which are glaciers
Longest Run: 7 miles *(11.3 km)*
Lifts: 1 gondola, 6 high-speed quads (one covered), 3 triples, 7 surface lifts
Lift Capacity: 29,112 skiers per hour
Terrain Classification: 15% novice: 55% intermediate: 30% advanced
Night Skiing: 2% allowance
Snowmaking: 370 acres *(150 ha)*

Whistler

Base Elevation: 2,214 feet *(675 m)*
Summit Elevation: 7,160 feet *(2,183 m)*
Vertical Drop: 4,946 feet *(1,509 m)*
Primary Slope Direction: 360 degrees
Annual Snowfall: 360 inches *(914 cm)*
Skiable Days: 210
Skiable Terrain: 3,657 acres *(1,480 h)*
Runs: 100 marked trails plus unlimited options in seven Alpine bowls, one of which is a glacier
Longest Run: 7 miles *(11 km)*
Lifts: 2 high-speed gondolas, 6 high-speed quads, 2 triples, 1 double, 5 surface lifts
Lift Capacity: 29,895 skiers per hour
Terrain Classification: 20% novice: 55% intermediate: 25% advanced
Night Skiing: None
Snowmaking: 160 acres *(65 ha)*

Total Annual Visits: 2.14 million combined

With so many skiers and boarders slicing and dicing up the slopes it's easy to assume that finding lodging at Whistler is like trying to carve a turn on boiler plate ice with dull edges. But that's not the case, not with over 20,000 beds available. What's so remarkable is that 75 percent of these beds are located within 500 meters of the lifts, making Whistler-Blackcomb the largest ski-in/ski-out resort in North America.

And there's more. Whistler receives an average of 30 feet of snow per year and has one of the longest ski seasons anywhere. Both areas are usually open by Thanksgiving. Blackcomb shuts down in late April and then re-opens in June with skiing on the Horstman's Glacier until August. Whistler is open all the way through to mid-June in Glacier Bowl, conditions permitting. The best plan when skiing or riding in the summer months is to hit the slopes early in the morning before the snow turns to granulated sludge. Then, head down the hill for a round of golf, mountain biking, or swimming at nearby Lost Lake.

With so much to offer it's no wonder that Whistler-Blackcomb has won so many awards. For seven consecutive years, *Mountain Sports and Living*, formerly *Snow Country* magazine, named Whistler-Blackcomb "North America's Best Ski Resort." *Skiing* magazine editors agreed,

awarding the same distinction twice. And the list goes on. Whistler-Blackcomb has been honored for best overall design, as well as top resort on the continent for lift lines.

Background continued on page 64

Getting There

- **From Portland, OR, and Seattle, WA:** Take I-5 north to U.S./Canada border. *[Directions continued below.]*
- **From Spokane, WA:** Take I-90 west to I-405. Head north on I-405 to I-5. Take I-5 north to U.S./Canada border. *[Directions continued below.]*
- **From Boise, ID:** Take I-84 west to I-82. Take I-82 west to I-90. Take I-90 west to I-405. Follow I-405 to I-5. Take I-5 north to U.S./Canada border. *[Directions continued below.]*
- **[Continued.]** There are two routes available to Whistler. The first takes travelers through the heart of Vancouver. To explore the city, take I-5 north across the border. *Be aware. After the border I-5 turns into a small four-lane road with stoplights and congested traffic that requires an addi-*

tional 90 minutes of driving time. Avoid typical morning (8 A.M.–10 A.M.) and afternoon (3 P.M.–7 P.M.) rush hours. Avoid the main border crossing, which guarantees more traffic, between the hours of 6 P.M.–8 P.M. on Thursdays and Fridays and 4 P.M.–8 P.M. on Sundays when travel- ing back into the U.S. To bypass the city, take I-5 north to the border, but take the "Truck Crossing" exit—this bypasses the main border crossing and cuts down on the driving time. Once in Canada, take Provincial Highway 15 (PH 15) north. Stay on PH 15 until the Trans-Canada Highway 1 (TCH 1). Follow TCH 1 around the east side of Vancouver. TCH 1 ends near Whytecliff, but PH 99 continues. Follow PH 99 (the Sea to Sky Highway) to Whistler. Signs to Whistler are clearly visible. *This portion of the drive is best done during the day. PH 99 fol- lows the coastline of Howe Sound, which is sur- rounded by jagged peaks, glaciers, and lush green forests. Because PH 99 follows the sound, it twists and turns along the cliffs above the water and becomes increasingly winding as it heads in to the mountains. The road is not well lit and can be diffi- cult and stressful to drive, especially in rain or snow.*

Airport Services: Vancouver International (YVR) is the closest airport to Whistler. Perimeter's Whistler Express bus leaves regularly from the airport. Call (604) 266–5386 for times. Visit *www.whistler.net* for more options.

Ferry Services: The Victoria Clipper offers ferry service packages to Whistler from Seattle. Call 1–888–724–5223 (in BC) or (604) 444–2890 (in the U.S.) or visit *www.victoriaclipper.com*

Rail Services: BC Rail offers daily service to Whistler Village from North Vancouver. Call 1–800–339–8752 (in BC) or 1–800–663–8238 (in the U.S.) or visit *www.bcrail.com/bcr-pass/bcrpsca.htm* for more information.

Background*continued*

Despite over two million skier visits a year, Whistler-Blackcomb's modern lift system manages to shuttle guests quickly and efficiently across the mountain—though it should be said, the lines aren't exactly short. A suggestion to beat the lines and still cover the mountain: If the lifts in one area are experiencing difficulty, simply ski to the bottom and walk 100 feet (30 m) to the gondola on the other mountain. The top is only 20 minutes away.

True to its Canadian heritage, Whistler-Blackcomb excels in customer service as well. In fact, most ski areas in the States could learn a thing or two from Whistler-Blackcomb. Mountain hosts offer to carry skis, lift operators make an effort to clean snow off the lifts before guests sit, and guests are greeted with a smile every day.

Although the two mountains make up the biggest and best resort in the Western Hemisphere, they have not always been under the same ownership. Whistler was opened to the public as a ski destination in 1966. The BC government created the Whistler Resort Municipality in 1975, the first and only such entity in Canada. A few years later, in 1978, 53 acres of Crown Land were given to the municipality to develop the current town center. In 1980, Blackcomb opened its lifts. Whistler Village was built at the base of both mountains. Ever since then the two areas have been competing for snowriders. This fierce rivalry fueled the growth of both mountains, and snowriders have benefited tremendously.

Due to this competitive environment, the resorts grew faster than most. From the late eighties to 1996 each mountain tried desperately to top the other. Nearly $3 billion Canadian dollars were invested in the resort. Whistler installed a 10-person gondola. Blackcomb responded by installing their own eight-person gondola and several high-speed quads. Whistler remodeled Pika's Peak Restaurant. Blackcomb opened the Glacier Creek Lodge. Blackcomb installed the Glacier Express high-speed quad. Whistler installed a new six-person gondola. Talk about keeping up with the Joneses! Even though the two mountains are now under one flag, Intrawest, ownership has promised that each mountain will retain its distinct personality. So "Which one is best?" It really depends on the type of terrain you're looking for. Whistler-Blackcomb has it all.

Without question, Whistler-Blackcomb is the king of North American skiing. Those who argue otherwise probably haven't been here. However, it's Whistler-Blackcomb's awesome size and its unlimited amenities and worldwide reputation that may be its biggest drawback. Two million skier visits a year means crowds. On a busy day there might be as many as 25,000 people on the mountains. So much for getting away from it all.

With size come certain considerations for visiting families. For instance, it's not the best idea to let the children run unchecked in the village. And guests should remember not to leave skis or snowboards unattended. Local police report that on average 50 pairs of skis are stolen every day in the village. But such precautions are the unavoidable response to growth. What some view as a more upsetting change to the now mega-resort is the loss of regional identity. Much of the resort's old charm, many say, has been diluted by the influx of popular American retail franchises, like Starbucks and The Gap. Thankfully though, the resort continues to enforce strict guidelines regarding signage and building design, as well as building color. But say what you will, no one will deny that Whistler Village is pedestrian friendly. Most visitors leave their cars once they arrive and are able to walk it the rest of their stay: to the lifts, to the restaurants, to the shops, and ultimately back to their rooms.

Trail Profiles

Blackcomb

For years ski film producers Warren Miller and Greg Stump have made Blackcomb one of their signature winter studios. Why Blackcomb? Because it's loaded with supermodel-slim chutes, huge air drops, dangerously steep lines, cliffs, crags, couloires, cornices, and exquisite tree skiing. Advanced snowriders love the challenge that Blackcomb offers on nearly every run. Some favorites include *Couloir Extreme*; any number of narrow chutes in the *Pakalolo Rocks; Ruby, Garnet, Sapphire,* and *Diamond* bowls; and the *Blow Hole* at the entrance to Blackcomb Glacier.

The top of *Couloir Extreme* is Blackcomb's highest point, without hiking. Looking down the 1,000-foot (300 m) pitch can be intimidating. To the skier's left is the steepest section. Just a short way into the middle of the run there are a few jagged rocks sticking up through the snow. Though the grade is steep, the snow is usually consistent, thanks to the elevation. Mike Hatrup, Glen Plake, and Scott Schmidt made the *Couloir* famous in Greg Stumps' 1989 movie *Licensed to Thrill*. Since then, wannabe extreme skiers have flocked to Blackcomb to ski the *Couloir*, and many have discovered the hard way that it's not as easy as world-class pros make it look on the big screen. Those who fall in the *Couloir* usually don't stop until they hit the bottom. About a quarter of the way down, the run takes a wide turn to the skier's left, widens, and begins to level off. It's the first few hundred feet from the top that demand precise, controlled turns.

Ruby, Garnet, and *Diamond* bowls are accessed off the Glacier Express. From the chairlift, hang a left and stay high just under the ridge. Traverse below the ridge to *Spanky's Ladder*. The steps are kicked in the snow and the sign up on the ridge is easy to spot. *Spanky's*

Ladder requires clicking out of one's sleds and hiking the 15 to 20 feet to the top. All three bowls have steep, challenging entrances. In the middle of the run, however, snowriders find the goods…deep, untracked powder. At the bottom, hook into the *Blackcomb Glacier Road*. It's a long skate out, but it's well worth the turns in the bowls.

The *Blow Hole* is a short pitch but one of the coolest runs on the mountain. It's easy to spot when hiking from the top of the Showcase T-bar to the gate, which is the access point to the *Blackcomb Glacier*. Topography and conditions coalesce to form a crescent-shaped gash made of rocks on one side and a completely vertical wall of snow, shaped like a crescent moon on the other. Near the top, the opening between the rocks and snow is minimal. Near the bottom it's over 50 feet across.

Turns in the *Blow Hole* are some of the sexiest turns on the mountain. Skiers have to set their edges hard and fast because with each turn they drop several feet. Add to that, the wind has packed the snow tight against the rock face, and wind-packed snow does not check speed like deep powder. Sometimes the wall is so steep that even angry edge sets don't prevent skiers from sliding farther into the hole. As they slide, their skis shave off thousands of slivers of snow crystals. With each turn a thin cloud bursts from the skis, reducing visibility—so much so that they just have to trust their ability and make the next turn by instinct.

Watching a hot skier rip this line from the top is amazing. It's easy to lose sight of the skier briefly with each turn as he sets his edges and emerges from a fresh cloud of snow. Then as the crack opens up and bottoms out he gains speed in the middle and turns back up onto the wall, launching huge airplane turns. Though it is steep, the *Blow Hole* is not considered extremely dangerous. It bottoms out comfortably, with no dire consequences, but only advanced skiers will be able to make the quick, aggressive turns required near the top of the run. These are fun turns that make skiers giggle like a five-year-old after too much sugar.

Just beyond the entrance to the *Blow Hole* is *Blackcomb Glacier*. The wide-open face of powder is sure to become a favorite of anyone who skis it. Skiers and snowboarders find turn after turn in untracked snow—but only early in the morning. After a big storm, expect to see a line of snowriders waiting for ski patrol to open the *Glacier*. And by that afternoon, expect the powder to be cut up. The only drawback to riding the *Glacier* is the long, relatively flat *Blackcomb Glacier Road*. Skiers and boarders have to ride this out nearly two-thirds of the way down the mountain as it is the only way back to the chairlifts. To pass the time, check out the eerily beautiful lime-green colored moss hanging in the surrounding forest.

Intermediate skiers and boarders will find several exciting runs on Blackcomb designed just for them. From the top of nearly every chair is at least one intermediate trail down. And with the large fleet of snowcats keeping the hills buffed, these runs are fantastic for improving carving techniques. The Catskinner triple chair, the Solar Coaster Express, and the Jersey Cream Express all unload snowriders at the Rendezvous Lodge, which is also the central hub of the mountain. From here, skiers and riders can continue on to the top via the *Express Way* cat track and then the Seventh Heaven Express quad. Or, snowriders can explore any one of the less intimidating runs below the lodge. *The Choker, Ross' Gold, Cruiser, Jersey Cream, Honeycomb, Zig Zag,* and *Cougars Milk* are all intermediate runs that are kept in fantastic condition by trail crews.

Snowriders who like laying tracks in the trees should try *Bark Sandwich,* off the *Catskinner Trail.* The gladed trail features bumps, kinks, and short drops that keep skiers guessing. Because of its lower altitude on the mountain, most guests assume the snow is better else-

Snowboarding **Highlights**

Blackcomb Terrain Park

Located under the Catskinner chair on *Choker* and *Lower Catskinner*, the Blackcomb Terrain Park is used by snowriders of all abilities and disciplines. With 16 acres (6.5 ha) in total and 2,952 feet (900 m) in length, the park is huge, and even has its own lift access. The Catskinner triple chair gives riders the opportunity to survey the entire park, and will deposit them next to the top of the alpine halfpipe. There's also a school bus at the bottom of the park with a refreshment stand—a cool place to wind down and watch the action. A unique 14-speaker outdoor surround-sound system blasts music throughout the entire park. The stereo includes turntables for guest DJs to spin music and entertain fellow boarders.

Blackcomb's halfpipe, located at the top of the Catskinner chair, was regraded and extended to 400 feet (120 m) during the 1997/98 season. Two snow making hydrants support the pipe, and it's maintained by a full-time Pipe Dragon. As an added bonus, the Rendezvous restaurant is only a minute walk away.

Randy Lincks/Whistler-Blackcomb Resort

Whistler Terrain Park

Whistler's Terrain Park covers nearly 3,000 feet (900 m) and 2.5 acres (1 ha). It begins just below Whistler's competition pipe on the *Green Acres* trail. The park was designed by snowboard pros like Canadian Olympic Snowboarding Gold Medalist Ross Rebagliatti who conceptualized the ultimate synergy of freestyle and freeriding pleasure. Riders will find huge kickers, rollerz, tabletops, spines, banked turns, and hordes of other hits.

Whistler's halfpipe is located at the top of the Emerald Express and meets FIS World Cup competition standards. Groomed daily with the new Whistler Pipe Dragon, the pipe is supported by a snowmaking hydrant.

While both the Whistler's and Blackcomb's parks offer terrain for novice and expert riders, beginners may find Blackcomb's Alpine Halfpipe more suitable to their riding styles. The more advanced halfpipe at Whistler is longer, steeper, and has higher walls. Nonetheless, both pipes are kept in great shape. Two snowcat operators are scheduled each evening to maintain both halfpipes and both parks.

where, but resort regulars know there's usually a healthy portion of frosted flakes to go with their *Bark Sandwich*. Powder stashes can also be found next to the Solar Coaster chair. Don't be lured by the crowds into heading the other direction toward Jersey Cream.

Another cache of powder can be found off the high path to the Seventh Heaven chair. From the top of the Jersey Cream chair, take the high traverse on the skier's left. (It's on the right when unloading from the chair.) Once past the main runs, dropping off anywhere along the traverse is solid. There are quite a few open spots in the trees, as well as in the gladed areas. These are usually soft turns in untracked snow. Don't worry about getting lost.

Just keep heading down and hook into the low traverse to the Seventh Heaven Express quad. Daring skiers and borders also drop off this traverse as well, and eventually wind up on a lower traverse that takes them back to the bottom of Solar Coaster. DO NOT go off the third traverse. There is no way out from this one.

Another local favorite on powder days is a gladed area called *Outer Limits*. To get there, take the Crystal Ridge chair (a slow triple) and skate out to the top of *Ridge Runner*. *Ridge Runner*, incidentally, is one of the best cruising runs on the mountain. Follow *Ridge Runner* down and look for a long entrance-way on the right. Head in here and keep to the left. Venturing too far to the right takes you to the top of some big, bad, and ugly cliffs that are unskiable.

Bump skiers will love *Overbite*, which is accessed from the Crystal chair and completely visible from the bottom of the Glacier Express and the Jersey Cream Express. Ripping smooth turns on *Overbite* earns skiers loud cheers from the crowd. The run is steep and the fall line is consistent—which is why all the bump competitions at Blackcomb are held on *Overbite*.

Despite the impressive expanse of terrain, novice snowriders are not entirely thrilled with Blackcomb. Access to the mountaintop is easy for any skier or boarder, and there's always an easy way down, but most of the upper trails are intermediate or advanced. The beginner trails here are nothing to write home about, many of which consist mainly of cat tracks. The better green runs can be found on the bottom third of the mountain, though snow conditions here are somewhat inferior because of the elevation. In early and late season, skiers will likely find themselves skiing on artificial snow—or even skiing in the rain.

Shannon Falls Provincial Park

Along the way to Whistler-Blackcomb, stop and visit the Shannon Falls Provincial Park, located 36 miles north of Vancouver and just south of Squamish. Shannon Falls is the third highest waterfall in British Columbia and is simply spectacular. Each minute thousands of gallons of water rush over the edge of the 1,000-foot tall, 95 million year-old granite walls. The park, at the base, is filled with a deafening roar of water and a thick cold mist. Standing directly downstream from the falls will give you an icy shower—Shannon Creek originates in the BC Coast Range and is fed with melting snow and ice. During the late summer months, tourists hike nearly straight up the creek by skipping and climbing from small rocks to gigantic boulders.

Legend has it that the falls were created when an enormous two-headed serpent slithered up the mountain side and made its way inland, only to be met and beheaded by the son of the Great Chief of the Squohomish Indians. It's said that the route the serpent took is now the path the waters follow.

History says that Captain George Vancouver anchored and camped here in 1792 while charting Howe Sound. A century later, William Shannon laid claim to the area. He made bricks from the rich red clay soil near the mouth of Shannon Creek. These bricks were used to build some of the first homes in the nearby town of Squamish, many of which are still standing to this day.

Another century passed and the Falls were acquired by the Carling O'keefe Breweries. The park was established in 1984 when the Carling O'keefe Breweries donated the land.

Across the highway be sure to stop by for breakfast, lunch, or supper at the **Roadhouse Diner** at Klahanie. Owned by two families, the diner serves homestyle breakfast, crisp salads, seafood, pasta, and more. Reservations are requested: (604) 892-5312. For more information on Shannon Falls, contact the BC Parks Department at (604) 898-3678.

Whistler

Whistler, on the other hand, does a worthy job of welcoming novice skiers and boarders. Beginners will appreciate all the green trails located mid-mountain. At this elevation the snow quality is more consistent. The quickest method of transport to this part of the mountain is the Whistler Village gondola. The same area is accessible from the Creekside gondola but requires connecting with the Red Line Express quad.

From the Roundhouse Lodge and the top of the gondola, novice snowriders will enjoy runs like *Whiskey Jack*, *Porcupine*, *Pony Trail*, and *Ego Bowl*. Their shallow and finely manicured slopes provide a friendly environment where novice skiers and boarders can practice their techniques without having to worry about challenging terrain. Additionally, more of the mountain can be explored on trails instead of cat tracks.

From the gondola, head down *Pony Trail*. After the first pitch look for *Fisheye*. There's a sweet, sustained pitch here for intermediates, with a long run out toward *Franz's Run*. Farther down is *Banana Peel*—a fun, short ride that reconnects with *Pony Trail*. The entire mid-mountain offers seemingly endless green and blue runs that connect with one another.

More excellent novice track can be found on *Jolly Green Giant* and on nearby terrain, accessed from the top of the Whistler gondola or the Emerald chair. Located to the skier's right of *Ego Bowl*, the *Jolly Green Giant* is slightly tougher than *Pony* and *Fisheye*. The *Giant* flows into *Marmot*, *Chipmunk*, and *Coyote*. Another mix of blue and green runs, each deposits skiers and boarders onto *Sidewinder*, which eventually leads to the Emerald chair.

As their confidence builds, novices may explore the Peak chair—a new high-speed quad with a four-minute ride. From the top of the chair, glide straight onto *Highway 86* for a scenic feast of glaciers, snow-covered peaks, and ice blue alpine lakes. *Highway 86* winds around the *West Bowl* and deposits snowriders along the bowl's base and eventually onto *Franz's Run*. From here they continue all the way to the bottom of *Franz's* and then take the Creekside gondola back up the mountain—or they follow the *Traverse Road* over to the Big Red Express and do it over again. Intermediate riders and skiers should also hit *Highway 86* but then head right into *Bagel Bowl* for an ungroomed adventure. Not too worry, the fall line is moderately steep at worst.

A word to the wise: Don't turn left off *Highway 86*. It leads out of the ski area boundary. The wide-open field of powder is seductively inviting but it leads to an ugly line of cliffs and eventually the Cheakamus Valley and the icy waters of Cheakamus Lake. Many a snowrider has been enchanted by the siren call of this area only to spend a brutally cold night alone, wondering if they'll ever see the sun rise again.

On the other side of the Peak chair, hop into the *Saddle* or lay tracks on *Last Chance*. The *Saddle*, the third entrance off the top into *Glacier Bowl*, was widened in 1998 with dynamite and a lot of back-breaking work. The effort has paid off though. Now intermediate skiers and boarders have access to one of Whistler's biggest bowls of frosted flakes. The entrance

Paul Morrison/Whistler-Blackcomb Resort

is now wide enough and shallow enough to be groomed right down the middle every day. Trail crews leave just enough ungroomed terrain on each side to give inexperienced snowriders the opportunity to go off-piste without venturing too far. If they get into trouble, all they have to do is glide back onto the groomed slope.

When debating which mountain is best, advanced snowriders often rave about Whistler's massive bowls. All seven are accessible from the Peak chair. After big storms, skiing Whistler's bowls may be some of the best lines a snowrider ever carves. Imagine hundreds of turns in knee-deep light powder. Arriving early is a must though. By mid morning, the bowls are full of big soft bumps.

From the top of the Peak chair advanced skiers and boarders will find thrills by taking a sharp right traverse on the high road before *Highway 86*, known as *Frontier Pass*. This takes them to *Cockalarum*, a burly ridge that offers up to 20-foot drops into *West Bowl* below. Depending on where skiers and boarders enter, they either slide in or launch in! The higher up *Cockalarum Ridge*, the more extreme the entrance, and the more untracked the powder—let's just hope you survive the landing. Once in the *West Bowl* the terrain quickly mellows out into fun, fast, and frisky turns. Head down to reconnect with *Highway 86*. Take 86 to the Big Red Express and head back up to do it again.

Expert snowriders should try *Glacier Bowl*, which is accessed by taking a left off of the Peak chair. Besides the Saddle, there are two additional entrances and both are tricky. The *Glacier Cirque* is the first entrance into *Glacier Bowl*. The entrance is always funky and barely wide enough for a pair of sleds. Typically skiers have to side-slip the steep ramp, which then deposits them into the wide-open bowl with tons of turns. The uninviting entrance discourages many riders from even considering this part *Glacier Bowl*—which means awesome, crowd-free turns for the skiers who have the skills and the courage to take this line. The other entrance to *Glacier Bowl* is the *Glacier Couloir*—even more dangerous than *Glacier Bowl*, but again, rewarding to those who are willing to risk a fall. The pay off is fresh tracks once in the bowl. This is not for the faint of heart or the vertically challenged.

Just to the left of the Peak chair is *Whistler Bowl*. Take a right off of the chair and head downhill. Though steep, this entrance is less of a riddle to strong intermediate snowriders. Dive in and have fun in the bumps in the middle and on the left. Or, stay to the right for several turns on a steep pitch. *Whistler Bowl* is big and long. After a number of turns skiers and boarders are ushered into *Doom & Gloom*. The terrain is not as bad as it sounds. In fact, there are usually hidden stashes of snow on these two moraines. A moraine, by the way, is glacial detritus, formed over thousands of years by retreating and advancing ice flows. As the

foot of the glacier expands and contracts, large mounds of rock and sediment begin to col-
lect. The hills that form are called moraines. Ski the back-side of them for the best snow.

Skiers also traverse above *Doom & Gloom* and ski into the *West Bowl*. This accesses the
Christmas Trees—an amazing, lightly gladed slope usually filled with uncut powder. The area
gets its name from the trees that grow small and stunted because of the high elevation and
harsh weather. While *Christmas Trees* can't be found on any map, it's known by regulars as
a can't-miss area. This traverse is, however, hard on snowboarders due to the deep snow
depths and the flat terrain. Snowboarders who don't keep up enough speed find themselves
walking through thigh-deep snow. On the map, look for the black line that runs from
Whistler Bowl to the *West Bowl*, under the permanently closed area. It doesn't appear gladed, but it actually is. This slope deposits snowriders into the lower portion of *West Bowl*.
Head down from here and hit *Highway 86* and then ride back up the Big Red chair.

For less extreme entrances into Whistler's bowls, take the *Burnt Stew Trail* into *Symphony
Bowl*. The back bowl of Whistler offers a groomed piste all the way down to the Harmony
Express chair. Along the way, skiers and boarders can depart from the groomed area to get
fresh tracks or ride the crud. It's wide open and great for all levels. Intermediates should have
what it takes to negotiate the *Sun*, *Symphony*, and *Harmony* bowls. These three are also
accessible from the Harmony Express lift. For novices who reach the top of this chair but
don't want to give the bowls a ride, try *Harmony Ridge* or the *Burnt Stew Trail*. Both are
always groomed and in great shape.

Advanced intermediates can test their mettle in the trees of the *Glades*, *Boomer Bowl*,
and *Gun Barrels*. From the top of the Harmony Express, hang a left and follow the ridge. To
the right lies the *Glades*, a wide open run through the trees. To the left is *Boomer Bowl*,
which is more like a saucer when compared to *Glacier* and *Whistler Bowl*; and yet, there are
usually fresh tracks out here on semi-steep terrain. From *Boomer*, access the *Gun Barrels*,
which are tighter and steeper lines than the *Glades*. Or, choose to take the easy line out of
the bowl by staying to the left of the *Barrels*. All lines lead to *Sidewinder* and then back to
the Harmony chair.

More Fun in the Flakes

More than 17 miles (28 km) of trackset **cross-country skiing** trails wind through the
Lost Lake Park, Chateau Whistler Golf Course, and the North Nicklaus Golf Course. The
trails range from beginner to expert level. Additional trackset trails around the Whistler
Golf Course offer an ideal beginner's route. In the evening all the trails are lighted and your
access ticket is no longer required after 8:30 P.M. Cross-country ski trail maps and rental
equipment information are available at the Whistler Activity and Information Center, or
by calling one of the following companies direct: Sports Stop: (604) 932–5495; Mile High
Sport Shop: (604) 938–7736; or Wild Willies Ski Club: (604) 938–8036.

Whistler is about as complete a winter adventure as there is. They really do offer something for everyone. Even non-snowriders. In the villages there are several **snowmobile touring** companies, year round **fishing tours, sleigh rides, dogsledding, snowshoeing**, and flight-
seeing expeditions (**helicopter or airplane tours**). The Meadow Park Sports Center offers
swimming, a wading pool for children, hot tub, sauna, indoor **ice-skating**, drop-in **ice hockey**, a squash court, and fitness center. Call (604) 938–3133 for more information.

Skier Services

💲 Lift Tickets

Ages 19–64: $57 • **Ages 13–18:** $48 • **Ages 7–12:** $28 • **Ages 65+:** $48 • **Ages 6 and younger:** Free • Plan ahead and stop in at most any 7-Eleven convenience store to purchase discounted lift tickets. Discounts vary but range from $5–$10 • *Prices based on the 2000–2001 ski season using Canadian currency. See page 354 for conversion information.*

🎿 Rentals

Literally thousands of ski and snowboard packages are available. Virtually every make and manufacturer is available as there are over 20 rental shops spread out through the villages. There are also on-mountain rental shops • Generally skis run $20 and snowboards $33 • *Prices based on the 2000–2001 ski season using Canadian currency. See page 354 for conversion information.*

👥 Services

Ski School: 900 instructors; Private lessons $100/hour; Group lessons $30/hour; Beginner's package $89 (includes lesson, rentals, and half-day lift ticket) • **Snowboard School:** 300 instructors; Private lessons $100/hour; Group lessons $30/hours; Beginner's package $99 (lesson, rentals, and half-day lift ticket) • **Childcare:** There are two babysitting services in the resort: Tiny Tots Babysitting Agency, and the Nanny Network. Both offer in-suite child-care and hourly rates. Both Whistler and Blackcomb Mountains offer all-day programs for children from age three months and up; some include ski lessons, crafts, story-telling and afternoon nap. The resort's major hotels also provide lists of local babysitters • **For Kids:** Both mountains offer skiing and snowboarding programs for children and youths ranging in age from two to 16 years. Kids aprés-ski programs are offered several days a week from 3:30 P.M.–5:30 P.M.; and a special Kids' Night Out is offered twice a week. The Meadow Park Sports Center features an indoor swimming pool, children's wading pool/play area, and ice rink; and offers family drop-in rates. The Rainbow Theatre features first-run movies on a nightly basis and matinee's on weekends. Alpen Rock House, which opened in July of 1999, offers food and entertainment for all ages. Within the facility you'll find music, dancing, bowling, video games, and billiards. For more information call (604) 938–0082 • *Prices based on the 2000–2001 ski season using Canadian currency. See page 354 for conversion information.*

Room & Board

Skiing aside, Whistler-Blackcomb's five mountainside villages are worth a visit all by themselves. Each presents a variety of unique boutiques, trendy galleries, and countless restaurants to keep you busy while off the slopes. **Whistler Village,** sometimes referred to as the original village, is located at the base of Whistler and Blackcomb mountains and is connected by interwoven cobblestone pedestrian walkways. It offers the greatest selection of restaurants of the five villages. **Village North** is the most recently developed area with wide pedestrian-only promenades that wind through retail areas and fast-food restaurants. **Upper Village** is snuggled into the base of Blackcomb Mountain with paths that wind past the Blackcomb Day Lodge and some pricey restaurants. **Whistler Creek Side** is an eclectic area, reflecting the history and local flavor of the resort with funky cafes, a 24-hour convenience store, gas stations, a pharmacy, and medical and dental clinics. **Function Junction** is where locals shop for their household needs. This area is home to **Whistler Brewery**, the resort's own micro-brewery.

Lodging

On-site

Over 115 hotels, hundreds of condos, numerous bed & breakfasts, and private accommodations are available within walking distance from the lifts. Beautiful hotels built with marble and granite, towering logs, gigantic windows, and materials indigenous to the area are commonplace. Prices range from $99 to $900/night, depending on the season and type of accommodation. Your best bet is to either check out the resort website at *www.whistler-blackcomb.com* or call the central reservations line at 1–888–284–9999. This service will also recommend alternative lodging ideas and can arrange a complete package with lift tickets, air tickets, and ground transportation. If a stay at the resort is not for you, there are thousands of other accommodations within 10 minutes of Whistler, everything from five star hotels to youth hostels.

Dining

On-site

Whistler's reputation as a truly international resort is reflected in its variety of cuisine. From quaint coffee houses to five-star restaurants, there is something for everyone. There are over 90 restaurants, lounges, bars, and cafes, offering Italian, Thai, Chinese, Japanese, Indian, French, Greek, and Mexican cuisine. Guests can eat at chain restaurants like the **Hard Rock Café** and **The Keg**. They can get pizza delivered to

Alpine Dining

Few mountains have as many on slope options as the Whistler-Blackcomb combo. In fact, the resort offers more on-mountain seating than any other resort on the continent. Whistler Mountain has the **Roundhouse Lodge**, a 50,000-square-foot restaurant with 1,700 seats. Located at the top of the village gondola, the lodge offers everything from vegetarian to barbecue. The Roundhouse Lodge is also home of the popular Fresh Tracks Breakfast Program. Snowriders who are willing to roll out of bed a little early and spend a few extra bucks will earn a full buffet breakfast and first tracks on the mountain. At the top of the Harmony Express is the **Harmony Hut**. The Hut is a great place to grab a quick snack. On the Creekside try **Raven's Mountain Deli**. Located at the top of the Creekside gondola, Raven's is good for quick snacks and full-on lunches.

On Blackcomb Mountain the selection is just as diverse. The **Rendezvous Lodge** serves Mexican, burgers, pizza, and vegetarian items. **Christine's Dining Room** serves West Coast cuisine and has an elegant linen and silverware luncheon. The Glacier Creek Lodge, at the bottom of the Glacier and Jersey Cream quads, offers international fare at the **River Rock Grill**, while downstairs the **Glacier Bite** provides bistro-style counter service. Finally, the **Horstman Hut** offers a menu of chili, pizza, and pasta at the top of the Seventh Heaven Express and Crystal Hut.

their rooms that's easily on par with Dominos. The best breakfast can be found at small hole sin the wall called Bavarian cafés that serve homemade pastries. On the high-priced side, **Umberto's Italian Restaurant** is delicious. **Death by Chocolate** is the best place in the village for dessert. There are tons of bars that serve hamburgers, chicken wings, and fries. Many guests visit the village grocery store and take food back to their rooms and prepare it there. There are ice cream and candy parlors. Whatever type of cuisine a guest could want can likely be found at Whistler-Blackcomb. As far as evening entertainment, the village is alive with guests dancing, attending small music concerts, going to the movies, enjoying massages, eating delicious cuisine, and laughing it up with comedians at various clubs. There is also ice skating, horse drawn sleigh rides, dog sledding, and tons more. The following is a list of just a few of the more popular aprés ski destinations at Whistler-Blackcomb.

⑩ Restaurants

The Brew House's relaxed atmosphere, complete with a large fireplace and homemade bread and desserts, make you feel as cozy as it gets in this winter wonderland. In addition to their great homemade fare, Brew House brews lagers and ales on site. 4355 Blackcomb Way. (604) 905-BREW • **Sushi-Ya** offers Whistler's best traditional Japanese Sushi as well as other regional dishes. Above McDonald's MarketPlace. (604) 905-0155 • For a different restaurant experience, try **Crepe Montagne** where the crepes are made right in front of you. A family-owned restaurant, Crepe Montagne's menu offers crepes for all tastes, as well as raclette and cheese fondues. The strawberry and chocolate crepes are to die for! (604) 905-4444 • The upscale, award-winning **Araxi Restaurant, Bar and Wine Cellar** specializes in French and Italian regional cuisine. Also known for their extensive wine inventory, Araxi boasts a stock of over 12,000 bottles. Reservations recommended. Whistler Village Square. (604) 932-4540 • **Las Margaritas** specializes in traditional dishes from Northern Mexico and Southern California, Las Margaritas claims to have the best salsa (made fresh daily!) and margaritas anywhere, as well as the largest selection of tequila in British Columbia. Prices are reasonable. Whistler Creek Lodge, Creekside. (604) 938-6274 • **La Bocca** brings together east and west Argentinean dining with mid to high-end prices. Their exotic menu coupled with a friendly atmosphere and vibrant décor makes La Bocca an intriguing and delightful place to dine. Whistler Village Square. (604) 932-2112 • **Thai One On** is our spot for Thai food in British Columbia. Located in Le Chamois at the base of the Blackcomb upper village. (604) 932-4822 • **Alpen Rock** is a 40,000-square-foot adventure. The restaurant offers casual, high-quality dining with a variety of food, all of which is reasonably priced. After dinner, enjoy music and dancing, live entertainment, or traditional and new-age games such as glow-in-the-dark bowling. Located in Whistler Village courtyard under the Holiday Inn. (604) 552-5736 • **Rimrock Café** is a little out of the way, but is well worth the short drive. Consistently rated one of the best fine-dining restaurants in Whistler, Rimrock's dishes range from salmon and seabass to rack of lamb and steak. (604) 932-5565 • **Monk's Grill** is known for their outstanding Alberta prime rib, spicy hot chicken wings, and juicy burgers, Monk's Grill is perfect for a ski-in lunch or an evening of fine dining. With excellent service, Monk's Grill is known as Whistler's Premier Steakhouse. Slopeside at Blackcomb Mountain. (604) 932-9677 • Located aside Hoz's Pub, **The Creekside Grillroom** offers patio dining and a wine list with over 100 selections from the Northwest and around the world. Daily Chef Creations compliment an already extensive menu. Reservations recommended. 2129 Lake Placid Rd., Whistler Creekside. (604) 932-4424 • **Death By Chocolate.** Need I say more? Base of Whistler gondola. (604) 938-1323 • **Uli's Flipside Restaurant** specializes in fresh food, funky tunes, and local color—and the kitchen is open until 2 A.M! Upstairs across from body shop overlooking Village Square. (604) 935-1107

⊙ Bars and Clubs

The Savage Beagle claims to be "Whistler's Favorite Place to Party." Probably because they serve up some of the best drinks, dj's, and fresh-squeezed juices around. Whistler Village Center. (604) 938-3337 • **Black's Pub** has something for everyone. Upstairs catch the spectacular views of Whistler Resort from the atrium. While you're enjoying the views, enjoy a selection of more than 90 brands of international beer. Black's Pub also claims the widest selection of scotch in Whistler. And feel free to bring the kids. The restaurant downstairs serves families. Base of Whistler and Blackcomb gondolas. (604) 932-6945 • With a slogan like "Helping People Get Laid Since 1986," **Moe Joe's** probably could have helped even Austin Powers get his (mojo) back. Attracting local music and local people, this place is a blast at night. Around the corner from Village Square. (604) 935-1152 • **Buffalo Bill's** is a prime night spot with 13 video screens, pool tables, and a huge dance floor. If you're lucky, you might catch some big musical acts as well. Melissa Etheridge, The Tragically Hip, and Randy Bochman have all played here. Across from the conference center in Whistler Village. (604) 932-6613 • **Maxx Fish** is another club with a huge dance floor and pool tables. The difference here is that Maxx Fish features international dj's that spin house, hip-hop, and R&B. Occasionally, live bands will play. Wednesday nights are big with the locals. Village Center. (604) 932-1904 • **Hoz's Pub** is located in Whistler's "original" part of town. Hoz's features an extensive food, beer, and wine list with great views of Creekside Whistler. 2129 Lake Placid Rd., Whistler Creekside. (604) 932-5940 • Called "Whistler's Original Watering Hole," **The Boot Pub** was popular even before Whistler became Whistler. A favorite of the locals, the pub provides local live entertainment every Friday and Saturday night and The Boot Ballet Dancers every Tuesday and Wednesday. Nancy Green Way. (604) 932-3338

Apex Resort

Apex Mountain Resort

P.O. Box 1060
Penticton, British Columbia V2A 7N7

Ski Report: (250) 492–2929, ext. 2000
Information: (877) 777–2739
E-mail: *info@apexresort.com*
Website: *www.apexresort.com*
Credit Cards: Visa & MasterCard

Season: Late November to mid April
Operating Hours: 9 A.M.–3:30 P.M. daily.
Night Skiing: Wednesday, Friday, and
Saturday 6 P.M.–9:30 P.M.

Background

L ocated in the heart of the Okanagan-Similkameen Mountains, Apex Ski Resort collects more sunshine, on average, than any other resort in central British Columbia. The extra hours of daylight provide more time to explore the resort's 60 runs and 550-plus acres. Skiers and boarders will be thrilled to discover beastly mogul fields, steep chutes, bowls, and immaculately groomed slopes for cruising with the top down. In a 1995 issue, *Powder Magazine* described Apex as a "little area that rocks." While Apex won't conjure up comparisons to the seemingly boundless combination of Blackcomb and Whistler, there is nothing "little" about the skiing.

A quick drive from Penticton, British Columbia, Apex is spread out over the two faces of Beaconsfield Mountain, which reaches an elevation of 7,187 feet. A new detachable quad lift, aptly named Quickdraw, transports snowriders to the peak for spectacular views of four different mountain ranges, as well as nearly five percent of the entire province of British Columbia. The Monashee Mountains lie to the east, the Cascades to the south, the Cathedrals to the southwest, and the British Columbia Coast Range to the west. A combination of good service and great scenery, it's no wonder *Ski Canada* recently called Apex "Canada's Best Small Destination Resort."

Mountain Stats

Base Elevation: 5,197 feet *(1,585 m)*
Summit Elevation: 7,187 feet *(2,180 m)*
Vertical Drop: 2,000 feet *(605 m)*
Primary Slope Direction: North
Annual Snowfall: 200+ inches *(500 cm)*
Skiable Days: 125–140
Skiable Terrain: 550 acres *(223 ha)*
Runs: 60
Longest Run: 3 miles *(5km)*

Lifts: 1 high speed quad, 1 triple, 2 surface lifts (t-bar and platter), 1 tube tow
Lift Capacity: 4,029 skiers per hour
Terrain Classification: 16% novice; 48% intermediate; 18% advanced; 18% expert
Night Skiing: 10%
Snowmaking: 9%
Annual Visits: 100,000

Getting There

- **From Vancouver, BC:** Take Trans-Canada Hwy 1 (TCH 1) east to Hope, BC. At Hope, take Provincial Highway 3 (PH 3) east to PH 3A. Go North on PH 3A to Penticton. From the intersection of Channel Parkway and Fairview Road in Penticton, travel west on Green Mountain Road to Apex Mountain Road. Take Apex Mountain Road to the resort.

- **From Seattle, WA:** Take I-5 north to WA 520. Head east on WA 520 to I-405 and then go north to U.S. 2. Head east on U.S. 2 to U.S. 97. Cross the border and continue north on PH 97 to Penticton. From the intersection of Channel Parkway and Fairview Road in Penticton travel west on Green Mountain Road to Apex Mountain Road. Take Apex Mountain Road to the resort.

- **From Spokane, WA:** Take U.S. 395 north to PH 3, which is just across the Canadian border. Take PH 3 west to PH 97 and head north on PH 97 to Penticton. From the intersection of Channel Parkway and Fairview Road in Penticton travel west on Green Mountain Road to Apex Mountain Road. Take Apex Mountain Road to the resort.

Airline services: The closest regional airport is in Penticton, at Penticton Regional Airport (YYF). Most travelers fly into Calgary, Alberta, or Vancouver, BC, before changing to Air BC or Air Canada and continuing on to Penticton.

Shuttle services: This Ski Express Bus provides affordable transportation between the city of Penticton and Apex Mountain Resort. Call (877) 777–2739 for schedules.

Trail Profiles

From the 7,000-foot summit, snowriders have easy access to nearly every trail on the mountain. Experts will discover plenty of stomach-in-your-mouth steeps, chutes, and in-bounds tree-skiing. Try the area's less-frequented north side for runs, such as *Gun Barrel*—a narrow cut through dense pine trees that is dangerously steep and usually full of monstrous moguls. Additionally, *Make My Day* and *Twenty-Two* are both steep, narrow gashes that require a strong ability and extensive on-snow experience. On the south side, beyond the *Great Wall*, are the double black diamond runs *Sweet Sue*, *Tooth/Tusk*, and the surprisingly clean *Toilet Bowl*—each possessing a sharp pitch of 35 to 40 degrees.

For even steeper adventures, skiers and snowboarders can explore what locals refer to as "Proper." Officially, the area is known as Apex Peak, but identifying it as such alerts area residents that they're dealing with tourists. This area is best reserved for experienced to expert snowriders, and it's advised to hook up with a knowledgeable local who can serve as a guide in the beastly Proper. Located just south of Beaconsfield, Proper reaches another 200 feet above its in-bounds brother. Venturing out to Proper requires snow shovels and avalanche transceivers, not to mention the courage and skill to ride seriously steep terrain. Not only is the terrain fearsome, but the snow conditions are challenging as well. Most of Apex Peak is completely above treeline and is therefore exposed to the sometimes punishing weather of the BC interior. Over the course of any given run, snowriders may cut tracks through wind-blown crust, ice, and—with good timing—lots of powder.

Apex doesn't restrict itself to the elite snowrider, though. Less aggressive skiers and boarders can make their way to the summit and find a multitude of safe and sane trails. *Grandfather's Trail* is a designated, three-mile-long green run that winds down the area's north ridge all the way to the base lodge. Additionally, *Juniper* and *Ridge Run* are fantastically smooth cruising runs that also stem from the top of Beaconsfield, providing access to the lower mountain.

As good as the skiing is at Apex, what makes the area memorable are the locals. While they may or may not share their secret runs and powder stashes with outsiders, they are always willing to lend a hand and strike up a friendly conversation. This hospitality extends to the Apex staff, who are truly dedicated to making your ski experience the best it can be.

More Fun in the Flakes

There are two areas for **cross-country skiing**. "Apex Village" provides 7.4 miles (12 km), plus 0.6-mile (1-km) night-lit loop. Trails are not groomed or trackset and thus there's no trail access fee. The Nickel Plate Nordic Centre is located 4 miles (6 km) from Apex Village. It provides 18.6 miles (30 km) of groomed and trackset trails, with classic and skating tracks, as well as 12.4 miles (20 km) of backcountry trails. There is no cost, but donations are accepted.

Nickel Plate Adventure Company provides one- and two-hour **guided snowmobile tours**. Included in the package are boots, gloves, helmets, and suits. Group discounts are available. Nickel Plate Adventure Company also provides **horse-drawn sleigh rides** at Apex Mountain Village Stables. Catering available for groups of 10 or more. For more information on either of these activities, call (250) 292-8700.

The Apex Mountain Village outdoor **ice-skating** rink is open daily, with rentals available. It's lit for evening skating.

Snowboarding **Highlights**

At last Apex has set aside some terrain specifically for snowboarding. The Apex Mountain Dew Boardercross Terrain Park is now officially open for business, and business is thriving. Area crewmembers have turned the *Claim Jumper* trail into a terrain park replete with tabletops, spines, hips, and quarterpipes. Situated at the mountain's lower half, the park offers 750 feet of challenging fall-line riding and is accessible from the T-bar at the hill's base. The T-bar climbs up the *Okanagan* run, where the halfpipe is rebuilt each year. The Apex crew starts in the early season by blowing artificial snow onto *Okanagan*, giving them a solid base on which to sculpt a burly 300-foot halfpipe with a pipe grinder similar to the Bombardier. *Okanagan* is also equipped with lights on Wednesday, Friday, and Saturday nights. Terrain park and halfpipe aside, the most popular runs for one-plankers are the unnamed runs in the trees off the Quick Draw quad chair. The terrain is steep, the snow is deep, and the trees are tight. In a nutshell, it's free-riding nirvana.

Skier Services

Lift Tickets

Ages 19–64: $35/full-day, $29/half-day, $10/night • **Ages 13–18:** $31/full-day, $25/half-day, $10/night • **Ages 8–12 and 65+:** $25/full-day, $19/half-day, $7/night • **Ages 7 & younger:** Free • *Prices based on the 2000–2001 ski season using Canadian currency. See page 354 for conversion information.*

Rentals

Ski Rentals: Ages 13+: $24. Ages 8–12: $16. Ages 7 & younger: $13. Type of Gear: Volant and Dynastar • **Snowboard Rentals:** Ages 13+: $36. Ages 12 & younger: $27. 100 sets. Type of Gear: Aggression boards, Vans boots, and Switch bindings • **Nordic Ski Rentals:** $14/all ages • *Prices based on the 2000–2001 ski season using Canadian currency. See page 354 for conversion information.*

Services

Ski School: 25–30 instructors; Private lessons $45 for 2 hours; Group lesson $28 for 2 hours; Beginner's package $37 (includes poma lift, 60 minute lesson, and rentals) • **Snowboard School:** 10–12 instructors; Private lessons $45 for 2 hours; Group lesson $28 for 2 hours; 1st Turns Program $42 (includes poma lift, 60 minute lesson, and rentals) • **Childcare:** Kids Club, 18 months to 6 years old. Prices vary. Call (877) 777-2739 for more information • *Prices based on the 2000–2001 ski season using Canadian currency. See page 354 for conversion information.*

Room & Board

▣ Lodging

On-site

The Inn at Apex Mountain Resort lets you ski to and from your door with choice of standard unit, adjoining suite with fireplace, kitchenette, and loft—all with natural wood beams and peaked windows, hot tubs, and fitness room; rates $85–$129/night; 1–800–387–2739.

Penticton–20 miles *(32 km)* away

Winter or summer accommodations are available in private cabins, chalets, condos, and townhouses; (250) 292–8256 • **Apex Mountain Resort RV Centre** offers 32 sites equipped with electrical hook-ups, coin-operated hot showers, and clean restrooms; (877) 777–2739 • *Call the Penticton Information Center 1–800–663–5052 for more options.*

⒲ Dining

The Gun Barrel Saloon challenges you to hammer a nail into a log and get free drinks at this fun bar, or try the flaming hot coffee served from the mouth of a double barrel shot gun; located in the village, reservations are suggested; (250) 292–8515

Get Hammered at the Gun Barrel Saloon

Getting hammered at the Gun Barrel is a different experience than you might imagine. It's actually a game invented by some Austrian ski instructors looking to subsidize their drinking habit. The game is formally called Nageln (pronounced neg-lin). The object of the game is to use the thin end of a bricklayer's hammer and pound a nail into a giant log. Everyone gets one try and the last person to not get the nail down buys the drinks. Up to 10 people have been known to stand around the log at a time. Practice hammering a few nails before you visit Apex and you'll get to drink for free.

If alcohol is not your gig, you can try a swig of hot coffee. Flaming hot coffee that is. Even better, it's delivered to you from the mouth of a double barrel shot gun. Don't worry—the gun isn't loaded. But the experience is a must try. In addition to being a "party pub" the Gun Barrel includes a 120-seat full service dining room. Located in the village. Reservations are suggested.

Fairmont Hot Springs Resort

Fairmont Hot Springs Resort

Box 10
Fairmont Hot Springs, BC
Canada, V0B 1L0

Ski Report: (250) 345–6413
Information: (250) 345–6311
   1–800–663–4979
E-mail: *info@fairmontresort.com*
Website: *www.fairmontresort.com*
Credit Cards: Visa, MasterCard, & AMEX
Operating Hours: Mon–Sun 9:30 A.M.–4:30 P.M.
Night Skiing: Fridays only 4 P.M.–9 P.M. (in February only)
Season: Late November to late March

Background

Those who visit Fairmont Hot Springs tend to be less concerned with attacking the slopes than with stripping away the layers of stress put on by the work world. With only 13 runs and just 1,000 feet of vertical, the snowriding at Fairmont is good but modest. It's clearly not the main attraction. No, the 10,000 square feet of pools bubbling with natural sweet-smelling mineral water are. Fairmont's hot springs—Canada's largest all-natural hot springs—were created millions of years ago when deep, large fissures were left in the rocks as the tectonic plates worked to raise the Rocky Mountains. Snowmelt settled into the fissures and worked its way down to the mountain's center. Warmed by the earth's core, the waters rose to form surface pools. The process continues, and today these warm water pockets afford bathers a truly unique and relaxing experience. An hour or two in the pools may leave you wrinkled as a raisin, but it'll soothe your soul.

Water temperatures range from 102 to 108 degrees Fahrenheit and are controlled by adding colder water from the snow and nearby creeks. The pools are drained and refilled daily with fresh water, lessening the need for harsh chemicals. Jacuzzis just can't compare with Fairmont's hot springs. In addition to diving pools, lap pools, and kiddie-pools, the resort boasts several pools just for R&R. Visitors at Fairmont will find the hot tubs neither crowded nor reeking of chlorine.

The surrounding landscape, the huge bowls and ice-capped crags of the Fairmont Range, adds to the wonderfully invigorating waters of the hot springs. Nestled at the base of the spectacular Rocky Mountains, Fairmont Hot Springs Resort peeks west across the Columbia River Valley at the snow-covered peaks of the Purcell Mountains. To the south lie Columbia Lake and the headwaters of the mighty Columbia.

For guests who want more of an on-snow adventure, a good plan is to bunk at the Fairmont Lodge, enjoying the luxurious comforts of the resort, and day-trip it to the surrounding ski areas of Panorama, Kimberley, and Fernie. Each of these is more focused on snowriding than Fairmont, and they're only 35 to 90 minutes away. So enjoy the best of both worlds.

Mountain Stats

Base Elevation: 4,200 feet *(1,280 m)*
Summit Elevation: 5,200 feet *(1,585)*
Vertical Drop: 1,000 feet *(305 m)*
Primary Slope Direction: Southwest
Annual Snowfall: 150 inches *(381 cm)*
Skiable Days: 100
Skiable Terrain: 300 acres *(122 ha)*
Runs: 13

Longest Run: 1mile *(1.5 km)*
Lifts: 1 triple, 1 surface tow
Lift Capacity: 3200 skiers per hour
Terrain Classification: 20% novice; 60% intermediate; 20% advanced
Night Skiing: 30% allowance
Snowmaking: 55%
Annual Visits: 22,000

Getting There

- **From Portland, OR:** Take I-5 north to Seattle. *[Follow Seattle directions below.]*
- **From Seattle, WA:** Take I-90 to Spokane. *[Follow Spokane directions below.]*
- **From Spokane, WA:** Take I-90 east to Coeur d'Alene, ID. From Coeur d'Alene, take U.S. 95 north to the town of Invermere, BC. At the Canadian border U.S. 95 changes to Provincial Highway 3/95/93 (PH 3/95/93). Take the Invermere exit and proceed to Fairmont Hot Springs signs to the ski area.
- **From Vancouver, BC:** Take PH 3 east to PH 3/95/93. Follow this road north to the town of Invermere. Take the Invermere exit and proceed into town. Follow Fairmont Hot Springs signs to the ski area.

Airport Service: For guests traveling from outside the Northwest, the Calgary International Airport (YYC) is the closest major gateway airport. It's a 3.5-hour drive to the ski area. Most travelers fly into Calgary and connect with Air BC or Air Canada before continuing on to Cranbrook, BC, and the Cranbrook Regional Airport (YXC).

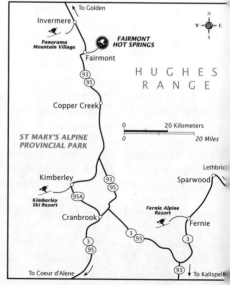

Trail Profiles

Fairmont has a smattering of trails that are accessible right out the back of the lodge. All 13 are named with a clearly Western theme in mind. Novice skiers will delight in *Moonshine*—a wide, gentle rolling slope groomed silky smooth every day. Equipped for night skiing, *Moonshine* branches off to the more lightly pitched *Crooked Tree*, which rolls into *Easy Rider*.

Easy Rider may be the resort's premier run because of its long, winding course and a launching pad near the finish, where a big roller suitable for all abilities tops off the trail. The mountain drops gradually, but with enough speed, skiers and boarders can achieve air as long as five to seven seconds while just a few feet off the ground.

High Plains Drifter skirts the area's boundary, inviting intermediates and novice snowriders for a tour over a mile and a half long. The trail is groomed every day and rides like a newly surfaced two-lane highway. *Snow Gun*, also groomed daily, offers a variety of pitches with one short but steep line at the bottom. It's a great place for intermediate riders to test their skills before moving on to more advanced terrain.

What Fairmont lacks in variety, it makes up for with a few noble challenges. Black-diamond *Two Gun*, with its double fall line, is usually full of powder or small bumps. Moguls tend to stay relatively small because the trail's steep pitch and off-piste conditions can intimidate many a skier.

Skiers who like to bang through the big bumps have *Desperado* and its combination of three separate pitches over 1,000 vertical feet. The top is steep and the bumps get nasty. A timely flat spot in the middle allows skiers to catch their breath before entering a second mogul field that drops to the base.

Snowboarding Highlights

For a small resort that does not focus on snowriding, Fairmont has done a good job at building snowboard-specific terrain. There's the *Kid's Pipe*, a halfpipe, and a terrain park. Plus there are various jumps built all over the mountain.

The *Kid's Pipe* is about 90 feet in length with six- to seven-foot walls and a shallow grade. The *Kid's Pipe* is located in front of the main Chalet. The halfpipe is near the base, as well, and is roughly twice the size of the Kid's Pipe. Locals love the unique tabletop entrance to the pipe, not to mention the 10-foot walls and 150 feet of vertical. The terrain park is just above the two  pipes and features 12 manmade obstacles including a tabletop, a spine, two rails, and jumps in various shapes and sizes.

More Fun in the Flakes

For information on **snowmobile tours, sleigh rides,** and the indoor **skating** rink, call 1–800–663–4979.

Skier Services

🅂 Lift Tickets

Adults: $26/full-day, $20/half-day; Juniors: $17/full-day, $13/half-day • **Senior:** $12/full-day and half-day • **Ages 5 & younger:** Free • *Prices based on the 2000–2001 ski season using Canadian currency. See page 354 for conversion information.*

🎿 Rentals

Ski Rentals: Adults: $20/full-day, $16/half-day; Junior: $13/full-day, $11/half-day. Type of Gear: Rossignol • **Snowboard Rentals:** $30/full-day and $25/half-day. Type of Gear: Rossignol and Kemper • *Prices based on the 2000–2001 ski season using Canadian currency. See page 354 for conversion information.*

🏠 Services

Ski & Snowboard School: 12 ski instructors and 8 snowboard instructors; Private lessons $40/hour; Group lessons $19/hour • **Childcare:** None • *Prices based on the 2000–2001 ski season using Canadian currency. See page 354 for conversion information.*

Room & Board

🛏 Lodging

The real draw here is the **Fairmont Lodge**, but other accommodations such as motels, B&Bs, and five-star villas may also be found by calling the main reservations line. (250) 345–6311 or 1–800–663–4979.

On-site

Fairmont Lodge, recently renovated, is rustic but luxurious, as evidenced by its four-and-a-half-star rating. Most importantly, rooms look out over the hot springs and down into the valley. Lofts, suites, and standard layouts are available. Enjoy complementary use of the hot mineral pools and free parking. Rates range from $99–$159/night. (250) 345–6311 or 1–800–663–4979 • Fairmont also offers a 311-site RV park; rates $17–$33/night. 1–800–663–4979.

🍽 Dining

On-site

Lodge Dining Room offers elaborate dining delights from breakfast to dinner, and a Sunday brunch, all served with flair in a comfortable setting overlooking the pools and lawns, with Norman Swain on the piano most evenings. A day lodge provides a restaurant and snack bar, as well as a Pizza Hut. There are après-ski facilities including lounges and a nightclub.

Manning Park Resort

Manning Park Resort
P.O. Box 1480
Hope, BC
Canada VOX 1LO

Ski Report & Information: (250) 840–8822
E-mail: *info@manningparkresort.com*
Website: *www.manningparkresort.com*
Credit Cards: Visa, MasterCard, & American Express

Operating Hours: 9 A.M.–4 P.M. Thursday–Monday
Season: Mid November to early April

Background

Manning Park Resort is a solid weekend alternative for Vancouver-area residents looking to avoid the expense and crowds of Whistler-Blackcomb. The resort lies within Manning Provincial Park, on the northern tip of the Cascade Mountain Range and at the end of the famous Pacific Crest Trail. In addition to alpine skiing and snowboarding, the rustic and family-oriented resort offers a taste of classically groomed cross-country skiing, Nordic skate skiing, snowshoeing, backcountry touring, telemarking, and outdoor ice-skating.

Skiers have been touring the park since 1951. The downhill area opened in 1965. Since then, area management has been more concerned with the experience of going downhill than up. There isn't a single high-speed quad on the mountain, just a well-maintained double chairlift circuit. The skiing, however, is excellent, and the scenery simply stunning. From the top of Manning Park, Mount Hozameen—which reaches nearly 10,000 feet—is the closest of 10 snow-capped peaks visible in the Cascade Mountains to the south.

85

Mountain Stats

Base Elevation: 4,339 feet *(1,323 m)*
Summit Elevation: 5,868 feet *(1,789 m)*
Vertical Drop: 1,417 feet *(432 m)*
Primary Slope Direction: Northeast
Annual Snowfall: 228 inches *(580 cm)*
Skiable Days: 100
Skiable Terrain: 183 acres *(74 h)*
Runs: 24

Longest Run: 1.9 miles *(3 km)*
Lifts: 2 doubles, 1 T-bar, 1 handle tow
Lift Capacity: 4,171 skiers per hour
Terrain Classification: 30% novice; 40% intermediate; 30% advanced
Night Skiing: None
Snowmaking: None
Annual Visits: 60,000

Getting There

- **From Spokane, WA:** Take I-90 west to I-405. Follow I-405 north to I-5. *[Follow Seattle directions below.]*
- **From Seattle, WA:** Take I-5 north to Exit 255, WA 542 (also known as East Sunset Drive and the Mount Baker Highway). Take WA 542 to WA 9. Head north on WA 9 to the town of Sumas. Cross into Canada and take Trans-Canada Highway 1 (TCH 1) east toward Hope. At Hope, follow Provincial Highway 3 (PH 3) to the ski area.
- **From Vancouver, BC:** Take TCH 1 west to Hope. At Hope, follow PH 3 to the ski area.

Trail Profiles

Manning Park's 24 runs are serviced by two double chairlifts and two surface lifts. Fortunately, with the exception of President's Day weekend, lift lines are minimal. The Blue Chair offers terrain for all abilities. *Wagon Trail* begins with a narrow track before the gentle slope opens wide, making it a great spot for novice skiers and boarders. *Blue Face* is rarely groomed and usually winds up fiercely bumped with moguls. Bigger bumps and sharper steeps are the hallmarks of *Blue Streak*, which runs directly under the chairlift.

The Orange Chair provides access to a majority of the remaining area where mid-level skiers can take on a variety of cruising runs. They include a narrow twisting trail called *HorseShoe* and the *Featherstone Special*—Manning Park's steepest groomed run. *Featherstone* is short but the turns are fast and fun. For more cruising, try *Orange Streak* to the skier's left of the chair. Manning Park regulars stop and frequent *ChitChat* about halfway down. A flat spot in the run, *ChitChat* is a perfect spot to stop and "shoot the chit" before breaking for the bottom.

To experience classic skiing the way nature intended it, look no further than the trees. From the top of the Orange Chair, head out to *Apple Bowl* from the top of the Orange Chair. It is off to the right and the path is easy to spot. There's usually a crowd of boarders and skiers leading the way. Don't expect a lot of vertical, but the variety of terrain and abundance of powder make the short hike worth the effort.

Snowboarding **Highlights**

Manning Park builds a small terrain park every year just below *Snag* and just above *Coming Home*. It offers eight manmade obstacles in a 400-foot vertical span, including tabletops, spines, berms, and jumps of various sizes. Crewmembers and local riders work together to construct the park, which is accessed from the top of the Orange Chair. Boarders also like to hike out to *Apple Bowl* and tear through the powder and trees.

Photo courtesy Manning Park

More Fun in the Flakes

Manning Park is a mecca of **backcountry skiing**, offering a series of open bowls and powder skiing. Within the park boundary there are over 118 miles (190km) of wilderness touring. In addition Manning Park offers 18.5 miles (30km) of machine groomed trails for **track skiing** and 18.5 miles (30km) of groomed trails for **cross-country skiing**.

Located adjacent to the beginner slope is a non-serviced lift area for **tobogganing** and **tubing**. There is currently no fee for use of the area. Toboggan rental is available at the main desk of the lodge. New to Manning are designated (marked) **snowshoe trails**—rentals are available. **Ice-skating** is also available.

In December of 1999 Manning introduced the Loon Lagoon Recreation Center, which houses changing rooms, an in-door hot tub, co-ed wet and dry saunas, and a fitness room. Manning also plans to build a new outdoor night-lit skating rink.

Skier Services

$ Lift Tickets

Ages 18–64: $31/day weekend, $20/day mid-week • **Ages 13–17:** $25/day weekend, $20/day mid-week • **Ages 7–12:** $19/day weekend and mid-week • **Ages 65+:** $20/day weekend and mid-week • **Ages 6 & younger:** Free • *Prices based on the 2000–2001 ski season using Canadian currency. See page 354 for conversion information.*

⛷ Nordic Trail Passes

Ages 18–64: $13; Ages 13–17: $12 • **Ages 7–12:** $10 • **Ages 65+:** $11 • Ages 6 & younger: Free • *Prices based on the 2000–2001 ski season using Canadian currency. See page 354 for conversion information.*

🎿 Rentals

Ski Rentals: Ages 13+: $21–$26; Ages 7–12: $15–$18; Ages 6 & younger: $11–$15; 400 sets. Type of Gear: Rossignol, Salomon, Elan, and Dynastar • **Snowboard Rentals:** Ages 13+: $36; Ages 12 & younger: $30; 200 sets. Type of Gear: K2, Rossignol, Burton, Option, Elan, and Nitro (now including step-ins) • **Nordic Ski Rentals:** Ages 18+: $18–$25; Ages 13–17: $14–$25; Ages 7–12: $12; Ages 6 & younger: $11 • **Telemark Ski Rentals:** Ages 13+: $28. Type of Gear: Rottefella, Garmont, and Rossignol • **Snowshoe Rentals:** $10–$25/all ages • **Snowblade Rentals:** Ages 13+: $16–$21; Ages 12 & younger: $14–$17. Type of Gear: Salomon • *Prices based on the 2000–2001 ski season using Canadian currency. See page 354 for conversion information.*

🏫 Services

Ski School: 15 instructors; Private lessons $35/hour; Group lessons $18/hour; Beginner's package from $38 (includes lift ticket and rentals) • **Snowboard School:** 4 instructors; Private lessons $35/hour; Group lessons $21/hour; Beginner's package from $53 (includes lift ticket and rentals) • **Nordic Ski School:** 3 instructors; Lesson package from $32 (includes lift ticket and rentals). *Call (250) 840–8822 for times and availability* • **Telemark Ski School:** Lessons $55 (includes day lift pass, Crispi buckled teleboots, Rottefella cable bindings, and shaped skis). *Available on guaranteed reservation basis only. Call (250) 840–8822 for times and availability* • **Childcare:** Fully licensed services. *Call (250) 840–8822 for more information* • **Tuning/Waxing/Repairs:** Basic tuning, waxing, and repairs available for snowboards, downhill skis and cross-country skis • *Prices based on the 2000–2001 ski season using Canadian currency. See page 354 for conversion information.*

Room & Board

🛏 Lodging

On site

The Main Lodge has 73 rooms, a fireside lounge, game rooms, saunas, nightly in-house movies, and meeting facilities. Guests have the option of large and small rooms, all of which are reasonably priced. Visitors can also stay in a more private setting in cabins equipped with kitchens, TV's, and fireplaces. Manning Park offers chalets that share single kitchens with three sleeping units. The Last Resort is one of the original buildings in the Park, built in 1949, and is popular for family gatherings and church, school, and youth groups. None of the lodging is ski-in ski-out, however Manning Park provides a shuttle bus to take guests the short distance of about three miles to the chairlifts. Rates run from $109–$550/night (excluding GST). Value Season and Mid-Week Packages available. Call 1–800–330–3321 or (250) 840–8822 for more information.

Hope–42 miles *(66 km)* away
Colonial 900 Motel offers king and queen beds and kitchenettes; rates $40–$50/night. (604) 869-5223 • **Evergreen Bed & Breakfast** features three delightful rooms with country decorations, queen and double beds, balconies, and patios; rates $65–$69/night. (604) 869-9918 • **Slumberlodge** offers 34 rooms with queen beds, pool, sauna, and restaurant; rates $49–$59/night. 1–800–757–7766 • **Sunshine Valley Bed & Breakfast** is the nearest B&B to Manning Park; two suites with private bath in a quiet country home; BC Tourism approved; rates $65 and $75. (604) 869-2143 or e-mail at *sunshinevlybnb@uniserve.com* • **Quality Inn** offers queen and double beds, indoor pool, hot tub, sauna, and breakfast; rates $64–$76/night. 1–800–899–5996.

⑪ Dining

On-site
The original **Pinewoods Lodge** was built in 1949 when the Hope-Princeton Highway first opened. As it was back then, it continues to be a favorite stop for visitors staying at the resort, visiting the park or traveling through. Today, it is home to the **Cascade Cafe, Pinewoods Dining Room**, the **Bear's Den Lounge, Manning's Country Store** and the **Similkameen Meeting Rooms**, and it's all smoke-free. Guests enjoy fresh & hearty breakfasts, baked treats like cinnamon buns, homemade soups and a fairly extensive lunch menu for big, small, and even health-conscious appetites.

Open for dinner from 5:30 P.M., the Pinewoods Dining Room is casual and rustic with a diverse menu featuring pastas, stir-fry, fresh salads, and house specialties like schnitzel and pacific salmon. For smaller appetites there are junior and appetizer menus. There is also a full bar and wine list featuring BC whites and reds.

The unique Bear's Den Lounge features the handiwork of BC craftsmen and artists. Lots of games and a cozy fireplace add to the casual and smoke-free (except firewood) environment. Full bar including Bear Beer on tap, and pub-style food menu. Specials nightly and theme nights monthly.

Hope–47 miles *(75 km)* away
Dogwood Valley Café serves standard Canadian cuisine. (604) 869-7082 • **Grammy's Pizza & Steakhouse** serves a delicious variety of pastas, pizzas, salads, and steaks. (604) 869-7141 • **Home Restaurant** offers home-style cooking, good pies and large portions. (604) 869-5558 • **Kibo Japanese Grill and Café** offers traditional Japanese cuisine featuring sushi and tempura. (604) 869-7317 • **Sandwich Tree** serves lunch-counter-style sandwich, soup, and salad joint. (604) 869-3834.

Red Mountain

Red Mountain
P.O. Box 670
Rossland, BC
Canada VOG1YO

Ski Report:
  Canada: (250) 362–5500
  Spokane, WA: (509) 459–6000
Information: (250) 362–7384
E-mail: *reservations@ski-red.com*
Website: *www.ski-red.com*
Credit Cards: Visa, MasterCard, & AMEX

Operating Hours: 9 A.M.–3 P.M. weekdays and
  8:30 A.M.–3:30 P.M. weekends

Season: Early December to early April

Background

Not only is Red Mountain one of Canada's oldest and most famous ski resorts, it is the home of Western Canada's first ski lift, installed in 1947. Nestled in the Kootenay Mountains of southern BC, Red has a long history of hosting big-time competitions and producing some of the world's best skiers. In fact, the first-ever World Cup race in Canada was held on the slopes of Granite Mountain. Rossland natives Nancy Greene and Kerrin Lee-Gartner both earned Olympic Gold Medals in 1968 and 1992.

For all its time-honored glory and tradition though, Red has remained true to its small-town, homegrown skiing heritage. The excessive development that has occurred at other winter resorts has yet to find its way to Red Mountain, and Rossland visitors won't find the decadent glitz and glamour of larger resorts like Whistler, Vail, and Aspen. Entering the mining town feels like stepping back in time to the gold rush of the late 1800s. Victorian houses and glorified mining shacks with bright, multicolored roofs line the narrow streets that wind up the valley walls toward Red Mountain. Brick cobblestone lines Main Street. Relics of the town's mining origin can be seen everywhere. Chain restaurants and major retail outlets are non-existent in Rossland. Visitors find that Red Mountain has a distinct personality and charm, most of which focuses on the best part of any ski experience—riding, sliding, and gliding downhill.

Mountain Stats

Base Elevation: 3,888 feet *(1,296 m)*
Summit Elevation:
Granite Mountain: 6,800 feet *(2,266 m)*
Red Mountain: 5,208 feet *(1,589 m)*
Vertical Drop: 2,900 feet *(970 m)*
Primary Slope Direction: 360 degrees
Annual Snowfall: 300 inches *(762 cm)*
Skiable Days: 130
Skiable Terrain: 400 groomed acres *(162 ha)*, 800 acres *(324 ha)* of trees

Runs: 83
Longest Run: 5 miles *(8.1 km)*
Terrain Classification: 10% novice; 45% intermediate; 45% advanced
Lifts: 3 triples, 1 doubles, 1 T-bar
Lift Capacity: 6,150 skiers per hour
Night Skiing: None
Snowmaking: None
Annual Visits: 130,000

Getting There

- **From Portland, OR:** Take I-5 North to I-90. *[Follow Seattle directions below.]*
- **From Seattle, WA:** Take I-90 east to Spokane. *[Follow Spokane directions below.]*
- **From Spokane, WA:** Take U.S. 395 north through Colville to WA 25. Take WA 25 north through Northport. Continue north to Canadian border where WA 25 becomes Provincial Highway 22 (PH 22). Rossland and Red Mountain are a short distance across the border.
- **From Vancouver, BC:** Head east on Trans-Canada Highway 1 (TCH 1) to Hope. From Hope take PH 3 east to Grand Forks. At Grand Forks, take PH 3 east to Christina Lake. At the Nancy Green Junction, take PH 3B to Rossland and Red Mountain.

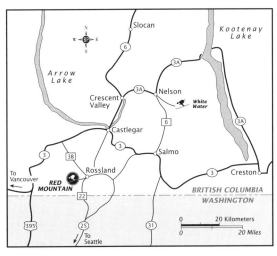

Airport Services: Air Canada can connect you to Castlegar Airport (YCG) from most international hubs. Shuttles to the ski area and rental cars are available from the airport. Most travelers from outside of the Northwest fly into Spokane International Airport (GEG), the closest international gateway to Rossland, and rent a car to make the two-hour drive to the resort. Red Mountain also provides a shuttle from Spokane Airport three times a week on Wednesdays, Saturdays, and Sundays.

Trail Profiles

Spread out over two distinct peaks—Red and Granite—the entire area is serviced by only five lifts, and one of these is a T-bar. At 6,150 skiers per hour, lift capacity pales in comparison to the bigger resorts that have sunk millions into new lift systems. And yet, Red still offers awesome snowriding, despite early morning lift lines at the Silverload triple chair. The best skiing and riding to be had at Red is on Granite Mountain and there is only one way to the top from the base of the lodge. After the initial early morning crowds have been transported up the mountain and spread out between the Paradise triple chair and the Motherload triple chair, lift lines are no longer a bother. The initial wait will never decrease as long as the area sticks with triple chairs instead of moving up to high-speed quads. Red will, however, expand farther away from the lodge when they

install two new chairs on Gray Mountain to the northeast of Granite. When the chairs are installed will depend on the area's ability to raise the capital. Lets hope it's soon. Locals who regularly hike up Gray claim the terrain and snow is fantastic.

Three of the resort's five lifts go straight to the top of Red and Granite. From there snowriders can choose lines that head in every possible direction. From the top of Granite and Red there's 360 degrees of skiing. Over 83 marked trails, 400 acres of groomed terrain, and 800 acres of tree skiing provide enough variety to last a lifetime. Don't be surprised to come across aging locals who claim that after 60 years of skiing they still find new stashes of turns.

Red also boasts BC's fifth-highest vertical drop (2,900 feet), third-largest amount of skiable terrain, and one of its longest runs (5 miles). It is pure quality, though, that makes Red one of the best snowriding experiences north of the border.

Advanced skiers and boarders relish the fact that over 60 percent of the terrain is off-piste. The area's constantly cool temperatures and dry air make for ideal snow conditions. Fresh turns in deep, light snow can be discovered days after snowfall ends. Some favorite local runs include the *Powder Fields*, *The Slides*, *Link's Run*, and *Cambodia*. All four are accessible from the top of Granite. *Powder Fields* is self explanatory while *The Slides* earned its moniker by being one of the steepest lines on Granite. Snowriders who fall down tend to slide all the way to the bottom. *Cambodia* is a series of several 10-to 15-foot drops. The only way down is to hurl one's sleds or board over each miniature cliff. *Link's Run* may be the steepest of the four—and there's the added pressure of skiing it right under the lift.

Less aggressive advanced skiers and boarders will find single black-diamond runs like *Papoose Bowl*, *Short Squaw*, *Ledges*, and *Jumbo* to be nearly as exciting. *Papoose Bowl* is a short

Snowboarding **Highlights**

Future plans include building a pipe and an elaborate terrain park. Seeing as 35 percent of Red's skier visits are snowboarders, this makes good sense. But whether or not the pipe and park actually open depends a lot on Red Mountain being in the black. For now, local riders are more than content to freeride the area. Granite is like one big park full of natural hits, jumps, drops, powder fields, and enough challenging terrain to keep even expert boarders satisfied.

distance down the mountain from *Link's Run*. However, *Papoose* has a less extreme entrance. *Short Squaw* is a steep cut through the trees on the backside of Granite. *Jumbo* is actually a steep open field of powder, full of lumps, bumps, and jumps. The run leads skiers and boarders to *Ledges*—a series of small shelves from which snowriders can hurl their bodies.

Intermediate skiers and boarders will also find plenty of terrain on which to improve their turns. *Southern Comfort*, *Sluice*, *Southern Belle*, and *Ruby Tuesday* all feature groomed ,medium fall-line skiing. Take them slow or fast, one thing is for sure, they are smooth. All of these runs are located in the Paradise Basin.

Only 10 percent of Red's runs are dedicated to novice snowriding. The good news is that the terrain is strategically laid out so beginners are not relegated to the base area. From the tops of both peaks there are gentle rolling runs down the mountain. On Granite, five-mile *Long Squaw* is a buffed cat track that starts at the top and doesn't end until it has explored nearly the entire mountain. From Red's peak, novice and intermediates will find *Dale's Trail* and *Ski School Alley* to be the gentlest way down. While *Ski School Alley* is a great place to learn the finer points of wedge turns, it, as its name might imply, can be overburdened with instructors and students.

As good as the skiing is in-bounds at Red Mountain, adventurous skiers and boarders find fantastic skiing in the surrounding backcountry. Several 6,000-foot peaks form a natural alpine playground with Granite Mountain in the center. *Kirkup*, *Record*, *Roberts*, and *Gray* are all accessible from the top of the resort. For skiers and boarders looking for a backcountry experience that is a little less extreme, take advantage of the Black Jack Cross-country Area, which offers 34 miles of machined groomed track. Two diagonals and one skating track are complete with warming huts, toilets, and first aid stations along the trail.

More Fun in the Flakes

Cross-country skiing is available at Red Mountain and in the surrounding area. The choice is between over 34 miles (55 km) of trails in two different areas. Call the following organizations for more information: Black Jack Cross country Ski Club at (250) 362-7301 and Paulson Cross-country Trails at (250) 365-8600.

Ice skating is available at the Rossland Arena. Call (250) 362-7191 for more information. **Sleigh rides** can be arranged by calling (250) 362-5895. **Snowmobiling** opportunities are available through High Mountain Adventures at (250) 362-5342.

Skier Services

⑤ Lift Tickets

Ages 19–65: $42/full-day, $30/half-day • Ages 13–18: $34/full-day, $24/half-day • Ages 7–12: $22/full-day, $15/half-day • Ages 65–74: $27/full-day, $17/half-day • Ages 6 & younger and 75+: Free • Single-ride tickets: $10 • *Prices based on the 2000–2001 ski season using Canadian currency. See page 354 for conversion information.*

🎿 Rentals

Ski Rentals: $31/adults, $26/kids. Type of Gear: Atomic, Volant, Salomon, Elan, Head, Rossignol, and Keniessel • Snowboard Rentals: $31/adults, $26/kids. Type of Gear: Rossignol, Elan, Arcane, Killerloop, and Heelside • Telemark Rentals: $31/all ages • *Prices based on the 2000–2001 ski season using Canadian currency. See page 354 for conversion information.*

🏫 Services

Ski School: 25 instructors; Private lessons $50/hour and $30 for second hour, Group lessons $30/two hours; Beginner's package $35–$45 (includes rentals, lesson, and lift ticket). Call (250) 362-7115 for reservations. Lessons available in French and English • Snowboard School: 10 instructors; Private lessons $50/hour and $30 for second hour, Group lessons $30/two hours; Beginner's package $50–$65 (includes rentals, lesson, and lift ticket). Call (250) 362-7115 for reservations. Lessons available in French and English • Childcare: Red Mountain Kindercare is open seven days a week, 8:30 A.M.–4 P.M. Ages 18 months to six years. Fully licensed programs and lunch options. Referrals available for 18 months and under. Call (250) 362-7114 for more information • *Prices based on the 2000–2001 ski season using Canadian currency. See page 354 for conversion information.*

Room & Board

While Red's old-fashioned ski experience is a soothing alternative to the massive development and hustle and bustle of resorts like Whistler-Blackcomb, it's also easily criticized. There are several hotels in Rossland, but none of them could be considered five or four-star establishments. The dining is a slightly different story. Many restaurants are starting to shine, particularly Olive Oyl's and the Mountain Gypsy, both of which serve modern cuisine. Though mostly a burger joint, Sunshine Cafè is sure to please the hungry carnivore. In a nut shell, the food can be good and the value is beyond reproach, but for those looking for a resort that offers it all, fine dining and fancy accommodations, Rossland is not your best choice. Drive an hour-and-a-half north to the town of Ainsworth Hot Springs for a real treat: Ainsworth Hot Springs Resort. The resort's natural hot springs sit above Kootenay Lake. The rejuvenating waters are heated at the earth's core and forced toward the surface spilling out into caves and pools. The lodge itself sits above the lake and provides the most luxurious accommodations in the area. Call 1-800-668-1171 for more information.

▣ Lodging

On-site

Red Mountain Cabins and Motel is situated 400 yards from the Granite lift, offers motel rooms and four-and six-bed cabins (each with kitchenette) nestled in the trees. Rates are from $85–$180 a night. 1–888–338–2299 or (250) 362–9000 • **Ram's Head Inn** combines fireside lounge, down duvets, hot tub, sauna, ski bench, and weight room in a hospitable and luxurious atmosphere. Rates are from $90–$107 a night. (250) 362–9577 • *Call Central Reservations at 1–877–969–SNOW or (250) 362–5666 for more options.*

Rossland–3 miles *(5 km)* away

Uplander Hotel is located in the heart of downtown, offers patio dining, lounge, pub, hot tub, sauna, and fitness center. Rates are from $86–$105 a night. 1–800–667–8741 or (250) 362–7375 • **Rossland Motel** offers large two-bedroom suites and bachelor units with fully equipped kitchens. Rates are from $49–$75 a night. (250) 362–7218 • **Mountain Shadow Hostel** is located in downtown with 40 beds, a kitchen, laundry, and storage. Rates are $17 a night. (250) 362–7160 • *Call the Rossland Chamber of Commerce at (250) 362–5666 or visit www.rossland.com for more options.*

Ainsworth Hot Springs–1.5 hours away

Ainsworth Hot Springs Resort offers standard rooms with kitchenettes, suites, and honeymoon suites. Rates are from $106–$131 a night. 1–800–668–1171 or (250) 229–4212.

ⓘ Dining

On-site

Sourdough Alley is the main lodge cafeteria • **Rafter's Lounge** is located upstairs from Sourdough Alley and serves tasty pizza and Mexican food • Paradise Lodge serves soups, stews, and sandwiches.

Rossland–3 miles *(5 km)* away

Amelia's Restaurant in the Uplander Hotel offers family-style meals with hearty breakfasts, homemade soups, burgers, sandwiches, pastas, and full dinners. (250) 362–7375 • **Clansey's Cappuccino** serves excellent specialty coffees, soups, sandwiches, pizza melts, veggie roll-ups, bagels, and muffins. (250) 362–5273 • **Idgie's Restaurant** is home to Misty Mountain Pizza (Rossland's first pizza delivery), which makes hearty, delicious pizza. (250) 362–5266 • **Louis Blue Room** in the Uplander Hotel serves beautifully presented appetizers and salads, continental cuisine, pastas, seafood, Thai, and Eastern dishes with mountain views. (250) 362–7375 • **Mountain Gypsy Café** is a creative fusion of various cuisines, specializing in light healthy lunches and inexpensive modern food. (250) 362–3342 • **Olive Oyl's** serves excellent contemporary cuisine with an international flair, gourmet pizzas, pasta, entrees, and desserts. (250) 362–5322 • **Rock Cut Pub** is a neighborhood pub with spectacular views of the mountains, eight beers on tap, and a delicious pub menu. (250) 362–5840 • **Sunshine Café** offers creative home-style cooking for breakfast, lunch, and dinner; featured in "Where To Eat in Canada" for 15 years. (250) 362–7630 • *Call the Rossland Chamber of Commerce at (250) 362–5666 or visit www.rossland.com for more options.*

Cypress Mountain

Cypress Mountain
P.O. Box 91252
West Vancouver, BC
Canada V7V 3N9

Ski Report: (604) 419–7669
Information: (604) 926–5612
E-mail: *contact@cypressmountain.com*
Website: *www.cypressmountain.com*
Credit Cards: Visa, MasterCard, & American Express
Operating Hours: 8:30 A.M.–11 P.M. weekdays; 8 A.M.–11 P.M. weekends and holidays. Hours are tentative, call snowphone at (804) 419–7669
Season: Early December through mid April

Background

J ust 10 miles from North Vancouver and less than an hour from downtown, Cypress Mountain lies on the edge of the supernatural British Columbia wilderness and the bright lights of the big city. Cypress offers snow junkies a quick fix in a distinctly urban, yet completely natural setting. Strachan Mountain's 4,750-foot elevation (Cypress' high-point) affords panoramic views of the surrounding area. To the southeast lies a urbanesque cityscape: Streets and alleys full of automobiles, neon lights, tall buildings, posh neighborhoods, and industrial areas. To the west is the maritime view of Howe Sound and the Burrard Inlet, where visitors can spot ferries, boats, yachts, and barges navigating the waters between Vancouver Island and the smaller Gulf islands. In the opposite direction, the BC Coastal Range leads the eyes north past the Lions Peaks, all of which peak at over 5,200 feet. The mountains continue to rise as they extend northward, and peaks such as Mount Garibaldi and the Tusk are easy to spot from the top of the area's Sky Chair.

Cypress unfolds over three of the BC Coastal Range's lower peaks: Black Mountain (4,000 feet), Mount Strachan (4,750 feet), and Hollyburn Peak (3,978 feet). While each is relatively low-lying, there's plenty of snowfall here—albeit mostly of the moist variety. Rain in Vancouver usually means snow at Cypress during winter.

Due to the area's size and proximity to such a large city, Cypress can be crowded on the weekends and on Friday evenings. The Sunrise quad does a good job of distributing snowriders across the three mountains quickly.

The amenities at Cypress are geared toward night riding and quick day-trips. There are no on-site accommodations or formal restaurants at Cypress. But, not to worry; Vancouver is close enough and well stocked with all the trappings of an international city.

Mountain Stats

Base Elevation: 3,000 feet *(915 m)*
Summit Elevation: 4,750 feet *(1,449 m)*
Vertical Drop: 1,750 *(534 m)*
Primary Slope Direction: West and east
Annual Snowfall: 236 inches *(600 cm)*
Skiable Days: 120
Skiable Terrain: 205 acres *(83 ha)*
Runs: 25

Longest Run: 2.2 miles *(3.5 km)*
Lifts: 1 quad, 3 doubles, 1 surface tow
Lift Capacity: 5,800 skiers per hour
Terrain Classification: 23% novice; 47% intermediate; 40% advanced
Night Skiing: 100% allowance
Snowmaking: None
Annual Visits: 200,000

Getting There

- **From Portland, OR, and Seattle, WA:** Take I-5 north to U.S./Canada border. *[Directions continued below.]*
- **From Spokane, WA:** Take I-90 west to I-405. Head north on I-405 to I-5. Take I-5 north to U.S./Canada border. *[Directions continued below.]*
- **From Boise, ID:** Take I-84 west to I-82. Take I-82 west to I-90. Take I-90 west to I-405. Follow I-405 to I-5. Take I-5 north to U.S./Canada border. *[Directions continued below.]*
- **[Continued.]** Take I-5 north across the border. Once in Canada, take Provincial Highway 15 (PH 15) north. Stay on PH 15 until Trans-Canada Highway 1 (TCH 1). Follow TCH 1 through Vancouver—you're actually bypassing the city—to Exit 8. Follow Cypress Bowl Road to the ski area.

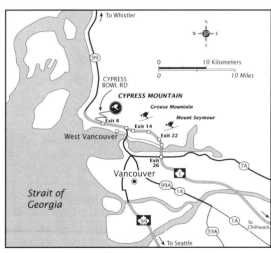

Be sure to make this drive before or after morning rush hour (7–10 A.M.) or prior to afternoon rush hour (3–7 P.M.). Traffic around Vancouver can be brutal, not to mention border congestion.

Airport Services: Vancouver International (YVR) is the closest airport to Cypress Mountain.

No shuttles run directly to Cypress from the airport. Cypress Mountain offers daily shuttle busses during the winter season from Park Royal Center, Horseshoe Bay Ferry Terminal, Caulfield Village, and the North Vancouver SeaBus terminal. You can take an airport shuttle to one of these shuttle points. For schedule and price information call (604) 878–9229. Or you can just rent a car to drive the 40 miles to the ski area.

Trail Profiles

All of Cypress's 25 trails are below the treeline. As skiers and boarders descend from the top of the double lift Sky Chair, the trees grow continuously taller and thicker, providing shelter and visibility from the harsh storms that can roll in off the waters of Howe Sound.

Panorama, at 1,000 feet wide, serves up ideal terrain for novice snowriders. It begins on the front side of Black, at the top of the Eagle chair. The gentle, undulating terrain is groomed daily, making the trail a favorite direct run to the base. Roughly one-third of the way down, the trail hangs a big left, offering the best vantage to view Vancouver's city streets. On the other side of Strachan, the *Collins* run—another highway-wide trail groomed daily—drops another 1,000 feet to the bottom of the Sunrise quad. The trail gives novice skiers and boarders the opportunity to explore more than just the mountain's front side.

Intermediate skiers often link turns on upper and lower *Fork*. Accessible from the top of the Eagle lift, the trail shoots away from the lift towers before winding its way back to the base of the lift. More often than not *Fork* is groomed, though on busier days it can become bumped up. From top to bottom, skiers and boarders will encounter several spots with steeper pitches—but not so steep that lower intermediates can't handle them. On the opposite side of the mountain, from the top of the Sunrise quad, *Horizon* offers mid-level snowriders more worthy terrain. The top half is velvety smooth while the black-diamond-rated lower half turns steeper, sometimes forming a difficult maze of moguls when the trail is saturated with skiers—which is usually on weekends and holidays. Both *Horizon* and *Fork* drop 1,000 feet from the top.

Advanced skiers will find more than enough challenging terrain at Cypress. Directly below the Eagle chair is the inconsistent fall line of *Trumpeter*. It has at least two different fall lines, in addition to flat spots, a few small gullies, and buried stumps used for catching air and ripping through the snow. From the top of the Sunrise quad the another local favorite is *Bowen*, which gradually drops one-third of the way down the trail before hitting a constant 40-degree pitch. Because it is peppered with small trees, the trail is never groomed. Add in tracked up snow and bumps in between snowfall, and *Bowen* gets big, bad, and burly.

Cypress's toughest challenge and signature run is *Top Gun*. With 1,750 feet of vertical, *Top Gun* is the longest run of Vancouver's three nearby areas (Cypress, Mount Seymour, and Grouse Mountain). It's also the most difficult. From the top of the Sky Chair hang a right and hit *T33*, which serves as the top section of *Top Gun*. Named after a naval fighter trainer that crashed in 1962, *T33* is a rolling run that connects with the rest of the *Top Gun* trail. Completely ungroomed, the trail plunges down a steep line as skiers and boarders descend, offering up 1,750 feet of stumps, jumps, hits, drops, and crud.

Another insider's choice lies between the bottom of the Sky Chair and the top of the Sunrise quad. To the skier's right, black-diamond *Humpty Dumpty* cuts through the trees, connecting the top of one lift to the base of the other. *Humpty Dumpty* follows a natural narrow gully that is a nest of nasty bumps and fickle terrain. It's a fun area for playful-minded skiers and boarders before the trail dumps onto *Horizon*.

Snowboarding Highlights

Cypress rolls out the red carpet for snowboarders. There's a halfpipe, boardercross trail, and terrain park. In the spring, Cypress builds yet another terrain park near the top of the Sky Chair. The main terrain park is located on the top half of *Bowen*, and contains a half-dozen manmade hits such as tabletops, spines, and other jumps. The 300-foot halfpipe lies next to the top of the terrain park on *Bowen* and features smooth six- to eight-foot trannies and five- to seven-foot verts. Cypress recently purchased a Pipe Grinder, ensuring a consistently smooth track.

On the Black Mountain side, accessible from the Eagle chair, snowboarders take on the *Windjammer*—Cypress's very own boardercross run. On *Windjammer* snowboarders cop air off rollerz and tabletops while carving phat turns through the manmade berm between the launch pads. *Windjammer* is at least a quarter-mile long, and while not considered a pro boardercross, it gives amateurs a taste of the real thing.

Every April Cypress builds the *BoardZone* at the top of the Sky Chair and *T33*. A half-dozen hits, tons of high-performance demos, a kickin' sound system, and barbecue and prizes combine to make the *BoardZone* a daily jam session on the snow. Riders of all abilities are welcome to prove their skills while an announcer calls the action over a PA system. The competition is friendly and relaxed, and prizes are routinely awarded to boarders of all abilities. Guests are handed prizes right on the spot for performing tricks, landing big air, and just plain going for it.

And just like the rest of the mountain, all of Cypress's snowboard terrain is lit for night riding.

More Fun in the Flakes

Cypress Mountain has 10 miles (16 km) of groomed trails and **cross-country skiing** lanes that lead through tracts of old-growth forest. Cypress' Discover Cross-country program allows newcomers to the sport an easy entry. Call (604) 922–0825 for more information on times and availability. The trails are open 8 A.M. to 10 P.M.

Self-guided **snowshoeing** trails are open from dawn until dusk. Cypress organizes **snowshoe tours** from the cross-country ski area base. Hop on the Fondue Snowshoe Tour or customize your own trip.

Cypress offers snowriders a **tubing** area complete with a tube lift and two groomed runs to slide down. The cost is $11/day (tubes included). Enjoy the groomed toboggan area for $5/day. Both the tubing and **tobogganing areas** are located adjacent to the cross-country area, which is 1.5 miles (2.5 km) before the parking lot of the alpine area. There is also an ungroomed snow play area open free to the public.

Skier Services

🅢 Lift Tickets

Ages 19–65: $35 • Ages 13–18: $29 • Ages 6–12: $17 • Ages 5 and Under: :$2 • Ages 65+: $15 • *Prices based on the 2000–2001 ski season using Canadian currency. See page 354 for conversion information.*

🔳 Nordic Trail Passes

$12/day for adults and $10.50/day for youth (13–18) • *Prices based on the 2000–2001 ski season using Canadian currency. See page 354 for conversion information.*

🔳 Rentals

Ski Rentals: $24/adults; $13/ages 12 & younger; 800 sets. Type of Gear: Rossignol and Salomon • **Snowboard Rentals:** $36/adults and youths for full-day, $30/ages 12 & younger, 400 sets. Type of Gear: Rossignol and Burton • **Telemark Ski Rentals:** $22 • **Snowshoe Rentals:** $13/adults and $10/ages 6–12 • **Clothing Rentals:** Everything you'd need to hit the snow • *Prices based on the 2000–2001 ski season using Canadian currency. See page 354 for conversion information.*

🔳 Services

Ski & Snowboard School: 60 ski instructors and 45 snowboard instructors; Private lessons $55/hour up to four people; Group lessons $30/two hours up to eight people. *Call the ski school at (604) 926–5346 for reservations and times* • Nordic Ski School: Private lessons $55/hour. *Call the ski school at (604) 922–0825 for reservations and times* • **Childcare:** Kids Camp. Call (604) 926–6346 for more information • *Prices based on the 2000–2001 ski season using Canadian currency. See page 354 for conversion information.*

Room & Board

There are no on-site accommodations at Cypress. The Vancouver area accommodates over 2 million people, and offers all the amenities of a big city. Hotels, motels, B&Bs, and restaurants in North and West Vancouver offer the closest accommodations. There are some restaurant options between Cypress and Vancouver, but your best bet is to go on to Vancouver since it is so close. Call the BC Tourism Bureau at 1–800–663–6000 or visit *www.tourism-vancouver.org* for more information.

🔳 Lodging

Vancouver–40 miles *(64 km)* away

See the Grouse Mountain chapter *(on page 106)* for lodging and dining options in Vancouver.

🅒 Dining

On-site

Cypress Mountain offers a day cafeteria, a heated and covered sundeck, **Hollyburn Lodge and Cafeteria** near the cross-country trailhead, and **Growlies Bar and Grill**, but no formal dining room.

Forbidden Plateau

Forbidden Plateau
P.O. Box 3268
Courtenay, BC
Canada V9N 5N4

Ski Report: (250) 338-1919
Information: (250) 334-4744
E-mail: *info@forbidden.bc.ca*
Website: *www.forbidden.bc.ca*

Operating hours: 9 A.M.–3:45 P.M. daily.
Night Skiing: 6 P.M.–10 P.M. Friday–Saturday

Season: December to April

Background

Hundreds of years ago, two feuding tribes went up to the plateau to work out their differences, peacefully everyone thought. No one knows exactly what happened next but it seems that one tribe "fell" off the side of the mountain. That gruesome event sort of made the plateau taboo for the tribe that didn't "fall." From that point on, the tribe elders forbade anyone in the tribe to visit the plateau—hence the name. But that's not the weirdest part of the story. Each spring the trees in the area shed a gray/green moss from their branches. When the moss hits the snow it reacts, turning the snow a light shade of pink. Legend-spinners say this is the blood of the ancient warriors who clumsily "fell" off the plateau.

While Forbidden Plateau may sound a little intimidating to potential visitors, this family-focused, family-owned, and family-operated ski area has laid out the welcome mat for all snowriders. Inexpensive lift tickets, majestic scenery, and first-class customer service are just a few of the reasons to visit Forbidden. Located just a half an hour from friendly downtown Courtenay, BC, on Vancouver Island, Forbidden Plateau is the oldest ski area on the Island. It offers visitors a relaxing atmosphere away from crowded lift lines and bright lights.

The view alone is worth the trip to Forbidden. Located on the east side of Vancouver Island, Forbidden looks over at the BC Coastal Range, which is full of snow-covered crags, ice blue glaciers, and satin-white snowfields. In between the Island and the coast runs the Georgia Strait, Butte Inlet, and Desolation Sound. From Forbidden's 3,450-foot perch, the Gulf Islands to the south look like a lush green tropical paradise. Up the mountain is the awesome and intimidating Comox ("co-mox") Glacier.

Mountain Stats

Base Elevation: 2,300 feet *(700 m)*
Summit Elevation: 3,450 feet *(1,050 m)*
Vertical Drop: 1,150 feet *(350 m)*
Primary Slope Direction: Southeast
Annual Snowfall: 130 inches *(330 cm)*
Skiable Days: 150
Skiable Terrain: 340 acres *(138 ha)*
Runs: 22

Longest Run: 1.3 miles *(2 km)*
Lifts: 1 double, 3 surface tows
Lift Capacity: 3,400 skiers per hour
Terrain Classification: 50% novice; 35% intermediate; 15% difficult
Night Skiing: 30% allowance
Snowmaking: None
Annual Visits: 12,500

Getting There

- **From Portland, OR, and Seattle, WA:** Take I-5 north to U.S./Canada border. *[Directions continued below.]*
- **From Spokane, WA:** Take I-90 west to I-405. Head north on I-405 to I-5. Take I-5 north to U.S./Canada border. *[Directions continued below.]*
- **From Boise, ID:** Take I-84 west to I-82. Take I-82 west to I-90. Take I-90 west to I-405. Follow I-405 to I-5. Take I-5 north to U.S./Canada border. *[Directions continued below.]*
- **[Continued.]** Take I-5 north across the border. Once in Canada, take Provincial Highway 15 (PH 15) north. Stay on PH 15 until Trans-Canada Highway 1 (TCH 1). Follow TCH 1 through **Vancouver, BC**—you're actually bypassing the city. TCH 1 ends near Whytecliff, but PH 99 continues. Follow PH 99 (also known as the Sea to Sky Highway) to the Nanaimo Ferry Terminal. Ferry signs are very visible. From Nanaimo take PH 19 north to Courtenay and follow signs to Forbidden Plateau.

Be sure to make this drive before or after Vancouver's morning rush hour (7–10 A.M.) or prior to afternoon rush hour (3–7 P.M.). Traffic around Vancouver can be brutal, not to mention the border congestion.

Ferry Services: For schedule and price information call British Columbia Ferries at 1–888–223–3779.

Airport Services: For guests traveling from outside the Northwest the closest major airport is Victoria Airport (YYJ). Most travelers, however, connect to Air BC or Air Canada through Vancouver International Airport (YVR) and continue on to Courtenay (YCA) and the ski area.

Besides the stunning views, and despite the menacing name, Forbidden is a warm inviting family area. Because it serves a small community, it safe to turn young kids lose on the slopes. There is only one chairlift and all runs funnel back to the day lodge. Let them go off on their own and meet them at the bottom of every run. It's important to note that Forbidden is not a manic joint of skiers. Snowriding there is like stepping back to a simpler, more trusting time. Ski theft, for instance, is not a concern. In terms of equipment, the one double chair is old but well maintained. But because of lack of expensive high-speed quads, lift tickets are inexpensive.

The only real concern one might have before visiting Forbidden is: Will it be open? The ski area always seems to be teetering on the edge of closure. This is not to say it's likely to go out of business—it is Vancouver's oldest ski area after all—but during slow spells it's not unheard off for management to pull the plug on the phone lines and abandon ship. Needless to say, if you want to plan a trip to this great ski area, call ahead to see if someone's home.

Trail Profiles

Skiers and snowboarders will find over 20 wide-open runs on 1,150 vertical feet. Eighty-five percent of the terrain is dedicated to beginners and intermediates. With their focus on family skiing, Forbidden grooms every run, every day, right up to 40-degree point. In fact, they groom about 30 percent more per skier than any other mountain in British Columbia. Management spends what money they have on grooming to provide a great family ski experience. This extra grooming is, in part, a necessity. Forbidden lies on the leeward side of the Comox Glacier. Weather systems cut across the glacier from the west side and unload on the ski area. It's not uncommon to have 10 to 20 feet of snow in a ten-day period. The area has to be groomed or the mountain would be nearly impossible to ski. And being so low Forbidden can receive any type of snow from elephant snot to powder. With so much grooming it doesn't much matter what the snow conditions are.

Novice skiers love the fact that they can ski right from the top of Forbidden. From the top of the chair take *J-Way* or the *Logging Road*. The gentle slopes are at least five snowcats wide and wind way down mountain like a big corkscrew.

Intermediate skiers should try the big open bowl skiing of *Comox Bowl, Main Bowl* and *The Chute.* All three have roughly 20-degree slopes and are always groomed. Moreover the pitches are consistent without fall away slopes.

For a fast cruising run try *Middle Boston.* It is a big, wide, sweeping top-to-bottom with a 25- to 30-degree pitch. *Middle Boston* is popular with advanced skiers who like to make fast turns. More advanced skiers will want to check out the *Cardiac Express, Bone Shaker,* and *Old Red.* All three are roughly 35- to 40-degree slopes with consistent fall lines for about 1,000 feet. *Cardiac* and *Old Red* start above the treeline. All three get bumped out fairly quickly providing a solid challenge to most advanced skiers. Advanced skiers will also enjoy *Outer Boston* and *Kandahar.* Both are steep with roll-over pitches that keep snowriders from seeing the bottom of the run until they commit to going over the top. The fact that they are groomed and just over 40 degrees makes them super fast trails. Try *Upper Boston* and *Cathedral Grove* for tree skiing and more constant fall-line skiing—both run through a lightly treed area with a 30-degree pitch.

Forbidden is the only mountain on the Island to offer night skiing—30 percent of their terrain is lighted. The Blue T-bar and the handle tow are both open for night skiing access.

Forbidden offers full-service facilities including ski and snowboard rentals and a CSIA certified ski school. Skiing at Forbidden will be easy on the pocket book. At $28 a day for adults (Canadian dollars) Forbidden is a great value. Getting there, however, is a little difficult. From any of the major cities in the Northwest, visitors have to endure at least one long ride in the car, a ferry ride (you're going to an island, remember), and then another ride in the car. Even if you fly to the island you'll have to change planes or stop over at least once. If visitors leave from the U.S. they'll be subject to two flights and going through customs on their way in and out of Canada.

Snowboarding Highlights

Snowboarding has recently become more of a priority at Forbidden. Now there is a terrain park and two halfpipes. The terrain park covers 20 acres and has six to 10 features, making for great expression sessions. Boarders will find big air jumps, tabletops, spines, rollerz, and a quarterpipe. Forbidden also builds one halfpipe for advanced riders and one for first-time pipers. The location of the pipes changes from year to year, and they are constructed by the area crew and local riders.

More Fun in the Flakes

Forbidden offers 19 miles (30 km) of free **cross-country skiing** trails as well as a **snow tubing** park that offers surface lift access for $5 to $10 a person.

Skier Services

🅂 Lift Tickets

Ages 19–64: $28/full-day, $18/half-day, $12/night • **Ages 13–18 and 65+:** $22/full-day, $15/half-day, $11/night • **Ages 7–12:** $16/full-day, $12/half-day, $10/night • **Ages 6 & younger:** Free • *Prices based on the 2000–2001 ski season using Canadian currency. See page 354 for conversion information.*

🎿 Rentals

Ski Rentals: $19.50/adult; $18.25/ages 13–18; $12.50/ages 7–12; $6.85/ages 6 & younger. Type of Gear: Dynastar and Solomon • **Snowboard Rentals:** $35.50/all ages • *Prices based on the 2000–2001 ski season using Canadian currency. See page 354 for conversion information.*

🏠 Services

Ski School: 20 instructors; Private lessons $25/hour; Group lessons $16; Beginner's package $30 (includes lift ticket, lesson, and rentals) • **Snowboard School:** 10 instructors; Private lessons $25/hour; Group lessons $16; Beginner's package $45 (includes lift ticket, lesson, and rentals) • **Childcare:** None is available, but there is a Kids Camp that takes kids from 3 years of age up • *Prices based on the 2000–2001 ski season using Canadian currency. See page 354 for conversion information.*

Room & Board

🛏 Lodging

Forbidden is a small ski area with mostly community visitors, so there is no on-site lodging. The town of Courtenay is nearby, though, and offers plenty of lodging and dining options.

Courtenay–19 miles *(30 km)* away

Forbidden Plateau Bed & Breakfast affords a peaceful country setting only minutes from Courtenay; 3 bedrooms; on five acres of farmland; access to hiking trails and water holes; rates $60–$70. (250) 703-9622 or 1–888–288–2144 • See Mount Washington, BC, *(see page 34)* for additional lodging and dining.

🍽 Dining

On-site

Forbidden has a high-quality cafeteria, **Kandahar Lounge**, and the **Trickle Creek Café**. Each serves tasty and affordable fare for skiers in a friendly atmosphere. The view from the dining rooms of the **Comox Valley** below is beautiful.

Grouse Mountain

Grouse Mountain

6400 Nancy Greene Way
North Vancouver, BC
Canada V7R 4K9

Ski Report: (604) 986–6262
Information: (604) 980–9311
E-mail: *info@grousemtn.com*
Website: *www.grousemountain.com*
Credit Cards: Visa, MC, & AMEX

Operating Hours: 9 A.M.–10 P.M. daily;
9 A.M.–5 P.M. Christmas Day
Night Skiing: 4 P.M.–10 P.M. daily

Season: Mid November to mid April

Photo courtesy Grouse Mountain

Background

A mere 15 minutes north of Vancouver, Grouse and its lighted trails resemble more of an airplane runway than a ski resort. However, it is the view in the opposite direction, from the top of Grouse Mountain back to Vancouver, that attracts tourists and locals alike. The "Peak of Vancouver" provides an unbelievable view of Canada's biggest and brightest West Coast city. From anywhere on the 4,100-foot peak, the megatropolis spreads out in nearly all directions complete with the Lion's Gate Bridge, ships in the harbor, city lights dancing on the Georgia Strait and several thousand headlights navigating the streets, bridges, and alleys of Vancouver.

Come nightfall, the adventure begins at the base of the Skyride Tram at 900 feet, where snow mongers clad in Gore-tex® and goggles wait with couples decked out in tuxedos and evening gowns. The couples are headed up to the restaurant for an evening of fine dining while the snow mongers yearn to cut moonlit tracks. From there the tram climbs 2,800 feet up a jagged cut through majestic spruce, cedar, hemlock, and Douglas fir trees. Upon exiting the tram, tourists and snowriders are greeted with a small skating pond, intricate carvings, a remodeled chalet, and trees painted white with pristine snow. First-time visitors are stunned by the drastic change in scenery—and with good reason. One minute visitors are escaping an urban jungle and the next they are entering a winter wonderland.

Grouse Mountain is not a destination ski resort. Those seeking quality snow, open bowls, and steep terrain might look elsewhere. However, if a winter adventure with variety and an urban twist is the goal, Grouse Mountain is a must-ski. Making turns and looking down into the streets of Vancouver is a sight to be remembered forever.

Mountain Stats

Base Elevation: 900 feet *(274 m)*
Summit Elevation: 4,100 feet *(1,250 m)*
Alpine Station: 3,700 feet *(1,128 m)*
Vertical Drop: 1,210 feet *(369 m)*
Primary Slope Direction: East
Annual Snowfall: 315 inches *(800 cm)*
Skiable Days: 120
Skiable Terrain: 202 acres *(82 ha)*
Runs: 22

Longest Run: 1 mile *(1.6 km)*
Lifts: 2 aerial trams, 4 doubles, 4 surface tows
Lift Capacity: 5,500 skiers per hour
Terrain Classification: 40% novice; 40% intermediate; 20% advanced
Night Skiing: On 13 runs
Snowmaking: 75%
Annual Visits: 355,000

Getting There

- **From Portland, OR:** Take I-5 north to Seattle. *[Follow Seattle directions below.]*
- **From Seattle, WA:** Head north on I-5. *[Directions continued below.]*
- **From Spokane, WA:** Take I-90 west to I-405. Go north on I-405 to I-5 north. *[Directions continued below.]*
- **From Boise, ID:** Take I-84 north to I-82. Take I-82 to I-90. Take I-90 west to I-405. Go north on I-405 to I-5 north. *[Directions continued below.]*
- **[Continued.]:** Take I-5 north into Canada. Once across the border, take Provincial Highway 15 (PH 15) north. Stay on PH 15 until Trans-Canada Highway 1 (TCH 1). Follow TCH 1, which also becomes PH 99 through Vancouver. Take the North Vancouver Exit 14 to Marine Drive and then left onto Capilano Road. From there follow the signs to Grouse Mountain.
- **From Vancouver, BC:** The aerial tram at Grouse Mountain can be reached by car or by public transit. Follow Georgia Street west through Stanley Park and across the Lion's Gate Bridge. Take the North Vancouver exit to Marine Drive and then left onto Capilano Road. From there follow the signs to Grouse Mountain. In North Vancouver, Grouse Mountain can be reached by the metro bus, which runs every half-hour. Take Bus #236 from Lonsdale Quay/Seabus or #232 from Phibbs Exchange.

✈ **Airport Services:** For guests traveling from out side of the northwest, the Vancouver International Airport (YVR) is a major gateway for Canadian, U.S., and Pacific Rim carriers. An assortment of rental car companies are available.

🚍 **Bus Services:** TRANSLINK, the public bus service, provides regular service every half-hour to the base of Grouse. For schedule and price information call (604) 521–0400.

Trail Profiles

Grouse Mountain offers 22 marked trails with 13 of them open after the sun goes down. The snow at Grouse is often moist and heavy due to its low elevation and proximity to Howe Sound and the Georgia Strait.

Novice snowriders spend most of their time on *The Cut*—Grouse's signature trail. Voted "Best Urban View" in *Ski Canada*, *The Cut* is groomed perfectly for wide-open cruising. The scenery from top to bottom is stunning, particularly at night when the lights of Vancouver twinkle and sparkle in the distance. To reach *The Cut* from the main lodge, take the *Chalet Road*. This short traverse enters *The Cut* near the top of the run. Hang a left and enjoy the view all the way to the bottom of Chair Two.

Blue run *Centennial* is a choice run for skiers and boarders looking to slide and glide over groomed, rolling terrain. More adventurous snowriders often turn right about halfway down *Centennial* to *Dogleg* for a taste of powder or possibly some crud.

For the more advanced skier, black-diamond tracks can be found off the top of Peak Chair on the *Peak Run*. The summit view is arguably the best Grouse has to offer. In every direction there is something beautiful to admire—from the BC Coast Range to the streets of Vancouver to the Georgia Strait. The view is so striking that it can prove distracting to skiers pounding through the bumps down the *Peak Run*.

Snowboarding Highlights

Snowboarding at Grouse Mountain is in full stride, and the resort capably delivers the goods. Grouse Mountain's Terrain Park features a challenging mix of hits, spines, tabletops, quarterpipes, pyramids, rollerz, and gap jumps. The park is 624 meters in length, 750 meters of vertical, and was designed to take advantage of the topography of the run *Side Cut*. The park also features a border-cross style area complete with berms, rollerz, and man-made obstacles. The park is accessible from the Cut Chair and the Blueberry Chair.

Photo courtesy Grouse Mountain

More Fun in the Flakes

Grouse Mountain's **cross-country skiing** trails feature a 3km-beginner track and a 2.3-km advanced loop around Blue Grouse Lake and beyond the Peak Plateau. The trails are groomed daily for single track or skate skiing.

Snowcat-drawn **sleigh rides** are available with lift tickets or Skyride tickets. Call (604) 980–9311 for more information.

A newly introduced option to Grouse is the Munday Alpine Snow Park 10-km network of marked and patrolled trails for **snowshoeing**. Traverse the alpine meadows of Dam Mountain, the well-traveled trail around Grouse Lake or tour the 16-foot chainsaw sculptures that make up the Tribute to the Forest, where you'll learn about the native plants and wildlife.

A new 8,000-square-meter outdoor **ice-skating** rink is located at the base of the ski area next to the upper tram terminal. The rink is open from 9 A.M. to 10 P.M. daily. Skating is free.

Skier Services

🅂 Lift Tickets

Ages 13–64: $25/weekend & holidays, $19/mid–week • **Ages 7–12:** $15/weekend & holidays, $9/mid-week • **Ages 65+:** $15/weekend & holidays, $13.50/mid-week • **Ages 6 & younger:** Free (with a ticketed adult) • *Day Prices based on the 2000–2001 ski season using Canadian currency. See page 354 for conversion information.*

🄰 Rentals

Ski Rentals: $22–$27/adults; $12–$16/kids; 1500 sets. Type of Gear: Rossignol and Salomon • **Snowboard Rentals:** $35/adults; $25/kids; 600 sets. Type of Gear: Rossignol, K2, Heelside, and Vans • **Nordic Ski Rentals:** $13/adults; $8/kids • **Snowshoe Rentals:** $13/all day • **Snow Blades:** $15. Type of gear: Salomon • **Ice Skate Rentals:** $4/hour • *Prices based on the 2000–2001 ski season using Canadian currency. See page 354 for conversion information.*

🏢 Services

Ski School: 95 instructors; Private lessons $45–$55/hour; Private group lessons $90/hour; Group lessons $20–$25 • **Snowboard School:** 95 instructors; Private lessons $45–$55/hour; Private group lessons $90/hours; Group lessons $20–$25 • **Nordic Ski School:** Learn to cross-country ski $45 (includes lift ticket, lesson and rentals) • *Prices based on the 2000–2001 ski season using Canadian currency. See page 354 for conversion information.*

Room & Board

🛏 Lodging

There are no on-slope accommodations at Grouse, but justifiably so. No worries, Vancouver is just minutes away. The city is home to over 2 million people and offers its guests an assortment of hotels, motels, and bed and breakfasts too large to mention. Plus, the international city of Vancouver has a virtual smorgasbord of restaurants, including sushi, Indian curry, Chinese, Thai, Italian, Pakistani, Gregorian, Mexican, and nearly every other cuisine known to man. For more information, call BC Tourism Bureau: 1–800–663–6000 (U.S. and Canada) or visit their website at *www.tourism-vancouver.org*.

Vancouver–7 miles *(10 km)* away

This city offers numerous choices for motels, hotels, and bed and breakfasts. Call the BC Tourism Bureau at 1–800–663–6000 for an exhaustive list of options.

🍽 Dining

On-site

There are numerous restaurants to choose from at the Peak Chalet at Grouse, including **The Observatory, Bar 98 Bistro,** and **Lupin's Café.** Each has a romantic atmosphere with delicious food and spectacular views of Vancouver.

Vancouver–7 miles *(10 km)* away

Again, there are so many choices of restaurants with every type of cuisine here that it's difficult to recommend only a few. However, if you would still like some guidance, call the BC Tourism Bureau at 1–800–663–6000.

Grouse Mountain: A Century of Urban Ski Adventures

Vancouver locals have enjoyed the splendors of Grouse Mountain for over one hundred years. A party of hunters gave the mountain its name in 1894 after shooting a blue grouse bird on the summit. Thirty years later, entrepreneur W.C. Shelley foresaw the attraction of the mountain's wilderness setting and panoramic views, setting the wheels in motion for a mountain roadway. A paved toll road was completed during the Roaring Twenties, as high society took to the hills. With white-gloved dinner service, Grouse Mountain became the St. Moritz of Canada.

From the late forties to the mid-sixties, Grouse expanded its services and underwent a series of changes that put it at the forefront of winter recreation in western Canada. The construction of the Village Chair—North America's first double chairlift—created a boom at Grouse. In 1948, the Grouse Mountain Ski School exploded with the introduction of the Vancouver Sun Free Ski School. For eight consecutive years over 8,000 students graduated from the program. In 1951 a second chairlift was installed, providing the highest lift-serviced vertical in British Columbia. And in 1965, Grouse erected Canada's first aerial tram, called Blue Skyride, and finished construction of a new mountain chalet.

Since the early eighties, more emphasis has been placed on developing the area's summer activities. To complement the natural beauty and spectacular views, the resort added the Rusty Rail Barbecue, Blue Grouse Lake nature trails, paved walking paths, and marked hiking trails. The biggest upgrade and the one that benefits snowriders most is the restoration of the Peak Chalet. The multi-million-dollar project recreates the original beauty of the 1920s chalet. A giant atrium boasts two intricately carved columns depicting Grouse Mountain history, a granite fireplace, and plenty of BC Douglas fir. The chalet features The Observatory restaurant, Bar 98 Bistro, Lupin's Café, the Spirit Gallery, and the Theater in the Sky. Bar 98 and The Observatory provide unforgettable views of Vancouver. Grouse's restaurants are dangerously romantic, providing the perfect setting for a first date, a marriage proposal, or the actual ceremony, despite its current two-year wait.

Harper Mountain

Harper Mountain

2042 Valleyview Drive
Kamloops, British Columbia
Canada V2C 4C5

Ski Report: (250) 828–0336
Information: (250) 573–5115
E-mail: *harperski@bc.telus.net*
Credit Cards: Visa & MasterCard

Operating Hours: 9:30 A.M.–4 P.M. weekdays
(chair opens at 12:30 P.M.); 9:30 A.M.–4 P.M.
weekends and school holidays.
Night Skiing: 6:30 P.M.–10 P.M. Wednesday–
Friday nights (surface lifts only)
Season: Mid December to mid March

Background

J ust outside the downtown of Kamloops, BC, is the tiny, family-owned Harper Mountain ski area. Harper is fueled mainly by skiers from the nearby community who have limited time and funds and are just looking to cut some turns. Tickets are relatively inexpensive, and the area is equipped with decent lighting for night skiing. And while nearby Sun Peaks is often the choice for area snowriders, Harper provides a good base for novice skiers and a quick fix for others when they only have a few hours to ride.

Trail Profiles

Harper's 15 short trails are all below treeline and are serviced by one triple chair and two surface lifts. All of them funnel back to the lodge, making the area safe to turn the kids loose. The mild terrain of the learning area is also in front of the lodge. Once they have learned the craft of linking turns, novice skiers and boarders will enjoy *Big Bend*. The 2.5-mile (4 km) trail drops 1,300 vertical feet (396 m) with a huge turn in the middle of the run.

Popular with intermediates is a gentle giant-slalom run called *Spillway*. It's composed of several pitches—some steep and others more easily negotiated. The rolling trail is lit for night skiing and visible from the lodge.

Advanced snowriders like to slide and glide underneath the chair lift. The challenging terrain offers several different fall lines. Bump bashers like to test their skills on the north side of *Cliff Hanger*, which features 1,000 vertical feet (305 m) of steep moguls. Sloped out at 30 degrees, it is the mountain's steepest run.

Mountain Stats

Base Elevation: 3,600 feet *(1,098 m)*
Summit Elevation: 5,000 feet *(1,524 m)*
Vertical Drop: 1,400 feet *(427 m)*
Primary Slope Direction: North
Annual Snowfall: 150 inches *(385 cm)*
Skiable Days: 100
Skiable Terrain: 400 acres *(162 ha)*
Runs: 15

Longest Run: 2.5 miles *(4 km)*
Lifts: 2 surface lifts, 1 Triple
Lift Capacity: 3,600 skiers per hour
Terrain Classification: 25% novice; 50% intermediate; 25% advanced
Night Skiing: 2 runs open
Snowmaking: 2%
Annual Visits: 30,000

Getting There

- **From Kamloops, BC:** Follow Provincial Highway 5 (PH 5), also named the Yellowhead Highway, north for 2 miles (3.2 km). Turn east on the designated road, following the signs to Harper Mountain.
- **From Vancouver, BC:** Take Trans-Canada Highway 1 (TCH 1) east to Hope. Take PH 5 north towards Kamloops. Please note that a toll is required to travel on portions of PH 5. From Kamloops take PH 5 north. Turn east on the designated road, following the signs to Harper Mountain.

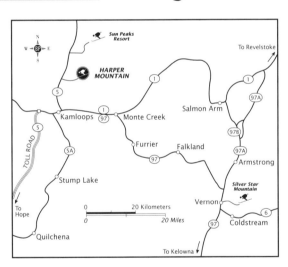

More Fun in the Flakes

Harper offers 13 miles (21 km) of free ungroomed and unpatrolled **cross-country skiing** trails.

Snowboarding Highlights

For a small non-destination area Harper has done a good job at providing terrain specific to snowboarding. One-plankers will find two halfpipes and a terrain park at Harper. The *Kid's Pipe* is located directly above the lodge. It is 90 feet long, with a gentle slope and five- to seven-foot walls. The *Halfpipe* can be found just outside the back door of the lodge. Excavated into the ground with 10-foot shelves on each side, the pipe is just over 150 feet long and is built and maintained each year with the help of a simple snowmaking system and a resilient crew.

The real treat at Harper is the *Maxi Pipe*. The natural pipe is accessible from the top of the lift and drops roughly 1,200 feet through a snow- covered creek bed. The walls twist and turn downhill, and it is by far the best place to ride here. The terrain park sits at the top of the *Maxi Pipe* trail and consists of a tabletop, a spine, whoop de do's, and a few jumps.

Skier Services

🅢 Lift Tickets

Ages 15–64: $25/full-day, $18.50/half-day, and $18/night • **Juniors & Ages 65+:** $18/full-day, $13.50/half-day, $12/nights • *Prices based on the 2000–2001 ski season using Canadian currency. See page 354 for conversion information.*

🅡 Rentals

Ski Rentals: $22–$25/day; 200 sets. Type of Gear: Rossignol, Elan, and Kestle • **Snowboard Rentals:** $33/adult, $29/child; 60 sets. Type of Gear: Kemper and Elan • *Prices based on the 2000–2001 ski season using Canadian currency. See page 354 for conversion information.*

🅢 Skier Services

Ski School: 10 instructors; Private lessons $36/hour; Group lessons $20/hour. Call (250) 374-0448 for availability and reservations • **Snowboard School:** 3 instructors; $95–$104/four hours of lessons • **Childcare:** None • *Prices based on the 2000–2001 ski season using Canadian currency. See page 354 for conversion information.*

Room & Board

Harper Mountain is primarily a day/evening ski area so there is no on-site lodging. Downtown Kamloops is nearby if you're looking for a place to stay or eat. You can also go to other nearby ski areas, such as Sun Peaks (*see page 54*), which offers more variety for dining.

■ Lodging

Kamloops–14 miles (*23 km*) away

Davy Crockett Motel offers 35 rooms with kitchen units, sauna, hot tub, and special winter rates; rates $35/night. (250) 372–2122 • **Riverland Motel** is located on the river, offers comfortable rooms, laundry, mountain views, and Jacuzzi suites; rates $55–$85/night. 1–800–663–1530 or (250) 374–1534 or *www.kamloops.com/riverlandmotel* • **Coast Canadian Inn** offers nicely decorated, comfortable rooms, fitness center, pool, and laundry service; rates $120/night. (250) 372–5201 or *www.coasthotel.kamloops.com.*

⑪ Dining

On-site

There is a cafeteria in the Day Lodge at Harper Mountain.

Kamloops–14 miles (*23 km*) away

Rock'N Firkin is a popular sports pub with a gourmet pizza bar, live entertainment, and lively atmosphere. (250) 376–6121 or *www.rocknfirkin.kamloops.com* • **Storms Restaurant** lets you choose from a variety of dishes from around the world while dining alongside the Thompson River. (250) 372–1522.

Hemlock Valley Resort

Hemlock Valley Resort
Agassiz, British Columbia
V0M1A0

Information: (604) 797–4411
Ski Report: (604) 520–6222
E-mail: *hvrsales@uniserve.com*
Credit Cards: Visa, MasterCard, & AMEX

Operating Hours: 9 A.M.–3:30 P.M. Friday–Sunday and Holidays.
Night Skiing: 3:30 P.M.–8:30 P.M.

Season: December to mid-late April

Background

Only 90 miles northwest of Vancouver, Hemlock Valley is a quiet alternative to the larger, glitzier resorts of British Columbia. Hemlock looks out over Harrison Lake and is composed of log cabins, town houses, condominiums, and a day lodge. The resort is an intermediate skier's paradise. Nearly two-thirds of Hemlock's 34 trails are designated blue runs. Two double and one triple chair lift transport snowriders to the top of finely groomed trails and two medium-sized bowls. Most of the terrain is above the treeline; nearly all of the trails serviced from the Skyline Double are rated advanced. The Sasquatch Triple accesses intermediate trails, most of which are straight shots back to the base.

Mountain Stats

Base Elevation: 3,300 feet *(1,006 m)*
Summit Elevation: 4,500 feet *(1,372 m)*
Vertical Drop: 1,200 feet *(366 m)*
Annual Snowfall: 180 inches (462 cm)
Skiable Terrain: 300 acres (122 ha)
Runs: 34
Longest Run: 7460 feet *(2,274 m)*

Lifts: 2 doubles, 1 triple, 1 surface lift
Lift Capacity: 4,000 skiers per hour
Terrain Classification: 20% novice; 60% intermediate; 20% advanced
Night Skiing: Yes *(call ahead)*
Snowmaking: None

Getting There

• **From Vancouver, BC:** Take Trans Canada Highway 1 (TCH) west to Provincial Highway 9 (PH 9). Head west on PH 9 to Agassiz. Follow PH 9 through Agassiz to PH 7 (also the Lougheed Highway). Proceed west on PH 7 to Morris Valley Road. At Morris Valley Road, turn right and follow the signs to the ski area.

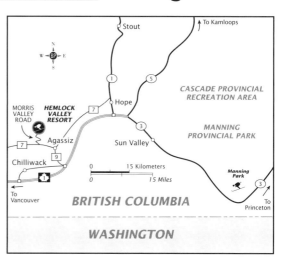

Snowboarding Highlights

Hemlock has supported snowboarding since the early 1980s and has a super halfpipe for freeriders.

More Fun in the Flakes

Cross-country skiing also available on 4.3 miles (7 km) of machine-groomed trails. Call the information line for more details.

Hemlock also offers **tobogganing, snowshoeing,** and a **biathlon** range. The **snow tubing** area is open 9 A.M. to 3 P.M. for $5/two hours and $9/all day.

Skier Services

Lift Tickets

Ages 18–64: $30/full-day, $24/half-day, $10/night • **Ages 13–17:** $25/full-day, $20/half-day, $10/night • **Ages 6–12:** $16/full-day, $14/half-day, $10/night • **Ages 5 & younger and 65+:** Free • *Prices based on the 2000–2001 ski season using Canadian currency. See page 354 for conversion information.*

🔥 Nordic Trail Pass

$8/all ages • *Prices based on the 2000–2001 ski season using Canadian currency. See page 354 for conversion information.*

🎿 Services

Ski & Snowboard School: Private lesson $32/hour; Group lesson $18 for 90 minutes • *Prices based on the 2000–2001 ski season using Canadian currency. See page 354 for conversion information.*

Room & Board

With limited lodging and dining, it's nice to know that Hemlock Valley is only 90 miles (145 km) from Vancouver—and so you're never far from excellent lodging or dining.

🛏 Lodging

On-site

Hemlock offers privately owned log cabins, condos, and townhouses; rates $120–$250/night. (604) 797–4444

Agassiz–55 miles *(90 km)* away

Harrison Crossroads Motor Inn offers rooms with queen beds, bath, shower, and color TV; rates $49–$100/night. (604) 796–8311 • **Pathfinder Motel and RV Park** has rooms equipped with single or queen beds, bath, shower, and cable TV; rates $40–$65/night. (604) 796–9345

🍽 Dining

On-site

The day lodge offers a cafeteria and lounge.

Agassiz–55 miles *(90 km)* away

Out to Lunch Café serves standard Canadian fare, breakfast and lunch only. (604) 796–2456 • **Seabird Island Café** serves all three meals of the day, with burgers, sandwiches, pancakes, buffalo burgers, chicken and pork dishes, and homemade fries. (604) 796–9852 • **Silvano's Restaurant** serves a bit of everything from Greek and Italian to stir-fry, schnitzels, steaks, and burgers. (604) 796–9565

Mount Seymour

Mount Seymour
1700 Mount Seymour Road
North Vancouver, British Columbia
Canada V7G1L3

Ski Report: (604) 718–7771
Information: (604) 986–2261
Website: *www.mountseymour.com*
Credit Cards: Visa & Master Card

Operating Hours: 10 A.M.–10 P.M. weekdays; 9 A.M.–10 P.M. Saturday, Sunday, and holidays.
Night Skiing: 4 P.M.–10 P.M. daily
Season: December to mid April

Background

Mount Seymour is the last area adjacent to Vancouver. While Seymour offers gentle slopes that are adequate for learning the basics of snowboarding and skiing, its most outstanding feature happens to be the largest terrain park and the only ISF in-ground halfpipe on the North Shore. It's no wonder that half of the area's clientele are snowboarders. Area management has committed to the sport like few resorts ever have. Boarders have the choice between three parks and the halfpipe, which is one of the best in British Columbia. As a result, local riders have made Seymour their number one choice for riding. Seymour also offers a snow tubing park complete with groomed slopes and a special handle tow, to take tubers back to the top of the runs.

Like Grouse and Cypress Mountains—Vancouver's other two ski areas—Seymour provides stunning views of the Vancouver skyline, the Georgia Strait, Howe Sound, and the Coast Mountains. And like its two neighbors, Seymour offers night skiing within minutes of downtown Vancouver. Residents and guests of Canada's largest West Coast city can literally be making turns in less than an hour after leaving downtown.

119

Mountain Stats

Base Elevation: 3,300 feet *(1,006 m)*
Summit Elevation: 4,600 feet *(1,402 m)*
Vertical Drop: 1,300 feet *(396 m)*
Primary Slope Direction: Southwest
Annual Snowfall: 120 inches *(305 cm)*
Skiable Days: 120
Skiable Terrain: 60 acres *(24 ha)*
Runs: 21

Longest Run: 1.5 miles *(2.4 km)*
Lifts: 3 doubles, 1 rope tow
Lift Capacity: 3,700 skiers per hour
Terrain Classification: 40% novice; 40% intermediate; 20% advanced
Night Skiing: 85% allowance
Snowmaking: None

Getting There

- **From Vancouver, BC:** Cross the Second Narrows Bridge and take Exit 22. Take Mount Seymour Parkway and follow signs to the provincial park. Turn left at Mount Seymour Road (in front of the Mohawk Station). Follow Mount Seymour Road to the ski area. Call (604) 718–7771 for road conditions.

- **Bus Services:** Guests can take a shuttle bus from several spots in North Vancouver. For schedule times and price information call the Snowphone at (604) 718–7771.

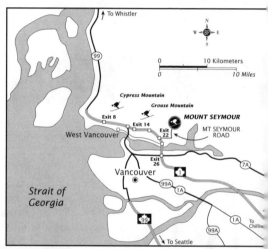

Trail Profiles

Seymour's 21 trails are spread out over 90 acres of terrain on Mystery Peak (4,600 feet) which provides 1,300 vertical feet of riding, gliding, and sliding. Nearly half of these trails are for novice snowriders. Best of all, beginners can explore the entire mountain. From each of Seymour's three double chairs, there is a designated green trail back to the lodge. The Mystery Peak lift takes novice skiers and borders to the top of *Manning* and *Brocton Gully*. *Manning* makes serpentine turns back to the lodge over wide gentle terrain. To reach *Brocton Gully*, snowriders must take the short blue run *Back Door* to the base of the Brocton Chair lift. From the top *Brocton Gully* is another wide, gentle slope through the forest. Closer to the lodge and accessible from the Goldie rope tow and the Lodge Lift, beginners will find several wide-open, gentle runs. *Goldie Meadows* and *Flower Basin* are perfect for learning and gaining confidence.

Intermediates will also find several trails to explore at Mount Seymour. *Northlands* is the longest intermediate run and is accessible from the top of Mystery Peak. It winds back and forth toward and away from the lift as it cuts down through the forest over undulating terrain. From the top of the Lodge Lift, intermediates can test their skills on *Trapper John's, Lower Unicorn,* and *Seymour 16's. Trapper John's* and *Seymour 16's* are straight shots from the top of the lift to the lodge where skiers and boarders will find super-wide groomed slopes. *Lower Unicorn* is a short run toward Mystery Peak and the top of the Goldie rope tow that cuts through the trees.

Advanced skiers will not find enough terrain at Seymour to keep them challenged for long. From the top of Mystery Peak their choices are limited to *Unicorn* and the gladed area between *Unicorn* and *Manning. Unicorn* is a long run on the backside that is usually bumped up. The gladed area between the two runs is not overly steep but the tightness of the trees does provide a challenge.

Snowboarding Highlights

Mount Seymour welcomes snowboarders with open arms. Area crew members construct three terrain parks every winter complete with tons of hits, including table tops, spines, kickers, rollerz, and banked turns. The Brockton Park, is designed for intermediate and advanced snowboarders. The six-acre park is located near the top of the Brockton lift. The Northlands Park, eight acres in size and also for intermediate and advanced riders, is accessible from the Mystery Peak lift. The beginner park is called Mushroom and inexperienced riders can find it near the top of the Goldie Rope Tow. However, the most popular feature at Seymour is the ISF in-ground halfpipe. Located near the base of the area, the halfpipe is 100 meters long with a 17 percent grade. While the basic pipe foundation is laid right into the ground, it is groomed nearly every day with a pipe grinder. Boarders spend all day and night in the pipe copping huge air and pulling sweet tricks. Yes the pipe is lit for night riding, as are the terrain parks.

More Fun in the Flakes

For those who'd rather be **snow tubing**, the Enquist Snow Tube Park is located above Parking Lot Two. Western Canada's first snow tubing park offers four lanes that drop over 100 feet and a fifth lane that is much more gentle for riders under 48 inches tall. The park offers tubes for rent and a unique lift system to take tubers back to the top of the tubing lanes. The snow tube park is open from 10 A.M. to 8 P.M. Fridays through Sunday and holidays. Rates are for individuals $9/two hours and $15/all day; and for families $40/two hours and $60/all day.

Skier Services

$ Lift Tickets

(Weekend/Holiday rates) Ages 19–64: $26/full-day, $24/half-day, $19/night; Ages 13–18: $21/full-day, $20/half-day, $17/night; Ages 6–12: $12/full-day, $9/half-day; $9/night; Ages 65+: $15/full-day, $15/half-day, $14/night; Ages 6 & younger: Free • (Midweek) Ages 19–64: $19/full-day, $15/night; Ages 13–18: $19/full-day, $15/night; Ages 6–12: $9/full-day, $9/night; Ages 65+: $15/full-day, $13/night; Ages 6 & younger: Free • *Prices based on the 2000–2001 ski season using Canadian currency. See page 354 for conversion information.*

Rentals

Ski Rentals: Ages 13–64: $20.50–$24/full-day, $16-$18/evening; Ages 6–12 & 65+: $12.50-$24/full-day, $10–$18/evening; Ages 6 & under: $9.50/full-day, $9.50/evening. Type of Gear: Rossignol and Salomon • Snowboard Rentals: $32/adults; $27/kids. Type of Gear: Rossignol, Morrow, and Burton • Snowshoe Rentals: $8 to $15 • Snowblade Rentals: For all ages: $13/day, $11/evening • *Prices based on the 2000–2001 ski season using Canadian currency. See page 354 for conversion information.*

Services

Ski School: Private lessons $45/hour; Beginner's package $50 (includes lift ticket, lesson, and rentals). For information on times and availability call the ski school at (604) 986–2261 • Snowboard School: Private lessons $45/hour; Beginner's package $60 (includes lift ticket, lesson, and rentals) • *Prices based on the 2000–2001 ski season using Canadian currency. See page 354 for conversion information.*

Room & Board

Lodging

There are no on-site accommodations at Mount Seymour. The Vancouver area accommodates over 2 million people, and offers all the amenities of a big city. Hotels, motels, bed and breakfasts, and restaurants in North and West Vancouver offer the closest accommodations. Call BC Tourism Bureau for more information; 1–800–663–6000 or *www.tourismvancouver.org*.

Dining

On-site

The Rock Chute Inn and Seymour Café offer a variety of fare for skiers.

Ski Smithers

Photo courtesy Ski Smithers

Ski Smithers

P.O. Box 492
Smithers, BC
Canada V0J 2N0

Ski Report: (250) 847-2550
Information: 1-800-665-4299;
(250) 847-2058
Website: *www.skismithers.com*
Credit Cards: Visa & MasterCard

Operating Hours: 10 A.M.–4 P.M. weekdays;
9:30 A.M.–4 P.M. weekends & holidays

Season: December to mid April

 Background

Location, location, location. Whoever coined this phrase must have been thinking of Ski Smithers. Only one other BC ski area, Shames Mountain, lies farther north than Smithers. And if Smithers wasn't so far north and the drive didn't take snowriders right past Whistler Resort to get there, it would surely be more popular. While it is a long drive to Smithers this means there aren't any lift lines. Ever. Not even on New Year's Day, Spring Break, or any other holiday. Never.

Hudson Bay Mountain rises 8,800 feet from the center of Bulkley Valley. Thousands of years ago the top of Hudson Bay—then another 6,000 to 8,000 feet higher—was blasted away by an eruption, bringing to it a resemblance to Washington State's Mount St. Helens. And just like the popular tourist spot, Hudson Bay attracts visitors who hike to the top to peek into the crater. In the summer it's full of water, and in winter its contents are a collage of ice, water, and snow. From the edge of the crater, the view in the opposite direction is amazing. The snow-covered crags of the Babine and Telkwa Mountains frame Bulkley Valley.

The lifts at Ski Smithers climb 5,500 feet, with another 3,000 feet of vertical still available up the mountain. Any plans to open the upper Hudson Bay, though, are contingent on the almighty investment dollar. And it doesn't look promising considering Smithers' remote location and stunted growth. In the meantime, many skiers and boarders hike up above the chair lift to gain more vertical and lay tracks in fresh snow. Just be sure to stay away from the large cornice that builds up on the lip of the crater. Walking out on to the edge could result in falling into the crater if the cornice breaks, which happens on a regular basis.

Mountain Stats

Base Elevation: 3,700 feet *(1,128 m)*
Summit Elevation: 5,500 feet *(1,677 m)*
Vertical Drop: 1,750 feet *(534 m)*
Primary Slope Direction:
  South and northeast
Annual Snowfall: 72 inches *(183 cm)*
Skiable Days: 118
Skiable Terrain: 292 acres *(113 ha)*
Runs: 34

Longest Run: 2 miles *(3.2 km)*
Lifts: 1 double, 2 t-bars, 1 rope tow
Lift Capacity: 2,900 skiers per hour
Terrain Classification: 25% novice; 55%
  intermediate; 20% advanced
Night Skiing: None
Snowmaking: None
Annual Visits: 45,000

Getting There

- **From Vancouver, BC:** Drive north to Trans-Canada Highway 1 (TCH1). Follow TCH 1 to Cache Creek. At Cache Creek, go north on Provincial Highway 97 (PH 97) to Prince George. At Prince George, head west on PH 16 to Smithers. Follow signs in Smithers for the ski area.

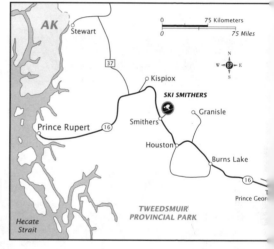

Airport Services: There are daily flights from Vancouver to Smithers International Airport (YYD).

Trail Profiles

Expert boarders and skiers will find more than enough challenging terrain at Smithers. There's *Cold Smoke*, a double-black-diamond run with steep drop-offs and glades on each side. The *Dahlie Double* is a steep narrow cut through the trees. From early on in the season it is full of big bad moguls. *Alpenhorn* is another narrow mogul run, but it is not as steep as *Dahlie's*. For warp speed super G turns try *Chapman's Challenge*, a wide open freeway that is long, steep and groomed everyday.

Intermediate snowriders will love *Ptarmigan's* super buffed consistent slopes and easy-going fall line. Other intermediate runs include *Turkey Shoot*, a shorter run that heads back to the lodge, and *Cinderella* which has a few steep drops, and narrow alleys through the trees.

The area serviced from the Prairie T-bar is best for novice skiers and boarders. Try *Twinkletoes* and *Cabin Runs*. *Twinkletoes* is another wide-open groomed trail with a shallow fall line. *Cabin Runs* are the children's favorite trails because they wind around cabins and trees where the kids have built several small jumps.

Lastly, many backcountry skiers will don their skins and hike up to the massive crater. From the top, these trekkers can ski all way down to the lodge taking in the magnificent view of BC's Coast Mountains.

The problem with Smithers is that getting there isn't easy. While its northern location almost guarantees super light snow, reaching the area is quite a haul. True, flights are available from Vancouver and Prince George to Smithers. Greyhound Bus and Amtrak reach Smithers as well. But why go so far and pass right by one of North America's biggest and best resorts in Whistler-Blackcomb? But therein lies the answer. While Smithers takes some effort to reach, there are not any lift lines, crowded slopes, or blows to the pocketbook. The question still remains however, is it worth the drive?

Snowboarding Highlights

Like the rest of the mountain, the Alpine Snowboard Park rarely sees a large crowd. Boarders usually have the park's 20 features all to themselves and at their own pace. Accessible from the Panorama T-bar, the park offers roughly 200 feet of vertical. Features are made with a cat and include jumps, spines, banked turns, tabletops, rollerz, kickers, and a quarterpipe with a 10-foot wall.

Skier Services

Lift Tickets

Adults: $31 • **Child:** $18 • **Youth:** $24 • **Senior:** $21 • *Prices based on the 2000–2001 ski season using Canadian currency. See page 354 for conversion information.*

Rentals

Ski Rentals: $20/adult; $17/youth; $15/child; for shaped skis add $5; 200 sets. Type of Gear: Rossignol • **Snowboard Rentals:** $34/adult; $29/youth; $21/child; 57 sets. Type of Gear: Rossignol • *Prices based on the 2000–2001 ski season using Canadian currency. See page 354 for conversion information.*

Services

Ski School: 15 instructors; Private lessons $28–$35/hour; Group lessons $12–$17/hour • **Snowboard School:** 15 instructors; Private lessons $28–$35/hour; Group lessons $12–$17/hour • **Childcare:** Available for children 16 months to 8 years old • *Prices based on the 2000–2001 ski season using Canadian currency. See page 354 for conversion information.*

Room & Board

🛏 Lodging

On-site

Windsong Guest House has ski-in, ski-out access, hot tub, sauna, rec room with pool table, and home-cooked meals; call for current rates and packages. (250) 847-9438

Smithers–15 miles *(24 km)* away

Aspen Motor Inn has an indoor pool, hot tub sauna, restaurant, and kitchenettes; rates $65–75/night. 1–800–663–7676 • **Douglass Motel** has family suites with fireplace, log cabins, kitchenettes, saunas, and whirlpools; rates $75/night. (250) 846–5679 or *www.monday.com/douglasmotel* • **Florence Motel** has kitchens in some units; rates $46–$55/night. (250) 847–2678 • **Hudson Bay Lodge** offers non-smoking rooms, whirlpool, sauna, restaurant, and pub; rates $81–$91/night. 1–800–663–5040 • **Sorrento Inn** has kitchenettes and suites available; rates $50–$65/night. 1–888–847–2601 • **Stork Nest Inn** offers free breakfast, a European-style steam room, and free movie channels. (250) 847–3831 or *www.storknest.com*

🍴 Dining

Smithers–15 miles *(24 km)* away

Alpenhorn Pub & Bistro serves burgers, pasta, sandwiches, soups, salads, and great beers; no minors. (250) 847–5366 • **Rainbow Alley and Gallery** serves vegetable dishes, pizzas, soups, and other specialty items. (250) 847–6121

Photo courtesy Ski Smithers

Whitewater

Whitewater Ski & Winter Resort
Nelson, British Columbia
V1L 5P7

Ski Report: 1–800–666–9420
Information: (250) 354–4944
Fax: (250) 354–4988
E-mail: *info@skiwhitewater.com*
Website: *www.skiwhitewater.com*
Credit Cards: Visa & MasterCard

Operating Hours: 9 A.M.–3:30 P.M. daily
Season: Early December to late March

Background

Nestled in the southeast corner of British Columbia, Whitewater Ski & Winter Resort may be the sweetest powder playground in the Northwest that does not mandate a ride in a helicopter or snowcat. While the area's 30-plus feet of average annual snowfall is enough to bury most Canadian ski towns without a trace, it's the quality of the snow conditions that guests rave about. All the old clichés about great powder apply to Whitewater—never-ending face shots in cold smoke, bone dry, feather-light champagne powder: it doesn't get any better than this.

Whitewater gets its fluffy flakes thanks to its location on Ymir (Why-mur) Peak, which rises to 8,000 feet. Whitewater tops out at 6,700 feet but the area is positioned between two distinct ridges on Ymir that produce the fantastic snow conditions. Whitewater lies in the bowl between the two ridges that form the apex of Ymir. The bowl/ski area acts as a natural catch basin of all the westerly storms in the area and turns the water vapor sucked off of nearby Kooteney Lake into loads and loads of light-dry snow. Roughly 95 percent of all the storms in the area have a westerly flow, which virtually guarantees that Whitewater will get hammered every year. Even in a year with half the normal snowfall Whitewater still receives more snow than many other northwest ski areas.

While the snow quality at Whitewater is tremendous the aprés-ski experience is all but non-existent. The area relies on nearby Nelson, BC for lodging and nightlife. Many snowriders may have already seen Nelson in the Steve Martin and Daryl Hannah comedy *Roxanne* as the old mining town served as the set for the movie. Located on the shore of Kooteney Lake, Nelson is a charming community with classic Victorian architecture, museums, an active local artisan and crafts industry, and a working 100-year-old streetcar. Visitors will find several comfortable inns, and restaurants with international fare.

Mountain Stats

Base Elevation: 5,400 feet *(1,646 m)*
Summit Elevation: 6,700 feet *(2,043 m)*
Vertical Drop: 1,300 feet *(396 m)*
Primary Slope Direction: North and south
Annual Snowfall: 400 inches *(1,026 cm)*
Skiable Days: 130
Skiable Terrain: 600 acres *(243 ha)*
Runs: 38

Longest Run: 5,280 feet *(1,610 m)*
Lifts: 1 surface tow, 2 doubles
Lift Capacity: 3,400 skiers per hour
Terrain Classification: 20% novice; 40% intermediate; 40% advanced
Night Skiing: None
Snowmaking: None
Annual Visits: 70,000

Getting There

- **From Vancouver, BC:** Take the Trans-Canada Highway 1 (TCH 1) east to Hope. At Hope, take Provincial Highway 3 (PH 3) east through Castlegar. Take PH 6 on to Nelson. At Nelson, follow Highway 6 south for six miles (10 km) to the Whitewater turnoff. Follow the mountain road for six miles (10 km) to the ski area. Winter tires and/or tire chains are required on the mountain road.

- **From Spokane, WA:** Follow U.S. 2 east to Newport. At Newport, take WA 20 west to WA 31. Follow WA 31 across the U.S./Canadian border to PH 3. Take PH 3 west to Salmo. At Salmo, follow Highway 6 north toward Nelson to the Whitewater turnoff. Follow mountain road for six miles (10 km) to the ski area. Winter tires and/or tire chains are required on the mountain road.

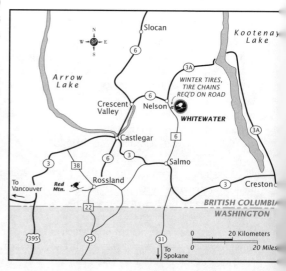

Trail Profiles

Whitewater is not regarded as a beginner's area. Just 20 percent of its 38 trails are designated for learning snowriders. On the other hand, novices from Western Oregon and Washington who are more accustomed to Cascade Concrete (heavy snow) will appreciate just how soft and forgiving the snow is at Whitewater. All beginner terrain can be accessed from the top of the Silver King Double Chair. Hang a right off the top and glide down *SluiceBox*, *Yankee Girl*, or *Kooteney Flats*. Each offers a gentle slope of soft, light, ridges of corduroy.

Intermediate snowriders have more terrain to choose from as they can access trails from both the Silver King and Summit Chair. To the skier's left of the Silver King try *Jack Pot*, which winds down the slope following the lift towers. On the other side of the chair take the Silver King Sky Way, which pushes out to the boundary of the ski area. Combined with the Quartz Skyway this is the longest run at Whitewater. Always groomed, these two trails are popular with guests, local riders, and skiers.

Other worthy mid-level runs include *Mother Lode*, *Joker*, and *Bonanza*—all of which are accessible from the Summit Chair. On the other side, from the top of the Summit Chair, take *Mother Lode*, *Joker*, or *Bonanza*. Mother Lode is a long twisting trail to the skier's right of the lift. *Joker* is still farther out the ridge but connects back into the *Mother Lode*. *Bonanza* starts to the skier's left of the chair but cuts back underneath the lift and heads back to the base. *Mother Lode* is an intermediate trail with one steep section that is groomed on a regular basis. More often than not Joker is covered in powder. Whitewater powder is simply some of the best, but *Joker* is located on a north-facing slope. This makes the powder on *Joker* the best of the best. *Bonanza* is similar to *Mother Lode* without the steep section.

A noteworthy expert run can be found off the Summit Chair by hiking to the top of *Powder Keg Bowl* and dropping into the tightly packed trees of the *Enchanted Forest*. Both are black-diamond runs topped with fabulously frosty flakes. Or, cut under the Powder Key on the Catch Basin Skyway to *Catch Basin*. Another black-diamond run, the *Basin* is loaded with lines of deep light powder and funnels through the *Enchanted Forest* as well.

To the skier's left of the Summit Chair snowriders can explore *Glory Basin*, *Dynamite*, or *Diamond Drill*. *Glory Basin* opens up with a few trees at the top of a steep pitch that is always loaded with powder. It funnels skiers and boarders through a lightly gladed tree area before bursting into *Dynamite*. The steep narrow chute cuts between the rocks and can be full of burly bumps. *Diamond Drill* runs parallel to *Dynamite* and is just as steep but much wider and through the trees instead of the rocks.

From the top of the Silver King lift, try *Concentrator Trees*, *Tramline*, or *Nugget*. An intermediate tree-lined run, *Concentrator Trees* consists of thick forest at the top. As the trees thin out, the pitch becomes steeper. *Tramline* is a straight shot from the Silver King Skyway to the bottom, and is replete with moguls on a steep slope. Lastly, *Nugget* runs extremely wide with several steep sections that roll over from milder terrain until it levels near the bottom.

With only two chair lifts one might expect long lift lines at Whitewater. Not to worry because *Nelson* is off the beaten path of the larger areas. On most days visitors are amazed by how few skiers and boarders they have to share the hill with. Usually it's only locals.

Snowboarding Highlights

Currently there is no terrain park or halfpipe at Whitewater. While there are a few man-made jumps and a couple of tabletops the area crew cannot keep up with the snow fall. Local riders don't care. Riding at Whitewater is about carving huge waves of snow in Mother Nature's winter bounty. The experience is as close to heli-skiing as it gets from a chairlift, but without the helicopter and the big-money ticket. A wise choice for snowboarders is *Concentrator Trees*, where it is simply heaven to free ride the natural hits and carve smooth sweet turns.

Skier Services

Lift Tickets
Ages 19–63: $36/full-day, $26/half-day • **Ages 13–18:** $27/full-day, $20/half-day • **Ages 7–12:** $21/full-day, $15.50/half-day • **Ages 65+:** $27/full-day, $20/half-day • **Ages 6 & younger:** Free • *Prices based on the 2000–2001 ski season using Canadian currency. See page 354 for conversion information.*

Rentals
Ski Rentals: $25/adults; $20/ages 13–18; $15/ages 12 & younger; 150 sets. Type of Gear: Rossignol • **Snowboard Rentals:** $25/adults; $20/ages 13–18; $15/ages 12 &younger; 50 sets. Type of Gear: Rossignol • **Telemark Rentals:** $25/adults; $20/ages 13–18; $15/ages 12 & younger • *Prices based on the 2000–2001 ski season using Canadian currency. See page 354 for conversion information.*

Services
Ski & Snowboard School: 15 ski instructors and 15 snowboard instructors; Private lessons $35/hour, $60/hour for two people; Group lessons are not available; Beginner's package: $42.95–$52.95 (includes lift, lesson, and rentals) • **Discover Skiing/Snowboarding/ Telemarking:** $43 (includes beginner's lift ticket, lessons and rentals) • **Childcare:** $4/hour; Ages 18 months to 6 years • *Prices based on the 2000–2001 ski season using Canadian currency. See page 354 for conversion information.*

Room & Board

While there are no on-slope accommodations at Whitewater, *Ski Canada Magazine* says Nelson, BC, is one of the best little ski towns that has managed to keep its charm. With a vibrant arts community, restaurants and entertainment for every taste, "aprés-ski" takes on a whole new meaning. Reservations can be made by calling the individual lines below, or by calling the Whitewater central reservations line at 1–800–666–9420.

▆ Lodging

Nelson–12 miles (*22 km*) away

Alpine Motel offers basic accommodations; rates $55–$75/night. 1–888–356–2233 or (250) 352–5501 • **Best Western** offers a free continental breakfast, hot tub, exercise room, and a restaurant; rates $79–$139. 1–888–255–3525 or (250) 352–3525 • **Dancing Bear Inn** is a hostel with a fireplace, book and video library, ski packages also available; rates $17–$20/night. (250) 352–7573 • **Heritage Inn** serves a complimentary full breakfast; rates $64–$84/night. (250) 352–5331 or *www.heritageinn.org* • **Inn the Garden Bed & Breakfast** has single rooms, suites, and a private cottage with a full breakfast; rates $70–$150/night. 1–800–596–2337 or (250) 352–3226 or *www.innthegarden.com* • **Lord Nelson** features a sport club, game room, and a restaurant; rates $59/night. (250) 352–7211 • **Viking Motel** is located twenty minutes from Whitewater ski area and offers a hot tub; rates $70–$120/night. 1–800–663–0102 or (250) 352–3595 • **Villa Motel** has a restaurant on premises, a heated whirl pool and hot tub, and refrigerators in each room; rates $55–$110/night. 1–888–352–5515 or (250) 352–5515 • *Call the Nelson Chamber of Commerce at (250) 323–3433 or visit them at www.city.nelson.bc.ca for more options.*

ⓘ Dining

On-site

Whitewater offers a few restaurants on the slopes as well as a gourmet-fare cafeteria just steps from the Silver King Chair.

Nelson–12 miles (*22 km*) away

All Seasons Café serves continental favorites and has Sunday brunch. (250) 352–0101 • **Fiddler's Green Restaurant** offers fine dining in a romantic atmosphere in a heritage home and garden. (250) 825–4466 • **Chez Oti's** serves continental cuisine made from scratch. (250) 505–2152 • **Main St. Diner** is open for lunch and dinner serving diner classics and hearty entrees. (250) 354–4848 • **New China Restaurant** serves traditional Chinese fare. (250) 352–9688 • **Rickaby's Restaurant** offers international cuisine such as Thai, Mexican, and American. (250) 354–1919 • *Call the Nelson Chamber of Commerce at (250) 323–3433 or visit them at www.city.nelson.bc.ca for more options.*

Major Alpine Resorts

Day Ski Areas

ALPINE RESORTS:
WASHINGTON

Other Ski Areas

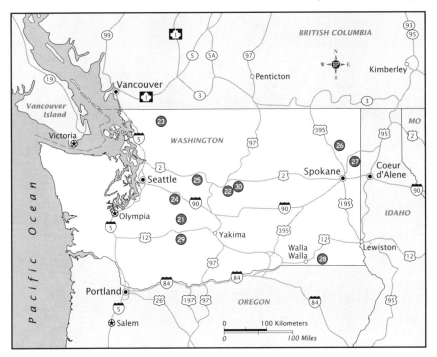

ew places in North America can match Washington's stunning beauty. Mount Rainier, Mount Baker, Mount Adams, and what's left of Mount St Helens, all volcanoes, tower above lush emerald green forests, the mighty Columbia and Snake Rivers, the ice blue Lake Chelan and the green giant Lake Washington. From the shores of Puget Sound the Cascades start climbing and reach their apex forming the backbone of the "Evergreen State" some hundred miles east and thousands of feet above sea level.

The combination of large bodies of water, volcanoes, and a glut of major peaks turns the Cascades into a virtual snow machine. In fact, two different areas in Washington hold the official and unofficial world records for most snowfall in a single season. Paradise Camp at Mount Rainier held the record for nearly 30 years at 1,122 inches until Mount Baker unofficially broke the record at 1,124 inches in 1999.

Snowriders throughout the country are often surprised to hear this fact, likely because the snow quality in Washington just doesn't attract skiers like the dusty, dry powder of the Colorado Rockies and the Utah Wasatch Range. Despite the nickname "Cascade concrete," Washington's soggy snow does produce some of the world's best snowriders. Olympic medalists Steve and Phil Mahre grew up skiing at White Pass, which literally sits in the shadow of Mount Rainier. Bill Johnson, the first American to win a gold medal in the downhill, spent several years training at Mission Ridge just outside of Wenatchee, Washington. And Craig Kelly, one of snowboarding's true pioneers and arguably one of its best all-time riders, put Mount Baker on the map, launching it into cult status among snowboarders.

Soggy conditions aside, the Cascade Mountains are downright rugged. All of Washington's major ski areas offer insane terrain. World-renowned filmmaker Warren Miller habitually employs

133

the Crystal Mountain backcountry in his flicks, while Alpental at the Summit serves up some of the craziest lines in the state. Snowboarders make the trek to Mount Baker to ride the legendary Banked Slalom course, which is literally a nasty gash of a creek bed filled with snow. Steven's Pass, Mission Ridge, 49° North, and White Pass also offer up adrenaline-charged skiing. Even tiny Badger Mountain, with just three rope tows run by old automobile engines, features steep terrain.

That's not to say that novice and intermediate snowriders won't find plenty of skiing to keep them busy. Three of the state's largest ski areas are within 90 minutes of the Seattle area, while three others lie within a half-hour of Eastern Washington's largest communities. All of them host a multitude of ski schools and offer terrain highly conducive to learning the basics.

Though the snow quality is ever-changing, Washingtonians don't seem to mind. They're used to skiing in the rain, over ice, through blizzards, and every other condition the wacky topography of the Cascades and heavy precipitation levels can dish out. Many of them take pride in the fact that they can ski and ride in less than ideal conditions. When they leave the state to visit other areas throughout the country, they have no problem tearing up the slopes and keeping up with the locals, just like the Mahre Brothers, Bill Johnson, and Craig Kelly.

Getting Around Washington

❶ AREA CODES

Washington currently has five area codes. The Seattle area uses **206**; Tacoma and south Seattle suburbs including Auburn use **253**; north Seattle suburbs including Everett, Bellevue, Redmond, and Kirkland use **425**; western Washington except Seattle and surrounding areas use **360**; and Spokane and eastern Washington use **509**.

🚍 ROADS

To contact the Washington Department of Transportation, call 1–800–695–7623 or visit *www.wsdot.wa.gov*. For Pass reports, visit *www.traffic.wsdot.wa.gov/sno-info*.

✈ BY AIR

Two major airports service the state of Washington: **Sea-Tac International Airport** (SEA) in the Seattle-Tacoma area and **Spokane International Airport** (GEG) in Spokane. The resort/ski area or a travel agent can best advise you on the cheapest and/or most direct way to connect from wherever you're departing. They can also arrange transportation from the airport to the ski area.

To book reservations on-line, check out your favorite airline's website or search one of the following travel sites for the best price: *www.cheaptickets.com*, *www.expedia.com*, *www.previewtravel.com*, *www.priceline.com*, *http://travel.yahoo.com*, *www.travelocity.com*, *www.trip.com*—just to name a few. Many of these sites can connect you with a shuttle or rental service to get you from the airport to the ski area.

🚌 BY BUS

Washington is well covered by bus service. **Greyhound** services Seattle, Spokane, and Snoqualmie Pass. Schedules and fares are online at *www.greyhound.com* or by phone at 1–800–231–2222. **Northwestern Trailways** provides service between Everett, Seattle,

Wenatchee, and Spokane. Schedule information is available online at the Greyhound website or by calling 1–800–366–3830 or (206) 728–5955. **Link Transit** services the Mission Ridge Ski Area, Waterville, and Chelan from Wenatchee. Contact them through their website at *www.linktransit.com* or by phone at (509) 663–6223. **Olympic Bus Lines** runs between the Olympic Peninsula and Seattle. Contact them through their website at *www.northolympic.com/ovt/shuttle.html* or by phone at 1–800–550–3858.

⊞ BY TRAIN

Amtrak's Cascade Corridor trains serve Seattle, Tacoma, and Olympia four times a day from Portland, OR. From the north there are two trips a day between Seattle and Vancouver, BC. The Empire Builder runs daily to Seattle, Wenatchee, and Spokane from Chicago, IL, and Minneapolis, MN. The Coast Starlight services Seattle every day from Los Angeles, San Francisco, and Sacramento, CA. Amtrak information and reservations are available online at *www.amtrak.com* or by calling 1–800–872–7245.

⊟ BY FERRY

The **Victoria Clipper** is a high-speed ferry service between Seattle and Victoria, BC. For more information and schedules, visit *www.victoriaclipper.com* or call (206) 448–5000 (in Seattle), (250) 382–8100 (in Victoria, BC), or 1–800–888–2535 (outside of Seattle & Victoria only). **Washington State Ferries** has many routes that cross Puget Sound. Most connect Seattle with the Islands and the Olympic Peninsula. Visit their website at *www.wsdot.wa.gov/Ferries* or call 1–888–808–7977. The **Coho Ferry** runs between Port Angeles and Victoria. For fare and schedule information call (360) 457–4491or visit their website at *www.northolympic.com/coho.* (Most ferries accommodate bikes.)

❓ VISITOR INFORMATION

For visitor information or a travel brochure, call the Washington State Tourism Division at 1–800–544–1800 ext. 800 or visit their website at *www.tourism.wa.gov.* The state's official site is *www.access.wa.gov.*

Crystal Mountain

Crystal Mountain
33914 Crystal Mountain Blvd.
Crystal Mountain, WA 98022

Ski Report: 1–888–754–6199
  Seattle: (206) 634–3771
  Tacoma: (253) 922–1832
Information: (360) 663–2265
E-mail: *comments@skicrystal.com*
Website: *www.skicrystal.com*
Credit Cards: All major

Operating Hours: 9 A.M.–4 P.M. Monday to Friday; 8:30 A.M.–4 P.M. Saturday, Sunday, and holidays

Night Skiing: 4 P.M.–8 P.M. Friday, Saturday, and Sunday
Season: Mid November to mid April

Background

I n the decade prior to 1996, Crystal Mountain Resort experienced only one major improvement—the installation of the Rainier Express chair lift, a high-speed quad. During that lackluster decade the area was a victim of poor management and a lack of capital. In March of 1996, all that changed. Crystal Mountain Resort was sold to the Michigan-based company, Boyne, USA. Under the terms of the sale, Boyne had to invest a minimum of $15 million in the area over the next 10 years. Already Washington's premiere resort, Crystal Mountain will lead Washington's ski areas into the new millenium.

Boyne's most noticeable contribution thus far is the installation of the Northwest's first six-passenger high-speed chairlifts—the Forest Queen and Chinook Express. Forest Queen—a state-of-the-art Doppelmyer lift—replaced the Rendezvous chair that serves much of Crystal's beginner and intermediate terrain. The lift transports 3,600 guests per hour and travels 1,000 feet per minute. The Chinook, boasting the same lift time and capacity, replaced the Midway Shuttle lift. The lifts are big enough to sleep two comfortably on each chair, and fast enough to keep snowriders from catching their breath. Consequently, surrounding trails have been expanded to accommodate the increased activity. Don't sweat the long weekend lines. The new "six packs" move even large crowds swiftly.

The rental shop has also undergone major reconstructive surgery, doubling its size. Other scheduled projects include development of a new restaurant in Campbell Basin, paving of the upper parking lot, expansion of the heated plaza in the base area, and reconfiguration of the Quicksilver chairlift to create more space on the beginner slopes.

Mountain Stats

Base Elevation: 4,400 feet *(1,342 m)*
Summit Elevation: 7,012 feet *(2,139 m)*
Vertical Drop: 3,100 feet *(946 m)* includes backcountry return
Primary Slope Direction: Various
Annual Snowfall: 340 inches *(863.6 cm)*
Skiable Days: 140
Skiable Terrain: 2,300 acres *(932 ha)*, including 1,000 acres *(405 ha)* of backcountry skiing

Runs: 50
Longest Run: 3.5 miles *(5.9 km)*
Lifts: 4 doubles, 2 triples, 1 high-speed quad, 2 high-speed six-passenger, 1 handle tow
Lift Capacity: 17,310 skiers per hour
Terrain Classification: 13% novice; 57% intermediate; 30% advanced
Night Skiing: 3 chairs
Snowmaking: 35 acres *(14 ha)*
Annual Visits: 330,000

Getting There

- **From Seattle, WA:** Take I-5 south to WA 18. Follow WA 18 east to Auburn. Take the Enumclaw exit and head south through Auburn to WA 410. Follow WA 410 through Enumclaw to the Crystal Mountain Access Road. Go left and follow the road to the ski area.

- **From the East Side area:** Take I-405 south to Renton, then take WA 169 (Maple Valley Highway) south to Enumclaw. At Enumclaw, follow WA 410 east to Crystal Mountain Access Road. Go left and follow to ski area.

Bus Services: Beeline Tours offers a variety of ski packages with roundtrip bus service from Seattle. For more information call 1-800-959-8387 or check out *www.beelinetours.com*.

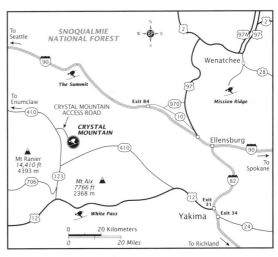

The downside of all the renovations and upgrades is increased lift ticket prices. Prior to the new ownership, Crystal offered a skier guarantee in which guests not satisfied with their experience could return their tickets within 75 minutes and receive a voucher good for another day of skiing. Not any more. Additionally, the resort said goodbye to midweek discounted tickets, which used to cost about 60 percent of the weekend price from Monday to Thursday. Crystal is one of the state's highest-priced areas, and yes, it's a pretty good trek from Seattle. But don't let that be discouraging. A bad day at Crystal is better than most good days elsewhere.

The improvements will certainly attract more skiers, but Crystal Mountain's biggest draw is, and will probably always be, its breathtaking vantage of Mount Rainier. The perennially snowcapped mountain is visible from just about anywhere in the state. But from Crystal, located on the northeast edge of Mount Rainier National Park, the 14,000-foot peak is up close and personal. The view from the Crystal Summit House—which at 6,872 feet is Washington's highest restaurant—is so grand that skiers often find themselves crowded out of the lift lines by sightseers. Lift operators are frequently heard politely asking the crowds to move away from the lift. Young and not so young alike can't seem to get enough of Washington's prized natural wonder.

Aside from serving as the ultimate backdrop, Mount Rainier is responsible for Crystal's unusually light snow. Ask any Washingtonian about their snow and the answer is sure to include the term "Cascade Concrete." And generally speaking, this is justified. The low altitude of Washington's ski areas and the Northwest's tendency for rain tends to produce heavy, wet snow. But Crystal lies in a weather pocket. Mount Rainier, just 12 miles southwest of Crystal, tends to catch most of the heavy snow on its west side, allowing only light snow to fall over and around the mountain, and on the slopes of Crystal. Though the snow quality is good, snow levels can be on occasion low, relative to other Washington resorts. When the snow is low, be sure to look out for rocks hiding just under the snow at the top of *Green Valley* and *High Campbell Basin*.

Trail Profiles

From the top of "Rex"—the local name for the Rainier Express lift—skiers and snowboarders can access terrain for all ability levels, including the local-favorite *Green Valley* area. This medium-sized bowl faces northeast and shelters skiers from harsher weather. The bowl frequently has the best snow on the mountain—without having to hike into the backcountry or ski Crystal's steep *Campbell Basin*. Families of varying ability levels find *Green Valley* to be a great family run. The resorts' snow cats do a fine job laying down a smooth corduroy track for strong novices while leaving plenty of off-piste and tree skiing for more aggressive snowriders. *Iceberg Ridge* is probably the easiest way into *Green Valley*. The superwide cat track stays above the bowl as it gradually drops in elevation. At the end of the ridge, the trail flows into *Green Valley* over a gentle pitch.

The largest amount of novice-friendly terrain is located on the other side of the mountain—Forest Queen provides access to nearly all of these slow-skiing areas. *Queen's Run* is the longest, and area groomers make sure it's velvety smooth every day. Beginners and lower intermediates love this run because of its rolling fall lines and wide-open spaces.

Another popular trail is *Lucky Shot*. Both speed junkies and intermediate skiers find *Lucky Shot* an exciting run. *Lucky Shot* faces north and is always carefully groomed. Early in the morning, before the crowds arrive, speed freaks carve up *Lucky Shot* with top-to-bottom runs that cover the 1,500 feet in less than three minutes. Strong novices and intermediates enjoy the gentle rolls and short, semi-steep pitches.

Intermediate skiers and boarders thrive at Crystal because they can explore nearly the entire mountain. From the top of every lift but one (Chair Six), there are seemingly unlimited options. From the top of Rex, snowriders can cruise wide-open runs like *Green Valley* or the ungroomed but not-too-steep *Northway Ridge*. *Downhill*, *Mr. Magoo*, and *GMAC*—each groomed with twists, turns, and undulating terrain—are accessed off Forrest Queen.

Colin Meagher/Crystal Mountain

What Crystal is truly regarded for is its steep, stomach-in-the-throat chutes and big-air cliffs. Locals find it crazy that so many other Washington skiers and boarders spend hours driving to Whistler or Sun Valley when Crystal has all the big drops, rowdy chutes, and super G turns a snowrider could want. At the top of the High Campbell chair, skiers and snowboarders alike drop into the main chute of *Powder Bowl*. The steep and narrow line faces east and is usually filled with soft, forgiving snow. Still, riders have to make powerful, aggressive turns to navigate the encroaching sides of the chute as snow slides down around them. Taking a fall in *Powder Bowl* often results in a slide of its own, all the way to *Lucky Shot*, not to mention a messy yard sale.

Also accessible from the High Campbell chair is the super fun and super cool *South Backcountry*. Skiers and boarders willing to hike anywhere from 20 to 60 minutes will be rewarded with more than enough narrow couloires and cliffs to fix even the deepest addiction to adrenaline. Just for thrill seekers is *Pinball*, at the top of King Peak. It's a 50-degree pitch with a twisted dogleg about one-third of the way into the chute. The trail is aptly named for snowriders who have experienced falling and bouncing off the series of jutting rocks that poke out of the snow.

Crystal offers more than 1,000 acres for backcountry travelers. The North Backcountry, accessible off Rex and the Green Valley chair, is simply unbelievable. Laying tracks out here requires a ride back to the lodge via a shuttle service that runs every half-hour. Powder mongers can still find untracked snow days after the last snowfall. It's a good idea to consult with the Ski Patrol or a local before venturing into the backcountry. The promise of a beer at the Snorting Elk in the lodge often serves as payment for the consultation. An aerial map of the backcountry is available for purchase in the sport shop for $5.

Snowboarding **Highlights**

Crystal offers a dedicated area of terrain to snowboarders. The *Boarder Zone Snowboard Park*, located under the Quicksilver chairlift, provides riders with easy to more difficult terrain. Designed and maintained for freestyle riding, the *Boarder Zone* features jumps, slides, and a halfpipe constructed with a Pipe Dragon. Crystal even offers "skill builder" programs in which snowboarders can learn freestyle tricks such as a jibe and a nosebone.

Though Crystal is putting more of its resources toward snowboard-specific terrain, many boarders ride Crystal for its natural hits and deep powder in the backcountry. *Campbell Basin* may be the most popular. Full of natural hits, small to big drops and ungroomed snow, the basin sees more than its share of snowboarders.

Skier Services

§ Lift Tickets

Ages 18–69: $38/full-day (includes night skiing), $33/half-day, $20/night • **Ages 11–17:** $33/full-day (includes night skiing), $28/half-day, $15/night • **Ages 70+:** $10/full-day (includes night skiing), $7/half-day, $5/night • **Ages 10 & younger:** Free (when accompanied by a paying adult; half-price otherwise) • *Prices based on the 2000–2001 ski season.*

▥ Rentals

Ski Rentals: $25–$33/adults; $15/children (ages 10 & younger); 700 sets. Type of Gear: K2. Call the rental shop at (360)–663-3040 to reserve equipment • **Snowboard Rentals:** $31/adults; $15/children (ages 10 & younger); 250 sets. Type of Gear: K2. Call the rental shop at (360)–663-3040 to reserve equipment • **Telemark Rentals:** $25/all ages. Call the rental shop at (360)–663-3040 to reserve equipment • **Rainier Rides Ski & Snowboard Demo Shop:** Located in the Alpine Inn. Offers the best quality and selection of skis and snowboards combined with expert service, as well as backcountry accessories such as avalanche beacons and snowshoes • *Prices based on the 2000–2001 ski season.*

⛑ Services

Ski School: 180 instructors; Private lessons $60/hour, $110/two hours, $160/three hours; Group lessons $30/two hours and $40/four hours; Beginner's package $39/two hours and $49/four hours (includes lift ticket, lesson, and rentals) • **Snowboard School:** 30 instructors; Private lessons $60/hour, $110/two hours, and $160/four hours; Group lessons $30/two hours and $40/four hours; Beginner's package $39/two hours and $49/four hours (includes lift ticket, lesson, and rentals) • **Childcare:** Kids Club for ages 4–11 is $65/full-day, includes lift ticket, lesson, lunch, and supervision. $45/half-day, includes all of the above except lunch and half a day of supervision. Handprints Daycare is a state-licensed facility for ages 1 year to 12 years. Staff is certified in first aid and CPR. Open Thursday through Sunday, hours vary. For rates and reservations call (360) 663-3037 • *Prices based on the 2000–2001 ski season.*

Room & Board

Crystal's variety and amount of terrain, incredible view of Mount Rainier, and easy access to the backcountry make the on-snow experience one of the best in the Northwest. Unfortunately for destination skiers, the resort lacks the large, plush hotels and après-ski activities that make Whistler and Sun Valley so popular. Besides the area restaurants and bars, the closest eating and drinking establishments are more than 20 miles down the highway. So, for now, Crystal remains mostly a day area happily filled with local skiers—at least until Boyne decides to develop a few new hotels. There are a few hotels in Enumclaw, which is 39 miles away, but at that distance skiers are better off staying a bit farther away in larger cities with many more hotels, restaurants, and entertainment venues.

▣ Lodging

On-site

Alta Crystal Resort offers a 1920's lodge, chalets with fireplaces and fully equipped kitchens, log cabins, hot tub, and heated pool; call for current rates and packages; 1–800–277–6475 or (360) 663–2500 or *www.altacrystalresort.com* • **Crystal Mountain Hotels** offers three hotels, the **Alpine Inn**, **Quicksilver Lodge**, and the **Village Inn**, with ski to your door convenience, large stone fireplace, balconies, and continental breakfast; call for current rates and packages; 1–888–SKI–6400 or (360) 663–2262 or *www.crystalhotels.com* • **Crystal Mountain Lodging Suites** offers chalets and condominiums with fireplaces, heated pool, beautiful landscape, and access to lower ski lifts; call for current rates and packages; 1–888–ON–THE–MT or (360) 663–2558 or *www.crystalmtlodging-wa.com* • **RV** electrical hook-ups are also available in Parking Lot B, first come, first serves basis; rates $15/night.

ⓘ Dining

On-site

Each of the following restaurants is run by Crystal Mountain Hotels, 1–888–SKI–6400 or *www.crystalhotels.com* • **The Summit House** offers an on-mountain lunch of gourmet pizza and pasta, soups, and salads, with a breathtaking view of Mount Rainier.

Silver Creek Lodge

Cascade Grill is close to the slopes so you can fuel up with breakfast or a quick lunch and still get in all the runs you possibly can • **Silver Creek Deli** has an espresso bar and serves made-to-order deli sandwiches, pizza, beer, wine and more • **Sourdough Sal's** serves satisfying fare for lunch and dinner and offers full cocktail service in a festive atmosphere with a great view of the slopes.

Alpine Inn

Alpine Inn Restaurant serves breakfast and dinner daily, and lunch on weekends where you can enjoy gracious service, gourmet food, and a wide selection of fine wines in an atmosphere of subtle sophistication • **The Snorting Elk Deli** lets you ski in and savor the fresh homemade soups, sandwiches, pizza, and pastries, sip an espresso or micro-brew; takeout menu is available • **The Snorting Elk Cellar** lets you warm up next to the roaring fire in this cozy European-style cellar. Enjoy wonderful food from the deli menu along with full cocktail service and a terrific assortment of microbrews and wines • **The Market at Crystal Mountain** is where you'll find all the basic essentials, including deli selections, baked goods, film, beer, wine and more.

Mission Ridge

Mission Ridge
P.O. Box 1668
Wenatchee, WA 98807

Ski Report: 1–800–374–1693
Information: (509) 663–6543
E-mail: *info@missionridge.com*
Website: *www.missionridge.com*
Credit Cards: All major, except Discover

Operating Hours: 9 A.M.–4 P.M. daily

Season: Late November to early April

Photo courtesy Mission Ridge

Background

Located on the eastern slopes of the snow-laden north Cascades, Mission Ridge is best known for its exceptionally dry, light snow. It may be Washington State's finest, and is often compared to Utah's world-famous powder. That's heady company. Mission's snow stays light due to the area's 4,570-foot base elevation (the highest base in the state), the dry climate of central Washington, over 300 days of sunshine per year, and the average low temperature of 20 degrees Fahrenheit. On the down side, Mission suffers through occasional winters of low snowfall. But the question becomes one of quality verses quantity. The mountain averages roughly 200 inches per year, and it would take a desert-dry season to affect the on-snow experience. Even in a sub-par year, the choice is 100 inches of light fluffy snow here or 300 inches of chunky cottage cheese elsewhere in the Cascades.

Mission recently celebrated its 30-year anniversary by joining forces with Washington's Stevens Pass. Shortly after, Harbor Mountain Company also purchased Schweitzer Ski Resort in Sandpoint, Idaho. The merger is sure to bring many positive upgrades to all three mountains. In Mission's case, expanded snowmaking and new lifts, trails, and lodges are under review by the U.S. Forest Service and the Washington Department of Fish and Wildlife. The Environmental Assessment for the area's future plans was approved during summer of 1998. Construction of the new lifts and lodges will follow once Harbor lines up the capital to make the improvements. In the meantime, snowriders will find Mission to be a magical place to lay tracks. Two thousand acres, 35 designated trails, 3 bowls, 2 ridges, and fantastic gladed tree skiing are the perfect compliment to Mission's dusty, dry snow.

Mountain Stats

Base Elevation: 4,570 feet *(1,394 m)*
Summit Elevation: 6,770 feet *(2,065 m)*
Vertical Drop: 2,200 feet *(671 m)*
Primary Slope Direction: East
Annual Snowfall: 200 inches *(508 cm)*
Skiable Days: 130
Skiable Terrain: 2,200 acres *(891 ha)*
Runs: 35

Longest Run: 2.2 miles *(35.4 km)*
Lifts: 4 doubles, 2 surface lifts
Lift Capacity: 4,300 skiers per hour
Terrain Classification: 10% novice; 60% intermediate; 30% advanced
Night Skiing: None
Snowmaking: Chairs 1 and 4
Annual Visits: 100,000

Getting There

• **From Seattle and Tacoma, WA:** Take I-5 to I-90. Head east on I-90 to Exit 84 (Cle Elum/Wenatchee). At Exit 84, take WA 970 north to U.S. 97. Continue on U.S. 97 to U.S. 2. Follow U.S. 2 east to Wenatchee and follow directions above from there.

• **From North Puget Sound:** Take U.S. 2 east to Wenatchee. Take WA 285 (Mission Street) to the end of town and take Squilchuck Road. Follow signs to Mission Ridge.

• **From Spokane, WA:** Follow I-90 west to WA 281 to Quincy. At Quincy, take WA 28 to Wenatchee. Take WA 285 (Mission Street) to the end of town and take Squilchuck Road. Follow signs to Mission Ridge.

Airport Services: Guests can also fly into Pangborn Memorial Field (EAT) in East Wenatchee. Horizon Air and United Express both service the airport with connecting flights from around the country. Rental cars are also available.

Bus Services: SkiLINK is a free bus service from Wenatchee to Mission Ridge. For schedules and more information call 1–800–851–5465.

Trail Profiles

Mission's advanced and intermediate terrain makes up 90 percent of the mountain. The only green skiing area is near the lodge. *Compromise* and *Mimi*—for novice skiers and children—are to the skier's right of Chair One, on the lowest third of the mountain. Terrain beyond that is suited to intermediates on up, though the resort keeps a close eye on the family experience. Anyone who can link wedge turns can explore many of the blue trails. Also, as a small-town resort, Mission is a safe, inexpensive place to turn the kids loose for an afternoon.

Some of the most heavily traveled advanced trails can be found from the top of Chair Two (6,770 feet). Try *Windy Ridge* and *Bomber Bowl*, whose names are more intimidating than the terrain. Before heading off to carve turns, be sure to check out the magical views of Mount Rainier, Mount Adams, the Columbia River, and Wenatchee Valley. To reach *Windy Ridge*, stay high to skier's right along the area boundary. It dips down and then back up. A quick skate/hike is necessary and then there are several lines off the *Ridge* from which to choose. Each heads through gladed trees and deposits skiers and boarders back into the gut of the area. Mission veterans claim this is some of the best powder skiing on the mountain. Only strong advanced snowriders should venture onto this ungroomed slope.

A short distance and a hike past *Windy Ridge* provides egress to *Microwave Bowl* and *Bowl Four*. Both are usually full of frosted flakes, and the hike usually means fresh tracks for those willing to make the effort. *Bowl Four* may have the mountain's best snow because it's north facing and doesn't receive much sunlight until late season. *Microwave* often has a loaded cornice at the top and feather-light powder in the bowl. Enter through the gates only when they are open, and be sure to check with the ski patrol for weather and snow conditions. Information regarding backcountry skiing or snowboarding, along with avalanche and weather conditions, may be obtained by checking with the ski patrol stations on top of Chairs 2, 3, and 4. At Mission it is completely legal and completely fun to explore areas beyond the ski area boundary, but they're not patrolled or maintained. Avalanche slopes, unmarked obstacles, and other natural hazards exist. Rescue in the backcountry, if available, is the responsibility of the Kittitas County Sheriff. It may take considerable time and it will be costly.

Kent Kerr/Mission Ridge

Snowboarding Highlights

Mission's terrain park has been around just a short time, but the resort is working to give boarders what they want. Accessible from Chair One, the park covers about four or five acres with six to eight obstacles that include a tabletop, rollerz, kickers, a small quarter-pipe, and jumps of various sizes. In the mean time, there is incredible free riding at Mission in *Bowl Four* and the *Outback*.

Traversing into the big wide bowl will get the adrenaline flowing fast since looking down on the untracked pristine slope is a thrill unto itself. *Bowl Four* is shaped like a fan with the wide end at the top. From here, *Bowl Four* provides a perfect pitch for carving big arcs through deep snow. As riders near bottom, the fan funnels into a gladed tree area with rolling terrain. Right before entering the trees there is a bench, or flat spot, that makes a perfect pit stop to rest and marvel at the beautiful signatures in the snow. After passing through the trees, Bowl Four deposits riders onto a groomed blue run called *Chak Chak*. Take *Chak Chak* to the base of Chair Four to start all over again.

Traversing right from the bench area opens up into a snowboarders paradise. *The Outback* is full of natural kickers and halfpipes, steep pitches, jumps, stumps, bumps, hops, and drops. Mission regulars love this area and routinely claim to find new lines with each entrance. Cut to the right from the bench and then head down, following the terrain. Snowboarders can only go so far to the right, as huge rock walls frame the area in. Near the bottom and at the top of the left pitch, a fence below is visible. From here, head back to the left, which deposits boarders into lower *Chak Chak*. Boarders who reach the fence find they have a difficult traverse over to *Chak Chak*.

On the skier's left from the top, there are runs for both intermediate and advanced snowriders. *Boundary Road* and *Katsuk*, both blue trails, provide access to *Bomber Bowl*. A challenging pitch, *Bomber Bowl* was named for a B-24 bomber that crashed on Mission Ridge in 1944 (*see page 147 for story*). *Bomber Bowl* opens up into *KaWham*, *Hidden Valley*, and *Nastar*.

Advanced and expert skiers will also get a charge out of the *Bomber Cliffs*. This ridge of exposed rock is far to the skier's left of the top of Chair Two. Take *Boundary Road* to just above *Bomber Bowl* and hang a left. Most of the rocks are too big to jump off, but there are several steep chutes between them.

Chairs Three and Four transport snowriders to the base of *Microwave Bowl* and *Bowl Four*. Most of this area is for intermediate skiers or skiers who like cruising on groomed trails. These lower runs are perfect for family skiing. In fact, they are designated as a slow-skiing zone. Guests of any age or ability are welcome so long as they ski slowly. The relaxed pace is perfect for socializing in between turns. Look for the runs on the trail map that are highlighted with the yellow grid. The slow-skiing zones have gentle pitches and lots of elbowroom for timid turns.

Bumps skiers should check out *Tyee* and *Lower Tyee*, plus *Lower Lip Lip*. Local bump skiers like to take Chair 3 to the top and start with *Tyee* by hanging a right off the chair. Pass the *Kiwa* run, and *Tyee* is the next trail. *Tyee* is a short, fierce pitch filled with big, bad, and burly bumps. There is a brief respite in the middle due to a short traverse over to *Lower Tyee*, which is longer than *Tyee* but not quite as steep. The bumps, however, are even bigger. Just when the legs are ready to blow out, *Lower Tyee* deposits skiers onto *Tumwater*, a groomed run. Cut across *Tumwater* to *Lip Lip*, which covers groomed terrain until the last pitch. *Lower Lip Lip* is directly under the lift.

More Fun in the Flakes

Mission Ridge offers a 3.5-mile loop for **cross-country skiing**. For those interested in **snow tubing**, the Squilchuck Tubing Park is located four miles (6 km) down Mission Ridge Road from the ski area and about eight miles (13 km) from Wenatchee. Eight dollars a day includes use of tube and tow.

Skier Services

§ Lift Tickets

Ages 18–64: $34/full-day weekend, $27/full-day mid-week; $29/half-day weekend, $24/half-day mid-week • **Ages 7–17:** $19/full-day and half-day • **Ages 65 & older:** $19/full-day and half-day • **Ages 6 & younger:** Free • *Prices based on the 2000–2001 ski season.*

Nordic Trail Pass

$5/all ages • *Prices based on the 2000–2001 ski season.*

Rentals

Ski Rentals: $17–$32; 500 sets. Type of Gear: Volant, K2, Rossignol, Volkl, Salomon, Dynastar, Elan • **Snowboard Rentals:;** $23–$32; 250 sets. Type of Gear: Rossignol and K2 Salomon Snowblades also available • *Prices based on the 2000–2001 ski season.*

Services

Ski & Snowboard School: 46 ski instructors; 24 snowboard instructors; Private lessons (includes lift ticket) $65–$70; Group lessons $38–$49; Beginner's package $35 (includes lift ticket, rentals, and lesson). Call (509) 663-7631 for more information • **Childcare:** Licensed services for children three months to six years. $10–$12/hour for 3–24 months; $8–$10/hour for ages 2–6. Call for reservations: (509) 663-6543 • *Prices based on the 2000–2001 ski season.*

The Tale of the Bomber Bowl

On the evening of September 30, 1944, a B-24 bomber on a training flight from the Walla Walla, Washington army base became lost in fog and rain. Around 8 P.M., the Beehive Lookout reported hearing a plane pass overhead and seeing flames through the fog. The following morning, investigators found the remains of the plane scattered throughout the rocky area that would later become known as Mission Ridge's Bomber Bowl. The Army packed out the deceased crewmembers, but most of the plane remained on the mountain.

It wasn't until 1992, nearly 50 years later, that the Bomber legend began. Area owners decided to return a section of the B-24's wing, which had hung in the Hampton Lodge since 1985, back to the crash site. Ski patrol members mounted the wing on two steel poles at the entrance to the Bomber Bowl trail, which has since served as a memorial to the young pilots who lost their lives. Miraculously, within an hour snow began to fall. And following seven years of below-average snowfall, the 1992–93 ski season marked a record year. Winters have been strong ever since.

Additionally, skiers have returned pieces of the wreckage collected as souvenirs over the years, and the Wing Site Memorial has become a popular spot. In the fall 1994, a local Boy Scout designed a commemorative sign featuring the story of the crash and the names of the crewmen who perished. Meanwhile, every winter, the snow keeps falling at Mission Ridge.

Room & Board

There is no on-site lodging at Mission Ridge, but there are four dining facilities on the mountain. The ski area is only 12 miles from Wenatchee, where guests will find numerous hotels, motels, bed and breakfasts, restaurants, cafés, and pubs. Many of the hotels offer discounted lift tickets and lodging packages, and some allow children ages 6 and younger to stay free.

Lodging

Wenatchee–12 miles *(19 km)* away

Comfort Inn Wenatchee is located two blocks from Riverfront Park and ice rink with 81 rooms; rates $59–$95/night. (509) 662-1700 • **Warm Springs Inn** is a B&B in a beautiful, updated 1917 mansion on the edge of Lake Wenatchee, offering five extravagantly decorated theme guestrooms, and a deck overlooking the river; rates $85–$110/night. (509) 662-8365 or *www.warmsprings.com* • *Call Visitor Information at 1–800–57–APPLE for more options.*

Leavenworth–22 miles *(35 km)* away

The romantic Bavarian town offers numerous choices for lodging and dining. You'll also find cross-country skiing, sleigh rides, dogsledding, ice-skating, and snowmobiling. Because of its location, Leavenworth is also a good base camp to ski Stevens Pass *(see page 156)* one day and then head to Mission Ridge the next. Each area is less than an hour in either direction. For more call visitor information at (509) 548-5807 • **Evergreen Motel** is an old-fashioned roadside inn with rooms that can sleep up to six people, including fireplaces, kitchens, and free continental breakfast; allows pets; rates $65–$135/night. (509) 548–5515 or *www.evergreeninn.com* • **Bosch Garten** boasts three lovely rooms with direct access to the deck and hot tub, a Japanese tea house, close proximity to shops and cross-country ski areas, and a delightful host; rates $98–$105/night. 1–800–535–0069 • **Hotel Pension Anna** offers a small, Austrian-style pension with a farmhouse atmosphere, rooms, suites, and free breakfast; rates $89–$189/night. 1–800–509–2662 • **Kinney Suites** offers three fully equipped and furnished condos; rates $175–$310/night. 1–800–621–9676.

⑩ Dining
On-site
The **Lost Prop** offers full service dining with beer, wine, and Northwest cuisine in the Hampton Lodge • **The Tamarack Grill** is adjacent to the Last Prop serves a skier's menu with a cafeteria style • **The Border's Café** located in the skier services building and serves a south-of-the-border style menu • **The Mountain Roost** is located at mid-mountain and serves pizza, soups, and salads.

Leavenworth–22 miles *(35 km)* away
Alley Café and Vintage Decadence features delicious Italian cuisine. (509) 548–6109 • **Andreas Kelley** serves German cuisine, chicken, and spaghetti. (509) 548–6000 • **Café Restaurant Mozart** serves a variety of tasty traditional German dishes. (509) 548–0600 • **Kristall's** serves traditional American food, such as burgers and sandwiches. (509) 548–5267.

Mount Baker

Mount Baker Ski Area
1019 Iowa Street
Bellingham, WA 98226

Ski Report:
   Bellingham: (360) 671–0211
   Vancouver, BC: (604) 688–1595
   Seattle: (206) 634–0200
Information: (360) 734–6771
E-mail: *snow@mtbakerskiarea.com*
Website: *www.mtbakerskiarea.com*
Credit Cards: Visa & MasterCard (not accepted in food service areas)

Operating Hours: 9 A.M.–4 P.M. daily, including holidays, except Christmas

Season: Mid November to May

Background

Ask a skier or snowboarder what ski area receives the most snowfall every year, and their response will likely be Utah's Snow Bird and Alta, or any number of Colorado resorts. The titleholder, believe it or not, is Washington's Mt. Baker, which receives the highest annual snowfall of any lift-serviced ski area in the world. In fact, Baker holds the world record for the greatest verifiable snowfall in a season, with a reported depth of 1,140 inches recorded for the 1998–99 season. The previous record of 1,122 inches was set at the Rainier-Paradise National Weather Service Cooperative station during the 1971–72 season. What makes the record even more astounding is that snowfall at Rainier is measured at an elevation of 5,420 feet, while Baker's snowfall is measured at 4,300 feet.

Baker lies in one of the highest portions of the Cascade Mountains, surrounded by peaks such as the ski area's namesake Mount Baker (10,750 feet) and neighboring Mount Shuksan (9,270 feet). These colossal mounds rise dramatically from the coastal lowlands much like Mount Rainier and Mount Adams. The two towering peaks and surrounding terrain act like a mainline injection of steroids to the local precipitation levels. Area crewmembers spent much of their time during the winter digging out trail signs 20 feet tall, or even extending them. Baker simply gets buried every single year.

Mountain Stats

Base Elevation: 3,500 feet *(1,068 m)*
Mid Elevation: 4,300 feet *(1,312 m)*
Summit Elevation: 5,050 feet *(1,540 m)*
Vertical Drop: 1,550 feet *(472 m)*
Primary Slope Direction: Northwest to northeast
Annual Snowfall: 645 inches *(1,638 cm)*
Skiable Days: 150
Skiable Terrain: 1,000 acres *(405 ha)*

Runs: 38
Longest Run: 1.8 miles *(2.8 km)*
Lifts: 2 quads, 6 doubles, 2 rope tows
Lift Capacity: 11,000 skiers per hour
Terrain Classification: 24% novice; 45% intermediate; 31% expert
Night Skiing: None
Snowmaking: None
Annual Visits: 100,000–175,000

Surrounded by the Mount Baker National Forest, in the midst of the Northern Cascades, this isolated ski area is too far removed from major cities and lacks the amenities to be a destination resort. Baker only receives approximately 150,000 skier visits per year, mostly because the nearest lodging is roughly 20 miles down a narrow two-lane road that is about as extreme as it gets once the snow starts falling. There's also the snow's poor reputation. While it's deep, it isn't exactly light. Snowboarders, on the other hand, have no problem with the deep, moist snow of the Cascades.

As one of the first areas to embrace snowboarding in North America, Baker soon became a Mecca for one-plankers. In fact, Baker has achieved cult status among riders and hosts quite possibly the world's most respected event—the Mt. Baker Banked Slalom. Snowboarders have filled the void created by skiers' lack of interest in Baker. They now account for 25 percent of skier visits every year. One of the reasons boarders are so enamored of Baker is because some of the biggest names in the history of snowboarding, including Craig Kelly, Jim Rippey, Amy Howat, Robbie Morrow, and Shaun Palmer, got their start at Baker. It's Baker's challenging terrain, though, that keeps them coming back. The mountain is riddled with cliffs, narrow gaps, steep open bowls, and deep snowfields—the quintessential snowboarder's playground.

Mt. Baker has also been working to attract more skiers. The area recently finished a four-year, $5 million expansion project that culminated with the opening of the $2.5 million White Salmon Day Lodge. It offers spectacular views of Mount Shuksan and the ski slopes. The lodge was constructed with materials indigenous to the Cascade Mountains such as hand-peeled timber logs, clay-fired custom tiles, columnar basalt rocks, and cedar shake shingles. It is almost worth the trip to Baker just to see the lodge, which is a testament to how far the area has come in the last few years. The lodge hosts a pro shop, limited rentals, ticket sales, and changing areas. The expansion project also doubled the size of Baker's intermediate terrain with the addition of two new quad lifts: Chair #7 and the Hemispheres Chair #8.

Trail Profiles

The Baker lift circuit stretches out over two peaks within spitting distance of Mount Shuksan and Mount Baker. Chairs 1, 2, 3 and 6 provide access to the 5,000-foot Panorama Dome, while 4, 5, 7, and 8 service the 5,540-foot Shuksan Arm. Baker operates two major parking lots, each servicing one of the two peaks. From each lot, the top is just two chair rides away. Shifting from one peak to the next is just a couple of chair lifts as well.

Getting There

- **From Seattle, WA:** Take I-5 north to Bellingham. At Bellingham, take Exit 255 and head east on U.S. 542 (Mount Baker Highway) to Mount Baker.
- **From Vancouver, BC:** Head south to the U.S./Canada border on I-5. Continue on I-5 to Bellingham, WA. At Bellingham take Exit 255 and head east on U.S. 542 (Mount Baker Highway) to Mount Baker.

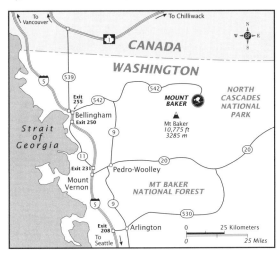

Bus Services: Beeline Tours offers a variety of ski packages with roundtrip bus service from Seattle. For more information call 1-800-959-8387 or check out *www.beelinetours.com*.

While the snow tends to be heavy, it is Baker's terrain that makes the area. In-bounds from the top of Panorama Dome and Chairs 1 and 6, there are numerous black diamond runs like *Sticky Wicket*, *The Chute*, and *Razorhone Canyon*. *The Chute* begins in an open powder field and closes on a narrow gash through the rocks. Brave or foolhardy snowriders straight run it, while others make 10 crisp, precise turns since it's just wide enough for a pair of skis.

Sticky Wicket, accessible from Chair 6, is a local favorite. From the top, hang a left off the lift and take the third trail to the right off *Canuck's Deluxe*. *Sticky* drops through an old growth forest of towering cedar and Douglas fir trees perfectly spaced for powder skiing. Skiers and

boarders have to react quickly, as the terrain is replete with quick drops, gullies, and snow-covered logs.

World Record!
Mount Baker holds the world seasonal snowfall record with **1,140 inches**, set in 1999.

Sticky Wicket drops into the lower portion of *Razorhone Canyon*. Most snowriders prefer to run the length of the canyon by entering it from the top of Chair Six. One of the more adventurous and unique ski runs in the Northwest can be found on *Razorhone*. It begins in a wide-open powder bowl, then closes in a steep, narrow canyon with 100-foot rock walls for about three-quarters of a mile. *Razorhone* gets a black-diamond rating because there's no chance to bail out once inside. Skiers and boarders must make precise turns and be aware of other riders.

Baker has all the challenging terrain an expert would expect, but there are also enough trails to keep novices and intermediates happy as well. From the top of both peaks there is an easy way down. Guests who can link wedge turns can tour the top of the mountain. Off the peak of Panorama Dome, accessible from Chair 6 or 1, the *Blueberry Cat Track* and *Austin* deposit skiers and boarders at the base lodge after 1,500 feet of vertical of smooth corduroy. Chairs 2 and 3 begin at the Heather Meadows Day Lodge and provide access to at least 10 different trails that are always groomed. With nearly flat terrain, *Heather Meadows* is the best area for novice snowriders who are still learning to stop and turn.

More adventurous intermediates will enjoy the *Shuksan Arm*—Baker's intermediate area. Guests reach the top by taking Chairs 8, 4, and 5. *Easy Money* and *White Salmon* are wide-open cruisers with rolling terrain, cat tracks, and short steep pitches. The *Oh Zone* provides stunning views of Mount Shuksan and the peaks just beyond the Canadian Border, not to mention the top-of-the-world view back toward the ski area.

Snowboarding Highlights

Despite Mt. Baker not having to lift a finger to build any snowboard terrain, riders all over the world consider the resort a snowboarding mecca. The entire mountain, snowboarders say, is a terrain park. The central feature and biggest draw is the 1,500-foot natural halfpipe located at the top of Chair 5. With walls averaging 10 to 30 feet high, even pro riders will find enough natural hits to satisfy them. To top it off, the distance between the walls is nearly perfect in that it is not so wide that riders lose speed in the transitions. Nor is it so tight that controlling their speed is an issue either. The natural, frozen, snow-covered creek bed drops into the *Nose Dive* trail, but only after some serious riding.

More Fun in the Flakes

Mt. Baker has 4 km of **cross-country skiing** trails, which are sometimes groomed, sometimes ungroomed, depending on the weather.

Skier Services

🟢 Lift Tickets

Ages 16–69: $32weekend/holiday; $22/Monday–Wednesday; $24/Thursday–Friday • **Ages 7–15:** $24.50/weekend/holiday; $18/Monday–Wednesday; $19/Thursday–Friday • **Ages 65–69:** $24.50/weekend/holiday; $18/Monday–Wednesday; $19/Thursday & Friday • **Ages 70+:** $5 • **Ages 6 & younger:** Free • *Prices based on the 2000–2001 ski season.*

🔘 Nordic Trail Passes

$5 donation suggested • *Prices based on the 2000–2001 ski season.*

🔘 Rentals

Ski Rentals: $22/adults; $18/ages 13–15; $15/ages 12 & younger; 500 sets. Type of Gear: Rossignol, Elan, K2, Volkl, Atomic, Salomon, Dynastar, and Olin ($34/all ages for performance skis) • **Snowboard Rentals:** $30–$39/all ages; 300 sets. Type of Gear: Gnu, Lib Tech, Murrow, K2, Palmer, Burton • **Telemark Ski Rentals:** $24/all ages. Type of Gear: Rossignol • **Nordic Ski Rentals:** $18/all ages • **Snowshoes Rentals:** $16/all ages • *Prices based on the 2000–2001 ski season.*

🔘 Services

Ski School: 60 instructors; Private lessons $50/1.5 hours; Group lessons $16/1.5 hours; Beginner's package $36 (includes lift ticket, rentals, and lesson) • **Snowboard School:** 30 instructors; Private lessons $50/1.5 hours; Group lessons $16/1.5 hours; Beginner's package $43 (includes lift ticket, rentals, and lesson) • **Childcare:** Limited schedule; call for information at (360) 734-6771 • *Prices based on the 2000–2001 ski season.*

Room & Board

Mt. Baker is primarily a day ski area as there are no on-slope accommodations. The closest lodging is roughly 20 miles (32 km) away in the small town of Glacier. Overnight parking for self-contained RVs is permitted in designated areas only.

🔘 Lodging

Glacier–20 miles *(32 km)* away

Snowline Inn offers 39 condos that are fully equipped and furnished with decks, satellite TV, fireplaces in some rooms, and can sleep up to six people; rates $45–$85/night. 1–800–228–0119 • **Cabin Country B&B** features a cozy mountain-lodge atmosphere with a comfy common room, deck, stone fireplace, and delicious breakfast; rates $75/night. (360) 599–2903 • **Mount Baker Chalets & Condos** offers a variety of fully equipped and fur-

nished condos and chalets with fireplaces, hot tubs, and an indoor pool; rates
$60–$200/night. (360) 599–2405 • **Mount Baker Cabin Rentals** offers one- to three-bedroom cabins with fully equipped kitchens, microwaves and dishwashers, living rooms with
gas fireplaces, VCR, video games, decks with private hot tubs, wooded locations, easy parking, towels and linens provided, some mountain views. (17 miles from the ski area) Web
access only at: *www.nas.com/baker/cabin.html* or *bridgel@nas.com*.

Bellingham–56 miles *(90 km)* away
   Big Trees Bed and Breakfast is located on two acres of old growth cedar and firs, it offers
   rooms with views of Lake Whatcom with window seats, complimentary drinks, and comfortable furniture; rates $95–$115/night. (360) 647–2850 or *www.nas.com/~bigtrees* • **De
   Cann House** is a Victorian B&B with two rooms, private baths, antique furniture, and a
   common room with a pool table; rates $60–$80/night for two people. (360) 734–9172 or
   www.pacificrim.net/~hudson.

⑪ Dining

Glacier–20 miles *(32 km)* away
   Milano's Market and Deli is a convenient stop on the way to Mount Baker offering homemade Italian cuisine, sandwiches, and wine. Take-out menu also available. (360) 599–2863.

Bellingham–56 miles *(90 km)* away
   The Archer Ale House serves classic European brews, Northwest microbrews, and pub fare.
   (360) 647–7002 • **Il Fiasco** serves a variety of Asian, northern Italian, and seafood, with
   fresh homemade desserts and soups, and Italian and Northwestern wines. (360) 676–9136.

Maple Falls–25 miles *(40 km)* away
   The Frosty Inn serves delicious standard American food. (360) 599–2594.

The Mount Baker Legendary Banked Slalom

With an open-entry system, limited sponsorship, and zero television coverage, the Mount Baker Banked Slalom is still regarded by many to be the best snowboard contest in the world. How can this be when the prize money is non-existent and riders earn zero world cup points? The answer: Riders gain the respect of the entire snowboard community while being recognized in the company of the sport's biggest names: Shaun Palmer, Craig Kelly, Terje Haakonsen, and Robbie Murrow. Racers hurl themselves down eight wide-bermed, gigantic, giant slalom turns. Then they drop into a natural halfpipe that is actually a snow-covered creek bed with intimidating walls and an undulating bottom. They race against each other down the mile-long course without any judges. The event is so popular and so well respected among the world's elite riders that many of them gave the 1998 Olympics their middle digits rather then miss this race. The reason? The Olympics are established, organized, and de-individualized. Team members must all wear the same uniforms and suspend contracts with their regular sponsors in lieu of Olympic sponsors. The Banked Slalom grand prize—golden duct tape on a chain—is the sport's Holy Grail. It represents the free-spirited-go-your-own-way attitude of snowboarding, which is how the sport began in the first place.

Stevens Pass

Stevens Pass Ski Area
P.O. Box 98
Skykomish, WA 98288

Ski Report:
   Seattle: (206) 634–1645
   Everett: (425) 353–4400
   Eastern WA: (509) 782–5516
Information: (206) 812–4510
Email: *info@stevenspass.com*
Website: *www.stevenspass.com*
Credit Cards: Visa & MasterCard

Operating Hours: 9 A.M.–10 P.M. daily; 9 A.M.–4 P.M. spring hours.
Night Skiing: 4 P.M.–10 P.M. daily

Season: Late November to mid April

Scott Wicklund,/Stevens Pass

Background

Established way back in 1937 in the Mount Baker-Snoqualmie and Wenatchee National Forests, Stevens humbly began with a Ford V-8 engine, an assortment of wheels and shafts, and a hunk of rope. Total investment for the two young founders from Seattle—Don Adams and Bruce Kehr—was less than $600. Tickets sold for 5 cents per ride, and gross ticket sales were $88 for the first season. Because Highway 2 was closed during the winter at the town of Scenic, determined skiers would hike the last six miles or buy an 18-cent, one-way train ticket.

While Stevens Pass has undergone several transformations, many of the original elements that made Stevens popular in the early days remain the same. A wide variety of terrain, proximity to the Seattle area, over 400 inches of snow annually, and a management philosophy that continually focuses on making the skiing experience as good as it can possibly be makes Stevens one of Washington's best snowriding venues.

During the Fifties, Stevens operated over 20 rope tows. The Sixties ushered in the Seventh Heaven lift, and with it some of the steepest and most advanced skiing in the state. The Seventies brought along a new day lodge, while two more lodges were built and Mill Valley opened the following decade. Serviced by the Southern Cross and Jupiter lifts, Mill Valley added another 400 acres of skiing on the backside of the area.

Mountain Stats

Main Base Elevation: 4,061 feet *(1,238 m)*
Mill Valley Base Elevation: 3,821 feet
(1,165 m) back side of mountain
Summit Elevation: 5,845 feet *(1,783 m)*
Vertical Drop: 1,800 feet *(549 m)*
Primary Slope Direction: 360 degrees
Annual Snowfall: 450 inches *(1,143 cm)*
Skiable Days: 150
Skiable Terrain: 1,125 acres *(456 ha)*
Runs: 37

Longest Run: 1mile *(1.6 km)*
Lifts: 2 high-speed quads, 1 quad, 4 triples, 4 doubles
Lift Capacity: 15,800 skiers per hour
Terrain Classification: 11% novice; 54% intermediate; 35% advanced
Night Skiing: 35% allowance (6 lifts)
Snowmaking: None
Annual Visits: 380,000

The Nineties featured installation of two new high-speed quads, upgrades of the Tye Mill lift, and a brand-new day lodge to end the millennium. In 1996 the SkyLine Express replaced the old Barrier Double chairlift. Two years later, the Hogsback Express high-speed quad replaced the Blue Jay and Hogs Back chairs.

More recently, Stevens replaced the old T-Bar Lodge by building a new $5 million dollar lodge with a distinctly Cascadian look and feel. Construction materials include large wood beams and granite rocks taken directly from the Cascade Mountains. The new lodge forms the centerpiece of the base area and provides seating and dining for 150 more skiers and boarders than the old lodge did. The Tye Mill double chair was upgraded to a triple chair.

Getting There

- **From Seattle, WA:** Take I-90 to I-405. Follow I-405 north to Exit 23 to WA 522 east. Then take U.S. 2 east to Steven's Pass.

- **Bus Services:** Beeline Tours offers a variety of ski packages with roundtrip bus service from Seattle. For more information call 1–800–959–8387 or check out *www.beelinetours.com*.

Trail Profiles

Stevens is spread out over two mountains, providing snowriders with five distinct terrain areas: *Mill Valley, Big Chief Mountain, Tye Bowl, Seventh Heaven,* and the intermediate and novice terrain on the area's front side. Both *Mill Valley* and *Big Chief* can be reached by taking the Big

Scott Wicklund/Stevens Pass

Chief lift from the base and then the Double Diamond triple chair to the peak and its outstanding view. To the north lies Glacier Peak and to the southeast is Mount Stuart. In between, there are two national forests and the Pine Lakes, Henry M. Jackson, and Glacier Peak wilderness areas.

On the front side, to the left of the lift, is the *Double Diamond* run. *DD* is a long, steep pitch usually covered with moguls. Get ready for a thigh-burning-bump-banging experience. Farther left, try *Wild Katz* or *Schims Meadow*. *Katz* is a narrow cut through the trees, just as steep as *DD*, and even more challenging because the run is so narrow. *Schims* is a little less intimidating and opens up into *Tye Bowl*. To the right of the *DD* lift is *Big Chief Bowl*. This is not a designated trail, but it is an extraordinary run within the area boundary. Plus, because of its steep entrance, traffic will be minimal.

From the top of the DD chairlift, *Mill Valley*—the backside of the area—is readily accessible. Most of this terrain is advanced. In fact, there are only four intermediate trails and zero novice trails here. *Polaris Bowl* and *Andromeda Face* are both visible from the Southern Cross lift. *Polaris* drops skiers and boarders onto *Andromeda*, making this a long run full of ungroomed snow, bumps, and gladed tree skiing. For excessively steep riding in *Mill Valley*, stay high on the ridge until reaching the *Corona Glades*. These pitches are short, but steep and ungroomed. For long cruising runs or less aggressive terrain in *Mill Valley*, continue past *Corona Glades* and hit *Gemini* and the *Outer Limits*. These two trails combine for a wide-open freeway of gently rolling slopes.

Tye Bowl and the *Tye Mill* lift are each accessible from Big Chief. Skiers and boarders in search of air flock to this chair because of all the natural hits directly under the lift. While riding the chair, visitors see riders hurl themselves off of Tye Rock. Not only is this not a designated run, but it is also illegal—and dangerous. Needless to say, when the snow is deep, many rebellious skiers and boarders slip the rope lines and jump off the rock with little regard for the rules.

Also accessible from Tye lift is *Tye Bowl*, skied mostly by locals who can rip. Getting there requires skiing through a natural obstacle course of trees, short jumps, and rocks. Once into the bowl, there are several turns in untracked pow pow, even late in the day. This is a particularly good area to hit once the more accessible trails are skied out. From the top of the Tye lift, looking down the hill, stay directly under the chair lift. Only a few yards down,

Snowboarding **Highlights**

Stevens has built a killer terrain park dubbed *The Bent Monkey*. Accessible from the Brooks Chair, *The Bent Monkey* includes over 12 features. Boarders start at the top of *Broadway* and follow the park into *Brennan's Trail* while hitting tabletops, spines, jumps, and other manmade obstacles.

Stevens also builds a burly halfpipe about two-thirds of the way down *Broadway*. Approximately 300 feet long and covering 200 feet of vertical, the pipe is built and maintained by area crew members with a halfpipe grinder. The pipe features four- to six-foot trannies with seven- to eight-foot verts and 10- to 15-foot shelves.

take a hard right; cut under the chair here, and head into the trees. This is where the obstacle course begins. The trail, if it can be called that, gets narrow and steep. The best plan of attack is to find someone who knows the area well. After negotiating the obstacle course, snowriders are usually rewarded with a bowl full of fresh frosted flakes.

The Tye Mill chair is perfect for families of different ability levels. Aggressive skiers can ride under the chair and intermediates can make turns on *Skid Road* or *Crest Trail*. Both are superbly groomed, designated blue trails.

Seventh Heaven is likely the most popular trail for advanced and expert snowriders. From the top, there are several steep chutes that give a whole new meaning to double black diamond. On the front side, directly underneath the chair, lies the steepest in-bounds pitch on the mountain. Make sure the snow conditions are good when riding this run. Frequently, rain or daily temperature increases cause the snow to melt and then refreeze when the temperature drops during the night, and snowriders find themselves trying to set edges in ice. Wait for big snow days to tear up this gash of a run. A little further to the skier's left, snowriders charge down the *Bobby* and *Nancy Chute*. These steep, wooded runs give skiers and boarders much to contend with while ripping turns back to the chair. The backsides of *Seventh Heaven*, *Cloud Nine*, and *Rock Garden* are not as steep. However, they are much longer trails that provide several more turns.

Intermediate snowriders will find several finely manicured runs off the SkyLine Express. Most of the trails off SkyLine are long, rolling slopes perfect for laying tracks all day. The new quad services a large amount of gentle terrain near the base area. It is so gentle that skiers and boarders who don't carry enough speed have to pole and skate their way toward the next slope. This area tends to be a bit congested because most of the trails end here near the base area. Additionally, many of the lower-level ski and snowboard lessons take place on these runs.

Like all the major Washington ski areas, Stevens offers challenging terrain, tons of snow, and easy access from most of the major cities in the state. It's also like the others in that it doesn't offer much in the way of aprés-ski activities or mountainside lodging. Hence, the term *ski area* and not *ski resort*. Stevens is in the expansion mode, but only time will tell if the area can afford to develop mountain villages that offer more than just skiing—and attract thousands of visitors. On the other hand, Stevens still offers a great value. Skiers and boarders can ski for free on their birthday—yet another reason to call in sick or skip class.

More Fun in the Flakes

The Stevens Pass Nordic Center opened in 1992 and includes 15.5 miles (25 km) of broad, groomed terrain, with tracked **cross-country skiing** trails and an adjoining skating lane. The facility has a day lodge with rental equipment, food, retail, and instruction available. The center is five miles (8 km) east of the Stevens Pass summit, at Mill Creek. Rental equipment is available, including classic, skating, compact skis, and snowshoes.

Snow, Snow, Snow

The quality of the powder at Stevens, like the Summit, is highly dependent on the wind. An east wind blowing in the Strait of Juan de Fuca is a positive omen for Stevens Pass, as are colder temperatures in Wenatchee, which lies on the east side of the Cascades. The snow will be deep. Also, look for the weather person's observation of the Puget Sound Convergence Zone (CZ). The CZ is an area of moderate precipitation that usually occurs between Seattle and Everett after the passage of a cold front. Because Stevens lies downwind of the CZ, this pattern usually means the snow is falling at Stevens Pass.

Skier Services

🅢 Lift Tickets

Ages 13–61: $38/full-day, $33/half-day, $25/night • **Ages 7–12:** $25/full-day, $22/half-day, $21/night • **Ages 62–69:** $28/full-day, $25/half-day, $23/night • **Ages 6 & younger and Ages 70+:** $5/all times • **Beginner's Lift only:** $28/full-day, $25/half-day, $21/night • *Prices based on the 2000–2001 ski season.*

🅐 Nordic Trail Pass

$8/all ages • *Prices based on the 2000–2001 ski season.*

🚠 Rentals

Ski Rentals: Adults: $25/full-day, $21/half-day; Kids: $15/full-day, $13/half-day; 900 sets. Type of Gear: Rossignol, Atomic, Salomon, and Volant • **Snowboard Rentals:** $30/full-day, $26/half-day; 600 sets. Type of Gear: Rossignol, K2, Salomon, and Sims • *Prices based on the 2000–2001 ski season.*

🅑 Services

Ski School: 26 full-time, 200 part-time instructors; Private lessons $42/hour; Group lessons $50/hour; Beginner's package $44 (includes lift ticket, lesson, and rentals) • **Snowboard School:** 20 instructors; Private lessons $42/hours; Group lessons $50/hour; Beginner's package $42 (includes lift ticket, lesson, and rentals) • **Childcare:** Ages three months to 12 years. Reservations required. Call (206) 812–4510 for more information • *Prices based on the 2000–2001 ski season.*

Room & Board

▬ Lodging

Overnight accommodations are located throughout the Skykomish Valley area anywhere from 16 to 50 miles (26 to 80 km) away. The best bet is to head down the eastside of the mountains to Leavenworth. The romantic Bavarian Village is less than an hour away. See the Mission Ridge chapter (*page 142*) for lodging and dining options in Leavenworth.

On-site

Stevens has a designated RV overnight parking area with electrical hookups; rates $15/night.

Skykomish Valley–15 miles *(24 km)* away

SkyRiver Inn is a mid-range, family-oriented motel on the bank of the Skykomish River, 16 miles from Stevens Pass; rates $75–$150/night. 1–800–367–8194 or (360) 677–2261.

Sultan–42 miles *(68 km)* away

Dutch Cup Motel offers economy rooms with televisions and refrigerators in Sultan, 39 miles from Stevens Pass; rates $50–$85/night. 1–800–844–0488.

Wenatchee–58 miles *(93 km)* away

See the Mission Ridge chapter (*page 142*) for additional lodging and dining options.

⑪ Dining

On-site

Stevens Pass offers a total of five restaurants, two unique bars, three espresso bars, and a mini-market at the **Granite Peaks Lodge, Tye Creek Lodge**, and **Pacific Crest Lodge**. Cuisine includes deli sandwiches, pasta, oven-fired entrees, and grilled specialties.

The Summit at Snoqualmie

The Summit at Snoqualmie

P.O. Box 1068
Snoqualmie Pass, WA 98068

Ski Report: (425) 434–7669
Information: (425) 434–7669
E-mail: *thesummit.si@boothcreek.com*
Website: *www.summit-at-snoqualmie.com*
Credit Cards: All major

Operating Hours: 9 A.M.–10 P.M.
  Alpental and Summit West: Open daily
  Summit Central: Open Wednesday–Sunday
  Summit East: Open Saturday–Sunday in
  January and February
Season: December to mid April

Courtesy The Summit at Snoqualmie

Background

In the heart of the Washington Cascades, 52 miles east of Seattle, lies The Summit at Snoqualmie. Washington's largest resort is actually four separate ski areas: Alpental, Summit West (Snoqualmie), Summit Central (Ski Acres), and Summit East (Hyak). The Summit is also Washington's most accessible resort, which is its biggest draw. Any day of the week, Seattle-area skiers and boarders can escape the booming metropolis and its nightmarish traffic and literally be making turns in less than 75 minutes. Unfortunately, with an average elevation of 3,000 feet, the snow at The Summit is comparable to gloppy cottage cheese. And with the exception of three trails, The Summit also lacks long cruising runs, big open bowls, and powder fields.

But nighttime is the right time at The Summit, with snowriders rushing from work and school to get in a few evening turns. The Summit happens to be one of the largest night skiing facilities in the country. Roughly 70 percent of the area's skiable terrain can be skied after sundown. Those willing to ride under the light of the moon can even lay tracks on most of the remaining terrain.

Though now under one name and one owner (Booth Creek, Inc.), all four ski areas have distinct personalities, histories, and terrain. Alpental is a hard-core snowrider's mountain. Steep, challenging terrain and minimal amenities attract aggressive, high-caliber skiers and snowboarders. In contrast, Summit West is a gentle sloped hill, perfect for novice and lower intermediate skiers. Ask almost any Seattle native where they learned to ski, and most will say Summit West. Summit Central is somewhere between Alpental

Mountain Stats

The Summit at Alpental
Base Elevation: 3,200 feet *(976 m)*
Summit Elevation: 5,400 feet *(1,647 m)*
Vertical Drop: 2,200 feet *(671 m)*
Trail Classification: 10% beginner; 40% intermediate; 50% advanced/expert

Summit West
Base Elevation: 3,000 feet *(915 m)*
Summit Elevation: 3,900 feet *(1,189 m)*
Vertical Drop: 900 feet *(275 m)*
Trail Classification: 35% beginner; 45% Intermediate; 20% advanced/expert

Summit Central
Base Elevation: 2,860 feet *(872 m)*
Summit Elevation: 3,900 feet *(1,189 m)*
Vertical Drop: 1,040 feet *(317 m)*
Trail Classification: 50% beginner; 20% intermediate; 30% advanced/expert

Summit East
Base Elevation: 2,620 feet *(800 m)*
Summit Elevation: 3,700 feet *(1,128 m)*
Vertical Drop: 1,080 feet *(329 m)*
Trail Classification: 42% beginner; 40% intermediate; 18% advanced/expert

Primary Slope Direction: North
Annual Snowfall: 400 inches *(1,016 cm)/* all 4 areas
Skiable Days: 150
Skiable Terrain: 1,916 acres *(776 ha)*, plus 750 acres *(304 ha)* in the Alpental backcountry
Runs: 65
Lifts: 4 high-speed quads, 4 triples, 12 doubles, 2 magic carpets
Lift Capacity: 33,890 skiers per hour
Annual Visits: 400,000

and Summit West. The area has several challenging pitches but also has a fair amount of terrain that is novice/intermediate friendly. Summit East is the smallest of the areas and the least crowded.

In 1980, all four areas were purchased and consolidated by Ski Lifts Inc., which recently sold its stock to Booth Creek, Inc.—a Colorado-based corporation owned by the Gillette family. A demonstrated leader in the ski-resort industry, Chairman George N. Gillette, Jr. is responsible for bringing to prominence such world-renowned areas as Vail and Beaver Creek. Seattle area snowriders are already enjoying The Summit's recent upgrade—and still more improvements are on the way.

Over the next seven years, Booth Creek plans to pump another $30 million into the area. To date upgrades have included 12 new grooming machines, including a halfpipe grinder and two winch cats—a definite plus considering how inconsistent the weather can be at The Summit. Now, snowriders can count on excellent grooming no matter what the weather is doing.

All of the lodges have been remodeled as well: the new Timber Wolf Pub at Summit West; Rosita's Mexican restaurant (which replaces the old Alpenhaus cafeteria); and Trattoria Giorgio (an Italian restaurant that opened at Summit Central). But the best upgrades may be the addition of three new high-speed quads—the Pacific Crest quad at Summit West, the Armstrong's high-speed quad at Alpental, and the Central Express at Summit Central. Additional improvements are on the agenda but are ultimately contingent on the resort's budget and approval from the Forest Service. If things go well, guests will likely see more new lifts installed at The Summit.

Getting There

- **From Seattle, WA:** Take I-90 east to Exit 52 for Alpental and Summit West, and Exit 53 for Summit Central and Summit East. Follow signs to the ski area.
- **From Ellensburg and Cle Elum, WA:** Head west on I-90, using Exit 54 for Summit East and Exit 53 for all other areas. Follow signs to the ski area.
- **From Tacoma and South Puget Sound area:** Take I-5 north to U.S. 18. Follow U.S. 18 to I-90. Take I-90 east to Exit 52 for Alpental and Summit West and Exit 53 for Summit Central and Summit East. Follow signs to the ski area.

Bus Services: Beeline Tours offers a variety of ski packages with roundtrip bus service from Seattle. For more information call 1–800–959–8387 or check out *www.beelinetours.com*.

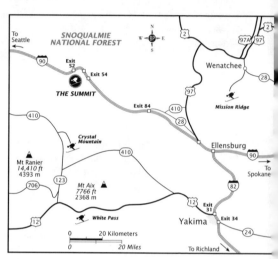

Resort Transportation: The Summit Shuttle Buses provide a free and convenient link between all the base lodge facilities at the Summit Friday night through Sunday day, and holidays.

Trail Profiles

Alpental at the Summit

Snowriders who learn to ski and snowboard at Alpental are equipped to ride anywhere in the world. From the top there is no easy way down. All the trails are steep and demanding. Every named run is rated with at least one black diamond, and many are double black diamonds. Moreover, the snow conditions at Alpental are erratic—a result of the fluctuations in temperature, a relatively low altitude, and the frequent rainfall. Which is why Alpental skiers and boarders have no choice but to become proficient snowriders.

At the peak, the snow can be wind-blown and—more often then not—skied off. The terrain is so steep that with each turn, the quality snow is shaved off and pushed down the fall line. Also, Alpental frequently receives rain at the top of the mountain. When followed by freezing temperatures, rain may turn the first 10 to 15 turns to ice—rock-hard and ice blue on occasion.

Typically mid mountain is where the best snow is found. As the runs bottom out, the fall lines are less serious. The lighter snow that has been pushed down the mountain because of the steepness tends to build up, creating a soft blanket of hero snow. In addition, many of the lower narrow chutes are somewhat sheltered from the changing weather conditions. More stable temperatures make for more consistent snow. Because the temperatures at the top of Alpental are consistently five to 10 degrees colder than at the bottom of the mountain, expect to finish your run in the notorious "Cascade Concrete."

From the top, riders and skiers have two major choices: *Edelweiss Bowl* or *International*. *Edelweiss* is a medium-sized bowl with four steep, narrow chutes and just one semi-open run. Jagged peaks and huge cornices surround 75 percent of the bowl. Wanna-be extreme snowriders often pull

What Snow Will It Be Today?

The overall snow quality at The Summit largely depends on which direction the wind is blowing. Winds originating in the east bring cold air into Snoqualmie Pass creating conditions that favor dry snow. West winds bring in warm, moist air from the Pacific Ocean, producing the infamous "Cascade Concrete." For light, quality snow, Washington's coastal dwellers should look for an east wind in the Straits of Juan de Fuca. East winds in the Strait most likely mean east winds at The Summit. Also, pay attention to the temperatures in Yakima and Wenatchee. The colder it is on the east side of the Cascades, the colder the air blowing through The Summit. The result is lighter and softer snow.

off illegal stunts on the cliffs that surround trails like *Rollen* and *The Fan*. On big powder days they can cop as much as 40 feet of air. For some, the best part is that most of the cliffs are visible from the bottom of the chairlift. Big drops are guaranteed to earn loud cheers from folks standing in line. However, the reason these no-guts-no-glory skiers and riders can pull maneuvers like this is because they have the skills and the chutzpah!

"*Nash*," the local's affectionate nickname for *International*, is as steep as it gets in-bounds. The upper third of the trail is at least a 50-degree pitch. And even trickier are the two entrances to *International*. Both are intimidating. The first 20 feet or so are usually scraped off due to the high traffic in the entrances and the steepness of the terrain. The first few turns may be on rock-hard ice, but the gut of *International* is a fabulous ride. Each edge set

causes miniature avalanches of cascading snow. It's terrain like *International* that makes for spectacular footage in Warren Miller ski flicks. In fact, Alpental was featured in Miller's 1998 film *Freeriders*. The steepest pitch on *International* is to the skier's right.

Following the right side of *International* will leads skiers and boarders to the entrance of *Adrenaline*. A narrow traverse between a high rock band and several evergreen trees spits them out onto its steep face. Ski far right again, and it becomes abundantly clear just how appropriate the name *Adrenaline* is. It's even steeper than *International*. Because of its location on the mountain, the far right side of *Adrenaline* is less cut up than the rest of the trail. Here lies the best snow on the mountain.

After surviving the intensely cool but somewhat hairball descent of *Adrenaline*, skiers and boarders find themselves on *Lower Nash*. *Lower Nash* is typically a mixture of wicked bumps and sloppy mashed potatoes, and it couldn't come at a worse time. Carving up *International* and *Adrenaline* is hell on the thighs. Next comes monstrous moguls with a layer of heavy crud on top. After abusing their knees at Alpental, skiers can take pride in knowing that they can ride almost anywhere in the world under any conditions.

After big dumps, this upper area is often closed in the early morning to allow the ski patrol to conduct avalanche control work. On good snow days, however, powder mongers stand in line at the bottom of Chair 2, the Edelweiss double, to ride to the top. They know just how good first tracks can be when the upper runs are blanketed in fresh snow. Hardcore Alpental fans have been known to wait as long as two hours to carve a bowl of freshies. There is nothing quite like linking turns in a foot of fresh light powder on Alpental's precariously challenging pitches.

Alpental also offers snowriders a uniquely old-fashioned ski experience. Over 750 acres of cliffs, steep chutes, and 500-year-old forest are open for skiing in the Alpental backcountry. While unpatrolled and unmarked, Alpental's backcountry is a wicked adventure. A high, narrow traverse takes skiers and boarders out to lay tracks in untouched virgin snow nearly every day of the week. Just be sure to check in first with the Pro Patrol. Before snowriders can legally enter the backcountry on their own, they must sign up for and take a backcountry tour with the patrollers. After the tour, the patrollers will provide backcountry passes. Always carry avalanche beacons and snow shovels and only venture into the backcountry with an experienced guide.

Courtesy The Summit at Snoqualmie

Summit West

Summit West, or Snoqualmie, was the first of the four areas to begin operating. During the early 1930s, a hardcore group of world-class jumpers hiked to the top of the Beaver Lake Hill and competed on a jump built by the Seattle Ski Club. Interest in the sport by both jumpers and skiers grew rapidly, prompting the Seattle Parks Department to apply for a permit from the United States Forest Service to establish an official ski area. In 1937, Webb Moffett founded Ski Lifts, Inc. and installed a rope tow near the site of the present-day Pacific Crest quad. When World War II erupted, Webb and his partner continued to run the area, gambling on the hope that Northwest skiers would maintain their enthusiasm for the sport. The gamble paid off. Devoted skiers pooled their gas ration coupons and continued to make the drive up Snoqualmie Summit. The biggest draw at The Pass, as it would later be known, was its quick and easy access to Seattle.

Encouraged by his success in the face of war times, Webb focused his attention and energy on further developing the area. In an innovative move, Snoqualmie became the country's first night-skiing area. Webb installed old gas-station lights so his employees could ski after the customers had gone home. Today, many skiers strap on their boards to make turns under the midnight sun.

The terrain at Summit West is perfect for novice and lower intermediate skiers. With the exception of the *Thunderbird* trail, the area consists of gently rolling hills that bottom out into a wide-open flat area in front of the lodges. Anyone who can link turns and stop can ski nearly anywhere on the hill. The terrain is mostly devoid of trees and obstacles and groomed into smooth corduroy.

Seven ski schools operate at Summit West, and on weekends there are numerous instructors teaching the finer points of wedge turns. For aggressive skiers the biggest attraction at Summit West is its City League Racing programs. The slopes are good enough for fast but not too heavily pitched slalom courses. Snowboarders are attracted to the interesting terrain park and 600-foot halfpipe.

Summit Central

Summit Central (Ski Acres) grew and prospered right next door to Snoqualmie. Ray Tanner purchased privately owned land (unlike Summit West, which is primarily on Forest Service land) and opened Ski Acres in 1948. Tanner installed two rope tows near the current location of the Holiday chairlift. One year later, he built the first chair lift in the Washington Cascades—an old single chair to the top. This marked the beginning of a friendly competition with Moffett that would last until 1980.

In the late 1970s, Ski Lifts, Inc. acquired Ski Acres, combining the area's two largest ski areas into a single operation. Since then, Ski Acres made an enormous improvement by adding the Triple 60 chair, which replaced the single chair in 1983. The area expanded significantly when the Silver Fir triple chair was completed and the Nordic Center opened in 1988.

Summit Central offers excellent night riding. Almost everything skiable during the day is skiable at night. Several of the runs provide aggressive fall-line skiing. While they are short runs—only about 1,100 feet—they are a blast. Groups of local ski instructors chase each other around the mountain trying to squeeze in as many runs before the lifts close for the night.

Triple 60 is always full of wacky moguls, making its gut a tough line—even for expert skiers. More often than not, the bumps are as big as Volkswagen Beetles. *Rip Cord* is basically a stump farm. Daring skiers line up to catch air off the snow-covered stumps. *Parachute* is also a local favorite. The steep pitch usually has the best snow on the mountain and the most consistent bumps. Additionally, this is where the Summit West *Cross Over Trail* enters into Summit Central. Many intermediate snowriders who are intimidated by *Parachute* cut a traverse right across the upper third of the run, making for a great launching pad. The area to the skier's far left of *Parachute* offers the best snow and is usually less skied out.

Summit East

Summit West and Summit Central are connected via a crossover trail, accessible from the top of Triple 60 chair and the Thunderbird chair. One lift ticket allows visitors to ski both areas. The same ticket also gets them on to the lifts at Alpental, via a shuttle bus. For that one low price, skiers can also lay tracks at Summit East (Hyak)—the last and smallest area of the four. Summit East can be reached via the Silver Fir chair and the *Cross Over Trail* on the far east side of Summit Central.

Ski Lifts Inc. purchased Summit East in 1992 from Pacific West. The area's biggest draw is its lack of crowds. There are no lift lines here—zero, zilch, nada. Summit East is open on Saturdays and Sundays in January and February. And though the area's best skiing is in the trees, Summit East is the lowest of the areas, and the snow quality can suffer considerably because of its elevation.

Snowboarding Highlights

Snowboarders have also benefited from The Summit's new owners, as evidence by a newly purchased halfpipe grooming machine. The area now sports two halfpipes and a terrain park at Summit West and a halfpipe at Summit Central. All three pipes and the park are lit for night riding. They are so popular that even after the area shuts down for the season, boarders continue to ride them as long as the snow remains.

Each halfpipe has been built to Olympic specifications, including 60-foot-wide decks. The extra large walkways kept the area from having to rebuild the pipes. Instead, the resort just groomed it four or five times a week with a pipe grinder. Snowboarders may remember the old halfpipe at Summit West, near the base of the Triple 60 face. This pipe has been moved to the midway point of *Alpine Bowl*. The move ensures not only more snow, but better quality snow from which to construct the halfpipe.

The terrain park is at Summit West. Known as *Area 52* because it's located off Interstate 90's Exit 52, the park is full of tabletops, jumps, banked turns, rollerz, tri-angle jumps, and spines. Depending on snow conditions, there may be as many as 25 obstacles in the park. The Pacific Crest quad services both pipes and *Area 52*.

More Fun in the Flakes

The new Nordic Center, formerly the Ski Acres & Hyak Cross Country Center, offers **cross-country skiing** on 34 miles (55 km) of machine-groomed trails. The lower trails, best suited for beginners, are open for night skiing and also host a popular, season-long Wednesday night racing series. The upper trails are accessible from the Silver Fir Trail. Roughly 31 miles (50 km) of trails wind around the base of the beautiful Mount Catherine.

The Nordic Center is located at the base of the Silver Fir and offers rentals, a learning center, a trailside café, and an accessory shop. For those looking to make their first tracks, private and group lessons abound for skiers of all abilities. There is also a Nordic Tuesday Night Race Series on a lighted trail system. Leave work by 5:00 P.M. and leave the competition in the frost by 6:30 P.M.

For those interested in **snowshoeing**, snowshoes are available at the Nordic Center to rent or purchase, and $5 covers the trail fee pass. Combination rental and trail pass packages are also available.

For **snow tubing**, visitors should seek out The Summit Tubing Center, located on what area management calls Mount Tubemore, on the east side of the Summit Central parking lot. Kids of all ages will love piloting their tubes down smoothly groomed runs. At the bottom, a tow takes tubers back up the hill. Open Friday to Sunday, the Tubing Center charges $7/session for ages 12 and older and $5/session for ages 11 and younger—includes both lift access and tube rental.

Skier Services

🅢 Lift Tickets

Ages 18–64: $34/day and $20/night • **Ages 12–17:** $27/day and $15/night • **Ages 7–11:** $20/day and $15/night • **Ages 6 & younger:** $7/day and $7/night • **Ages 65+:** $15/day and $15/night • *Prices based on the 2000–2001 ski season.*

🏔 Nordic Trail Passes

Adults: $9 • **Children and Seniors:** $7

🎿 Rentals

Ski & Snowboard Rentals: $17–$24/adults; $13/ages 6 & younger • *Prices based on the 2000–2001 ski season.*

🏂 Services

Ski & Snowboard School: Private lesson $45/hour; Group lesson $35/hour; Beginner's package $45 (includes lift ticket, lessons, and rentals) • **Nordic School:** Group Lesson $20; Nordic package $30 (includes trail pass, lesson, and rentals) • *Prices based on the 2000–2001 ski season.*

Room & Board

Though the area is just an hour from Seattle, on-site accommodations are available at the Summit Inn. There are also a few choices for lodging and dining in nearby Snoqualmie.

🛏 Lodging

On-site

Summit Inn is located at The Summit at Snoqualmie Ski Resort. The lodge offers 80 quiet rooms, king and queen beds, a restaurant, lounge, pool, sauna, and hot tub; prices and package deals vary. 1–800–557–7829 or (425) 434–6300 or *www.summit-at-snoqualmie.com/winter/lodging*.

Snoqualmie

Frantzian Mountain Hideaway Bed & Breakfast has a cozy Bavarian Alpine setting with private apartment, close proximity to skiing, washer and dryer, and plenty of room for the family; rates $75–$125+/night. (425) 434–6370 or *www.moriah.com/frantzian* • **Salish Lodge** is a lodge from olden times complete with a large stone fireplace, overstuffed chairs, and a beamed ceiling; rates $129–$429/night. 1–800–826–6124 or (206) 888–2556.

🍽 Dining

On-site

The Summit offers at least three or four choices for dining before and after skiing at each of the following areas: **Alpental, Summit West, Summit Central, Summit East, Nordic Center,** and **Tubing Center.** Fare includes Mexican, Italian, and American cuisine, and lounges, cafes, and delis.

Snoqualmie

The Herbfarm is a small country restaurant with an herb-dominated menu; reservations recommended. (206) 784–2222 • **Salish Lodge Restaurant** overlooks the falls and serves Northwest seafood and game. (206) 888–2556.

Team Ski Racing: City League

The City League Series is one of the largest amateur ski race leagues in the country. The side-by-side format, adult team ski and snowboarding race program is composed of nine leagues in Washington and Oregon: four leagues at Alpental at the Summit, three leagues at Summit West and one league at Mount Hood Meadows and Mount Hood Ski Bowl in Oregon. Participation includes over 175 teams with over 20,000 races per season. Races are held mid-week at night.

It's drag racing at its best. Each team member races opponents on other teams of equal speed and ability. Teams are made up of mixed ability skiers and can have up to 10 members. Six members on each team race each week and are "pre-paired" prior to racing. Racers ski two runs each, once on each dual course.

City League is a seven-week team ski racing series for skiers and snowboarders of all abilities. Courses are wide open GS Style and are negotiable for intermediates with no race experience. For more information, call or write to: **City League**, 2405 ½ 10th Avenue E, Seattle, WA 98102 • (206) 323-4573 • 1-888-323-4573

49° North Mtn Resort

49° North Mountain Resort
3311 Flowery Trail Road
Chewelah, WA 99109

Ski Report: (509) 880–9208
Information: (509) 935–6649
E-mail: *ski49n@ski49n.com*
Website: *www.ski49n.com*
Credit Cards: Visa, MasterCard, & AMEX

Operating Hours: 9 A.M.–4 P.M. Friday–Tuesday

Season: Late November to early April

Photo courtesy 49° North Mountain Resort

Background

Situated on the southern border of the Colville National Forest in Northeastern Washington, 49° North Mountain Resort is named for its location on the 49th parallel from the equator. While it may be thousands of miles away from the tropics, 49° North is only an hour from Spokane. Snow riding here is like stepping back in time when there weren't any big cities, miles of highways, and billions of people on the planet—meaning, it's a rare day that guests find lift lines waiting for them at the bottom of the area's 42 runs.

Two million acres of pristine forest spread out in all directions from Chewelah Peak (5,774 feet), which is located in the lower region of the Selkirk Mountain Range. Roughly 300 inches of annual snow blanket the 1,100 acres of terrain that form the ski area. On a clear day, the view of the Pend-Orielle River Valley and the Kettle Range to the northeast is spectacular and free of even a hint of freeway traffic noise. The only access into 49° North is on two-lane Flowery Trail Road. Guests are alone with the sound of their boards carving arcs through the soft, dry snow of the Inland Northwest.

New ownership has aggressively pursued transforming this virtually unknown winter playground into a family ski destination. Amenities are adequate, but visitors find some unique perks to make their ski experience at 49° North all the more worthwhile, including relatively cheap lift tickets, free midweek childcare, complimentary group beginner lessons, and Friday-night group skiing lessons for teenagers 13 and older—no parents allowed!

171

Mountain Stats

Base Elevation: 3,956 feet *(1,207 m)*
Summit Elevation: 5,774 feet *(1,761 m)*
Vertical Drop: 1,852 feet *(565 m)*
Primary Slope Direction: North
Annual Snowfall: 300 inches *(762 cm)*
Skiable Days: 120
Skiable Terrain: 1,100 acres *(446 ha)*
Runs: 42

Longest Run: 2.5 miles *(4 km)*
Lifts: 4 doubles, 1 rope tow
Lift Capacity: 4,200 skiers per hour
Terrain Classification: 25% novice; 40% intermediate; 30% advanced; 5% expert
Night Skiing: Special occasions only
Snowmaking: None
Annual Visits: 55,000–60,000

Getting There

- **From Spokane International Airport:** Travel east on U.S. 2 to I-90 East. Take the Division Street exit and go north through Spokane. Division Street becomes U.S. 395. Take U.S. 395 approximately 48 miles (77 km) to Chewelah, WA, and turn right at the traffic signal onto Flowery Trail Road. Follow this road for 10 miles to the ski area.

- **From Seattle, WA:** Take I-90 east to Spokane. Take the Division Street exit and go north through Spokane. Division Street becomes U.S. 395. Take U.S. 395 approximately 48 miles (77 km) to Chewelah, WA, and turn right at the traffic signal onto Flowery Trail Road. Follow this road for 10 miles to the ski area.

- **From Coeur d'Alene, ID:** Take I-90 west to Spokane. Take the Division Street exit and go north through Spokane. Division Street becomes U.S. 395. Take U.S. 395 approximately 48 miles (77 km) to Chewelah, WA, and turn right at the traffic signal onto Flowery Trail Road. Follow this road for 10 miles to the ski area.

Airport Services: Spokane International Airport (GEG) is serviced by most major carriers and is clearly the best place to land if flying in to the resort. 49° North is about one hour's drive north of Spokane. Rental cars are available at the airport.

Trail Profiles

At the base of the resort there are four chairlifts and a rope tow providing access to the area. The chairlift circuit is in good working condition, but there aren't any high-speed quads on the mountain. Despite the chairs being a little slow, the good news is that there usually aren't any lift lines.

All 42 trails are almost completely below the treeline, which allows for consistently good visibility, relatively gentle weather conditions, and high-quality snow. With just over 300 inches of snowfall a year, it's no wonder *Powder Magazine's* readers voted 49° North the best-kept powder secret in the Northwest.

Snowriders of all abilities often start with a ride up Chair One, which transports them to the top of Chewelah Peak and provides access to every type of terrain the resort has to offer. Novice skiers and boarders enjoy *Silver Ridge*—the area's signature run. *Silver's* wide cut through the trees and easy grade provide hundreds of confidence-building turns. The length of the run is a welcome contrast to the typical bottom-of-the-mountain turf beginners get at other resorts. The combination of the finely groomed slope and serpentine twist near the end keep things interesting without putting novices in over their heads. More experienced snowriders find *Silver Ridge* to be a great warm-up run.

Terribly timid beginners can spend their time on *Payday*, the resort's third chair. There are six trails to choose from in this quiet, isolated tract. Each lies near the base and offers just a touch of pitch to allow for a comfortable learning experience.

Adventuring intermediates should include *Mahres Gold*—accessed from Chair One—on their list of runs. Named after the Washington Mahre Brothers, who captured Olympic Gold and Silver medals in the mid 1980s, this challenging run is fast at the top and gentle as it winds toward the base of the resort. To reach *Mahres Gold*, unload from Chair One, hang a left, then cut back underneath the chair near the top. Blue-run skiers might also try *Lost Dutchman* on the mountain's far side. One of the longest runs on the hill, *Lost Dutchman* is off-camber from top to bottom. Skiers treasure the wide-open cruising, but for snowboarders, the trail is tough on the calves.

Experienced skiers and boarders won't be able to resist the trees of *Powder Keg* or the burly terrain on *Klondike*. *Klondike* follows the Chair One towers with a rock n' roll mogul field down its right-hand side. Farther to the right, *Powder Keg* is a fairly steep gladed tree area. The run earned its name from the explosive nature of the bone-dry snow found in the trees. We're talking face shots all day long.

Photo courtesy 49° North Mountain Resort

More unreal tree skiing can be found in *Cy's Glades*, named for Cy Levine, who introduced skiing here in the late 1920s. These glades offer the mountain's steepest skiing, and as such, they see little traffic.

49° North regulars spend tons of time in the *Sluice Box* and in the treeline along *Last Chance*. Both are rated black-diamond and are accessible from Chair Four. They offer up 1,200 feet of perfect fall-line snowriding, with no cat track disturbances or funny angles. It's just straight up and down through fabulous wind-shielded snow. Because there's almost never a line on Chair Four, skiers and boarders can churn and burn laps on these runs all day long.

More Fun in the Flakes

49° North offers 6.2 miles (10 km) of **cross-country skiing** trails. In particular, there's the 1.2-mile (2-km) *Little Larch loop* and an out-and-back on the 4,800-foot *Road Trail*.

Snowboarding **Highlights**

Chair Two, the Grubstake, provides an exclusive entrance into 49° North's snowboard park. With the only Pipe Dragon in the Inland Northwest, the resort pulls off an Olympic-size halfpipe every year that runs 350 feet long, 12 feet tall, and 48 feet wide. Above the pipe is a snowboard park replete with natural and manmade obstacles, including tabletops, spines, a quarterpipe, and hits both big and small. The park continues to grow each year as the new owners dedicate more resources and time. Their goal is to develop the park into the region's best, and they're well on their way to accomplishing that.

49° North also offers intense backcountry freeriding in the *East Basin*. The steepness of the terrain keeps traffic to a minimum, allowing fresh turns all day long. From the top of Chair One, hang a right, stay above *Silver Ridge*, and head into the trees. Both the sign and the trail are easy to spot. After a few hundred yards, the trail opens up to a large gladed area. By virtue of its eastern location on the mountain, the snow tends to be drier here than anywhere else. It may just be the best snow on the mountain.

Skier Services

🔊 Lift Tickets

Ages 18–61: $25/midweek, $30/weekends and holidays • **Ages 62–69 and Students (Ages 16 & older):** $22/midweek, $24/weekends and holidays • **Ages 7–15:** $20/midweek, $22/weekends and holidays • **Ages 70 & older:** $6/day • **Ages 6 & younger:** Free • *Prices based on the 2000–2001 ski season.*

🎿 Rentals

Ski Rentals: Ages 16 & older: $20/day; Ages 7–15: $18/day; Ages 6 & younger: $12/day; 300 sets. Type of Gear: Elan, Olins, and Rossignol • **Snowboard Rentals:** Ages 16 & older: $25/day; Ages 7–15: $20/day, Ages 6 & younger: $18/day; 150 sets. Type of Gear: K2, Burton, Morrow, Killer Loop, and Rossignol • There's a demo center for snowblades and snow bikes are available • *Prices based on the 2000–2001 ski season.*

🏫 Services

Ski, Snowboard, Nordic, & Telemark School: 60 instructors; Private lessons $28/hour or $48/ two hours; Free beginner group lessons • **49ers Club:** Ski and snowboard lessons for ages 5–10; Lessons are $19–$29 depending on time of day and length of lesson; lift tickets and rentals are an additional $10 • **Childcare:** The resort's licensed daycare program is free to guests midweek (non-holiday periods) and is $3.50/hour on weekends and holidays. Call (509) 935-6649 for more information • *Prices based on the 2000–2001 ski season.*

Room & Board

The quaint town of Chewelah, roughly 10 miles down Flowery Trail Road from 49° North, hosts the closest accommodations. Surrounded by mountains, Chewelah is home to friendly people who understand what living in a small community is all about. Chewelah offers its guests a handful of restaurants and a couple of comfortable motels. Begin the day with a cup of coffee and a bite to eat at **The Neighbors Café** on the corner of Main Street and U.S. Route 395. The price is right, the food is hearty, and the pastries are out of this world. When it's time to hang up the sleds, the **Nordlig Motel** has an inviting hot tub and warm, comfortable beds for your tired muscles. There isn't any nightlife to speak of in town, but early to bed and early to rise means first tracks in the morning.

■ Lodging

Chewelah–10 miles *(16 km)* away

New 49er Motel and RV Park offers 13 rooms, a pool, Jacuzzi, kitchenettes, and 28 RV spaces; rates $35–$50/night. (509) 935–8613 • **Nordlig Motel** offers a spa, free continental breakfast, and affordable prices; rates $39–$60/night. (509) 935–6704 or *www.panorama-land.com/nordlig* • Call the Chewelah Chamber of Commerce toll-free at 1–877–243–9352 or visit them at *www.chewelah.org* for more options.

Colville–28 miles *(45 km)* away

Colville Comfort Inn is located in the center of activity with 53 rooms; rates $44–$125/night. (509) 684–2010 • **Downtown Motel** has 18 rooms; rates $36–$66/night. (509) 684–2565 • **Lake House** is a fully equipped and furnished cabin on the lake with two bedrooms, two baths, a hot tub, canoes, deck, and barbecue. Rates depend on number of nights of occupancy, decreasing with number of nights; rates $90–$110. (509) 684–5132.

⑪ Dining

Colville–28 miles *(45 km)* away

Angler's Grill & Trophy Room serves seafood, burgers, and sandwiches. (509) 685–1308 • **Cookie's Café** serves burgers, sandwiches, soups, daily specials, and delicious pie. (509) 684–8660 • **Pizza Factory** serves a variety of pizzas, pastas, sandwiches, lasagna, and calzones. (509) 684–5000 • **Whistle Stop Diner** has an eclectic atmosphere and serves a delicious eggs, potatoes, and meat breakfast, and lunch with home-baked turkey, the best meats, and sandwiches. (509) 684–3424.

Mount Spokane

Mount Spokane Ski & Snowboard
Spokane, WA 99021

Ski Report: (509) 443–1397
Information: (509) 238–2220 ext. 215
E-mail: *ski@mtspokane.com*
Website: *www.mtspokane.com*
Credit Cards: Visa & MasterCard

Operating Hours: 9 A.M.–4 P.M. daily
Night Skiing: 4 P.M.–9 P.M. Wednesday–Saturday

Season: Early December to mid April

Background

A noted teaching resort, Mount Spokane sits only 30 miles from Washington's largest eastern city, Spokane, and within shouting distance of the Idaho/Washington border. Ask many of the local Spokanites where they learned to turn, and they'll likely fess up that it was at Mount Spokane. The area's focus on providing a solid foundation of skiing and snowboarding fundamentals, proximity to Spokane, and night skiing on 60 percent of the mountain are the main reasons snowriders frequent the area. Despite lift tickets being so cheap, roughly $27 on weekends and holidays, the area stays financially healthy.

As a nonprofit, managing entity Spokane 2000 pumps all profits into improving the resort. A five-year plan has Spokane 2000 slated to develop the backside of the mountain and add additional tree runs. Mount Spokane has been known to have its share of fog, so more trails through the trees will provide more visibility as well as additional terrain.

177

Mountain Stats

Base Elevation: 3,818 feet *(1,164 m)*
Summit Elevation: 5,883 feet *(1,794 m)*
Vertical Drop: 2,065 feet *(630 m)*
Annual Snowfall: 180 inches *(457 cm)*
Skiable Terrain: 2,500 acres *(1,013 ha)*
Runs: 38
Longest Run: 8,000 feet *(2,439 m)*

Lifts: 5 double chairs
Lift Capacity: 5,000 skiers per hour
Terrain Classification: 20% novice; 50% intermediate; 30% advanced
Night Skiing: 60% allowance
Annual Visits: 100,000

Getting There

- **From Spokane, WA:** Travel north on U.S. 395 (Division Street). Follow U.S. 395 to U.S. 2. Head east on U.S. 2 until you reach WA 206. WA 206 ends at the ski resort.
- **From Coeur d'Alene, ID:** Take I-90 west to the Argonne Road exit. Follow Argonne Road, which changes to Bruce Road, north for 4 miles (6.4 km). Turn right on WA 206. WA 206 ends at the ski resort.

Trail Profiles

Novice and intermediate snowriders love Mount Spokane. And with good reason: 70 percent of the area comprises blue and green trails. In addition, the area recently purchased two state-of-the-art grooming machines. Trails are groomed nightly, making beginners and intermediates even happier.

Novice riders will spend most of their time on *Ego Flats* learning edge control and steering techniques. Accessible via a short lift on Chair 5, *Ego Flats* is a football-sized area that is parking-lot flat—making it a perfect place to learn.

Chair 3 provides great access to a good chunk of the mountain, most of which is intermediate terrain. *Northwest Passage, Nastar,* and *New Bowl* are all wide-open blue runs with fun fall lines. They also deposit skiers and boarders back at the base of Chair 3. To reach Chair 4 and the outer boundary of the area, cruise down the long intermediate trail of *Lamonga Pass.* On the other side of Chair 4, *Ridge Run* is another long blue trail.

Bump-runners will want to check out the *Two Face* slope below Chair 2. It's a perfect pitch of moguls for hotshot ski instructors to show off their abilities and win the respect of their students. *Two Face* earns its name from the resort grooming one side flat, with steep terrain ideal for carving, and leaving the other side open for moguls. Chair 2 is just above the main lodge at the end of the road. Take Chair 5 and then slide over to 2.

At the top of Chair 2, the wind can whip, but the views on a clear day are spectacular. Coeur d'Alene, downtown Spokane, and at least 17 lakes can be seen from the peak of Mount Spokane. When skiers and boarders have finished gawking, there's a great tree run through the *Meadows* that leads virtually all the way downhill. There's also the *Northwest Passage*, which snowboarders can take to reach the *Terrain Park*, as well as a few off-shoots to *Gates Park* and *Lost 200*—narrower runs banked by tight forest.

Via Chair 2, the western side of the hill is also accessible. Super-wide *Tea Kettle* run or *No Alibi* are less crowded most days than the runs along Chairs 2 and 3. From this area, drop down to the base of Chair 1 and the old lodge, creatively called Lodge Number One. There are plenty of runs and plenty of room to spend a good portion of the day on Chair 1.

Snowboarding Highlights

Mount Spokane has laid out the welcome mat for snowboarders, despite lacking a halfpipe. Riders will discover a killer terrain park best described as a boardercross course. Over 500 yards long, the park drops 750 vertical feet as it winds its way down the mountain through multiple hits and manmade obstacles, including tabletops, banked turns, spines, rollerz, and an old car that riders rail off. The park is accessible from the top of Chair 3, about a third the way down the *Northwest Passage* trail. The park is constructed by area crew members and local riders, groomed twice a week, and is lit for night riding as well.

More Fun in the Flakes

There are 15.5 miles (25 km) worth of track for **cross-country skiing**, operated by the State Parks Department and available on the other side of valley, only two miles from Mount Spokane. The trails are groomed five days a week and require just a snow park permit to ski. For Nordic ski conditions call (509) 239-4025.

Skier Services

Lift Tickets

Ages 21–61: $27/full-day, $24/half-day, $12/night • **Ages 16–20, students, and Ages 62+:** $24/full-day, $21/half-day, $12/nigh • **Ages 7–15:** $21/full-day, $18/half-day, $12/night • **Ages 6 & younger:** Free • *Prices based on the 2000–2001 ski season.*

Rentals

Ski Rentals: $22/all ages; 500 sets. Type of Gear: Dynastar shaped skis, DNR, Osin, and Nidecker • **Snowboard Rentals:** $26/all ages; 400 sets. Type of Gear: Original Sin • *Prices based on the 2000–2001 ski season.*

🏫 Services

Ski School: 30 instructors; Private lessons $35/hour; Group lessons $15/90 minutes; Beginner's package $35 (includes lift ticket, lesson, and rentals) • **Snowboard School:** 35 instructors; Private lessons $35/hour; Group lessons $15/90 minutes; Beginner's package $39 (includes lift ticket, lesson, and rentals) • *Prices based on the 2000–2001 ski season.*

Room & Board

🛏 Lodging

Spokane–30 miles *(48km)* away
Park Lane Motel, Suites & RV Park offers full kitchens, two-bedroom suites, continental breakfast, and 18 RV stalls; rates $45–$85/night. 1–800–533–1626 or *www.cet.com/~parklane* • **Travelodge** offers rooms and suites, a fitness room, complimentary breakfast bar, and 80 rooms; rates $60–$110/night. 1–800–578–7878 or *www.spokanetravelodge.com* • **Angelica's Bed & Breakfast** is a turn-of-the-century mansion with four guestrooms, accommodates overnight stays, corporate events, and special occasions; rates $90–$110/night. 1–800–987–0053 or *www.angelicasbb.com* • **Oslo's Bed & Breakfast** features two guest rooms in a comfortable Norwegian atmosphere with Scandinavian cuisine, and a large terrace overlooking the garden; rates $65–$85/night. (509) 838–3175 • **Solar World** offers fully equipped and furnished townhouse suites at daily, weekly, and monthly rates. 1–800–650–6530 or (509) 468–1207 or *www.rent.net/ads/solar* • *Call Spokane Visitors and Tourism at 1–800–248–3230 or visit them at www.visitspokane.com for more options.*

Deer Park–23 miles (37km) away
Love's Victorian Bed & Breakfast offers a romantic country setting with waterfalls, a pond, private baths, and three guestrooms; rates $85–$125/night. (509) 276–6939 or *www.bbhost.com/lovesvictorian.*

🍴 Dining

On-site
The ski area has a day lodge with a large cafeteria for a quick bite to eat and a nice bar area for a more relaxing time.

Spokane–30 miles *(48km)* away
Patsy Clark's is a turn-of-the-century mansion, lavishly decorated, and serves continental cuisine. (509) 838–8300 • **Cannon Street Grill** serves a delicious traditional breakfast, a Sunday brunch, and a lunch of burgers, sandwiches, specialty salads, and entrees. (509) 456–8660 • **The Downtown Onion** serves burgers and beer; a pressed-tin ceiling and affordable prices make this a good eat. (509) 747–3852 • **The Elks Lodge** serves delicious traditional American food like burgers, pizza, chicken, seafood, and ribs. (509) 926–2328.

Ski Bluewood

Ski Bluewood
262 East Main
Dayton, WA 99328

Ski Report: (509) 382–2877
Information: (509) 382–4725
 Tri-cities: (509) 545–6651
 Walla Walla: (509) 529–9585
E-mail: *bluewood@bmi.bet*
Website: *www.atplay.com/bluewood (unofficial)*
Credit Cards: Visa & MasterCard

Operating Hours: 9 A.M. to 4 P.M. daily (closed Mondays except on holidays)

Season: Mid November to mid April

Background

Ski Bluewood is one of Washington's best-kept secrets. Perched high atop the Blue Mountains, just 54 miles northeast of Walla Walla in Southeast Washington, Bluewood has the second-highest base elevation (4,450 feet) in the state—and possibly the best snow as well. The Blue Mountains rise out of a desert region, providing clear skies and cold, smoke powder that totals over 300 inches annually. With only 24 trails on its 400-plus acres and no high-speed quads, Bluewood is hardly a large resort, but snowriders searching for soft, dry, forgiving pow pow need look no farther than Bluewood.

Mountain Stats

Base Elevation: 4,450 feet *(1,357 m)*
Summit Elevation: 5,650 feet *(1,723 m)*
Vertical Drop: 1,200 feet *(366 m)*
Primary Slope Direction: North
Annual Snowfall: 300 inches *(762 cm)*
Skiable Days: 150
Skiable Terrain: 430 acres *(174 ha)*
Runs: 24

Longest Run: 2 miles *(6.4 km)*
Lifts: 3 triples, 1 tow lift
Lift Capacity: 3,950 skiers per hour
Terrain Classification: 27% novice; 43% intermediate; 30% advanced
Night Skiing: None
Snowmaking: None
Annual Visits: 54,000

Getting There

- **From Walla Walla, WA:** Take U.S. 12 north to Dayton. At Dayton, take the North Fork Touchet River Road east to Ski Bluewood.
- **From the Tri-Cities, WA:** Take WA 124 east to U.S. 12. Follow U.S. 12 to Dayton. Then take North Fork Touchet River Road east to Ski Bluewood.

Trail Profiles

Bluewood is entirely below treeline and located in a heavily forested north-facing bowl. The contour of the mountain and the trees forms a natural buffer against the most severe weather while allowing the snow to pile up. Days after big storms, skiers and boarders find protected stashes of powder in the trees. Offer a local a stout micro-brew, and they're sure to show the way to their personal stashes. Just don't talk to strangers wearing orange coveralls blazed with five-digit numbers—nearby Walla Walla is home to the state penitentiary.

Bluewood has one main chairlift, the Skyline Express triple chair, that transports snowriders to the top (5,650 feet) and provides access to the entire mountain. At two miles, *Country Road* is the mountain's longest run, and it's perfect for novice snowriders learning the fine art of wedge turns. The boulevard-width trail is a virtual Sunday drive in the country.

Advanced skiers will find *Jack Hammer* and *Scorpio* to be more than enough challenge. Both are loaded with bumps and steep enough to keep the heart thumping. Egomaniacs can show off under the Skyline Express on the mogul run *Ego*.

For challenging off-piste skiing, try *Green Giant* and *Rated R*, to the skier's left of the triple chair; and *Champagne* and the *Stump Farm*, to the right. *Green Giant* and *Rated R* dump snowriders into a gully, but only after laying tracks through a tight maze of trees. *Champagne* and *Stump Farm* have slightly less vertical and are a bit more open.

Intermediates can make quick runs on *Huckleberry*, which goes straight to the base of the Skyline Express, or head out to the *Tamarack Trail* for even more turns. Light, dry snow and excellent grooming make for buttery-smooth, buffed corduroy.

More Fun in the Flakes

Bluewood does not offer **cross-country skiing**; however, there are trails outside of the ski area boundary popular among Nordic skiers. Maps and other information concerning those trails are available at Bluewood's Information Desk on the mountain.

Snowboarding Highlights

Despite being a small ski area, Bluewood recognizes the importance of snowboarding in a big way. For the last few years, Bluewood has focused on building an amazing terrain park. The park used to cover an entire 1,500-foot run and 350 feet of vertical, offering a virtual smorgasbord of obstacles like a large tabletop, quarterpipe, halfpipe walls, kickers, and smaller tabletops. Its black diamond rating came as a result of the terrain enhancement that the staff built into the run. Currently, Bluewood is planning on constructing a bigger park and a halfpipe for the coming season. The location has not yet been set.

Skier Services

🅢 Lift Tickets

Adults: $27/full-day, $21/half-day • **Students:** $23/full-day, $19/half-day • **Children (grades 1–8):** $20/full-day, $17/half-day • **Ages 65 & older:** $20/full-day, $17/half-day • **Preschool & younger:** Free • *Prices based on the 2000–2001 ski season.*

🎟 Rentals

Ski Rentals: $17/adults; $14/children; 300 sets. Type of Gear: Rossignol and K2 • **Snowboard Rentals:** $26/adults and students, $22/children; 100 sets. Type of Gear: Burton and Murrow • *Prices based on the 2000–2001 ski season.*

🏂 Services

Ski School: 50 instructors; Private lessons $34/90 minutes; Group lessons $17/90 minutes; Beginner's package $24 (includes lift ticket and rentals) • **Snowboard School:** 20 instructors; Private lessons $34/90 minutes; Group lessons $17/90 minutes; Beginner's package $28 (includes lift ticket and rentals) • *Prices based on the 2000–2001 ski season.*

Room & Board

🏠 Lodging

Dayton–21 miles *(34 km)* away

Weinhard Hotel is a Victorian hotel with 15 rooms decorated with antique furniture, one suite with Jacuzzi, and a rooftop garden; welcomes families and pets; rates $75–$125/night. (509) 382–4032 • **Purple House Bed & Breakfast** is a restored nineteenth century house with four guestrooms in a Victorian residential neighborhood; rates $85–$125/night. (509) 382–3159 • **Blue Mountain Hotel** offers a country atmosphere with 23 rooms and queen beds; rates $36–$80. (509) 382–3040.

🍴 Dining

Dayton–21 miles *(34 km)* away

Woodshed Bar & Grill serves comfort food, darts, pool, and microbrews. (509) 382–2004 • **Patit Creek Restaurant** offers a casual atmosphere with gourmet meat dishes, carefully selected local wines, and delicious desserts. (509) 382–2625 • **Gasoline Alley** is a 50's & 60's style drive-in serving burgers, shakes, and fries. (509) 382–2775 • **Cracker B's Pub** serves deep-dish pizza, burgers, steaks, wine, cocktails, and microbrews. (509) 382–2364.

White Pass

Mark T. Peterson/White Pass

White Pass
U.S. Route 12
White Pass, WA 98937

Ski Report:
 Seattle: (206) 634–0200
 Yakima: (509) 248–6966
 Tacoma: (253) 572–4300
Information: (509) 672–3100
E-mail: *info@skiwhitepass.com*
Website: *www.skiwhitepass.com*
Credit Cards: All major

Operating Hours: 8:45 A.M.–4 P.M. daily
Night Skiing: Friday and Saturday

Season: Mid November to mid May

Background

L ocated in Washington's Southern Cascade Mountains, White Pass receives 300-plus inches of the Cascade's best snow, and the views of Mount Rainier, the Tattoosh Range, and the Goat Rocks are simply awe-inspiring. But White Pass is most recognized as the home of Steve and Phil Mahre—two of the greatest American skiers to ever click into a pair of sleds. Natives of nearby Yakima, the brothers spent their youth learning how to carve perfect turns on White Pass' 32 trails. In 1984, they won the silver and gold medals in the Winter Olympics at Sarajevo. Since then, the area has undergone the usual lift upgrades, but the aura of White Pass hasn't changed. The family-friendly attitude is still a focus of the area staff.

Admittedly, White Pass is a small, day-ski area. There are only four chairlifts, but they sufficiently access the entire mountain. The Great White Express high-speed quad transports skiers and boarders to the top, providing 180 degrees of challenging skiing for snowriders of all abilities. Because of its relatively isolated location, White Pass is almost never crowded. Yakima is the only sizable town nearby and its population is only 60,000. Lift lines are the exception and not the rule. The area has such a friendly, small-town mentality that it's a safe place to turn the kids loose for the afternoon. And if you do have young kids, you'll be happy to know that children age six and younger stay and ski free of charge.

Mountain Stats

Base Elevation: 4,500 feet *(1,372 m)*
Summit Elevation: 6,000 feet *(1,829 m)*
Vertical Drop: 1,500 feet *(457 m)*
Primary Slope Direction: North
Annual Snowfall: 350 inches *(889 cm)*
Skiable Days: 150
Skiable Terrain: 635 acres *(257 ha)*
Runs: 32
Longest Run: 2.5 miles *(4 km)*

Lifts: 1 high-speed quad, 3 doubles, 2 surface lifts
Lift Capacity: 6,225 skiers per hour
Terrain Classification: 20% novice; 60% intermediate; 20% advanced
Night Skiing: 10%
Snowmaking: 15% allowance
Annual Visits: 100,000

Getting There

- **From north Seattle area:** Take I-90 east to I-82. Follow I-82 toward Yakima. At Yakima, head west on U.S. 12 (Exit 31). The ski area is off of U.S. 12.
- **From Spokane, WA:** Take I-90 west to I-82. Follow I-82 toward Yakima. At Yakima, head west on U.S. 12 (Exit 31). The ski area is off of U.S. 12.
- **From Olympia, WA:** Take I-5 south to U.S. 12 and travel east. The ski area is off of U.S. 12.
- **From the Tri-cities:** Take I-82 toward Yakima. At Yakima, head west on U.S. 12 (Exit 31). The ski area is off of U.S. 12.

Trail Profiles

White Pass has the highest base elevation of any ski area on the Washington Cascade Crest—yet nearly all of the area's 32 trails are completely below treeline. Now, consider that White Pass is located in one of the driest regions in the state. What does this all mean? Guests will discover some of the best snow the Cascades have to offer. The higher elevation and arid climate produce light snow, while the protection provided by the trees gives the snow a longer life. At the same time, the trees form a barrier against harsh Cascade winter storms. White Pass has managed to strike a solid balance between pulse-quickening steeps, wide-open cruisers, and gentle learning zones.

Novice snowriders will find *Holiday* fits their comfort level because it is virtually flat. The 2.4-mile trail features mild, serpentine terrain from top to bottom. Skiers and boarders who don't keep up enough speed in the middle section, though, may find themselves poling and pushing out—maybe even hiking. Be sure to straight-run *Holiday*.

More aggressive beginners will make an easy transition to *Ptarmigan*. Located on the back side under Chair Four, the wide trail offers a slightly higher degree of difficulty than *Holiday*, with a couple of fun rollers mixed in. To return to the base, take Chair Four back to the top and ski back down *Holiday*, or glide all the way down *Main Street*. *Main Street* spins around the back of the mountain and connects to *Paradise*—another big, blue cruiser.

Intermediate snowriders have satiny-smooth rides on *Cascade*, *Holicade*, *What?*, and *Tucker*—all on the east side of the mountain. They're loaded with rollers and big turns. Near the bottom, below the *Cascade Cliffs* and within sight of the lodge, the trails turn into a slightly tilted golf course. The terrain is gentle and as wide as the back nine.

Advanced intermediates should be able to handle the steeper pitch of *Mach 5*, located to the skier's right, near the top of the Great White quad. From the top, hang a sharp right off the chair and ride the ridge for 40 to 60 feet. Hang another right under the chair and drop over the ridge and down into *Mach 5*. The slope is wide and steep enough for most intermediate skiers, but not steep enough to prove dangerous. In fact, it bottoms out rather quickly, so taking a fall usually means it's not far to reach the bottom. However, the farther out the ridge, the steeper the lines become. Skiers and boarders also have to contend with a few tight turns in the trees. Intermediate snows riders might strongly consider avoiding this area altogether.

For more intermediate adventures, take *Holiday* and cut into the trees, anywhere near the top. The pitch is mild but the trees and natural bumps make the detour a challenge. Try the same on the other side of the hill. Take the Great White quad to the top and head straight off the chair to *Quail*. It's the last trail on the right. Near the top, duck into the trees again. Snowboarders call this area *Disney Land*. It's filled with bumps, stumps, little jumps, and twists and turns through the forest. Near the bottom it funnels into a creek bed that, when full of snow, serves as a curving, natural halfpipe. (The advent of shaped skis helps skiers ride anything a snowboarder can, so don't be intimidated by any halfpipe!) Be sure to follow only the paths through the trees that have clearly had a lot of traffic. They lead back out onto *Quail* near the bottom of Chair Four.

Snowboarding Highlights

Plans are still in the works to build a halfpipe and a terrain park at White Pass, but the best riding is still off in the trees on runs like *Holiday* and *Quail*. These areas are filled with whoopties, rollerz, natural kickers, and obstacles. Boarders can cut almost anywhere into the trees and find sweet riding. Just be sure to head back in the same direction before running into a cliff. Many experienced one-plankers link up with *Disney Land*, which is accessed off the top of Great White by heading directly to *Quail*, taking the last trail on the right, and ducking into the trees). Boarders can play on a variety of terrain twists through forest before hitting the natural halfpipe near the bottom (snow conditions permitting).

Advanced snowriders will find plenty of rowdy terrain to explore, as 13 of 32 trails are rated black diamond. On the first ride up Great White, hardcore riders can't help but spot the first cliff band right under the chair. To huck or not to huck is the question when considering whether or not to ski *Execution*. There is a line through the rocks or a launch pad onto a pretty solid landing. It's a big one, so be sure there is plenty of soft snow at the bottom before taking off. It's also the steepest pitch on the mountain, and therefore either the perfect spot to win glory or make a total spectacle.

Nearly all of the runs down the center of the hill under or near Great White hold advanced terrain. From the ridge that Great White follows, skiers and boarders can drop anywhere into the trees. *Star Wars* is full of steep lines through a sardine-packed tight forest. Though not marked on the map, this area lies roughly halfway down the *Roller Cattrack*. Just be sure to stay to the left before eating up too much vertical. *Star Wars* ends above a serious cliff band. Also be aware of the two creek beds that have to be crossed. They can be tricky, and snowriders unfamiliar with the area may end up taking an ice-cold bath.

For more expert terrain, skiers can jump onto *Raven's Haven* right off the top of Chair Four. The best line is right under the chair, as it is steep with a short drop over a stump or two and a couple of rocks—a definite crowd pleaser if the jumper can stick the landing. *Hour Glass* is a thigh-pounding, knee-punishing mogul run formerly shaped like an hourglass. The bottleneck was quite severe in the old days, but tree removal and blasting have opened the bottle up a bit. Take *Mach 5* and stay to the right to reach *Hour Glass*.

More Fun in the Flakes

White Pass offers an 11-mile (18-km), groomed **cross-country skiing** trail, which is double tracked with a 10-foot skating lane. The trail is renowned among Northwest Nordic skiers for its impeccable grooming and pristine wilderness setting—the *Cascade Crest Trail* bisects the area and is bordered by USFS-designated wilderness areas. The track is maintained Thursday through Sundays and all holidays, and is left in its natural state Monday through Wednesday, when access to the track is free.

Mark T. Peterson/White Pass

Skier Services

🅢 Lift Tickets

Adult and children: $33/weekend and holiday, $22/mid-week • Ages 6 & younger and 73+: Free • *Prices based on the 2000–2001 ski season.*

🄰 Nordic Trail Passes

$7 • *Prices based on the 2000–2001 ski season.*

🎿 Rentals

Ski Rentals: $17/adults; $12/kids; 600 sets. Type of Gear: Elan • Snowboard Rentals: $25 • Nordic Ski Rentals: $14/adults; $10/kids • *Prices based on the 2000–2001 ski season.*

🄸 Services

Ski School: 100 instructors; Private lessons $38/hour; Group lessons $20/hour; Beginner's package: $35 (includes lift ticket, lesson, and rentals) • Snowboard School: 25 instructors; Private lessons $38/hour; Group lessons $20/hour; Beginner's package $45 (includes lift ticket, lesson, and rentals • Nordic Ski School: 10 instructors; Private lessons $38/hour; Group lessons $20/hour • Childcare: Unlicensed daycare available daily from 8:30 A.M.–4:30 P.M. for ages 2–6. Call (509) 672-3106 • *Prices based on the 2000–2001 ski season.*

Room & Board

White Pass offers some on-site lodging with ski-in/ski-out convenience. More lodging is available 20 miles away in Packwood along with various dining options.

🛏 Lodging

On-site

Village Inn, across the road from the ski lifts, is a privately owned condominium facility that features fully equipped kitchens, private baths, and balconies with great views; rates $85–$185/night. (509) 672-3131.

Packwood–20 miles (32km) away

Tattoosh Motel is within easy driving distance to Mount Rainier National Park, Mount Saint Helens, and White Pass, and features a common hot tub, a common room, and one- or two-bedroom cabins; rates $35–$95/night. (360) 494–6710 or http://landru.myhome.net/krsharp • **The Inn of Packwood** offers 34 wood paneled rooms, indoor heated pool, Jacuzzi, and kitchenettes available; rates $50–$145/night; (360) 494–5500 or www.innofpackwood.com • **Cowlitz River Lodge** offers a continental breakfast, standard motel accommodations, and shared hot tub; rates $50–$85/night. (360) 494–4444 • **Crest Trail Lodge** has a common hot tub, 27 rooms, and continental breakfast; rates $45–$65/night. 1–800–477–5339 • **Silver Beach Resort** offers a motel, cabins, and camping for tents and RV's, with a common outdoor hot tub; rates $13–$75/night. (509) 672–2500.

🍴 Dining

Packwood–20 miles (32km) away

Ambrosia serves soups, salads, and pastries for lunch. (360) 494–4422 • **Packwood Club Café** serves all kinds of food with a lighthearted attitude. (360) 494–5977 • **Peter's Inn** serves a variety of American food, burgers, shakes, omelets, and more. (360) 494–4000.

Badger Mountain

Badger Mountain
Waterville, WA 98858

Ski Report & Information:
(509) 745-8273 or (509) 745-8409
Website: *www.douglascounty.org.badger*
Credit cards: Cash only

Operating Hours: 11 A.M.–4 P.M., only open weekends and holidays

Season: January to mid March

Background

B adger Mountain is a miniature ski area serving the small community of Waterville, Washington. In fact, Badger and the town are tied closely together. The Lions Club runs the cafeteria, a local farmer owns a hopped-up tracker that acts as a snowcat, and the city owns the hill. The result of such community involvement is that the area has a definite family feel to it. Everyone knows everyone on the mountain, which makes it a super-safe place for children. Badger is run completely by volunteers.

The rope tows are run by old automobile engines, which means low priced tow tickets ($6). A season's pass is only $35 for individuals and $75 for entire families. They offer lessons on an as-needed basis with season passes, but not on a daily basis. The Badger Mountain season's pass also provides discounts at Mission Ridge, Washington *(see page 142)*. There are only a few trails at Badger, but they're groomed every day the ski area's open. The runs are short—only 800 feet—but they're steep.

Mountain Stats

Base Elevation: 3,000 feet *(915 m)*
Summit Elevation: 3,800 feet *(1,159 m)*
Vertical Drop: 800 feet *(244 m)*
Primary Slope Direction: North
Annual Snowfall: 100 inches *(254 cm)*
Skiable Days: 50
Skiable Terrain: 20 acres *(8 ha)*
Runs: 4

Longest Run: 1,700 feet *(518 m)*
Lifts: 3 rope tows
Lift Capacity: 1,800 skiers per hour
Terrain Classification: 33% novice: 34% intermediate: 33% advanced
Night Skiing: None
Snowmaking: None
Annual Visits: 4,000

Getting There

🚌 • **From Seattle and Tacoma, WA:** Take I-5 to I-90 and then head east to Exit 84 (Cle Elum/Wenatchee). Take WA 970 north to U.S. 97. Continue on U.S. 97 to U.S. 2. Follow U.S. 2 east to Waterville. *[Directions continued below.]*
 • **From Spokane, WA:** Follow I-90 west to WA 281 to Quincy. Then take WA 28 to U.S. 2. Take U.S. 2 east. *[Directions continued below.]*
 • **[Continued.]** Take U.S. 2 east toward Waterville. Approximately 1.5 miles before Waterville, take a right (south) onto Planetz Road NW. Follow Planetz Road until Baseline Road. Take a right (west) onto Baseline Road. Continue on Baseline Road until Badger Mountain Road. Take a left onto Badger Mountain Road and head to the ski area.

✈️ **Airport Services:** The Waterville Municipal Airport provides access for small planes only.

More Fun in the Flakes

Badger Mountain offers 3 miles (5 km) of fully-groomed **cross-country skiing** trails.

Skier Services

💲 Lift Tickets

Day Pass: $6/day; Season Pass: $35 • **Family Pass:** $75 • **Ages 6 & younger and 73+:** Free • *Price based on 2000–2001 ski season.*

🎿 Rentals

Currently there are no rentals, but maybe in the future.

🏠 Services

Ski School: $60/individual; $100/family; Lessons are available only for season pass holder • *Price based on 2000–2001 ski season.*

Room & Board

Since Badger Mountain is a day ski area only, there are no on-site lodging accommodations. However, the nearby towns of Waterville and Wenatchee offer choices for lodging and dining. Badger operates a day lodge with concessions sold by the local Lions Club.

ALPINE RESORTS:
OREGON

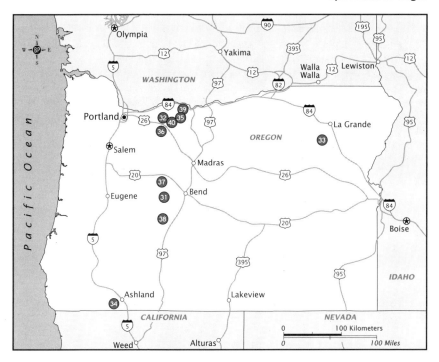

With 13 national forests, dormant volcanoes, hundreds of rivers, deep lakes, and miles of hidden beaches, Oregon is one of North America's premier outdoor playgrounds. Each year thousands of mountain climbers and snowriders flock to the slopes of Oregon's highest spot Mount Hood. On the north side of the mountain, water thunders through the basalt cliffs of the Columbia River Gorge and plummets 620 feet over Multnomah Falls as the mighty river winds its way to the Pacific Ocean. The gorge forms a wicked wind tunnel at the town of Hood River—the Promised Land for wind surfers. Many hardcore outdoor athletes spend their summer mornings carving turns on the slopes of Mount Hood and their afternoons riding the wind across the Columbia River. Crater Lake National Park, another favorite attraction, sits at 6,200 feet in a massive caldera left when a volcano blew its top thousands of years ago. The Newberry National Volcanic Monument is a harsh reminder of just how powerful Mother Nature can be. For miles the land is covered with razor-sharp mounds and peculiar rolling formations of basalt, the result of molten lava bubbling up from the earth's crust.

Several of the Oregon's ski areas are within 90 minutes of Portland, the state's largest city. The remaining ski areas lie within four hours. The two most famous are Mount Bachelor and Timberline. Mount Bachelor was the first resort in the Pacific Northwest to create a family ski area. Its smooth slopes, tame terrain, high-speed quads, and kids programs attract families from all over the country. Millions of people across North America are familiar with Mount Hood's historical Timberline Lodge, though they may not know it. Stanley Kubrick's The Shining, starring Jack Nicholson, used the lodge as the film's backdrop.

Snowriding in Oregon is fantastic, and skiers and boarders can easily find and access the terrain best suited to them. Being so close to the coast, the snow tends to be moist and heavy, but this doesn't stop skiers and boarders from hitting the slopes. And why should it? If there's a drawback to skiing in Oregon it's that Timberline Lodge is the only ski-in/ski-out facility in the state, which is why Oregon skiing has been kept out of the limelight. The reason for this lack of resort lodging is that most of the ski areas sit on national forest land. Local snowriders seem to delight in the lack of on-slope accommodations. Fewer visitors mean more trackless snow and fewer crowds on the slopes—which is just the way the locals like it. It's hard to argue with logic like that.

Jay Carroll/Mt. Hood Meadows

Getting Around Oregon

● AREA CODES

The area code 503 covers Portland, Salem, and Northwestern Oregon, and is now overlaid with the recently added 971 area code. The area code 541 serves the remainder of Oregon.

● ROADS

For winter road conditions, call 1–800–977–6368. To contact the Oregon Department of Transportation, call (503) 986–4000 or visit *www.odot.state.or.us* for current road closings and openings, traffic updates, and road construction plans and timetables.

● BY AIR

Portland International Airport (PDX) is Oregon's main airport. A number of smaller airports throughout the state have connections through Portland International. The resort/ski area or a travel agent can best advise you on the cheapest and/or most direct way to connect from wherever you're departing. They can also arrange transportation from the airport to the ski area.

To book reservations on-line, check out your favorite airline's website or search one of the following travel sites for the best price: *www.cheaptickets.com*, *www.expedia.com*, *www.previewtravel.com*, *www.priceline.com*, *http://travel.yahoo.com*, *www.travelocity.com*, *www.trip.com*—just to name a few. Many of these sites can connect you with a shuttle or rental service to get you from the airport to the ski area.

● BY BUS

Greyhound services Portland, Eugene, Bend, Sisters, and Ashland. Schedules and fares are available online at *www.greyhound.com* or by phone at 1–800–231–2222. The RAZ Trax Airporter connects Amtrak, Greyhound, and downtown Portland with the Portland International Airport. Call (503) 684–3322 for schedules and pick-up info. Pierce Pacific Stage services Portland, Cannon Beach, Seaside, and Astoria. Call 1–888–483–1111 for information and fares. Pacific Trailways connects Portland with Lincoln City. Call (503) 692–4437.

● BY TRAIN

Amtrak's Cascade Corridor trains service Portland and Eugene four times a day from Seattle, WA. The Empire Builder train runs daily to Portland from Chicago, IL; Minneapolis, MN; and Spokane, WA. The Coast Starlight train services Portland and Eugene every day from Los Angeles, CA; San Francisco, CA; and Klamath Falls, OR. Amtrak offers connecting bus service to Bend, Ashland, and Boise, ID. Amtrak information and reservations are available online at *www.amtrak.com* or by phone at 1–800–872–7245.

● VISITOR INFORMATION

For visitor information or a travel brochure, call the Oregon Tourism Commission at 1–800–547–7842 or visit their website at *www.traveloregon.com*. The state's official site is *www.state.or.us*.

MAJOR ALPINE RESORTS: OREGON

Mount Bachelor

Kirk DeVoll/Mt. Bachelor Ski Resort

Mount Bachelor

P.O. Box 1031
Bend, Oregon 97709

Ski Report: 1–800–829–2442,
(541) 382–7888
Information: 1–800–829–2442,
(541) 382–2442
E-mail: *info@mtbachelor.com*
Website: *www.mtbachelor.com*
Credit Cards: All major

Operating Hours: 9 A.M.–4 P.M. weekdays; 8
A.M.–4 P.M. weekends and holidays
Season: Mid November to early July

Background

Central Oregon's Mount Bachelor is indisputably the biggest and the best the state has to offer. The dormant volcano, formed 30,000–50,000 years ago, is a giant compared to the other Oregon resorts. The summit reaches 9,065 feet and provides snowriders with 360 degrees of skiing, 70 runs, over 3,686 acres of terrain, and 3,365 feet of vertical. Considering the huge cache of terrain, skiers may presume that getting around the mountain is an arduous task. On the contrary, Bachelor has invested millions of dollars into its lift circuit, making navigating the mountain a snap. Of the 11 chairs on the hill, seven are high-speed quads. Each one provides access to the mountain's major areas. The design of the Bachelor's lift circuit is so efficient that waiting in line is a rare occurrence. Add to that over 300 inches of light, dry, high-desert powder that blanket Bachelor each year.

Another perk at Bachelor is that the resort only asks snowriders to pay for what they ski and ride. The high-tech Flextime lift ticket system deducts a pre-determined number of points for each run. Want to quit early? Kids tired? Something unexpected come up? The flexible system automatically deducts points with each chair ride, saving the balance for up to three seasons.

Despite its gargantuan size, the resort somehow maintains a warm, friendly atmosphere. Bachelor caters to families with slow-skiing zones and women-only and kids' programs. Moreover, the base area lacks the masses of condos, hotels, and retail establishments of more commercial resorts. The lodges are day-only, and the lack of glitzy development lends a relaxed pace to the winter playground experience. For nighttime activities and lodging, tourists must drive roughly 20 miles to the Sunriver Resort or the town of Bend. Here, snowriders will have no problem finding beds on which to rest after a hard day of skiing and boarding, and will also discover eating establishments to satisfy even the most finicky palate.

Mountain Stats

Base Elevation: 5,700 feet *(1,738 m)*
Summit Elevation: 9,065 feet *(2,765 m)*
Vertical Drop: 3,365 feet *(1,026 m)*
Primary Slope Direction: 360 degrees
Annual Snowfall: 250–300 inches *(635–762 cm)*
Skiable Days: 220
Skiable Terrain: 3,686 acres *(1,493 ha)*; 1,600 acres (648 ha) groomed daily
Runs: 70

Longest Run: 2 miles *(3.2 km)*
Lifts: 7 super express quads, 3 triples, 2 surface lifts, 1 double
Lift Capacity: 21,000 skiers per hour
Terrain Classification: 15% novice; 25% intermediate; 35% advanced/intermediate; 25% expert
Night Skiing: None
Snowmaking: None
Annual Visits: 570,000

Getting There

- **From Seattle, WA, and Portland, OR:** Take I-5 south to U.S. 26. Go east to U.S. 97. Take U.S. 97 south to Bend and follow the signs.
- **From Eugene, OR:** Take OR 126 east to OR 242. Take OR 242 east to U.S. 20. Follow U.S. 20 east to Bend and follow the signs.
- **From Salem, OR:** Take OR 22 east to U.S. 20. Follow U.S. 20 east to Bend and follow the signs.
- **From Northern California:** Take U.S. 97 north to Bend and follow the signs.

Airport Service: Guests traveling from outside the Northwest, the closest regional airport is Robert Fields Airport in Redmond/Bend (RDM). Bus, taxi, and limo service is available from the airport.

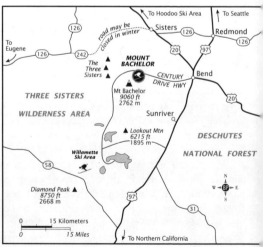

Bus Service: Guests can travel from both Bend and Sunriver to Mount Bachelor on the Super Shuttle. Tickets are available at the Mount Bachelor transit center in downtown Bend and Sunriver. For schedule and price information call 1–800–829–2442 or (541) 382–2442.

Trail Profiles

A word to the wise…better bring the long boards when visiting Bachelor. The mountain is a virtual Shangri La for snowriders who like to rip big, bold sweeping arcs. Every day a fleet of snowcats lays down 1,600 acres of velvety smooth corduroy. Add these buffed trails to an impressive 3,000 feet of vertical and Bachelor provides top-to-bottom screamers, huge turns, and phat phat grins. Bachelor's grooming is so good, and the terrain so varied, that even novice and intermediate snowriders will find plenty of hero snow laid out for them like a red carpet.

One of the Pacific Northwest's all-time great cruising trails can be found on the *West Ridge Run*. Take the Summit Express quad to the top of the mountain and traverse completely across the top until you reach the highest point of the mountain, the West Ridge. Diving into this high-speed cruiser shoots snowriders onto *Thunderbird* and lands them at the bottom of the Pine Marten Express. During major competitions, this run is used for downhill races and all high-speed events. The downhill course runs directly in front of the Pine Marten Lodge. In order to get the best coverage, television and media crews are placed on top of the lodge to get the feel of exactly how fast competitors go. Racers have reached speeds of over 60 mph.

The Outback Express also offers access to several cruising runs. *Ed's Garden, Kangaroo, Downunder,* and the upper section of *Bushwacker* are notoriously clean cruisers. All four provide 1,500 feet of vertical on well-groomed terrain and snow. Both intermediate and advanced snowriders will find these runs fun and fast. But perhaps the most popular cruiser at Bachelor is the *Spark's Lake Trail*. Accessed by taking the Outback Express and then the new Northwest Territories quad, *Spark's Lake* is the only groomed black diamond run at Bachelor. The pitch here is steep. And with the light, dry snow groomed smooth, snowriders can carve giant, sweeping arcs while rocketing down 2,400 feet of vertical.

Mike Houska/Mt. Bachelor Ski Resort

Bachelor doesn't stop their grooming here. The resort also offers great bump skiing with machine-made moguls. Yep…machine made. While many of the mogul runs are left ungroomed to be bumped up naturally, others are constructed by grooming machines with articulating blades. Ride the Pine Marten Express or Outback Express to ride machine-enhanced bumps on *Grotto, Shorty, Down Under West, Lower Bushwacker,* and the west side of *Boomerang.* Bachelors' groomers take advantage of the natural terrain to create a sculpted, undulating snow surface. The effect is a roller coaster ride on skis with experiences in weight-lessness and then compression. Machine-sculpted bumps usually mean a better line through the moguls. Traditional manmade bumps take longer to form and the lines through them are less consistent. At the end of the weekend, after everyone has had their chance on the bumps, moguls are usually plowed for safety reasons, and machine-sculpted bumps are formed.

For an all-natural snowriding experience, try the Summit Express. Nearly all of the ter-rain accessible from the top is above the timberline. This is ungroomed, challenging terrain, offering bowls, ridges, and steep chutes. Best of all, this area is a powder Mecca. After a big storm of fresh frosted flakes, this is the place to ski. Strong intermediates should not be intimidated by the single black diamond status of these trails. The barren terrain above the treeline is challenging mostly because it is ungroomed. The slopes are not that steep.

Bear in mind, though, that snow conditions above treeline can be dicey. Bachelor's tow-ering elevation leaves the summit well exposed and the snow frequently wind-packed and crusty, occasionally resulting in difficult conditions. With just a few clouds, the visibility can become poor, considering there are no trees for contrasting detail. A huge snowfall can bot-tom out visibility below zero. The summit area affords incredible terrain, but expect it to be closed 30 to 40 percent of each season. Many a salivating snowrider has spent an entire week at Bachelor without every reaching the summit.

Those fortunate enough to time their stay just right will experience some of the area's best off-piste skiing from the summit. Snowriders have three main options. A straight run off the backside deposits skiers and boarders into vast bowls that have never been named. Each of these bowls filter into trails and eventually lead back to the *Northwest Territory*—an area so colossal that few skiers ever seem to find the same run twice.

A second alternative for snowriders is to hike to the mountain's tip-top and plunge into the *Cirque Bowl* on the front side. This area is more well traveled, likely because it can actually be seen from the chairlift. Several unnamed runs in the *Cirque Bowl* offer ter-rific snowriding through the *Pinnacles,* toward the moraine, and onto the bottom of the Summit Express.

The final option is to drop off the mountain's right onto *Cow's Face.* This tract of terrain receives big snow dumps and is rarely crowded. Snowriders find hundreds of turns in the fresh pow pow. The first thousand feet runs through a wide-open powder field. Snowriders can explore the trees below *Cow's Face* and just to the skier's right of the *Flying Dutchman.* Here, the trees are lightly gladed and traffic is minimal. Just be sure to pay attention to all ski patrol catch lines. They act as the ski area boundary, and ignoring these ropes means skiing out of bounds through a dense forest and hiking back up the road to the lodge—and the loss of your ticket if caught.

Tree lovers will find the terrain off of the Outback Express a blast. *Outback* is full of twist-ing lines through the trees, with jumps, stumps, bumps, drops, and hops covered in untracked snow. There are far too many lines to count or name. Beyond the Outback Express lies the recently opened and well-worth-exploring *Northwest Territory*. Accessed by the new Northwest Express quad, the fresh terrain offers what many consider to be the state's best gladed tree skiing.

These runs are nearly two miles long from the summit and reflect the natural contours of the mountain. The *Northwest Territory* is loaded with superb backcountry terrain, covered by the mountain's best snow. Because many of the trails are unnamed, there's a good possibility snowriders will discover untracked lines in long-lasting virgin powder. Clearly, exploring this magnificent expanse is best experienced with a group of ski buddies. In fact, entering this area alone has resulted in a few lost skiers and snowboarders who strayed beyond the boundary line. A wise strategy is to start at the top, then divide and conquer. It's not uncommon for skiers and snowboarders to shred all 2,377 feet of vertical without ever spotting another soul. But they are reassured they are not alone by the yelps and whoops coming through the trees.

The local secret stash is the *Peckerwoods*. It's not on the map, and locals have been known to turn down large bribes rather than cough up the location of this snow-packed treasure. With a little explo-

Mount Bachelor Ski Education Foundation

The Mount Bachelor Ski Education Foundation (MBSEF) is a non-profit organization designed to support alpine, cross-country, and snowboard competition in Central Oregon. MBSEF provides for the development of all aspects of ski and snowboard sports by providing training programs and competition events for all ages and abilities. Most participants range from six to 21 years old and participate in a wide variety of programs and events. MBSEF's services range from introductory level courses, geared toward teaching the skills necessary to enjoy the sport, to full-time training programs, designed for athletes seeking national and international competition. Even though most athletes choose their preferred discipline (alpine, cross-country, or snowboard) to train, cross-training can be arranged in some programs. For more information call MBSEF at (541) 388-0002 or e-mail them at mbsef@bendnet.com.

ration and luck, though, *Peckerwoods* shouldn't be too hard to find. Take the Outback Chair to the top and then follow it back down on *Outback Way* for a couple hundred feet. Then, hang a right at the sign to *Ed's Garden*. Cut into the trees between *Ed's Garden* and *Down Under*. Herein lies the *Peckerwoods*, long revered by locals for its tree skiing, natural bumps, jumps and stumps, and deep light snow.

It's true that Mount Bachelor is a strong intermediate and advanced snowrider's paradise, but the resort doesn't forget the novice downhiller. Despite the area categorizing only 15 percent of the mountain as novice terrain, nearly anyone who can link turns can explore much of the mountain. Bachelor's grooming is so good the novice skiers can ski many of the blue runs as well as the 15 designated green trails. Lower intermediate and first-time skiers and boarders can play around in any of the family skiing zones, highlighted in yellow on the trail map. *Leeway, Skyliner,* and *Marshmallow* are some of the most popular. On the lower half of the mountain, these runs are sheltered from the more severe weather, and the trails are wide with shallow grades.

Snowboarding Highlights

Mount Bachelor has the distinction of being one of the country's first resorts to open its entire mountain to snowboarders, and today snowboarding is more of a priority then ever. Bachelor is the only resort in Oregon to employ a separate staff dedicated to maintaining their terrain park and halfpipes. Each pipe—one each for novices and experts—is sculpted with a Pipe Dragon. The novice pipe, located under Sun Rise Express, has six to eight-foot walls and is 200 to 300 feet long. The advanced pipe lies under the Yellow Chair and near the West Village. It's a standard Olympic competition pipe, running 300 feet long, with the verts sometimes reaching as high as 14 feet with six-foot trannies.

The terrain park is located near the top of *Pat's Way* to the right of the Skyliner Express. Open to both skiers and boarders, the park gets bigger and better every year and features 15 to 20 manmade obstacles including quarterpipes, spines, rollerz, kickers, and other natural hits. The expertly built park also features spacious drop-in areas with smooth transitions.

For great free riding head straight off the back side from the top of the Summit Express. At the top there are several big bowls of powder that lead into gladed tree runs and eventually to the *Northwest Territory's* cat track. Hit the cat track and follow it back down to the Northwest Quad.

The Mount Bachelor Snowboard Learning Center offers a variety of instructional programs for riders of all abilities and ages. The programs will help riders develop skills to ride the entire mountain, including steeps, bumps, cruisers, and powder.

Bachelor offers a 3,000-square-foot facility dedicated to snowboard retail and rentals. There are 550 sets of snowboard packages available, as well as a large selection of demo boards from top manufacturers. Rental inventory includes K2 or Morrow boards, and Air Walk or K2 boots.

More Fun in the Flakes

Because Mount Bachelor's slopes are not congested with condos, hotels, and restaurants, the **cross-country skiing** is simply amazing. A rustic but super-comfortable lodge lies at the head of 12 trails totaling 35 miles (56 km) of machine-groomed tracks. For miles in all directions there is nothing but unblemished wilderness full of wildlife and pristine forests. The Nordic terrain classifications are 5% beginner, 87% intermediate, and 8% expert.

Dogsled rides are also available. For reservations call 1–800–829–2442. Payment in full is required, all major credit cards accepted.

Skier Services

🅢 Lift Tickets

Ages 13–64: $43/full-day; $37/half-day • **Ages 7–12:** $22/full-day; $17/half-day **Ages 65+:** $31/full-day; $22/half-day • **Ages 6 & younger:** Free. • **Lower lift special:** $26. • **Racer:** $28 • *Prices are based on the 2000-2001 ski season.*

Nordic Trail Passes

Ages 13–64: $11/full-day; $9.50/half-day • Ages 7–12: $5.25/full-day; $4.25/half-day • Ages 65+: $6.50/full-day; $5.25/half-day • Ages 6 & younger: Free. • Groomed trail hours open are 8:30 A.M.–4 P.M. daily. • *Prices are based on the 2000–2001 ski season.*

Rentals

Ski Rentals: $18/all ages; 1,600 sets. Type of Gear: Rossignol, Lange, Salomon, Raichle, and Tyrolia • **Snowboard Rentals:** $28/all ages; 550 sets. Type of Gear: Rossignol, Burton, Morrow, and K2 • **Nordic Ski Rentals:** Adults range from $12–$20/full-day and $10–$16/half-day. Type of Gear: Rossignol • **Telemark Rentals:** Demos for adults are $25/full-day and $20/half-day. Type of Gear: Rossignol • *Prices are based on the 2000–2001 ski season.*

Services

Ski & Snowboard School: 90 ski instructors and 20 snowboard instructors; Private lessons $50/hour; Group lessons $30 and up • **Transportation:** The Mount Bachelor transit center is located in Bend on the corner of Colorado and Simpson. The shuttle fees are $1 each way. Tickets for the morning and afternoon shuttle can be purchased at the ticket window in the downtown transit center. The shuttle bus service operates weekends only beginning Thanksgiving weekend, then daily from roughly December 20 through April 20. Schedule information is available at all mountain information centers, or by calling (541) 382-2442 or 1-800-829-2442. • **Childcare:** Licensed. 1-800-829-2442 • **Racing:** NASTAR. Coin-Op Racing. Spring and Summer Race Training Camps. Call (541) 382-2442 extension 2146 for more information. • **Team Racing:** City League is one of the first programs of its kind in the America organized around team racing by league. The program is NASTAR format and includes team sponsorship. Each team has seven members aged 18 years and older. For team registration forms and fees, contact the Mount Bachelor Race Department at (541) 382-2442. See page 170 under The Summit/City League Side Bar. • *Prices are based on the 2000–2001 ski season.*

Did You Know...

Though dormant for thousands of years, the volcanic Mount Bachelor is heavily monitored for seismic activity, as is the rest of the Cascade Range.

Room & Board

Despite not having a single on-slope lodging facility, Bachelor still manages to make its guests comfortable after they hang up their boards for the evening. The town of Bend is just under a 30 minute drive and offers several B&Bs, numerous hotels, and even more restaurants and bars. Between Bend and Bachelor lie several year-round resort lodges. Places like the **Inn at the 7th Mountain** and **Sunriver Resort** are with in 20 minutes of Bachelor and offer quiet and extremely comfortable bedding. The Inn at the 7th Mountain is the closest. The accommodations at Sunriver are primarily in the second homes of various owners. All of them are kept up extremely well and come with everything expected in a home. Some have hot tubs, Jacuzzis, VCR's, stereos, and satellite dishes. Amazingly, Sunriver is not that expensive for large groups. Moreover, there is nearby shopping and dinning. And late in the season, early spring, there are several paved bike trails open for jogging, in-line skating, and walking—not to mention all of the golf courses in the area. Call Mount Bachelor Travel at 1–800–987–9968 for more information and reservations. They can book everything from daycare to airfare to lodging and lift tickets.

Lodging

Bend–(30 minutes away): The following locations are booked through Mount Bachelor Travel at 1–800–987–9968

Cimarron Motor Inn rooms have king- or queen-sized beds, and are equipped with microwave and refrigerator, continental breakfast offered, and heated pool; rates $49–59; 1–800–304–4050 • **Motel West** is centrally located, close to shopping, restaurants, and the downtown area, as well as just 25 miles away from Mount Bachelor. Ski packages are available, smoking and non-smoking rooms available, rooms equipped with microwave, refrigerator, cable TV, and telephone; rates $30–49; 1–888–291–4764 • **Pine Ridge Inn** has large upstairs rooms have Jacuzzi and living room, all rooms have gas fireplaces, king-sized beds, and bathroom, morning breakfast buffet, wine and cheese in the evenings, and turndown; rates $110–275; 1–800–600–4095 • **Elkai Woods** at Widgi Creek has queen studios and triple rooms, coffee service, TV, VCR, pool and Jacuzzi, guests receive golf discount as well; rates $90–250; (541) 317–5000 • **Shilo Inn** offers king-sized beds in rooms, and queen sleeper sofas, microwave, refrigerator, fireplaces in some rooms, in and outdoor pools, sauna, steam room, and fitness center; rates $109–175; 1–800–222–2244 • **Hawthorn Suites** are located 10 minutes from Mount Bachelor with suites available with either queen-sized bed or queen and fold out bed, computer desk, 25-inch TV, fully equipped kitchens in some rooms, hot and cold breakfast served; rates $74–99; 1–888–388–5006 • **Sunriver Resort,** 1–800–547–3922 • **Inn at the Seventh Mountain** offers a wide range of accommodations available from single bedrooms to eight person condos, rooms have refrigerators, desk, some have sofa beds, kitchens, and private decks; facilities include hot tub, sauna, gift shop, bike rentals, horseback riding, white water rafting, hiking, and a camp for children; rates $59–302; 1–800–452–6810.

Village Properties

Mount Bachelor Village offers one- two- and three-bedroom condos, and hotel rooms, with outdoor pool, access to gym, breathtaking views, Jacuzzis, and outdoor hot tubs; rates vary with special vacation packages; 1–800–452–9846 or (541) 389–5900 or *www.empnet. com/brc/mbvr.*

Dining

On-site

Mount Bachelor offers a variety of restaurants at each of its day lodges. For reservations or information on them call 1–800–829–2442.

Pine Marten Lodge
Scapolos is a casual restaurant on the first floor that serves gourmet pizzas and fresh soups •
Skiers Palate Restaurant is Mt. Bachelor's signature restaurant featuring Northwest cuisine,
daily specials, homemade desserts, and a great view • **Pine Marten Café** offers a choice from
the broiler, grill, deli, or yakisoba bar • **Beer & Wine Bar** is a walk-up bar with microbrews
from the Northwest, a variety of wines, and a spectacular view of the Mt. Bachelor summit.

West Village Lodge
Lower Castle Keep Restaurant is a family place with lunch buffet, soup and salad bar, full
service bar, satellite TV, and cozy fireplace • **Upper Castle Keep Bar** offers table service,
full bar, a fireplace, and a sundeck with views of the slopes • **Villa Cucina** serves a breakfast and lunch of bakery items, hand tossed pizza, pasta, and American cuisine • **Espresso
Bar** features coffees and specialty desserts.

Sunrise Lodge
Cocina Del Sol serves flavorful Mexican specialties and traditional American cuisine for
breakfast and lunch • **Sunrise Lounge** is a full service bar with microbrews and wines served
in a cozy lounge or the sundeck • **Espresso Bar** serves specialty coffees and desserts • **Jr.
Race Center** serves pizza and racer favorites.

Cross Country Center
Ullr Café serves energy food such as pasta, soups, and deli sandwiches in a cozy log cabin.

Courtesy Mt. Bachelor Ski Resort

Timberline Ski & Lodge

Timberline Ski Area & Lodge
Timberline Lodge, OR 97028

Ski Report: (503) 222–2211
Information: (503) 622–7979
Hotel Reservations only: 1–800–547–1406
E-mail: *info@timberlinelodge.com*
Website: *www.timberlinelodge.com*
Credit Cards: All major

Operating Hours: 9 A.M.–10 P.M. daily;
9 A.M.–1:30 P.M. summer hours.
Night Skiing: 4 P.M.–9 P.M. Friday and
Saturday; Mid December to March
Season: October to September

Background

Being the summer ski capital of North America makes Timberline one of the planet's most unique resorts. Where else in the Northern Hemisphere, or anywhere else for that matter, can snowriders ski and board for 12 months out of the year? The only other place on the continent that offers consistent summer snowriding is Blackcomb, British Columbia. Yes, even the gargantuan Whistler Resort doesn't offer as long a season as one of Oregon's oldest and most legendary resorts. At Timberline snowriding is possible on the permanent-lift-accessed *Palmer Snowfield* for 51 weeks a year. Over 50 separate race teams, clubs, and camps featuring world champion alpine freestyle snowriders from all over the world use Timberline as a training base during the summer months. And so can snowriders of all abilities.

Located just 55 miles outside of Portland on Mount Hood, Timberline Ski Area actually began as a lodge. On June 11, 1936, at the height of the Great Depression, ground was broken for a project unique in America. Timberline Lodge was built entirely by hand, inside and out, by skilled and unskilled craftspeople hired by the federally commissioned Works Projects Administration (WPA). The building is a tribute to their skills. It's also

Mountain Stats

Base Elevation: 4,800 feet *(1,830 m)*
Mid Elevation: 6,000 feet *(2,135 m)*
Summit Elevation: 8,540 feet *(2,605 m)*
Vertical Drop: 3,590 feet *(1,095 m)*
Vertical Drop Night Skiing: 1,050 feet *(320 m)*
Primary Slope Direction: South
Annual Snowfall: 400 inches *(1,016 cm)*
Skiable Days: 355

Skiable Terrain: 1,430 acres *(579 ha)*
Runs: 32
Longest Run: 3 miles *(4.8 km)*
Lifts: 2 high-speed quads, 1 triple, 3 doubles
Lift Capacity: 8,961 skiers per hour
Terrain Classification: 30% novice; 50% intermediate; 20% advanced
Night Skiing: 25%
Annual Visits: 280,000

Jon Tullis/Timberline Ski & Lodge

Getting There

- **From Portland, OR:** Take I-84 east to I-205 south. Take Exit 19 off I-205 onto U.S. 26. Follow to U.S. 26 for 40 miles (64.4 km) to Timberline access road. Turn left here. Lodge is six miles (9.7 km) up.
- **From Seattle, WA:** Take I-5 south to I-205. Take I-205 to I-84. Take I-84 east to Exit 16 at Wood Village. Turn right after 2.7 miles (4.3 km) on Burnside Street. Follow to U.S. 26 and turn left. Follow for 40 miles to Timberline access road. Turn left here. Lodge is six miles up.
- **From Boise, ID:** Take I-84 north to OR Rt. 35. Follow Rt. 35 to U.S. 26. Take U.S. 26 to Timberline access road.

- **From Spokane, WA:** Take I-82 south to I-84. Then go east on I-84 to OR 35. Take OR 35 to U.S. 26. Take U.S. 26 to Timberline access road.
- **From Vancouver BC:** Head south to the U.S. border. Take I-5 south to I-205. Take I-205 south to I-84. Take I-84 east to Exit 16 at Wood Village. Turn right after 2.7 miles on Burnside Street. Follow to U.S. 26 and turn left. Follow for 40 miles to Timberline access road. Turn left here. The lodge is six miles up.

209

a monument to a government program that responded not only to the more physical needs of Americans in a desperate time, but also to the needs of their spirits.

Now a National Historic Landmark and Oregon's only ski-in/ski-out resort, Timberline is located at 6,000 feet up the southwest side of Mount Hood. The lodge sits in the middle of the lift circuit, 3.6 miles from the 11,245-foot summit. Fifty years after its construction the lodge is still considered an architectural wonder. In it are hand-forged iron gates, massive hand-carved wooden beams, giant stone fireplaces, carved wooden sculptures, wrought-iron chairs upholstered in rawhide, crocheted rugs, and hand-painted murals depicting local wildlife and Native American art. Each year over one million people visit the lodge. Millions more have seen the lodge, possibly without even knowing it. The lodge served as the backdrop for Stanley Kubrick's sinister motion picture *The Shining*, starring Jack Nicholson. Timberline's outdoor structure is the only part of the lodge that was actually in the film. Despite Kubrick's menacing camera angles, the lodge is actually warm and inviting.

Be prepared for comfortable but spartan accommodations when staying at the lodge. Each room is a different size, shape, and color, and many can be small and cramped. Though management has done much to refurbish the lodge, there's only so much that can be done because of Timberline's status as a National Historic Landmark. The U.S. Forest Service must approve each and every improvement made to the structure. The fact that Timberline is frozen in time is part of the attraction. Many guests who visited as children come back years later and are pleased to find that nothing has changed.

Trail Profiles

From the lodge, two express quads transport snowriders up the *Palmer Snowfield* to 8,540 feet. Below the lodge, four other lifts provide access to what is mostly a family, intermediate, and novice paradise. Fewer than one-third of the area's 32 trails are listed as black diamonds—runs that at most other mountains would be considered blue runs. This means that skiers and boarders of all abilities can explore nearly the entire mountain. There are miles of open groomed

Scott Adams

Snowboarding **Highlights**

While skiers and boarders both get lots of turns and air out of *Paint Brush*, snowboarders tend to be the riders who head to Timberline's two winter halfpipes. Both are standard size Olympic competition pipes. Their location varies from year to year depending on the snow conditions. More often than not the pipes are located near the *Paint Brush* area. All of Timberline's halfpipes are built with a Pipe Dragon. In the summer, Timberline builds four more halfpipes up on the glacier. All day long you can catch the pros perfecting freestyle maneuvers in the halfpipes.

Dave Davidson/Timberline Ski & Lodge

trails, ideal for perfecting your skills. The *Magic Mile* is a classic cruiser and is accessible from the Magic Mile Super Express quad, which climbs to 7,000 feet. The *Magic Mile* is the gigantic snowfield directly above the lodge and was named back in 1939 after the original chairlift. To the skier's far right when looking up is *Coffels's Run*, another wide-open cruiser. Basically, anything off of the Magic Mile Express is wide open, relatively flat, and above the treeline.

When the weather is poor, drop down to the trails below the lodge to *Lift Line* (under the Blossom chair), *Alpine* or the *West Run* to *Back Way*. All of these are intermediate runs, with rolling fall lines through the forest that protect snowriders from the wind. During the summer months, however, all the runs below the lodge are usually closed—as are the runs serviced by the Magic Mile Express quad. Summer skiing and riding is usually confined to the *Palmer Snowfield*, which is serviced by the Palmer Express.

Novice snowriders will want to try *Conway's Corner*, *Glade*, and *Thunder*—all of which are green trails. Each run makes a wide cut through the trees over gentle terrain. Despite all of the runs on the *Palmer Snowfield* being designated as black diamond runs, most skiers who can link wedge turns are able to handle the terrain during the summer months. All three trails are groomed every day and their pitch just isn't that steep.

Runs reserved for advanced skiers and boarders in the winter are accessed from the Palmer Express above the lodge and the Victoria Station below the lodge. The first Palmer chair, built in 1978, ascends from 7,016 feet to 8,501 feet. The new high-speed quad opened in 1997 and provides winter access to the famous snowfield for the first time ever. This improvement added 300 acres and 1,560 vertical feet to Timberline's winter terrain. *Bean's Run* to the left and *Palmer* to the right are horizon-to-horizon wide, providing supersonic GS turns. From Victoria Station try *Wy'east*, *Molly's Run*, *West Pitch*, and *Cut Off*. All four are 35 to 40-degree pitches that wind through the trees.

The most fun for advanced snowriders is in the *Paint Brush Terrain Park*. Over a dozen features are spread from top to bottom on an intermediate trail. A conference-room-long tabletop, hip-style jumps with precise landings, rollerz, and spines make the *Paint Brush* a must for any advanced snowrider. Skiers and boarders make laps all day long on *Paint Brush*, copping air on each of the 10-plus jumps.

Skier Services

$ Lift Tickets
$34 • *Prices based on the 2000–2001 ski season.*

Rentals
Ski Rentals: Age 14+: $20; Age 13 & younger: $13; 1,700 sets. Type of Gear: Rossignol, K2, Dynastar, and Elan • **Snowboard Rentals:** $33; 300 sets. Type of Gear: Rossignol, Ride, and K2 • *Prices based on the 2000–2001 ski season.*

Services
Ski School: 60 instructors; Private lessons $45/hour; Group lessons $25 for two hours; Discover Skiing program $35 for two hours (includes rentals and a lift ticket on the Besty chairlift) • **Snowboard School:** 40 instructors; $45 for two hours and a lift ticket on the Besty chairlift • **Summer Camps:** Erich Sailer Ski Racing Camps: (612) 431–4477. Freestyle International: 1–800–805–8580. High Cascade Snowboard Camps: 1–800–334–4272. Hurricane Racing Team • **Summer Ski Racing Camps:** (616) 582–6163. Mount Hood Summer Ski Camp: (503) 337–2230. National Alpine Ski Camp: 1–800–453–NASC. Timberline Summer Ski Race Camp: (503) 231–5402. Windell's Snowboard Camp: 1–800–765–7669• **Childcare:** Licensed daycare is available on weekdays only. (503) 622–7979 • *Prices based on the 2000–2001 ski season.*

Snowriding in August?

Summer skiing at Timberline is something that every snowrider should experience. And it seems that many are doing just that. Believe it or not, Timberline has more visitors in the summer than in the winter. Standing in line on a 60-plus degree day without skis or a snowboard on takes a bit of getting used to. Snowriders step onto an astro-turf patch and click into their bindings. They then shuffle up to the chair. The Magic Mile Express quad transports them halfway up Mount Hood, above rocks and dirt, to where they unload and skate over to the Palmer Express. Palmer climbs to 8,540 feet, passing over the glacier and actual snow (Palmer Snowfield). The snow is old and more like crushed ice than anything else. Early in the morning it can be extremely firm. As the temperature warms the snow softens up, so the best riding is usually around mid-morning. In the summer the chairlift starts loading at 7 A.M. because by lunchtime the snow becomes heavy and piles up like snow cone slush. Add ruts from skiers and boarders turning in the same place and it's quittin' time.

While summer turns are a blast, the novelty can wear off quickly. Most of the hill is roped off for the race camps. This leaves one narrow alley of turns. It doesn't take long for boredom to set in. Be sure to use LOTS of sunscreen—with a high SPF. Stay hydrated and don't forget wrap-around sunglasses or goggles. While it is warm enough to go without gloves, it's not recommended. Putting a hand down in the course, granulated snow can leave the skin raw. A pair of batting gloves or leather work gloves are plenty protection, while still keeping one's hands cool.

Room & Board

🛏 Lodging

On-site

Timberline Lodge is a National Historic Landmark that has 71 rooms available to the public. Each room in the lodge features hand-done watercolors of the wild flowers native to the region, as well as hand-made furniture. In addition, Timberline Lodge is open for summer ski and snowboard camps; rates $75–190/night; 1-800-547-1406

Government Camp–6 miles (9 km) away

Mt. Hood Manor has four guestrooms with private baths, elegant furnishings, and a sitting room with fireplace; rates $95–$145/night; (503) 272-3440 • **Falcon Crest Inn** offers ski packages, live entertainment, weekend packages, free breakfast, exercise equipment, and Jacuzzi; rates $99–$179/night; (503) 272-3403 • **Thunderhead Lodge** offers 10 spacious units equipped with kitchen, recreation room, fireplace, pool table, fussball, and a geothermically heated pool; rates $95–$305/night; (503) 272-3368 • **Mt. Hood Inn** offers king and queen beds, indoor parking, ski lockers, ski tuning facilities, large indoor spa, movies and satellite TV; rates $129–159/night; (503) 272-3205 • **Englands Lodging** offers chalets with fully equipped kitchens, TV with cable, wood stoves, firewood, linens, some laundry facilities, and pets are allowed with prior notice; rates $180–$300; (503) 272-3350.

Parkdale–35 miles (56 km) away

Mt. View Home is a four-bedroom house, with two baths, fireplace, laundry, secluded yard, great views of Mount Hood, and ski packages available; rates $125/night or $800/week; (503) 579-5416.

Mount Hood–40 miles (64 km) away

Mt. Hood Hamlet B&B is an 18th century New England house with three spacious guest rooms, private baths, one with fireplace, one with Jacuzzi tub, an outdoor spa with heated deck, and mountain views; rates $95–$125/night; 1-800-407-0570.

Hood River–50 miles (80 km) away

The town of Hood River is worth the driving time if you're seeking a unique town full of pubs pouring local brews and restaurants serving delicious food. Also, be sure to look for hotels that offer discounted lift tickets with each night's stay. *For more on Hood River, see Sidebar on page 230.*

Meredith Gorge Motor Inn offers a panoramic view of the Columbia River, a '50s retro decorum complimentary coffee, three rooms with kitchens, and allows pets; rates $34–$65/night; (541) 386-1515 • **Oak Street Hotel** offers river view rooms and deck, queen beds, and proximity to downtown restaurants and shops; rates $45–$65/night; (541) 386-3845 • **Love's Riverview Lodge** offers suites with living rooms, microwaves, and/or refrigerators, and free morning coffee; rates $49–$72/night; 1-800-789-9568 or (541) 386-8719 • **Hood River Hotel** is a restored 1913 National Historic Landmark offering river views and suites, Jacuzzi, sauna, exercise facilities, spa, and allows pets; rates $49–$145/night; 1–800–386–1859 • **Avalon Bed & Breakfast** is a charming farmhouse with two guest rooms with queen beds, shared bath, one room with two twin beds, a splendid view of Mount Adams, and a full country breakfast; rates $65/night; (541) 386–3941 • **Comfort Suites** offers indoor pool, spa, sauna, fitness center, Jacuzzi suites, computer hookups, and mountain views; rates $69–$129/night; 1–800–228–5150 or (541) 308–1000 • **The Mosier House** is a Victorian house with four guestrooms with shared baths, a master room with a private bath, tea and baked goods served in the afternoon, and a full gourmet breakfast; rates $85–$100/night; (541) 478–3640 • **Columbia Gorge Hotel** is an historic,

Jim Carpenter

restored 1921 home located atop a 210-foot waterfall on the bluff of the Columbia River. It features a lounge, river views, and allows pets; rates $170–$270/night; 1–800–345–1921 or (541) 386–5566.

Dining 🔟
On-site

Timberline's **Cascade Dining Room** offers continental cuisine, prepared under the direction of Chef Leif Eric Benson, who has won several international and regional culinary awards. There are two lounges within the lodge: the **Blue Ox Cafe**, featuring glass mosaic murals from the '30s and serving microbrewed beer, and regional wines, along with a varied lunch menu. **The Ram's Head Bar**, located on the third level, offers a panoramic view of the Cascades to the south, as well as a most impressive view of Mt. Hood to the north. Timberline also has a special conference wing, a beautiful, large heated swimming pool and hydrospa; (503) 272–3700.

Government Camp –6 miles *(9 km)* away
Charlies Mountain View serves a variety of seafood dishes as well as steak and prime rib; (503) 272–3333.

Hood River–50 miles *(80 km)* away
Sixth Street Bistro serves delicious, reasonably priced lunch and dinner. (541) 386–5737 • **Horsefeathers** is usually closed in January, is reasonably priced, they make their own beer, offer a menu larger than most in town, and are kid-friendly; (541) 386–4411 • **Big City Chicks** has locals raving about the food but it is expensive; (541) 387–3811 • **Hood River Bagel Company** makes bagels that are as good as any big-city bagel place, with good coffee, too; (541) 386–2123.

OREGON'S **OTHER ALPINE RESORTS**

Anthony Lakes Mountain Resort

Anthony Lakes Mountain Resort
47500 Anthony Lake Highway
North Powder, OR 97867

Ski Report: (541) 856–3277
Information: (541) 856–3277
E-mail: *ski@anthonylakes.com*
Website: *www.anthonylakes.com*
Credit Cards: Visa & MasterCard

Operating Hours: 9 A.M.–4 P.M.
Thursday–Sunday and holidays; closed
Thanksgiving and Christmas

Season: Mid November to mid April

Walter Klages/Anthony Lakes Mtn. Resort

Background

Anthony Lakes is the little Hershey's Kiss of Oregon skiing. With only 900 feet (275 m) of vertical on 21 runs, the area is small but the snowriding is big. Located in northeast Oregon's Elkhorn Range of the Blue Mountains, Anthony Lakes is a powder paradise. The dry temperatures combined with the highest base in the state virtually guarantee light dry snow. Moreover, the setting is spectacular. Visible from its 8,000-foot summit are the Elkhorn and Eagle Cap Mountains, high granite bluffs, and miles of untouched wilderness covered with giant snow-laced pines.

Trail Profiles

Only four of the area's 21 trails are on novice-friendly terrain, but beginners need not feel shortchanged. The novice trails start at the top of the area's only chair, a triple, and allow novice skiers and snowboarders to explore most of the mountain. *Broadway, Variety,* and *Road Run* are the easiest trails back to the lodge. In addition to being the resort's longest trail, *Broadway's* slope is wide and gentle. *Variety* and *Road Run* are nearly as wide, provid-

with Rossignol step-in bindings • **Nordic Ski Rentals:** $10/ all adult rentals; $5/ ages 12 and younger; 40 sets. Type of Gear: Fischer Skis • **Snowshoe Rentals:** $10/ all adult rentals; $5/ ages 12 & younger; 20 sets. Type of Gear: Redfeather. • *Prices are based on the 2000–2001 ski season.*

Services
Ski School: 37 ski instructors; Private lessons $25/hour; Group lessons $15/hour • **Snowboard School:** 8 instructors. First Time Snowboarding program is $30 (includes one group lesson and rentals) • **Nordic Ski School:** Private lessons $25/hour; Group lessons $15/hour • **Childcare:** none.

Room & Board

The closest lodging is 19 miles (31 km) away in North Powder. North Powder is a small community with only the one option for lodging and just a few more restaurants to choose from. Aprés-ski activities are minimal at best as Anthony Lakes is primarily a day area, serving the residents in the surrounding communities.

Lodging
North Powder–19 miles *(31 km)* away:
Powder River Motel offers rooms with queen, twin, or bunk beds, suites with kitchen, futon, and a walk-in shower; rates $31–$42/night; (541) 898-2829.

Baker City–35 miles *(56 km)* away:
Best Western Sunridge Inn offers three restaurants, pool, hot tub, mountain-view or pool-side rooms available; rates $77–$86/night; (541) 523-6444 • **Geiser Grand Hotel** has deluxe, grand, parlor, and honeymoon suites available with king or queen beds; rates $79–$199/night; 1–888–GEISERG or (541) 523-1889 • **Super 8** (541) 523-8282 • *Call the Baker County Visitor and Convention Bureau 1–800–523–1235 for more options.*

La Grande–45 miles *(72 km)* away:
Howard Johnson Inn offers queen or king beds, refrigerators, coffee pots, cable TV, heated outdoor pool and hot tub, exercise room, sauna, and complimentary breakfast; rates $67–$77/night; (541) 963-7195 • **Sandman Inn** has basic rooms, pool and spa are open 24 hours, complimentary continental breakfast; rates $63–$68/night; (541) 963-3707 • *Call the Union County Visitor and Convention Bureau 1–800–848–9969 for more options.*

Dining
Baker City–35 miles *(56 km)* away:
Pizza a Fetta serves wonderful specialty pizzas, pastas, soups, and salads, in a very friendly atmosphere; (541) 523-6099 • **Main Event** serves burgers, chicken, some Mexican dishes, has a soup and salad bar, and a delicious selection of appetizers; (541) 523-6988 • **Phone Company Restaurant** serves a variety of tasty sandwiches, pasta, soups, salads, steaks, prime rib, seafood, chicken, and fresh baked breads; (541) 523-7997.

Mount Ashland Resort

Mount Ashland Resort
1745 Hwy 66
Ashland, Oregon 97520

Ski Report: (541) 482–2754
Information: (541) 482–2897
E-mail: *mta@mind.net*
Website: *www.mtashland.com*
Credit cards: All major

Operating Hours: 9 A.M.–4 P.M. daily.
Night Skiing: 4 P.M.–10 P.M. Thursday–Sunday

Season: Late November to mid April

Background

Mount Ashland is the Northwest's most literary ski resort. The trail map reads like an index of Shakespearean characters and plays, including *Caliban, Tempest, Ariel,* and *Romeo & Juliet.* It's no surprise then, that the town of Ashland is home to the Tony Award-winning Oregon Shakespeare Festival. Each February the Gemütlichkeit (German for warm and friendly) community becomes an Elizabethan theme park as bards and minstrels perform Shakespeare's most celebrated plays. Fortunately, for snowriders this is but an added attraction to the area.

Nestled in the magnificent Siskiyou Mountains, just eight miles from the town of Ashland, Mount Ashland Resort is a small ski area that delivers bold skiing and stunning vistas. Black diamond and intermediate terrain account for 85 percent of the area—the majority of which is for advanced snowriders. From the 7,500-foot summit, the view of the "Big Foot" country of Southern Oregon and Northern California includes the monolithic volcanic peaks of Shasta and McLoughlin, 13 wilderness areas, and 10 national forests.

With a base elevation of 6,350 feet, the 300-plus inches of snow falling on Ashland every year is typically softer than the "Cascade Concrete" routinely reported at other ski areas in the Northwest. Ashland's prime conditions are a result of the east-west alignment of the Siskiyou Mountain Range (one of only two such trending ranges in the U.S.) and the rain shadow effect of the coastal mountains, which dry and cool incoming Pacific storms before they hit the slopes of Mount Ashland. The rain shadow also provides bluebird days all winter long.

Mountain Stats

Base Elevation: 6,350 feet *(1,937 m)*
Summit Elevation: 7,500 feet *(2,288 m)*
Vertical Drop: 1,150 feet *(351 m)*
Primary Slope Direction: North
Annual Snowfall: 300 inches *(762 cm)*
Skiable Days: 120
Skiable Terrain: 200 acres *(81 ha)*
Runs: 23 plus bowl skiing

Longest Run: 1 mile *(1.6 km)*
Lifts: 2 doubles, 2 triples
Lift Capacity: 5,350 skiers per hour
Terrain Classification: 15% novice; 35% intermediate; 50% expert
Night Skiing: 35% allowance
Snowmaking: None
Annual Visits: 86,000

Getting There

- **From Seattle, WA, and Portland, OR:** Head south on I-5 to Ashland, OR. Take the Mt. Ashland Ski Road Exit and follow the signs along the 8-mile (13-km) paved access road leading to the Mt. Ashland ski area.
- **From Boise, ID:** Take I-84 north to U.S. 20. Go west on U.S. 20 to U.S. 395. Take U.S. 395 south to OR 140. Take OR 140 west to OR 62. Take OR 62 west to I-5, then go south to Ashland, OR. Take the Mt. Ashland Exit and follow the signs along the 8-mile (13-km) paved access road leading to the Mt. Ashland ski area.
- **From Redding, CA:** Head north on I-5 to Ashland, OR. Take the Mt. Ashland Ski Road Exit and follow the signs along the 8-mile (13-km) paved access road leading to the Mt. Ashland ski area.

Trail Profiles

Mount Ashland encompasses 23 trails and additional unnamed runs in an area called the *Bowl*, where advanced and expert snowriders flock to its menacing chutes and cliffs. From the top of *Ariel*, which is also the summit, simply hang a right when unloading from the chair. The *Circe* and the *Bowl* are not far.

Black diamond-rated *Upper Tempest* is ungroomed all season, with grooming exceptions for a few ski races. The trail's rough reputation stems not only from its steep pitch but also from its psychological challenge. The bottom of the trail is completely visible from the top, measuring roughly 1,100 feet (336 m). The entire run drops down to the hill, giving snowriders a quick sense of vertigo. The full-perspective view makes *Tempest* look steeper than it actually is.

Romeo and *Avon*, the easiest runs off the Windsor chairlift, are perfect for intermediates because of their width and easygoing fall line. *Dream* is similar but provides more vertical as it is accessed from the top of the mountain. Lower intermediates and athletic novice snowriders can expect to handle *Dream* without worry. *Winter*, another fun run for intermediates, is steeper than *Dream* and provides some shelter and visibility from poor weather conditions as it winds through the trees.

Snowboarding Highlights

Snowboarding has been a part of Mount Ashland since the resort's inception, and the area is furthering its commitment to the sport by relocating its halfpipe. In years past it has been near the lodge, but it will likely soon be built on *Dream*, where the snow conditions are usually more consistent. Size and vertical drop are standard at 300 feet and 110 feet. The resort also has plans to purchase a Pipe Dragon. In the meantime, the pipe is maintained by snowboard instructors and other local boarders willing to put in the work. As far as the trails are concerned, snowboarders might consider hitting *Ado* and *Upper Balcony*. Located on the crest of the mountain range, these runs produce considerable drifts and snow undulations, which are ideal for bonking.

More Fun in the Flakes

There is **cross-country skiing** available on the south side of the mountain; however, the trail is not groomed. The only other winter activities are organized **backcountry tours**, available through Siskiyou Adventures. Call them at (541) 488–1632 for more information.

Skier Services

Lift Tickets
Full-day: Adults (ages 13–64) $27/weekends and $23/weekdays; Junior/Seniors (ages 9–12 and 65–69) $19/weekends and $16/weekdays • **Half-day:** Adults $19/weekends and $16/weekdays; Junior/Seniors $13/weekends and $11/weekdays • **Night:** Adults $15/weekends and weekdays; Junior/Seniors $10/weekends and weekdays • **Swing Shift** (12:30 P.M.–10 P.M. Thursday–Saturday): Adults $27/weekends and $23/weekdays; Junior/Seniors $19/weekends and $16/weekdays. Children (ages 8 & younger) and Seniors (70+): Free • *Prices are based on the 2000–2001 ski season.*

Rentals
Ski Rentals: $15/ adults and $10/ kids for full-day; $10/ adults and $7 kids for half-day (same for night skiing); 400 sets. Type of Gear: Rossignol boots and skis • **Snowboard Rentals:** $14/ half day and $20/ full-day; 80 sets. Type of Gear: K2 and Burton snowboards • *Prices are based on the 2000–2001 ski season.*

Services
Ski School: 20 ski instructors; Private lessons $30/hour; Group lessons $15/hour; Free ski

lessons for women on Wednesdays and for men on Thursdays; Learn-to-ski packages from $27–$32 (includes rentals, lift ticket, and 90-minute lesson); Skiwee Program for kids ages 4 to 8 $20–$35 • **Snowboard School:** 10 snowboard instructors; Private lessons $30; Group lesson $15; Learn-to-board packages from $32–$37 (includes rentals, lift ticket, and 90-minute lesson) • **Childcare:** None • *Prices are based on the 2000–2001 ski season.*

Room & Board

Like the rest of the Oregon ski areas, with the exception of Timberline Lodge, Mount Ashland does not offer any ski-in and ski-out accommodations, but the town of Ashland lies only 18 miles (29 km) from the ski area. Guests will find several choices of restaurants, motels, hotels, and B&Bs. As the home of the Shakespeare Festival, staying in Ashland can be an adventure. Bards and minstrels abound and guests are more than welcome.

Lodging
Ashland–18 miles (29 km) away

Ashland Regency Inn & RV is located 2.5 miles away from Shakespeare Park, and offers a two story exterior corridor, heated pool, cable TV, and complimentary breakfast; rates $60–$75/night; 1–800–482–4701 • **Country Willows B&B Inn** is a 19th century farmhouse with rooms and suites in the house, a cottage, and a converted barn, heated pool, outdoor Jacuzzi, and ski packages; rates $76–$195/night; 1–800–WILLOWS or *www.willowsinn.com* • **Flagship Quality Inn** offers cozy rooms, a heated pool, and free movies; rates $55–$90/night; 1–800–334–2330 or *www.flagship-inn.com/ash1.htm* • **Lithia Springs Inn** is a luxurious romantic inn with rooms, suites, cottages, and special theme suites and honeymoon cottages, hot-springs-fed whirlpools, and a satisfaction guarantee; rates $95–$175/night for most rooms and suites; rates $195–$295/night for special cottage and suites; 1–800–482–7128 or (541) 482–7128 or *www.ashlandinn.com* • **Morical House Garden Inn** was originally a farmhouse in 1882, but now offers seven guest rooms with a three course breakfast; rates $110–$160, with off season rates; 1–800–208–0960 or (541) 482–2254 • **Mount Ashland Inn** offers five rooms and suites in a log cabin with a spa and sauna cabin along with complimentary skis, sleds, and mountain bikes for the active winter guest; rates $99–$190/night; 1–800–830–8707 or (541)–482–8707 or *www.mtashland.com.*

Dining
Ashland–18 miles (29 km) away

Ashland Bar and Grill serves casual American food including soups, salads, pizzas, and hamburgers, with everything priced under $7; (541) 482–4131 • **Blue Mountain Café** serves a delicious turkey meatloaf, burrito wraps, rice plates, soups, sandwiches, and lots of coffees and desserts; (541) 488–3151 • **Calientes Grill & Cantina** is a casual restaurant that serves a wide variety of Mexican food including tacos, enchiladas, burritos, salads, fish, chicken, and beef; (541) 482–1107 • **Giseppi's Pizzeria & Sports** serves a variety of pizza by the slice, specialty pizzas, sandwiches, and salads; (541) 482–5559 • **Mihama Teriyaki & Grill** offers an eclectic range of dishes including Japanese chicken and beef teriyaki and curry plates, American burgers and fries, and seafood; (541) 488–3530.

Mount Hood Meadows

Mount Hood Meadows Ski Resort
Highway 35
Mount Hood, Oregon 97041

Ski Report: (541) 386–7547
Portland Ski Report: (503) 227–7669
Hood River: (541) 386–7547
Vancouver: (360) 571–3919
Information: 1–800–SKI–HOOD (754–4663)
E-mail: *info@skihood.com*
Website: *www.skihood.com*
Credit Cards: All major

Operating Hours: 8 A.M.–4 P.M. Monday & Tuesday; 8 A.M.–10 P.M. Wednesday–Sunday.
Night Skiing: 4 P.M.–10 P.M.

Season: Late November to early May

Brian Robb/Mount Hood Meadows

Background

Another Pacific Rim volcano, Mount Hood rises up from Mount Hood National Forest to reach 11,235 feet into the sky. It is the highest peak in Oregon and the fourth highest in the Cascade Range. Tucked away on the sunny east side of the mountain, Mount Hood Meadows has carved 87 runs out of over 2,100 skiable acres. The terrain is accessed with 10 chairlifts, four of which are high-speed quads. While the quality of the snow at Mount Hood can be questionable, snow depths of incredible proportions often reach over 400 inches each year.

The Mount Hood Meadows moniker is extremely misleading. It implies gentle slopes, a relaxed atmosphere, and a day of easy-going-Sunday-driver turns. And while beginner terrain abounds for novices, Meadows is anything but gentle and relaxed. For over 30 years the resort has earned a reputation as Oregon's toughest and roughest ski area. Just 67 miles east of Portland, Mount Hood Meadows features vast amounts of slightly graded tree runs, bowls filled with bumps, wide-open powder fields, and the precarious steeps of *Heather Canyon*.

Mountain Stats

Base Elevation: 4,523 feet *(1,380 m)*
Summit Elevation: 7,300 feet *(2,227 m)*
Vertical Drop: 2,777 feet *(847 m)*
Primary Slope Direction: Primarily eastern exposure with some northern and southern due to terrain features.
Average Snowfall: 430 inches *(1,092 cm)*
Skiable Days: 160
Skiable Terrain: 2,150 acres *(871 ha)*
Runs: 86
Longest Run: 3 miles *(4.8 km)*

Lifts: 4 high-speed detachable quads, 6 doubles, 1 pony, 1 rope tow
Lift Capacity: 16,145 skiers per hour
Terrain Classification: 15% novice; 50% intermediate; 20% advanced; 15% expert
Night Skiing: on 22 runs, 6 lighted lifts (4 of which operate until 10 P.M., Wed.–Sun.)
Snowmaking: None
Annual Visits: 350,000

Getting There

- **From Portland, OR:** Take I-84 to Exit 64 in Hood River. Follow OR 35 south for 35 miles (56.3 km) to the entrance of Mt. Hood Meadows. Or take U.S. 26 east from Portland to Government Camp (about 53 miles or 85 kilometers). Continue on OR 35, then turn left to go over Barlow Pass. The access road will be on the left.

- **From Seattle, WA:** Take I-5 south to I-205. Take 205 to I-84. Take 84 to Exit 64 in Hood River. Follow OR Rt. 35 for 35 miles to the entrance of Mt. Hood Meadows.

- **From Boise, ID:** Take I-84 north to OR 35. Follow OR 35 for 35 miles to the entrance of Mt. Hood Meadows.

- **From Spokane, WA:** Take I-82 south to I-84. Then to OR 35. Follow OR 35 for 35 miles to the entrance of Mt. Hood Meadows.

- **From Vancouver BC:** Head south to the U.S. border. The I-5 south to I-205. Take 205 to I-84. Take I-84 to Exit 64 in Hood River. Follow OR 35 for 35 miles to the entrance of Mt Hood Meadows.

Parking fee at Meadows: $2.50/ day, or $10.50/season. (The government maintains the road and parking lot.)

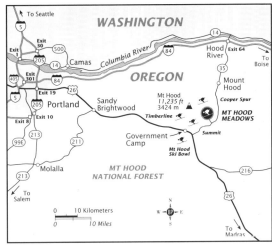

Bus Service: Guests can travel from Portland to Mount Hood by luxury coach bus. Tickets are available through the Ticket Master Outlet Store or the Mount Hood Meadows Portland Sales Office. Reservations required. For schedule and price information call (503) 287-5438.

Trail Profiles

For their own safety, first-time snowriders are shepherded to a specific area near the base of the resort. The terrain is not, however, the typical, flat, parking-lot variety to which many other ski areas relegate beginners. The trails are wide and gentle but with just enough of a pitch to challenge novice snowriders. They are real confidence builders. The Red, Buttercup, and Daisy chairs provide access to these trails and are located to the left of the lodge as you look up the mountain.

First-timers will also enjoy *The Zoo*, one of three terrain parks at Meadows. *The Zoo* is designed specifically for novice snowriders and consists of rolling terrain, small banked turns, and miniature jumps. The area is also home to a novice halfpipe, constructed with the first-

time piper in mind. Skiers and snowboarders alike are welcome in *The Zoo*.

The Blue Chair, the Mount Hood Express, and the Yellow Chair also provide access to novice terrain. For long cruising runs, take the Mount Hood Express and then head left to *Ridge Run* or right to *North Canyon*. Both trails wind back to the main lodge while offering wide, gradual descents—perfect for warming up stiff legs on the way to more challenging terrain. All six chairs are lit for night skiing.

And since Meadows is so close to Portland, many snowriders make the mid-week trek to get in a few turns in the evening. Twenty-two runs and four lifts operate until 10 P.M., Wednesday through Sunday.

Advanced intermediates should try *North Canyon* to *Tillicum* to *Kinniknick* to *Skyway*. This will take snowriders to the bottom of the recently installed Hood River Express. Combining the trails makes for a long, thigh-burning run. The base of the Hood River Express is actually lower on the mountain than the lodge area. When the weather's bad, head here to escape the wind and cold. During weekends this area tends to be less crowded than the area surrounding the lodges.

Intermediates can play almost anywhere on the mountain. From the Cascade Express, skiers and boarders can choose between the wide-open, above-treeline snowfields of *Texas Flats* or *Catacombs*. Oregon skiers voted *Texas Flats* the best intermediate skiing in the state because of its continuous fall line, which allows long, sustained, linked GS turns that seem to go on forever. The exceptional view from here is enough reason to take the run. Mount Jefferson, the Three Sisters Peaks, and Mount Bachelor rise up out of an ocean of clouds that roll in from the Oregon Coast at 4,000 to 5,000 feet.

Located on the other side of the Cascade Express, *Marmot Ridge* and *Elevator* are two of the tougher runs at Meadows. Both are above the treeline and are therefore exposed to the harsh winds that can whip across Mount Hood. The snow can be wind-packed crust, making it difficult to ski. On a calm day, though, with good snow conditions, both *Marmot* and *Elevator* are popular runs. Better get to them as soon as the Cascade Express opens, or the snow will be cut up quickly—especially on weekends.

Snowboarding **Highlights**

On big powder days, hot snowboarders head for *Heather Canyon* to carve wild waves of snow. The wall of snow busting up with each turn is a thing of beauty. When the snow is tracked-up, the boarders often head for *Park Place*—Meadows' advanced terrain park, located near the top of the Hood River Express. *Daisy Bowl* sports a big halfpipe that runs just over 400 feet in length and is 60 to 70 feet wide. The pipe is built and maintained by crewmembers with a Scorpion pipe-shaping machine. The walls are 10 to 12 feet high with six to eight feet of vertical and four- to five-foot trannies, depending on how much snow Mount Hood receives. *Park Place* also offers 12 hits, including tabletops, spines, berms, quarterpipes, and hip-style jumps where boarders can launch and land in at least three different directions. The area is so well groomed and maintained that local boarders who compete in Boarder Cross and Free Style events use it as a training center. The halfpipe and terrain features in *Park Place* are just like what you'll see on the pro tours. Next to *Park Place* is *Easy Rider*, an intermediate terrain park designed to help riders hone technique and step up to *Park Place*.

Each year Meadows will add more features all over the mountain as snow permits. Area management's goal is to give all snowriders an enhanced experience by using their groomers and pipe machine to make snowriding more challenging and exciting.

In between lies *Arena*, a blue run. Not nearly as steep as *Elevator* or *Marmot*, *Arena* is a good challenge for strong intermediate skiers. In order to remain in this area and ride the Cascade Express again, catch *Ridge Run* to the bottom. For more adventure on the way down, take *Cascade Skyway* to *Chunky Swirl*—a ridge riddled with small lumps, bumps, and jumps. This trail is perfect for big sweeping airplane turns. Dropping into the other areas of the mountain means more than one lift back to the top.

The Cascade Express also takes snowriders to the *Outer Limits*. A short blue run, *Outer Limits* serves as a connector to the lower half of *Heather Canyon*—Meadow's franchise terrain. Completely ungroomed, the upper half is for experts only. But from the *Outer Limits*, strong intermediate to advanced snowriders can handle the small bowls in the lower half of *Heather Canyon*. None of the bowls here feature eye-popping steeps, but the experience is one for the books. *Memorial, Twilight, Pluto,* and *Moon Bowl* are wide-open runs free of trees and other obstacles. When the snow is soft—and it usually is in *Heather Canyon*—turns in this area are fast and forgiving. Even when the snow is cut up, snowriders still carve big sweeping arcs across the hill.

The snow in *Heather Canyon* stays fresh for long periods of time because the canyon walls protect the snow from too much direct sunlight. This makes the temperatures in the canyon fairly stable, which means the snow is less susceptible to the continuous melting and freezing cycle experienced by many Northwest mountains. Additionally, *Heather Canyon* acts like a natural wind tunnel. The winds blow up

Brian Robb/Mount Hood Meadows

Scott Adams

the *Canyon* at night and deposits snow in the bowls from top to bottom. Moreover, the wind acts as a natural grooming mechanism because it fills in tracks and mows them down. Even when Meadows hasn't seen snow for days, the *Canyon* is usually silky smooth and ready to be ripped.

Be forewarned: While the *Canyon's* lower half can be handled by most intermediates, the upper half is, indeed, for confident and strong expert snowriders. From the top of the Cascade Express, hang a soft right and traverse high on the trail. The map lists this traverse as *Albert's Run*. *Albert's* is riddled with rocks and ice, making the entrance a bit tricky. To gain even more vertical, hike roughly 15 minutes toward the ridge's high-point. Skiers and boarders can choose several entrances into the *Canyon* from here, all of which are a steep, 45-plus degrees. *Confidence* is at the top, then *The Wall, Hot Rocks, Parachute, Way Out,* and *Super Bowl*. While the entrances are steep, most of them are smooth. What makes them dangerous is that a fall here usually means a slide all the way to the bottom of the *Canyon*.

The best way to get the most turns out of the *Canyon* is to start high, make several turns, and then head to the skier's right for more turns. This is possible because each run/bowl is lower on the mountain. Make turns up high and then cut across to the next run, before bottoming out in the *Canyon*.

Snowriders can also stay high and cut across the *Canyon* to the other side and explore *Low Lands, High Lands, Sunrise,* and *Hammer Bowl*. From any one of these runs, drop into *Heather Woods*. *Heather Woods* is full of steep pitches usually filled with primo powder in early winter and lush, spring-like corn snow in the spring. Snowriders need to be fleet of foot, on their edges, and proficient at linking turns to ride these runs.

Skiing the *Canyon* is heavenly, but guests have been known to spend more time on the lifts than snowriding as it takes three lifts to reach the top, although two of these are high-speed quads.

Advanced snow riders have even more options if they are looking for beefy terrain. Take the *Shooting Star Ridge* to the left of the Shooting Star Express and drop into *Absolute Magnitude*. The trees in this area are fairly open and the fall lines are roughly 30 to 35 degrees. Farther to the right, however, the trees get tighter and the pitches grow steeper.

Lower on the mountain, jump into any one of six bowls accessible from the Mount Hood Express. *Bowls One* through *Five* are more like teacups jammed together side by side. Despite the bowls being small, the runs are steep, off-piste, and lit for night skiing. Cut through the trees at the top of any one of them for steep, short runs of powder or crud.

228

More Fun in the Flakes

Cross-country skiers will find nine miles (15 km) of groomed track, plus a complete line of rental equipment and instruction. The Cross-country Learning Center is at the Hood River Meadows parking area, and is open daily Wednesday through Sunday. For more information call the Nordic Center at (503) 337–2222, ext. 222.

Skier Services

Lift Tickets

Day Skiing: Ages 6 & younger: $6/full-day; Ages 7–12: $21/full-day; Ages 13–64: $41 for 9 A.M.–4 P.M., 11 A.M.–7 P.M., or 1 P.M.–10 P.M.; $35/half-day; Ages 65+: $26/full-day • **Night Skiing:** $18/all ages from 4 P.M.–10 P.M. • *Prices are based on the 2000–2001 ski season.*

Nordic Trail Passes

$9/all ages for full-day • *Prices are based on the 2000–2001 ski season.*

Rentals

Ski Rentals: Adults $20/full-day; Children $15/full-day; 700 sets. Type of Gear: Rossignol **Snowboard Rentals:** $28 to $32; over 600 sets. Type of Gear: Features the largest snowboard rental facility in the state with over 600 MLY Snowboards and Emery One-step Boot Binding systems • **Nordic Ski Rentals:** $15/all ages for full-day; $10/all ages for half-day Telemark Rentals: $25/all ages for full-day • *Prices are based on the 2000–2001 ski season.*

Services

Ski School: Kids: Two hours of instruction in the morning, lunch, two hours of instruction in the afternoon: $70 w/out rentals $75 with rentals. Beginner program: ski or snowboard $45 (90-minute lesson, rentals, and beginner chairlift ticket). Private lessons: $50/hour or $110 for three hours. Group lesson: $30 for 90 minutes • **Snowboard School:** $45 for Beginner Special (90-minute lesson, rentals, and beginner chairlift ticket); Private lessons $50/hour; Group lessons $30 • **Nordic Ski School:** $30 for Beginner Special (includes track pass, 90-minute lesson, and rental); Private lessons $50/hour; Group lessons $30 • **Childcare:** Licensed. Will take as young as 6 weeks old. Call (503) 337–2222, ext. 374 • **Transportation:** Bus transportation is available from several metropolitan Portland locations; bus and lift package $50/adult, $40/child (12 & younger) • *Prices are based on the 2000–2001 ski season.*

Jay Carroll/Mount Hood Meadows

Hood River

Set against big mountain views on the shores of the Columbia River, Hood River is the closest thing to a ski town near Mount Hood Meadows. Though it's 35 miles down the highway, Hood River is worth the extra driving. Full of bars and pubs serving local brews, and restaurants serving delicious food, Hood River has a small, inviting ski-town feel to it.

Hood's roots are in agriculture, ranching, and lumber, but the spirit of the town is all about enjoying the surrounding country. Most of Hood River's inhabitants are gear-heads on the extended pro leisure tour. Skiers, snowboarders, bikers, paddlers, climbers, and sailboarders, all exist on menial jobs that don't dare interfere with skiing, snowboarding, and biking. It is perfectly understandable in Hood River to leave work in the middle of the day because it is snowing hard up the mountain.

In the summer it's difficult to find hotels with vacancies. Hood River is the Mecca of sailboarding, which is evidenced by the number of sailboard shops in town. But in the winter you can always find a comfortable, inexpensive room. Plus, most of the hotels offer $20 lift tickets to Meadows.

Call Meadows' Lodging Reservation Service at 1–800–SKI–HOOD (754–4663) to book a participating property and receive $20 lift tickets.

Room & Board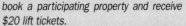

Due to its location on national forest land, the area cannot develop any ski-in/ski-out lodging. The closest beds are a few miles back toward Portland in Government Camp—a small community with a gas station, a small general store, and a few hotels. While the rooms are clean and comfortable they are not "resort" fare. For the most part Meadows is a day area. There is the famous Timberline Lodge nearby, but most Meadows skiers and boarders live in Portland. As such, it's easy to make the drive home since Portland is only 50 miles or so away. Out-of-town guests typically bunk in Hood River—a small farming and tourist community that sits on the north side of Mount Hood on the shores of the Columbia River.

⑪ Nearby

See the Timberline Ski & Lodge (*see page 208*) for additional lodging and dining options in the following locations.

Mount Hood Ski Bowl

Scott Adams

Season: Mid November to mid April

Mount Hood Ski Bowl

87000 E. U.S. 26
P.O. Box 280
Ski Bowl, OR 97028

Ski Report: (503) 222–2695
Information: (503) 222–2695
E-mail: *knorton@skibowl.com*
Website: *www.skibowl.com*
Credit Cards: All major

Operating Hours: 3:30 P.M.–10 P.M. Monday, Tuesday, & Wednesday; 9 A.M.–10 P.M. Thursday, Friday, & Saturday; 9 A.M.–11 P.M. **Night Skiing:** 3:30 P.M.–11 P.M. Saturday & Sunday; 3:30 P.M.–10 P.M. Sunday–Thursday

Background

Located only 52 miles east of Portland, Mount Hood Ski Bowl is Oregon's most accessible ski area and North America's largest night skiing facility. Skiers and boarders can leave the Portland area after work or school and literally be making turns in the moonlight in less than 90 minutes. But Ski Bowl's biggest strength may also be its biggest weakness. Because the area is so close to Portland, weekend crowds can be large. And with only four double chairs, lines may move very slowly.

Located in the southern Cascades and on the south side of Mount Hood, Ski Bowl's snow quality isn't exactly prime. In fact, with a base elevation of 3,600 feet, Ski Bowl's snow is typically water-laden and heavy. But with over 200 acres and 34 runs open each day until 10 P.M., it's still a great place to get away for just a few hours and lay some tracks.

In addition to great night skiing, the views at Ski Bowl are fantastic. Located on the south side of U.S. Route 26, the Ski Bowl looks north at Mount Hood's angry point and the Palmer Snowfield. Even farther north Mount Saint Helens and Mount Rainier are visible from the top of Tom Dick Peak (5,056 feet). To the south, Mount Bachelor and the Three Sisters look as if they are at arm's length.

Mountain Stats

Base Elevation: 3,600 feet *(1,098 m)*
Summit Elevation: 5,056 feet *(1,542 m)*
Vertical Drop: 1,500 feet *(458 m)*
Primary Slope Direction: North
Annual Snowfall: 300 inches *(762 cm)*
Skiable Days: 150
Skiable Terrain: 960 acres *(389 ha)*
Runs: 65

Longest Run: 3+ miles *(5 km)*
Lifts: 4 doubles, 5 rope tows
Lift Capacity: 4,600 skiers per hour
Terrain Classification: 20% novice; 50% intermediate; 30% advanced
Night Skiing: 45% allowance
Snowmaking: 3%
Annual Visits: 140,000

Getting There

- **From Portland, OR:** Take I-84 east to I-205 south. Take Exit 19 off I-205 onto U.S. 26. Follow U.S. 26 for 40 miles (64.4 km). Mount Hood Ski Bowl will be on the right.

Trail Profiles

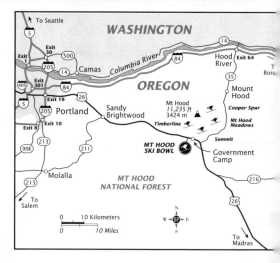

Most of the trails at Ski Bowl are wide open, but the area claims to have Oregon's most difficult snowriding in its upper bowls. This may well be true, as 37 of the 65 runs are designated black diamond runs. The Upper Bowl chair provides access to Ski Bowl Peak (5,026 feet) and Tom Dick Peak (5,056 feet). To the west on Tom Dick, the *West Wall* marks the area boundary and offers 850 feet of outstanding tree skiing down steep lines. More often than not snowriders are able to find fresh tracks in this area all day long. On the opposite side of the area, on Ski Bowl Peak, *Cannonball* serves up more steep terrain with several big rollers perfect for launching down the mountain. The most popular advanced terrain, however, lies in the *Outback*, with its steep lines, tight chutes, and open glades. A quick boot up *Treviso's Traverse* transports skiers and snowboarders to the top of Tom Dick and opens up 300 acres of radical snowriding.

Nearly all of the 14 intermediate runs are located on the east side of the ski area. Two of the most popular are *Mount Hood Lane* and *Fire Hydrant*. Mt. Hood Lane is accessible from the Multorpor chair and provides rolling terrain with a few challenging pitches. It serves double duty as the location for high school racing and other events. *Fire Hydrant* is accessible from the Lower Bowl chair, which means it lies far below the treeline. Its position offers natural shelter from the harsher weather. Snow conditions on *Fire Hydrant* tend to be consistent over the undulating terrain.

While the Ski Bowl terrain is primarily for advanced skiers and boarders, beginners can explore 3.5 miles of turns from the top of Ski Bowl Peak. The *Sky Line* trail explores the edge of the area boundary on Ski Bowl Peak, providing stunning views of Mount Hood and the gently groomed terrain. Novice snowriders will find more terrain on Multorpor Mountain (4,656 feet). *Easy Street* and *Roundhouse*, both accessible from the Cascade chair, explore the area's smallest peak on terrain that is groomed daily. From the Multorpor chair beginners can try *Skidaddle*, which offers more friendly runs on finely groomed slopes.

Snowboarding **Highlights**

Ski Bowl has laid out the welcome mat for snowboarders by building a terrain park that covers three runs and a halfpipe. Covering *Surprise, Easy Street,* and *Broadway*, the park drops 1,500 feet (458 m) from the top of the Multorpor lift and contains up to 20 features, depending on the snow conditions—which in the last few years have been outstanding. The result is that Ski Bowl has managed to build several banked turns, tabletops, rollerz, and spines. The park simply rocks. Located in the park, the halfpipe is 330 feet long with four- to six-foot trannies and the same size verts. The pipe and park are lit for night skiing and built with a pipe grinder by area crewmembers.

More Fun in the Flakes

Bungee Jumping. $25 per jump, 100-foot tower • **Snow Tube Park** includes tubes and tube lift

Skier Services

💲 Lift Tickets

Ages 13–64: $26/full-day, $16/half-day, $20/weekends • **Ages 7–12:** $26/full-day, $18/half-day, $11/weekends 8:30 A.M.–3:30 P.M. • **Ages 65+:** $15. **Ages 6 & younger:** Free • *Prices are based on the 2000–2001 ski season.*

Rentals

Ski Rentals: $20/adults and $14/kids for full-day; $13/adults and $11/kids for half-day; 400 sets. Type of Gear: Rossignol and K2 • **Snowboard Rentals:** $20–29; 180 sets. Type of Gear: Rossignol and MLY • *Prices are based on the 2000–2001 ski season.*

Erik Sanford

📖 Services

Ski School: 30 ski instructors; Private lessons $35 for the first hour and $20 for each additional hour; Group lessons $20/1.5 hours; Beginner's rate $26 for a 90 minute lesson (includes surface tow lift and rentals) • **Snowboard School:** 9 instructors; Private lessons $35 for the first hour and $20 for each additional hour; Group lessons $20/ 1.5 hours; Beginner's rate $34 for a 90 minute lesson (includes surface tow lift and rentals)

Childcare: For children ages six months to 12 years. Hourly and daily programs. Open Friday, Saturday, and Sunday during the ski season. For more information and reservations, call (503) 849–4117 • **Racing:** City League, 2405 1/2 10th Avenue E, Seattle, WA 98102. (206) 323–4573. Outside Seattle: 1–888–323–4573 (*See the side bar on page 166 for more information about City League.*) NASTAR coin-op dual-racing. Junior Racing. Training for 3 years and older. Call Mount Hood Race Team for more information. (503) 272–3503

Room & Board

🍴 Lodging/Dining

See the Timberline Ski and Lodge chapter (*see page 208*) for lodging and dining options. Meadows, Ski Bowl, and Timberline are within minutes of each other. As such the information is exactly the same.

Hoodoo Ski Bowl

Brian Robb/Hoodoo Ski Area

Hoodoo Ski Bowl

U.S. 20
Box 20
Sisters, OR 97759

Ski Report: (541) 822–3337
Information: (541) 822–3799
E-mail: *hoodoo@hoodoo.com*
Website: *www.hoodoo.com*
Credit Cards: Visa, MasterCard, & Discover

Operating Hours: 9 A.M.–4 P.M. Sunday–Tuesday; closed on Wednesday; 9 A.M.–10 P.M. Thursday–Saturday (hours apply from Dec 26th to March 31st); weekends only in April.
Night Skiing: 4 P.M.–10 P.M.

Season: Mid November to mid April

Background

The fact that Hoodoo is located in Central Oregon provides several advantages for snowriders. First, the interior of the Oregon is arid and dry, making for ideal snow conditions. Second, lift lines are non-existent at Hoodoo, thanks to its remoteness and Mount Bachelor's massive skier draw. Finally, Central Oregon is simply beautiful. At 5,703 feet, the top of Hoodoo provides visitors with a perfect vantage to admire Mount Jefferson and Three Fingered Jack to the north and the Three Sisters Wilderness area to the south.

Hoodoo Ski Bowl, the state's second oldest ski area, sits at the apex of Santiam Pass (4,700 feet), just outside the town of Sisters. Hoodoo welcomed its first paying customers in 1938 and installed the country's first double chair in 1942. Today, the resort welcomes guests with two full-service day lodges, three double lifts, one triple lift, and one new fixed-grip quad. In summer 1999, Hoodoo installed the Hodag lift, increasing its skiable terrain by almost 25 percent. The Hodag provides access to the northwest face of the mountain and its primarily intermediate and advanced terrain.

Mountain Stats

Base Elevation: 4,668 feet *(1,424 m)*
Summit Elevation: 5,703 feet *(1,739 m)*
Vertical Drop: 1,035 feet *(316 m)*
Primary Slope Direction: North
Annual Snowfall: 180 inches *(457 cm)*
Skiable Days: 120
Skiable Terrain: 806 acres *(326 ha)*
Runs: 29

Longest Run: 1 mile *(1.6 km)*
Lifts: 1 triple, 3 doubles, 1 new fixed-grip quad
Lift Capacity: 5,280 skiers per hour
Trail Classification: 40% advanced; 30% intermediate; 30% novice
Night Skiing: 25% allowance
Snowmaking: No
Annual Visits: 51,000

Getting There

• **From Portland, OR, and Seattle, WA:** Head south on I-5 to U.S. 20. Go east on U.S. 20 (Santiam Hwy) to Secondary Forest Route 2690. Follow 2690 to Hoodoo.

• **From Eugene, OR:** Take OR 126 east to U.S. 20. Take U.S. 20 east (Santiam Hwy) to Secondary Forest Route 2690. Follow 2690 to Hoodoo.

• **From Boise, ID:** Take I-84 north to Ontario, OR, then head west on U.S. 20 to Sisters, OR. Follow signs from Sisters to Hoodoo Ski Bowl.

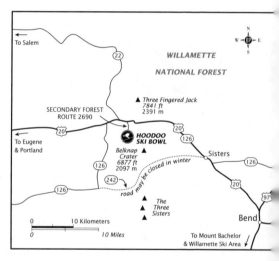

Trail Profiles

Make no mistake, Hoodoo is an intermediate to advanced ski area. In fact, 70 percent of the area is rated as such. All but two of the runs stemming from the top are designated black diamonds. *Crater* and *Face* are steep lines through tight to lightly gladed tree areas. *Grandstand* runs straight down the mountain next to the Green Chair and is regularly filled with monstrous moguls. On the other side of the lift snowriders hit *Dive* and *Mambo* for more turns on steep, ungroomed terrain. Both runs begin above the trees and then drop toward the waist of the mountain.

Thirty percent of Hoodoo is designated blue terrain, with plenty of trails that mid-level skiers and boarders can investigate. Intermediate *Hayrick* starts at the peak and winds around the backside before returning skiers and boarders to the base area. *Slalom Course* and *GS*, both wide open and with perfect pitches for racing, can be accessed here from the Red Chair. *Red Valley*, *Midway*, and *7 Stud* are quick shots back to the base. Steeper than typical blue runs, all three will test the ability of the average intermediate skier while providing fast turns for advanced skiers.

Novice snowriders can explore the top of Hoodoo by taking the *Backroad* to *Summit* or *Schuss Chute*. *Backroad* meanders around the mountain's backside and hooks up with both *Schuss Chute*, which features a straight shot to the base, and *Summit*, which offers a more circuitous path home. Additional green trails can be found off the Manzanita lift. *Top of the Wall*, *Powder Valley*, and *Blue Valley* are all short gentle runs that funnel back to the base lodge. In fact, all 29 trails at Hoodoo lead back to the base, making it a great area to let children run free. Parents can relax knowing that their kids have to return to the lodge with every run.

Snowboarding **Highlights**

Hoodoo is presently without any terrain exclusively for snowboarders, though the resort is in the midst of an expansion plan that includes a halfpipe and a terrain park. The details are not yet set, so in the meantime riders lay tracks on runs like *Boardwalk* and *Frank's Flight*, both of which are short and steep. Other local favorites include *Angel's Flight* and *Red Valley*. *Angel* is a steep trail with a natural roll running parallel to the fall line and nearly the length of the run. *Red Valley* starts out gentle and gets steeper as it nears the bottom.

Brian Robb/Hoodoo Ski Area

More Fun in the Flakes

Hoodoo has 11.4 miles (18.3 km) of maintained **cross-country skiing** trails. The Skyline Trail, which winds around the base of the mountain, is 5.2 miles (8.3 km) long and is open when weather permits. Each day 4.7 miles (7.5 km) are groomed and trackset. During weekends and holiday periods, 6.5 miles (10.5 km) are groomed. Trails are rated from novice to expert.

Skier Services

💲 Lift Tickets

Day (9 A.M.–4 P.M.): Adults (ages 13–64) $26 and Juniors (ages 6–12) $19.50 • **Late Day (1 P.M.–4 P.M.):** Adults $22 and Juniors $16. **Marathon (9 A.M.–10 P.M.):** Adults $29 and Juniors $22 • **Swing (1 P.M.–10 P.M.):** Adults $26 and Juniors $19.50 • **Night (4 P.M.–10 P.M.):** Adults $16 and Juniors $12 • **Seniors (65+):** $13/all times • **Ages 5 & younger:** Free

🅐 Nordic Trail Passes

$6 for adults $4 for children • *Prices are based on the 2000–2001 ski season.*

🎿 Rentals

Ski Rentals: $16/ all ages; 400 sets. Type of Gear: Elan skis and Salomon boots and bindings • Snowboard Rentals: $30/ all ages plus $250 returnable deposit; 120 sets. Type of Gear: Elan snowboards with Marker step-in bindings • Nordic Ski Rentals: $11/ adults; $9/ kids. Type of Gear: Fischer touring and skating skis with Salomon boots and bindings • Telemark Rentals: Demos are $20 • *Prices are based on the 2000–2001 ski season.*

🏅 Services

Ski School: 20 ski instructors; Private lesson $37 first hour, $25 each additional; Group lesson $39–$57 (includes rentals, lifts, and two hours instruction) • Snowboard School: 10 snowboard instructors; Welcome to Snowboarding lesson $50 (includes beginner lift and rentals) • Nordic Ski School: 2 Nordic instructors; Nordic first-time skier package $23 for 90-minute lesson (includes trail pass and rentals) • Childcare: Currently in the works • *Prices are based on the 2000–2001 ski season.*

Room & Board

🛏 Lodging

On-site
RVers can stay slope-side in sites with electrical hook-ups.

Camp Sherman–19 miles *(31 km)* away
Metolius River Lodges has cozy, fully equipped cottages with a kitchen, fireplace, and cross-country skiing from the doorstep; ski packages available; rates $65–$114/night; 1–800–595–6290 or *www.metoliusriverlodges.com* • Cold Springs Resort and RV Park offers five cabins situated on the riverfront, with queen beds and a private footbridge crossing over to Sherman's store; rates $98–$114/night; (541) 595–6271.

Sisters–20 miles *(32 km)* away
Sisters Comfort Inn and Mountain Shadow RV Park is decorated in an 1800's Western theme with modern décor in the rooms; rates $69–$99/night; (541) 549–7829 • Best Western Ponderosa Lodge offers queen beds, an outdoor pool, and a hot tub; rates $84/night; (541) 549–1234 • Black Butte Ranch, 8 miles (13 km) west of Sisters, offers one- and two-bedroom condos, cabins, and homes that are all fully furnished; some condos don't have kitchens; ski packages are available; rates $75–$315/night; 1–800–452–7455 • Squaw Creek B&B Inn has rooms equipped with TV, VCR, and coffee pot, and serves a delicious country breakfast; rates $85/night; (541) 549–4312 • Conklin Guest House offers five beautiful guest rooms with private baths, extra beds, comfortable furnishings, and a fireplace in one room; rates $75–$129/night; (541) 549–0123.

🍽 Dining

Camp Sherman–19 miles *(31 km)* away
Kokanee Café is open for dinner only and serves a variety of interesting dishes including quail, duck, lamb, various fish and seafood, and pasta; (541) 595–6420.

Sisters–20 miles *(32 km)* away

Black Butte Ranch serves all three meals in an upscale atmosphere, with a menu full of delicious selections including eggs benedict, fish and chips, duck, salmon, oysters, prime rib, and sirloin; (541) 595–1260 • **Three Creek Bar & Grille** serves homemade soups, salad, delicious sandwiches, burgers, chili, and ham; (541) 549–9670.

Willamette Pass Ski Area

Willamette Pass Ski Area

P.O. Box 5509
Eugene, Oregon 97405

Ski Report: (541) 345–SNOW
Information: (541) 345–SNOW
E-mail: *snowinfo@willamettepass.com*
Website: *www.willamettepass.com*
Credit Cards: Visa, MasterCard

Operating Hours: 9 A.M.–4 P.M. daily, including holidays.
Night Skiing: Available until 9 P.M. on Fridays and Saturdays from December thru February

Season: Mid November to mid April

Michael Kevin Daly/Willamette Pass

Background

Oregon's third largest ski area, Willamette Pass is best known as the home of the United States Speed Skiing Team. The long steep slopes of Eagle Peak are ideal for racing and training. In addition to watching the team compete, amateur snowriders can join recreational speed-skiing clinics and try out the track on special occasions.

Less than an hour's drive from Eugene, Oregon, Willamette Pass has one of the highest base elevations in the Northwest. The high elevation—5,120 feet on the south side and 5,823 feet on the backside—provides over 350 inches of light fluffy dry powder each year. But Willamette doesn't wait for Mother Nature's cooperation. Each year they lay down a solid base of manmade snow with "Pole Cat" snowmaking guns. Willamette's snowmaking system is the only fully operational installation in the state. The snowmaking system combined with a large fleet of Bombardier groomers allows Willamette to lay down miles of smooth ridged corduroy—even on several black diamond runs with pitches exceeding 35 degrees. But for all its reputation as a challenging mountain, Willamette caters to families by providing long, wide, gently sloped, tree-lined runs. With the exception of the occasional racer-head, the atmosphere at Willamette is relaxed and easy-going. Willamette has several programs catering to kids and race programs that encourage family members to ski, ride, and race together.

Willamette also provides more lift ticket options than any other area in Oregon. Snowriders can lay tracks by the hour, by the vertical foot, or by the day. Willamette Pass

Mountain Stats

Base Elevation: 5,120 feet *(1,561 m)*
Summit Elevation: 6,683 feet *(2,038 m)*
Vertical Drop: 1,563 feet *(477 m)*
Primary Slope Direction: 360 degrees
Annual Snowfall: 350 inches *(762 cm)*
Skiable Days: 140
Skiable Terrain: 550 acres *(220 ha)*

Runs: 29
Longest Run: 2.1 miles *(3.4 km)*
Lifts: 4 triples, 1 double, 1 tubing lift
Lift Capacity: 8,400 skiers per hour
Terrain Classification: 20% novice; 45% intermediate; 35% advanced
Snowmaking: 30%

was the original installation of the First Tracks™ electronic ticketing and Passport Ticket Option packages. They are able to track each skier's activities with real time access. Each time skiers touch their Ski Key to a reader at the head of the lift maze, the system records their lift access. Perhaps the best feature, in addition to tracking and messaging option is that snowriders can go directly from the parking lot to the lift lines without waiting in the ticket office lines.

From the top of Eagle Peak snowriders will find enchanting views of the spectacular Diamond Peak (8,744 feet) to the south. Diamond Peak is a multifaceted mountain that dominates the horizon. Odell Lake, located at the base of Eagle Peak and just across State Route 58, shines and sparkles year round, providing a view reminiscent of skiing at Lake Tahoe. Other landmarks that add to the view include Crescent Lake, Mount Thielson, and Mount Fuji.

From atop Peak 2 the view of the Oregon Cascades, stretching from Bachelor Butte to Mount Jefferson, is stunning. Nearby Maiden Peak lures backcountry skiers and snowboarders who are willing to cross the Pacific Crest Trail to reach its virgin bowl, only an hour or more from the slopes of Willamette Pass. Waldo Lake, one of the most pristine lakes in the United States, lies to the north west, and lends its name to one of our most popular cruising runs *Where's Waldo?*. This 360-degree panorama from Peak 2 offers a real sampling of the finest views available in Oregon.

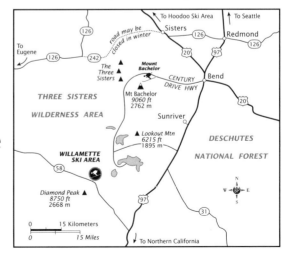

Getting There

- **From Portland and Salem, OR:** Head south on I-5 to Eugene, OR. From Eugene, head east on OR Rt. 58 until reaching the Willamette Pass Ski Area.

Trail Profiles

Just to the right of the lodge is the novice ski area called *Sleepy Hollow* and a slow-moving chairlift to help unsteady snowriders gain confidence. The *Sleepy Hollow* run consists of flat mild terrain placed out of the way of the intermediate and advanced runs, making it the perfect spot for nervous novices to learn the basics. There are only five other runs for inexperienced snowriders to explore at Willamette. While the runs to the skier's right of the Twilight Lift are wide, gentle tracks through the trees, novice skiers and boarders are relegated to this area until their skills improve. The rest of the area's 24 trails are dedicated to intermediate and advanced snowriding. All are long and uninterrupted by crossovers or cat tracks, allowing intermediate and advanced snowriders to explore Eagle Peak and Peak 2.

Local advanced snowriders love carving big high-speed turns from the top of Eagle Peak down runs like *RTS* and *High Lead*. *RTS*, whose pitch exceeds 52 degrees, doubles as the speed-skiing race course and has hosted three Subaru United States Speed Skiing National Championships. The slope is nearly 1,300 feet long with a 600-foot vertical drop. Skiers and snowboarders may slip into fantasy mode after eyeing the deep powder—a powder that falls here with more regularity than one might imagine.

High Lead is not quite as steep as *RTS*, but it offers similar fall-line skiing. The slope's grade exceeds 40 degrees for most of its length, offering a challenge even to expert skiers, without the stomach-in-the-throat feeling of skiing *RTS*. Odell Lake and Diamond Peak reflect their beauty as snowriders descend the slopes toward the base area. A catch line marks the ski area boundary and allows snowriders to access the Summit Chair and return for more excitement run after run—for as long as their legs and lungs permit.

From the top of Peak 2, *Northern Exposure* descends the mountain toward magnetic north. The run begins with a near cornice entrance to a pitch exceeding 40 degrees for several hundred feet before leveling out in an attempt to maintain that 10-foot-tall-bulletproof-I-can-ski-anything feeling of shredding perfect powder or corn on a challenging slope.

Michael Kevin Daly/Willamette Pass

Skiers enjoy the rush of hitting the monster moguls on the upper face of *Northern Exposure* and then ducking left onto *Down Under* for a traverse through some wild whoopdeedos. *Down Under* also provides access for many chutes and shots off rocks and ridges while leading to the base of the Peak 2 chair.

Intermediate snowriders will want to test their turns on *Rosary Run, Kaleidoscope,* and *Swoosh*—all of which are located on Eagle Peak. *Kaleidoscope* and *Rosary* are neat runs for the intermediate skier, tempting them to peek over the entrances to black diamond runs like *High Lead* and *Good Time Charlie. Rosary* has pitches that certainly put a little fear in the Blue Trail skier or rider—but, only enough to bring them back for more and maybe provide the rush that entices them to go to the next level. Otherwise, their gentle nature and beautiful scenery are pure fun.

Swoosh is a trademark run for Willamette Pass, both because of corporate ties to the famous shoemaker Nike, and for the heavily forested, somewhat narrow trails that provide the logo lines of the Willamette Pass image. A true blue square run by Willamette Pass standards, it will build confidence and encourage repeat runs.

Snowboarding Highlights

Snowboarding at Willamette Pass is omnipresent and awesome. Still, to meet the interests of the freeriders and park fanatics area management has built a boarder-cross-style course that offers continuous hits in a controlled area on the southern slopes off of *By George*. Mostly big rolls, banked turns, and quarterpipes, the park offers big air and carving terrain for snowboarders and skiers alike. Regular boardercross competitions and camps help riders develop their skills and compete for fun and prizes. The park is created by Willamette's grooming department under consultation from their International Ski Federation official and director of snowsports, Randy Rogers. Ski school staff riders perform routine maintenance. With the humongous snowfalls recorded at Willamette Pass most maintenance is by necessity performed with Bombardier snowcats. There is currently no halfpipe at Wilamette.

Peak 2 offers *Boundary Pass* and *Where's Waldo?* Both offer a gracious cruising experience to skiers looking for a challenging yet enjoyable "Blue Trail" experience. These two wide-open cruisers stand out from other ski areas' intermediate slopes. They wind along the ridges of Peak 2, offering occasional pitches that any other ski area would tag Black Diamond. The scenery is stellar, with views of lakes and volcanoes visible as you carve your way to the base of Peak 2 for another run toward ecstasy.

The prime bumps at Willamette Pass are found on *Success,* under the Summit Chair, and on *June's Run,* off of Peak 2. Both runs approach 40-degree grades, with the first few turns being the toughest. The slopes mellow with each turn.

But for the hardcore bump skier, *RTS* is it. There is no tougher test than skiing bumps where the natural slope hits 52 degrees. With bumps, some turns are over 60 degrees—causing a reality check in even the best skiers. One bad turn and it's ass and elbows all the way to the bottom.

Willamette Pass provides amazing tree skiing. The slopes described above are tame by comparison. With an average snowfall of over 350 inches, Willamette Pass lays to waste the bad image of Cascade Concrete. The trees between *Boundary Pass* and *Northern Exposure* are a good warm-up for what lies hidden between the pistes off *Junes*, *Timburr*, and most of all *RTS*. From *RTS*, north along the tree-covered bowl between the top of the Summit Chair and Peak 2, is an area known as *SDN* (*Steep Deep & Narrow*). *SDN* is easily some of the best-quality, lift-accessible tree skiing in the Northwest. Lined with monster hemlocks and Douglas firs, the space between is prime. The slopes reach and exceed 60 degrees. From the top of the Summit Chair head toward Peak 2 and then drop in left, anywhere. It may be a bit tight and narrow getting in, but once inside the lines are sublime.

From Peak 2 snowriders who climb the cornice above the lift, or drop in on the left from the top of *Where's Waldo?*, enter what's called *SDS* (*Steep Deep & Silent*). *SDS* offers more of what *SDN* has, but it's accessed by far fewer snowriders. With a little thinning, the hucking would be world class. Cliffs with a 55-degree landing offer serious hang time. Within the ski area boundary is the undeveloped West Peak, which offers off-piste skiing and riding for those willing to hike 10 to 15 minutes from the groomed slopes. The best plan is to hook up with a local to lead the way.

More Fun in the Flakes

There are 12.4 miles (20 km) of groomed and tracked cross-country trails within the Willamette Pass Ski Area. The Nordic center is located at the west end of the main parking lot.

Hourly snowtube rentals and lift access provide fun for the non-skiers who come to enjoy winter at Willamette Pass. The snowtubing center is located near the Nordic facility, at the west end of the main parking lot. Nordic and snowtubing hours are from 10 A.M.–4 P.M. weekends and holidays. Special arrangements can be made for groups by calling (541) 345–SNOW ext. 244.

Skier Services

🇸 Lift Tickets

Skiing/Snowboarding Rates: $29 for ages 11 to 64; $16 for ages 6 to 10; $14.50 for seniors 65 and older; $1 for ages 5 and younger. (All tickets require Ski Keys, a reusable $2 ticketing device.) • **Snowtubing Rates**: $5/hour with a two-hour minimum • **Nordic Trail Passes**: $6 for the day • *Prices are based on the 2000–2001 ski season.*

🎿 Rentals

Ski Rentals: $15/adults and $11/kids; 400 sets. Type of Gear: Fischer, Salomon, Dynastar, and Elan • **Snowboard Rentals**: 200 sets. Type of Gear: Rossignol • **Nordic Ski Rentals**: $8 for adults and $6 for kids • **Snowshoe Rentals**: $8 for the day • *Prices are based on the 2000–2001 ski season.*

🏂 Services

Ski School: 60 instructors; Private lesson $30/first hour and $10 for each additional hour; Group lesson: $15 for 90 minutes; First-timer Package $42 (includes rentals and beginner lifts); Women's programs available • **Snowboard School**: 25 instructors; First-timer Package $50 (includes rentals and beginner lifts) • **Racing**: Willamette Pass hosts the

Willamette Alpine Racing Program. WARP is a parent-run ski-racing organization dedicated to the development of ski racers ages 6 to 20. Coaches lead race training sessions throughout the season for Mitey-mites (ages 6 to 9), Buddy Werners (ages 10 to 12), and Juniors (ages 13 and older). For more information call (541) 345–SNOW ext. 357.

Room & Board

Willamette Pass has day facilities only. A variety of lodging options are available to meet the weekend or vacation needs of families, groups or individuals—and all can be found within 30 minutes of the pass. Many of the facilities offer mid-week lift-lodging packages that can save visitors up to 20 percent off regular rates. These are small communities without much nightlife or aprés-ski activities. The town of Eugene, home to one of Oregon's larger universities, is roughly an hour's drive. There you'll find several options for nighttime activities, including the world-reknowned Hult Center for Performing Arts.

◼ Lodging

Cascade Summit–9 miles *(14.4 km)* on Hwy 58

Odell Lake Lodge has twelve cabins and seven rooms with fishing and mountain bike rentals; rates $44–$95/night; (541) 433–2540 • **Willamette Pass Inn & RV** offers queen beds, kitchenettes, fireplaces, complimentary baskets of muffins and fruit and turn-down in the evening; rates $68–$98/night; (541) 433–2211 • **Shelter Cove Resort and Marina** has eight cabins with full housekeeping facilities, campsites, rental boats, and a general store; rates $65–$155/night; (541) 433–2548.

Oakridge–27 miles *(43.4 km)* west on Hwy 58

Westfir Lodge Bed & Breakfast offers ground floor rooms with queen beds and hall bathrooms, second-floor rooms with private baths, English country antique decoration in the sitting room and breakfast room; rates $80–$90/night; (541) 782–3103.

◉ Dining

On-site

The **main lodge** offers cafeteria style food including hamburgers, home-baked pizza, and Mexican fare. Breakfast is served until 10:30 A.M. daily. The lounge offers a full-service menu, plus items from the restaurant.

Cascade Summit and Oakridge–9 miles *(14.4 km)* and 27 miles *(43.4 km)* respectively

Crescent Lake Lodge and Resort offers in-lodge dining and full service bars; (541) 433–2505 • **Odell Lake Lodge** has in-lodge dining and full service bars; (541) 433–2540 • **Manley's Tavern** offers a dining and drinking atmosphere right out of the television show "Northern Exposure;" (541) 433–9637 • **Timber Jim's Pizza** has excellent pizza and a good deal on the salad bar; (541) 782–4310 • **Rosalina's** is the best Mexican restaurant this side of Tijuana with good food and even better margaritas; (541) 863–3140.

Cooper Spur

Cooper Spur Ski and Rec Area

11000 Cloud Cap Road
Mount Hood, OR 97041

Ski Report & information: (541) 352–7803
You can also contact Cascade Soaring for
more information: (503) 472–8805

Operating Hours: 9 A.M.–4 P.M. Saturday
Night Skiing: available to groups only, call to
make arrangements

Season: Late December to late March

Background

C ooper Spur sits on the northeast side of Mount Hood, with drier snow than the region's other areas. Its location also protects visitors from harsh weather. While the rest of Mount Hood is in the middle of a severe storm, Cooper Spur's guests might be lounging on the sun deck. The only downside to the location is that Cooper Spur receives less snow than other areas on the mountain's southwest side.

The family ski area has been operating since 1927, when it was developed as a ski jumping hill. Sixty years later Cooper Spur still retains its family atmosphere. Lift tickets are notably inexpensive. In fact, most of Cooper Spur's regulars are families who balk at the notion of $40 lift tickets. And with only 10,000 annual skier visits, parents can turn young kids loose on the mountain without fear. Parents who don't ski can also watch their kids from the warmth of Cooper Spur's relatively new day lodge. In 1996 the old day lodge burned down and has since been replaced by a new 3,000-square-foot day lodge, which includes a kitchen and snack bar, plus a lower-level maintenance shop.

Mountain Stats

Base Elevation: 4,500 feet *(1,373 m)*
Summit Elevation: 5,000 feet *(1,525 m)*
Vertical Drop: 500 feet *(153 m)*
Primary Slope Direction: Northeast
Annual Snowfall: 120 inches *(305 cm)*
Skiable Days: 100
Skiable Terrain: 150 acres *(61 ha)*
Runs: 7

Longest Run: 1,500 feet *(458 m)*
Lifts: 2 surface, 1 rope tow, 1 T-bar
Lift Capacity: 1,000 per hour
Terrain Classification: 50% novice; 40% intermediate; 10% advanced
Night Skiing: 75% allowance
Snowmaking: None
Annual Visits: 10,000

Getting There

- **From Portland:** Take I-84 to Exit 64 in Hood River. From Hood River follow OR 35 south to Cloud Cap Road. Go right on Cloud Clap and follow for 10 miles (16 km).

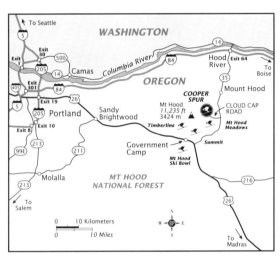

Trail Profiles

Most of Cooper Spur's seven trails are rated intermediate to lower advanced. *Round About* is the steepest run and tends to get bumped up after a busy weekend. The rest of the trails are groomed on a regular basis and cover short rolling slopes that are all below the treeline.

Novice skiers and boarders spend their time in the rope tow area. The slope is nearly flat and right outside of the lodge.

Snowboarding Highlights

Depending on the snow conditions, Cooper Spur will build obstacles for young snowboarders. In the past, these have included a short quarterpipe and a few jumps.

247

More Fun in the Flakes

There are 62 miles (100 km) of **cross-country skiing** trails in the Cooper Spur area. There's also a snow play area for **snow tubing** for $5/day.

Skier Services

🅂 Lift Tickets

Ages 12+: $12; **Ages 7–11:** $8; **Ages 5 & younger:** Free; **Night Skiing:** $5 • *Prices are based on the 2000–2001 ski season.*

🎿 Rentals

Ski Rentals: 250 sets; Type of Gear: Rossignol • **Snowboard Rentals:** 25 snowboard rental packages; Type of Gear: There's a collection of odds and ends, so it's best to bring your own board. • *Prices are based on the 2000–2001 ski season.*

🛎 Services

Ski/Snowboard School: 20 ski instructors and five snowboard instructors; Private lessons $30/hour; Group lessons $15/hour • **Childcare:** None. • *Prices are based on the 2000–2001 ski season.*

Room & Board

A humble mom-and-pop operation, Cooper Spur offers no slope-side accommodations. However, the **Inn at Cooper Spur** is comfortable, rustic, and just down the road from the ski area. For more options visit Hood River *(see page 230)*, just 26 miles (42 km) from Cooper Spur.

🛏 Lodging

On-site

The Inn at Cooper Spur is two miles from the ski area, with six rooms, three suites, and five cabins, sleeping up to eight; rates $69–$135/night; (541) 352–6692

Nearby

See Timberline Ski and Lodge *(page 208)* for additional lodging and dining options in the following areas: **Hood River** • **Government Camp** • **Parkdale** • **Mt. Hood**

🍽 Dining

On-site

Cooper Spur Day Lodge is located just off the slopes, with homemade meals and specials subject to the chef's daily whims.

Summit Ski Area

Summit Ski Area

P.O. Box 459
Government Camp, OR 97028

Ski Report: (503) 272–0256
Information: (503) 272–0256
E-mail: *susan@summitskiarea.com*
Website: *www.summitskiarea.com*
Credit Cards: Visa, MasterCard

Operating Hours: 9 A.M.–4 P.M. weekends and school holidays

Season: Late November to late March

Background

Summit Ski Area opened its slopes in 1927, making it Oregon's very first ski hill. Located on Mount Hood, amidst larger and more modern resorts like Mount Hood Meadows and Timberline, Summit manages to stick it out as one of Oregon's smallest areas.

For challenge seekers, the snowriding here is nothing to write home about. One well-maintained double chairlift and a few mild runs are the extent of what Summit has to offer. The area relies on natural snowfall, so be sure to call ahead for base-level reports before leaving.

So how does it stay in business? Summit's 400 feet of vertical surely isn't what brings area skiers back after all these years. The bargain price is. At a mere $20 a day, Summit is a great place to learn the basics or to just squeeze in a few turns without spending a fortune. In fact, if you can assemble 10 or more guests to buy a ticket, the standard fare for lift, rentals, and lesson runs drops to about $30.

Mountain Stats

Base Elevation: 3,900 feet *(1,220 m)*
Summit Elevation: 4,300 feet *(1,311 m)*
Vertical Drop: 400 feet *(91 m)*
Primary Slope Direction: Southeast
Annual Snowfall: 150 inches *(381 cm)*
Skiable Days: 60
Skiable Terrain: 52 acres *(20 ha)*
Runs: 6

Longest Run: 2,640 feet *(805 m)*
Lifts: 1 double
Lift Capacity: 1,200 skiers per hour
Terrain Classification: 85% novice; 15% intermediate
Night Skiing: None
Snowmaking: None
Annual Visits: 3,000

Getting There

- **From Portland, OR:** Take I-84 east to I-205 south. Take Exit 19 off I-205 onto U.S. 26. Follow to U.S. 26 for 40 miles (64 km) to Government Camp. The Summit Ski Area will be on the left at milepost 54.

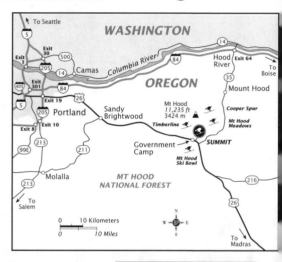

Did You Know...
U.S. Olympian Bill Koch is one of the owners of Summit Ski Area.

More Fun in the Flakes

There are 9 miles (15 km) of **cross-country skiing** trails available at the resort. **Innertubing** is also available.

Skier Services

S Lift Tickets

Adults: $20/full-day; **Children 5 & younger:** Free • *Prices are based on the 2000–2001 ski season.*

Rentals

Ski/Snowboard Rentals: There are two ski shops and two retail shops within 10 miles of the resort. • *Prices are based on the 2000–2001 ski season.*

🏫 Services

Ski/Snowboard School: Group lessons $10. Free for groups of 10 or more with purchase of a lift ticket • *Prices are based on the 2000–2001 ski season.*

Room & Board

🛏 Lodging

See the Timberline Ski and Lodge chapter *(page 208)* for lodging options.

🍴 Dining

On-site

The day lodge is cozy, though rustic and a bit cramped. An assortment of food is available, from omelets to quesadillas, all made to order.

Nearby

See the Timberline Ski and Lodge chapter *(page 208)* for dining options.

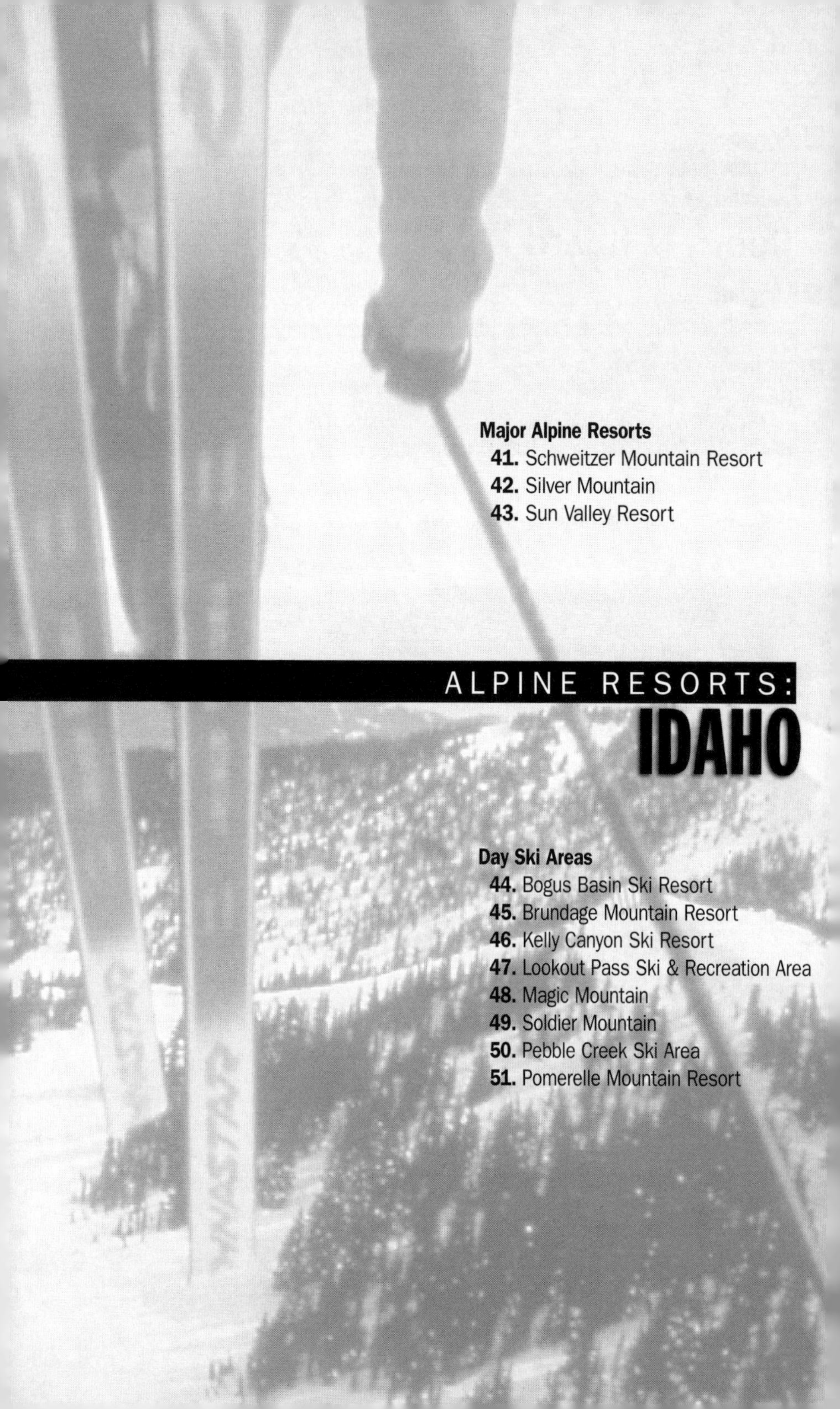

Major Alpine Resorts

ALPINE RESORTS:
IDAHO

Day Ski Areas

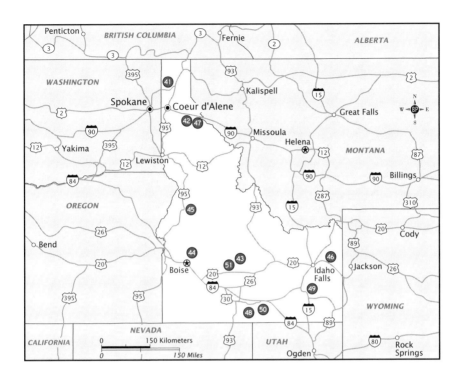

daho is a collage of contrasting beauty. Roughly 16 to 20 lush, green, national forests blanket the state's higher elevations, while the lowlands lie flat and covered in sagebrush and light, dry, bleached-brown sand. Visitors delight in the cool, clear waters of Lake Coeur d'Alene, Flathead Lake, and Lake Pend Oreille, then marvel at the harsh, drastic beauty of Hell's Canyon—the deepest gorge in America—and the eerily lonesome lunar landscape of the Craters of the Moon National Monument. Numerous rivers spread like a waving mass of tentacles around the state, while other areas appear parched. Even the seasons are drastically different from one another. Winters can be cold and bitter, and summers can be hot and suffocating.

Though winter and summer are relatively dry compared to the coastal states and the province of British Columbia—Idaho receives about 50 percent less precipitation—Idaho snowriders don't seem to mind. The harsh, dry conditions produce some of the country's best snow. The snow depths may not rival those in the Cascades of Washington and Oregon, or the Coastal Range of British Columbia for that matter, but the quality is far lighter and drier. Even at lower-elevation ski areas, Idaho's arid climate creates perfect powder on a regular basis. The constant, dry climate also works as a preservative, keeping the snow fresher for longer periods of time. Days after big storms, snowriders commonly find secret stashes of snow almost as good as the day it fell from the sky.

And then there's Idaho's incredible skiing, led by world-famous Sun Valley, whose tradition is being challenged by growing resorts like Silver Mountain and Schweitzer Resort. Sun Valley has always been a favorite of the rich and famous, particularly Hollywood, while Silver and

Schweitzer draw their fan base from all over the Northwest. There's no question, though; Sun Valley is one of the world's glitziest resorts, with stunning architecture, a high-tech lift system, and a snowmaking system that guarantees an early start to every season.

Silver and Schweitzer may never completely catch up to Sun Valley, but the skiing is fantastic and the amenities get better every year. About the only thing Idaho resorts lack are heart-pounding steeps. Instead, the name of the game is precision carving and superb grooming from top to bottom. Picabo Street grew up racing at Sun Valley and went on to dominate the World Cup skiing scene and the Olympics in the 1990s.

Several other smaller day areas are scattered throughout the state, most with limited amenities. But there are two things snowriders can routinely expect in Idaho: the snow will be light and dry, and crowds will be virtually non-existent—even at Sun Valley. Idaho's ski areas are harder for tourists to reach than other areas in the Northwest, and Idaho's population is sparse compared to those of Oregon, Washington, and British Columbia. Expect lift lines only briefly around the holidays.

Getting Around Idaho

● AREA CODES
The area code for all of Idaho is **208**.

⬛ ROADS
To contact the Idaho Transportation Department, call 1–888–432–7623 or visit *www.state.id.us/itd* for current road reports.

✈ BY AIR
Only one major airport services the state of Idaho: **Boise Municipal Airport** (BOI). The resort/ski area or a travel agent can best advise you on the cheapest and/or most direct way to connect from wherever you're departing. They can also arrange transportation from the airport to the ski area.

To book reservations on-line, check out your favorite airline's website or search one of the following travel sites for the best price: *www.cheaptickets.com*, *www.expedia.com*, *www.previewtravel.com*, *www.priceline.com*, *http://travel.yahoo.com*, *www.travelocity.com*, *www.trip.com*—just to name a few. Many of these sites can connect you with a shuttle or rental service to get you from the airport to the ski area.

⬛ BY BUS
Greyhound services most major cities in Idaho. Call 1–800–231–2222 for fare and schedule information or visit Greyhound's website at *www.greyhound.com*. **Northwestern Stage Lines** services Spokane, WA; Boise; Coeur d'Alene; and Kellogg. For information call 1–800–366–3830 or 1–800–366–6975 or visit their website at *www.nwadv.com/northw*.

⬛ BY TRAIN
Amtrak runs the Empire Builder daily from Seattle, WA, and Chicago, IL, to Sandpoint, which is adjacent to Schweitzer Mountain Resort. Amtrak also stops in Spokane with connecting bus service to Lewiston, Mcall, and Boise. Visit their website at *www.amtrak.com*.

❷ VISITOR INFORMATION
For visitor information or a travel brochure, call the Idaho Division of Tourism Development at 1–800–847–4843 or visit their website at *www.visitid.org*. The state's official site is *www.state.id.us*.

MAJOR ALPINE RESORTS: IDAHO

Schweitzer Mountain

Brian Robb

Schweitzer Mountain Resort
10,000 Schweitzer Mountain Road
Sandpoint, ID 83864

Ski Report: (208) 263–9562
Information: 1–800–831–8810;
    (208) 263–9555
E-mail: *ski@schweitzer.com*
Website: *www.schweitzer.com*
Credit cards: All major

Operating Hours: 9 A.M.–4 P.M. daily
Night Skiing: 3 P.M.–9 P.M. Friday–Saturday
and holidays

Season: Late November to early April

Background

In the narrow Panhandle of Northern Idaho lies a Northwestern gem. Spread over two monstrous bowls, Schweitzer Mountain Resort serves up over 2,300 acres of terrain; 2,400 feet of vertical; 58 named runs; a fistful of gladed timber runs; chutes, gashes, and secret stashes; and 300-plus inches of snow annually. The snow is dusty dry thanks to the arid clime of Northern Idaho. Considering the resort's expansive terrain and lack of crowds, snowriders will find plenty of pristine, powder in which to carve fresh tracks—even several days after big storms.

Unexploited does not mean undeveloped. Just a couple of years ago, Schweitzer finished a 10-year $100 million expansion period. Though Schweitzer has somehow managed to stay beneath the national radar, the area now has major-league facilities on the mountain, which are likely to improve after being purchased by Harbor Resorts of Seattle—which also owns Stevens Pass, Mission Ridge, and the Freestone Inn.

The area surrounding Schweitzer is equally impressive. Lake Pend Oreille lies 4,000 feet below the tip of the mountain and runs some 43 miles. On bluebird days, the lake causes the entire valley floor to shimmer and sparkle in the Idaho sun. Framed by the Cabinet and Green Monarch Mountains, the lake is 1,150 feet deep and offers fishing enthusiasts a chance at landing 25-pound-plus Kamloops trout.

Getting There

• **From Seattle and Spokane, WA:** Head east on I-90 to U.S. 95. Go north on U.S. 95 through Coeur d'Alene to Sandpoint, and follow signs to the ski area.

• **From Portland, OR:** Travel east on I-84 to I-82. Go north on I-82 to U.S. 395. Follow U.S. 395 to I-90. Head east on I-90 to U.S. 95. Follow U.S. 95 north to Sandpoint, and follow signs to the ski area.

• **From Boise, ID:** Take ID 55 north to U.S. 95. Continue on U.S. 95 to Sandpoint, and follow signs to the ski area.

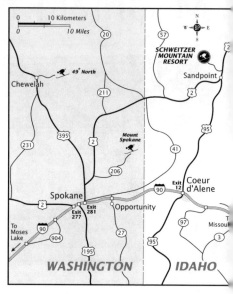

Airport Services: Schweitzer is 11 miles from downtown Sandpoint, ID, and only 86 miles northeast of Spokane, WA. The Spokane International Airport (GEG) is serviced by Northwest, Southwest, Delta, Horizon, and United Airlines. Rental cars are suggested, with most major companies operating out of the Spokane Airport.

Rail Services: Amtrak services Sandpoint from the east and west.

Trail Profiles

With over 2,300 acres, 58 named trails, and countless additional lines, Schweitzer has everything a snowrider could possibly desire in a mountain. That is, with the exception of intense steeps. Black-diamond trails here are indeed challenging for a large percentage of advanced snowriders, but Schweitzer doesn't quite deliver the goods like Alpental, Washington's *Upper International*, or Blackcomb, BC's *Extreme Couloir*.

Schweitzer does have its share of golden snowriding, including hundreds of twisting and turning powder lines through the trees of the *North Bowl*. *Kohlis Big Timber* is a steep glade area north of Chair Six. Locals say when the snow is right, it is simply awesome. *Siberia*, even farther north of Chair Six, takes skiers and boarders to the outermost reaches of the resort. Because of its remoteness, this gladed bowl remains untracked for much of the day.

Exit the trees, and you'll find bullet-train fast blues groomed to perfection. *Kaniksu, Have Fun, Vagabond,* and *Snow Ghost* are immaculately groomed daily and transport snowriders to the bottom of Chair Five or Six. Experts will find these runs a great place to catch their breath while keeping their turns interesting. These same runs also provide a challenge for lower intermediates. To access these runs without treading on the black-diamond trails, take the *Great Divide* from the top of the Great Escape quad.

Mountain Stats

Base Elevation: 4,700 feet *(1,220 m)*
Summit Elevation: 6,400 feet *(1,952 m)*
Vertical Drop: 2,400 feet *(732 m)*
Primary Slope Direction: North and south
Annual Snowfall: 300 inches *(762 cm)*
Skiable Days: 130
Skiable Terrain: 2,350 acres *(952 ha)*
Runs: 58

Longest Run: 2.7 miles *(4.3 km)*
Lifts: 1 high-speed quad, 5 doubles
Lift Capacity: 7,092 skiers per hour
Terrain Classification: 20% novice; 40% intermediate; 40%advanced
Night Skiing: 10% allowance
Snowmaking: Limited
Annual Skier Visits: 135,000

The *Great Divide* is an easy, Sunday-drive ride dividing the *North* and *South* bowl. Snowriders can hit the *Great Divide* and drop in on any number of runs, bowls, or glades on either their left or right. One side or the other always offers superb skiing, depending on the direction of the previous storm and where the sun is. The *Great Divide* is one of the resort's major highways. As such, it tends to see a lot of traffic. Nevertheless, intermediates and novices will love this run because it provides access to many blue-rated trails like *Zip Down*, *Cathedral Aisle, Loophole Loop*, and the *Teakettle Trail*. And advanced riders will like being able to drop off into either bowl for tougher runs like *Sun Dance* and *JR* on the south side, and *Whiplash* and *Shoot the Moon* to the north.

For the youngest of snowriders, Schweitzer has developed the *Enchanted Forest*. Located below the lodge near the base of Chair Two, it's out of the way of any fast, wild skiers. The mild terrain winds through old-growth trees and features a few natural obstacles such as small bumps and swells.

Be sure to check out the two recently cut trails in the *North Bowl: Kathy's Yard Sale* and *Glade-iator. Kathy's Yard Sale* was cut between *Cathedral Aisle* and *Zip Down*. It was named in honor of long-time Schweitzer and Alpine Shop employee Kathy Pelland, who lost her life in a tragic car crash in 1997. The second run, formerly *Hell Hole*, is now known as *Glade-iator*. Having been gladed and widened, it provides access routes to the bottom of Chairs Six and Five. Both runs offer 1,500 feet of vertical and are north facing, with plenty of tree coverage. This combination serves to protect the snow from wind and sun, creating long-lasting, fantastic conditions.

Sunbathers will want to stay in the *South Bowl*. The sunshine strikes earlier and stays longer on this side of the mountain. Try runs like *Stiles*, named for long-time Schweitzertonian Dr. Merrit Stiles. The natural bowl covers over 1,700 feet of vertical and offers gorgeous views of Lake Pend Oreille and the village. The *South Bowl* also has plenty of skill-testing steeps. From the top of Chair One, hang a left down the *South Ridge* and drop into the *ABC Chutes*. The fall lines are aggressive and narrow. To the right of the chair, the *Face* and *Sam's Alley* also provide formidable terrain.

Snowboarding Highlights

Each winter, Schweitzer breaks out its Scorpion Pipe Grinder to build a radical half-pipe. It sits just above the Selkirk Lodge at the bottom of the *South Bowl*, about a quarter of the way down the *Sparkle* trail. A blue run, *Sparkle* is about 1,000 feet long and 100 yards wide and is shaped like a big, natural gully with a vertical drop of 400 feet. The halfpipe is roughly 200 feet in length with 4- to 6-foot-high trannies and verts.

While the pipe is a bit short by competition standards, it is surrounded by an impressive terrain park. A work in progress, the park features several different manmade obstacles, including a triple takeoff, a spine, a tabletop, two quarter pipes, and a mound left over from an old chair tower that boarders love to hit. The triple takeoff is a big jump with three different angles from which to launch. Each one varies in height, amplitude, and distance. The biggest is 10 to 15 feet high. On the other side, boarders will find steep and safe landings. Schweitzer management understands how much fun it is to catch air. And rather than enforce a no-jumping mandate throughout the mountain, the top brass decided to give snowriders a place to cop air safely. The park is monitored, and all launch pads have landing zones on the other sides.

The park is accessible from Chair One. Boarders and skiers can unload from the chair at mid-station and make efficient laps through the park all day. New for the 1999–2000 season, the park is lit for night skiing and is serviced by a surface lift.

More Fun in the Flakes

Last summer Schweitzer added 12.4 miles (20 k) of new **cross-country skiing track**, creating an 18.6-mile (30-k) groomed system. Trails are groomed frequently.

Call the Selkirk front desk at 1–800–831–8810 or (208) 265–0257 (ext. 2280) for information on **snowmobile tours** and **horse-drawn sleigh rides**, plus **snowshoeing** and **snowblading** opportunities.

Skier Services

$ Lift Tickets

Ages 18–64: $35/full-day, $30/half-day, $20/night • **Ages 7–17:** $25/full-day, $20/half-day, $15/night • **Ages 65+:** $30/full-day, $25/half-day, $15/night • **Ages 6 & younger:** Free • *Prices based on the 2000–2001 ski season.*

Nordic Trail Passes

$8/all ages • *Prices based on the 2000–2001 ski season.*

Rentals

Ski Rentals: $23/all ages; 600 sets. Type of Gear: Rossignol • **Snowboard Rentals:** $29/all ages; 300. Type of Gear: Rossignol • **Nordic Rentals:** $17/all ages • *Prices based on the 2000–2001 ski season.*

🎿 Services

Ski & Snowboard School: 52 ski instructors and 12 snowboard instructors; Group lesson $25/hour; Private lesson $60/hour; Early Bird private lesson starts at 9 A.M. for $50/hour; Private $135/half-day, $300/full-day; Children ages 5–11 $50/full-day program (includes lift ticket, lunch, and 4 hours on-hill instruction) • **Nordic Ski School:** $25/all ages (includes lesson, trail pass, and rentals) • **Childcare:** Call 1–800–831–8810 for information • *Prices based on the 2000–2001 ski season.*

Room & Board

🛏 Lodging

Schweitzer Mountain offers a variety of on-site lodging and dining options that fit all price ranges. There are also many choices in nearby Sandpoint.

On-site

Selkirk Lodge is a luxurious hotel with a variety of rooms and suites, with pool, sauna, and more, located slopeside in the Schweitzer Mountain Resort Village; rates $90–$310/night; 1–800–831–8810 or (208) 265–0257 or *www.schweitzer.com* • **Schweitzer Mountain Condominiums** offers various accommodations from studios to four bedroom townhouses, with access to all the Selkirk Lodge facilities; rates $50–$415/night; 1–800–831–8810 or (208) 265–0257 or *www.schweitzer.com* • **Schweitzer Mountain Bed and Breakfast** located on top of Schweitzer Mountain, offers queen beds, a suite, private baths, cable TV, and sleigh rides; rates $90–$165/night; 1–888–550–8080 or (208) 265–8080 or *www.schweitzermtnbb.com* • **TKE Vacation Rentals** offers a variety of cabins, chalets, homes, and condos on and near the mountain, many with ski-in/ski-out convenience; rates $155–$340/night; (208) 263–5539 or *www.tkevacationsrentals.com.*

Sandpoint–11 miles (18 km) away

Lakeside Inn offers waterfront rooms with kitchenettes, hot tubs, sauna, balconies, free breakfast, recreational rentals, and ski packages; rates $49–$79/night; (208) 263–3717 • **Idaho Country Resorts** offers lakefront RV hook-ups and cabin rentals on Lake Pend Oreille; rates $25/night or $185/month for RV site, $150/night or $375/month for cabin; 1–800–307–3050 or (208) 264–5505.

🍴 Dining

On-site

Jean's Northwest Bar & Grill is located in the Selkirk Lodge and serves a wide selection of appetizers, specialty drinks, micro-brews, and cocktails • **Lakeview Café** serves breakfast, lunch, snack, or early dinner, located at the Lakeview Lodge • **Taps** offers a bar menu with live entertainment on weekends and holidays, located upstairs at the Lakeview Lodge • **New Pend Oreille Brewpub** is located in the Lazier Center in Schweitzer Village • **The Outback Inn** is located at the bottom of Chair 5 and is a great place to warm up and get a bite to eat when skiing the backside.

Sandpoint–11 miles *(18 km)* away

City Beach Bistro is similar to a French bistro, with intimate, informal style, extensive selection of wines, and ethnic dishes made with fresh ingredients such as seafood, filet mignon, and even special requests; (208) 255–1018 • **Eichardt's** is comfortable pub and grill located in a historic building mixes casual dining with a plentiful and refreshing menu, a dozen craft-beer taps, good wines, a full coffee bar, and pool table, darts, and board games upstairs; (208) 263–4005 • **Jalapeno's** serves delicious authentic Mexican food with one-of-a-kind huckleberry lemonade, and creek-side location; (208) 263–2995 • **Second Avenue Pizza** offers piled-high specialty pizzas that are loaded with special ingredients, calzones, salads, and sandwiches; (208) 263–9321 • **Swan's Landing** serves seafood, steak, homemade pastas, breads, and desserts, and a variety of microbrews in this rustic lodge with spectacular views of the sunset, reservations appreciated; (208) 265–2000 • *Call Sandpoint Information Center at 1–800–800–2106 or visit them at www.sandpoint.org for more options.*

Sandpoint

The small resort community of Sandpoint lies on the northern shores of Lake Pend Oreille. In addition to a plethora of off-snow activities, delicious dining options, and comfortable accommodations, Sandpoint has spawned a complementary artistic and cultural community. A number of nationally recognized artists make second homes here, and there is also an active performing arts society for music, dance, and drama. The Pend Oreille Arts Council brings national acts that include ballet, opera, classical music, and popular performance-art works. The historic Panida Theater, erected in the 1920s as a vaudeville theater, has been acquired by a nonprofit community group and operates as a performing arts center that attracts a wide range of musical and dramatic acts, including regular plays performed by the local Unicorn Theater. There's also the Performing Arts and Humanities of Sandpoint—a nonprofit group offering education in dance and the performing arts from its own new center downtown, with frequent shows.

Silver Mountain

Photo courtesy Silver Mountain

Silver Mountain
610 Bunker Avenue
Kellogg, ID 8387–2200

Ski Report & Reservations:
  1–800–204–6428
Information: (208) 783–1111
E-mail: *info@silvermt.com*
Website: *www.silvermt.com*
Credit Cards: Visa, MasterCard, & AMEX

Operating Hours: 8:15 A.M.–4 P.M.
Wednesday–Sunday; 8:15 A.M.–8 P.M.
Fridays in January and February

Season: Mid November to mid May

Background

L egend has it that old man Kellogg—father of Kellogg, Idaho—ventured into Northern Idaho's Bitterroot Range in the late 1800s in search of silver. As Kellogg approached the Silver Mountain area, his mule, whom he called "Jackass," became spooked by a noise and bolted. By the time Kellogg caught up with his mule he was ready to turn him into dog food. But Kellogg quickly realized that his Jackass stood atop a mountain bulging with silver. Jackass became somewhat of a legend thanks to his lucky strike, and Kellogg became a mining boom town. When the silver mines were finally exhausted in the early 1980s, residents turned their attention to their other precious resource: snow.

With over 300 inches of light fluffy snow annually, Silver Mountain has had little trouble delighting local snowriders who descend on the mountain each year. Today the abandoned mining caves still dot the hillsides and can be viewed by taking the Silver Mountain Gondola—the longest of its kind in the world—from the floor of the historic Silver Valley to the ski area's nearly 6,000-foot perch. Strung high above the town of Wardner and the abandoned mines, the transport takes guests the 3.1 miles to the slopes in just 20 minutes. Guests load the gondola in Kellogg, one-quarter mile off I-90. The ride allows visitors to relax and take in the stunning views of the valley below.

Mountain Stats

Base Elevation: 4,000 feet *(1220 m)*
Summit Elevation:
  Kellogg Peak–6,300 feet *(1,922 m)*
  Wardner Peak–6,200 *(1891 m)*
Vertical Drop: 2,200 feet *(671 m)*
Primary Slope Direction: North
Annual Snowfall: 300 inches *(762 cm)*
Skiable Days: 140
Skiable Terrain: 1,500 acres *(608 ha)*

Trails: 51
Longest run: 2.5 miles *(4 km)*
Lifts: 1 gondola, 1 quad, 2 triples, 2 doubles, 1 handle tow
Lift Capacity: 8,100 skiers per hour
Terrain Classification: 15% novice; 45% intermediate; 40% advanced
Snowmaking: 20% allowance

Getting There

- **From Portland, OR:** Head east on I-84 to I-82. Go north on I-82 to the Tri-Cities. Take WA 395 north to I-90. Take I-90 to Kellogg. Follow signs to the ski area.
- **From Seattle and Spokane, WA:** Travel east on I-90 to Kellogg and follow signs to the ski area.
- **From Boise, ID:** Take ID 55 north to U.S. 95. Continue on U.S. 95 to I-90. Follow I-90 east to Kellogg. Follow signs to the ski area.

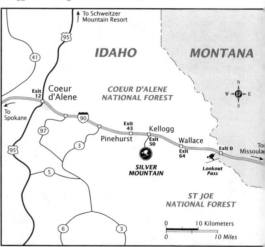

The gondola base, which transports guests to the Silver Mountain, is located in Kellogg, just two minutes off I-90. It's a 20-minute gondola ride to the slopes.

Trail Profiles

From Kellogg, the gondola transports skiers and boarders to the Mountain Haus day lodge, which at 5,700 feet is Silver's main hub. Three of Silver's five chairs either start or end here, and most of the skiing is within 1,500 vertical feet above and below this point on the mountain.

Silver is divided into two distinct areas of terrain: Kellogg Peak and Wardner Peak. From the Mountain Haus, head left (or south) to explore the north face of Kellogg Peak and the trails serviced by Chair Two. Chair One is also in this area but is used mainly to transport snowriders back to the Mountain Haus from the base of Kellogg Peak. The real snowriding, most of which is perfect for intermediates, is accessed from the top of Chair Two. *Sunrise* is the longest run, looping along the ski area's boundary on expertly maintained snow. Also from the top of Chair Two is *Silver Belt*—a dedicated slow-skiing zone. Groomed to perfection, *Silver Belt* provides access to four other intermediate runs: *Back Track, Northern Lights, Quick Silver,* and *North Star*. These runs are fairly broad with challenging pitches and lead back to the base of Chair Two. Overall the terrain is challenging but most intermediates should have no problem navigating around this area.

Thrill-seeking snowriders should pursue black-diamond runs like *Steep & Deep* and *Heaven*. *Steep & Deep* offers an 850-foot vertical line of near-perfect bump skiing. To access *Heaven*, skiers and boarders must thread through a line of tight trees. The intimidating narrow line rules out all but the best snowriders from entering the trail. The low volume of traffic usually means fresh turns.

On the other side of Kellogg Peak, advanced skiers drop into the *North Face Glades* and find excellent tree riding. The lines between the trees are narrow and steep nearly all the way to the bottom. Eventually, snowriders exit the forest onto *Centennial*, which follows to the base of Chair Three and later Chair Four.

Regrettably, Kellogg Peak doesn't offer much for the novice skier and boarder. The only green run here is *Alpenway*, and it's little more than a traverse. In fact, just a small percentage of the entire mountain's trails are set aside for beginners. Most of the eight novice trails are cut below the top of the gondola and lie within a short chair ride of the Mountain Haus. *Easy St. North* and *Ross Run* have moderate fall lines and are groomed flat and smooth daily. Both provide access to *Bear Grass* and *Huckleberry* before reaching the base of Chair Five, which returns to the Mountain Haus. Another option is continuing on *Dawdler* to the base of Chair Three, which also heads back to the Mountain Haus.

Photo courtesy Silver Mountain

Snowboarding **Highlights**

In the wake of the snowboarding phenomenon, Silver committed to riders a tract known as Noah's Park. Chair Five provides access to the park, which includes six to 12 different obstacles, depending on snowfall. Noah is 20 acres (8 h) strong and drops a good 600 vertical feet over banked turns, tabletop jumps, big kickers, and whoop de do's. Silver hasn't erected a halfpipe yet, but the resort does figure one into future plans. In the meantime, Silver intends to build the current park's features right into the mountain this summer. This will not only ensure more consistent and larger features, but the park should be able to open early with less snow.

The top of Chair Five (which is also the top of the gondola ride) is the launching base for three upper intermediates: *Paymaster, Collateral,* and *Saddleback.* These are designated blue/black diamond runs. *Paymaster* may be the toughest by virtue of its steepness and the large, deep moguls that form every year. While *Collateral* and *Saddleback* are groomed smooth, they are also quite steep. Turns on these runs are fast and furious. All three runs drop into the base at Chair Three. Double black diamond *Terrible Edith,* also accessible from the top of Chair Five, features a steep, wide pitch with a sprinkling of moguls. To reach this trail, take *Noah's Park* a short way and bang a left at the sign. *Terrible Edith* connects with *Centennial,* which leaves skiers at the base of Chair Four.

Intermediates and advanced skiers will discover plenty of challenges in the terrain accessed by Chair Four. Locals race to this area at the start of the day. One double-diamond mainstay is Wardner Peak—an expert-only, hike-to-the-top-and-ski-down area rich with deep powder, trees, and fast steep runs. *16 to 1* and *Sheer Bliss* get the legs going right off the top of Wardner. *16 to 1* drops down a steep line through a lightly gladed area and then into the intermediate trail *Gold,* which comes as a welcome relief after finishing the required series of hard, aggressive turns. *Sheer Bliss* rides the ridge of Wardner Peak before entering a crowded line of trees. Snowriders have been known to exit *Sheer Bliss* smudged with tree bark and sap and smelling like pine needles. Unlike *16 to 1,* however, *Sheer Bliss'* terrain doesn't let up. Additionally, *Silver Basin* and *The Meadows* are worthy black-diamond trails. From here, the only way back to the base of Chair Four is over another 1,000 feet of steep gladed trails.

Serious powder hounds might consider bribing a familiarized local into directing them to *South of the Boarder*—Silver Mountain's signature backcountry runs. Accessible from Kellogg Peak, *South of the Boarder* is packed full of powder and fresh turns. Understand, though, that exploring this area without an experienced local, avalanche beacons, and shovels can result in any number of dangers.

Snowriders of most ability levels will love shredding *Centennial* all the way from the top of Chair Four. At 2.5 miles, it's the mountain's longest run. Hit *Centennial* early in the morning before rush-hour congestion sets in. Young, old, advanced, or novice, the challenge is to make the run non-stop. Then try making each run faster than the previous one. *The Ridge,*

Tamarack, and *Gold* are also cool cruisers. A good strategy is to ride these runs to the mid-way loading zone on Chair Four. Below this point the snow tends to be heavier and less maneuverable.

More Fun in the Flakes

For **snowcat skiing** opportunities call Peak Adventures (208) 682–3200 or visit *www.nidlink.com/~snowcat.*

Skier Services

🄢 Lift Tickets

Ages 18–61: $29/full-day, $23/half-day • **Students (ages 18–23) & Seniors (ages 62+):** $23/full-day, $18/half-day • **Ages 7–17:** $20/full-day, $16/half-day • **Ages 6 & younger:** Free • *Prices based on the 2000–2001 ski season.*

🄡 Rentals

Ski Rentals: $24/adults; $12/kids; 200 sets. Type of Gear: Rossignol and Volant • **Snowboard Rentals:** $22; 100 sets. Type of Gear: Rossignol • *Prices based on the 2000–20001 ski season.*

Did You Know ...
To save $2 off lift tickets, go to Rosauer's Grocery Store in Kellogg. Be nice and buy something while you're there.

🄢 Services

Ski & Snowboard School: 80 ski instructors and 20 snowboard instructors; Private lessons $35/hour; Group lesson $15/hour; Beginner's package $35–$45 (includes lift pass, lesson, and rental) • **Childcare:** 1-800-204-6428 • *Prices based on the 2000–2001 ski season.*

Room & Board

Silver Mountain has no on-site lodging, so the town of Kellogg is as close as you can get. Kellogg is an old mining town turned to tourism. The hotels are clean and comfortable, but they're not quite four-star. A good option is to rent a cabin or small house in town. The gondola departs from town, so you're never more than 20 minutes from the slopes. There are also lodging and dining options in Kingston and Wallace. See the Lookout Pass chapter on page 292 for more details.

🛏 Lodging

Kellogg

Silverhorn Motor Inn offers an on-site restaurant and deluxe accommodations with queen beds, laundry, Jacuzzis, and cable TV; rates $56–$61/night; 1–800–437–6437 or (208) 783–1151 or *www.nidlink.com/~sminn* • **Sunshine Motel & Restaurant** offers economy accommodations; rates $36/night; (208) 784–1186 • **Super 8 Motel** offers family suites, pool, spa, laundry, continental breakfast, and free stay for kids under 12; rates $50–$63/night; 1–800–785–5443 or *www.nidlink.com/~super8klg* • **Mountain View Cabins** offers cabins that sleep 2–7 people, have fireplaces, laundry facilities, kitchen, and cable TV; rates $50–$60/night; (208) 786–1310 or *www.nidlink.com/~mtviewcabins*.

Kingston

Kingston 5 Ranch Bed & Breakfast is located near Silver Mountain, offers private baths, Jacuzzis, fireplace, outdoor spa, and delicious breakfasts; rates start at $100/night; 1–800–254–1852 or *www.nidlink.com/~k5ranch*.

Wallace

See **Lookout Pass** on page 292.

⑪ Dining

On-site

The Mountain Haus features the main-floor grille and the top-floor Moguls Bar • **Zanys Café Restaurant and Bar** is located at the Gondola Base.

Kellogg

Broken Wheel serves breakfast, lunch, and dinner fare such as pancakes, salads, and steaks; (208) 784–0601 • **Silver Spoon Restaurant** offers a full salad bar and serves steak, chicken sandwiches, and classic American cuisine; (208) 783–1151 • **Meister Burger** is open only until 2 P.M. with a full breakfast and lunch menu with burgers, seafood, and a variety of soups; (208) 783–5691 • **Sunshine Restaurant** offers breakfast, lunch, and dinner with a wide variety of choices on the menu; (208) 784–1186.

Don Weixl/Silver Mountain

Sun Valley Resort

Kevin Syms/Sun Valley Resort

Sun Valley Resort
P.O. Box 10
Sun Valley, ID 83353

Ski Report: 1–800–635–4150
Information: (208) 622–4111;
    1–800–786–8259
E-mail: *ski@sunvalley.com*
Website: *www.sunvalley.com*
Credit Cards: Visa, MasterCard, & AMEX

Operating Hours:
  Bald Mountain:
    Upper lifts: 9 A.M.–3:45 P.M.
    Lower lifts: 9 A.M.–4 P.M.
  Seattle Ridge: 9 A.M.–2:45 P.M.
  Dollar Mountain: 9 A.M.–4 P.M.

Season: Thanksgiving to late April

Background

On any given run down Sun Valley's Bald Mountain ("Baldy"), snowriders may find themselves skiing alongside celebrities like Arnold Scwartzenegger, James Cahn, Donna Karen, or Clint Eastwood. The "Valley," as local residents refer to Ketchum, Idaho's world-class resort, has always been a favorite of the rich and famous. And for good reason. Sun Valley is simply one of North America's best resorts. Magical scenery, a superbly designed trail system, five-star hillside amenities, light dry snow, the best grooming in the U.S., lots of sunshine, the world's largest computer-controlled snowmaking system, and seven high-speed quads combine to make the resort a must-ski.

Located in the Sawtooth National Forest, the Valley was first recognized for its commercial potential by Averell Harriman, a former New York governor who chaired the Union Pacific Railroad's board of directors in the 1920s. A long-time skier, Harriman decided the best way to attract passenger traffic to the West was to develop America's first grand ski resort. After an exhaustive search, he settled on the old mining town of Ketchum. Harriman coined the name Sun Valley and began construction of the world's first chairlift—a mutated machine previously used to load bananas onto cargo ships. He built glass-enclosed swimming pools, hired chefs to prepare haute cuisine, developed an impeccable service philosophy, and booked a sophisticated orchestra to perform nightly.

Mountain Stats

Base Elevation: River Run Plaza: 5,750 feet *(1,754 m)*
Summit Elevation: 9,150 feet *(2,791 m)* on Bald Mountain; 6,638 feet *(2,025 m)* on Dollar Mountain
Vertical Drop: 3,400 feet *(1,037 m)*
Primary Slope Direction: Various
Annual Snowfall: 200 inches *(508 cm)*
Skiable Days: 150
Skiable Terrain: 2,054 acres *(832 ha)*

Runs: 78
Longest Run: 3 miles *(4.8 km)*
Lifts: 7 high-speed quads, 5 triples, 5 doubles, 2 surface lifts
Lift Capacity: 28,180 skiers per hour
Terrain Classification: 36% novice; 42% intermediate; 22% advanced
Night Skiing: None
Snowmaking: 630 acres *(255 ha)*
Annual Visits: 400,000

Although the resort was clearly setting the standard, there was no way of getting around the fact that Idaho is in the middle of nowhere. To convince skiers around the nation that Sun Valley was worth traveling to, Harriman flew in several movie stars of the late 1930s, including Clarke Gable and Errol Flynn. To this day, the love affair between Tinsel Town and the Valley continues. The resort's recent 50th anniversary gala featured such stars as Clint Eastwood, Brooke Shields, and George Hamilton.

Why is Sun Valley so popular with the Hollywood stars? A stay in the Valley is what some would call roughing it in style. In the last five years the current owner has fuel-injected big-time money into the resort's lodges. The first time you walk through the door of any one of them you'll no doubt feel guilty for tracking snow on the carpet. Some snowriders even feel underdressed. One look at the elegant kitchens and the soft cushy chairs and you may think, "I should be wearing a tuxedo or gown for a place like this."

Completed in 1992, the Warm Springs Lodge was named "top day lodge in the nation" by *Mountain Sports and Living*, formerly *Snow Country* magazine. Building costs exceeded $4 million, but it was money well spent. The immaculate lodge features rustic, hand-notched, oversized logs, high ceilings, and towering glass windows. The Seattle Ridge Lodge made its debut in 1993. Construction of the 17,000-square-foot facility was a major engineering feat, because it was constructed at 8,680 feet. Complete with one of the worlds' largest mountaintop restaurants, Seattle Ridge is built with beautifully oversized hand-peeled, hand-notched, and hand-stacked logs. *Mountain Sports and Living* also designated the Seattle Ridge Lodge the best in the nation the year it opened. Baldy's third jewel, the River Run Plaza, was completed two years later. Like its two older siblings, the River Run Lodge features handcrafted logs, ancient river rock, and soaring glass walls. It has become the predominant access point to Bald Mountain thanks to the base-area high-speed quad that links with the Lookout Express quad to the top.

From the top of Baldy, guests can catch views of the Boulder Mountains to the northeast and the Pioneers to the east. Rising as high as 12,000 feet, these are some of the most photographed mountains in the world.

While Sun Valley ranks among the best ski mountains, the fame, success, and high degree of technology come at a price. Lift tickets are nearly $60 a day, and the resort offers no substantial discounts for multi-day passes. The lodges are beautiful and the food is delicious—the prices, however, are high enough to cause a severe stomachache to the thin-walleted skier. Additionally, the resort is more off the beaten path than other Northwest mountains. Most guests are in for a flight and/or a long drive. Only a few carriers fly into nearby Hailey, and tickets are usually pricey. It all adds up quickly, but for those who can afford it, Sun Valley is one of the best in the West.

Getting There

- **From Portland, OR:** Take I-84 east through Boise to Mountain Home. *[Follow Boise directions below.]*
- **From Seattle, WA:** Take I-90 east to I-82. Go south on I-82 to I-84. Follow I-84 through Boise to Mountain Home. *[Follow Boise directions below.]*
- **From Spokane, WA:** Take I-90 east to Coeur d'Alene. In Coeur d'Alene take U.S. 95 south to I-84. Head east on I-84. Continue on I-84 through Boise to Mountain Home. *[Follow Boise directions below.]*
- **From Boise, ID:** Take I-84 south to Mountain Home. At Mountain Home, take U.S. 20 east to ID 75. Follow ID 75 north to Ketchum. Drive through town and follow the signs to area parking.

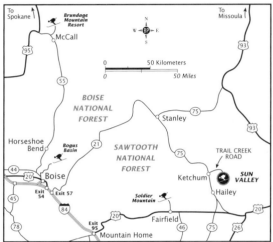

Airport Services: Daily flights into Sun Valley arrive just 12 miles south of the resort at Friedman Memorial Airport (SUN) in Hailey, ID. Horizon Air offers daily flights from Seattle and Boise to Sun Valley. The least expensive way to fly to Sun Valley is via Southwest Airlines to Boise (BOI), where car rentals are available. Flights from Seattle and Portland take under two hours, while the drive from Boise to Sun Valley is roughly 2.5 hours.

Shuttle Service: Daily shuttles from the Boise Airport to Sun Valley Resort can be arranged by calling Sun Valley Express at 1–877–622–8267.

Bus Service: Available to Sun Valley Resort from Boise, ID. For more information, contact Sun Valley Stages at 1–800–821–9064 or Sun Valley Express at 1–877–622–VANS.

Resort Transportation: The Ketchum Area Rapid Transit (KART) system provides free transportation throughout the Wood River Valley, including continuous roundtrips from the village to both Dollar and Bald mountains. Taxi service is also available on request. For information and reservations, call 1–800–786–8259.

Trail Profiles

Stunning amenities and scenery aside, the snowriding at Sun Valley is tremendous. The area map promises 3,400 vertical feet of skiing and boarding and that is exactly what it delivers. Without question, Sun Valley has some of the best fall-line snowriding in the world. From top to bottom it is all downhill—there are no major traverses or flat spots anywhere on the mountain. It's easy to rack up as much as 50,000 feet of vertical in a single day. The lift ride is no more than 15 minutes, and because high-speed quads serve all the major runs, there's virtually no waiting in line. In fact, the only truly busy times are New Year's Eve and a week or two around Spring Break.

Bald Mountain

Bald Mountain is broken into four major regions of terrain: *Seattle Ridge*, the *Bowls*, *River Run*, and *Warm Springs*. Each offers something for everyone, making Baldy a great place for families and groups of friends of different abilities.

Skiers and boarders of all levels can enjoy at least one of Baldy's bowls. Of the bowls,

Photo courtesy Sun Valley Resort

Broadway Face is the easiest and *Little Easter*, the most difficult. In between are six more snow-packed bowls, and each is full of corn flakes during spring. The bowls are accessible via the Mayday chairlift or by skating five minutes across the mountaintop. Mayday is just a seven-minute jaunt, but after riding high-speed lifts all day, Mayday will feel extremely slow. About one-third of the way up Mayday, be sure to check out the "Panty Tree"—a risqué depiction of a Christmas Tree. Guest-donated tree ornaments include racy women's lingerie and the occasional pair of boxers. To the skiers' right of Mayday, the bowls are designated blue runs. To the left, they are single black-diamond trails.

The morning after big storms finds snowriders racing to lay the bowls' first tracks. Making turns in dusty, dry Idaho powder is sheer pleasure. But waste no time. Within two hours of opening, most of the fresh snow is cut up. And by mid-afternoon, the bowls are full of bumps. In early and late-season months, be cautious of rocks and brush lurking just below the surface of the snow on all the south-facing slopes of the bowl—and anywhere else on the mountain for that matter. These slopes get burned all day long by the Idaho sun, resulting in a lower snow depth than on the north-facing slopes.

Novice snowriders will love the slow skiing zone on Seattle Ridge. *Gretchen's Gold* (named after Gretchen Fraser—America's first Olympic Skiing medalist), *Broadway*, and *Southern Comfort* are all wide-open avenues of superbly groomed corduroy. Many agree that the snow on Seattle Ridge is the best on the mountain, due to its location and the resort's superior grooming—even long after major storms. While the entire ridge is a designated slow-skiing zone, aggressive skiers and boarders blast down the ridge when they can't find quality snow anywhere else on the mountain.

Sun Valley: King of Corduroy

The best groomers in North America can be found at Sun Valley. The area's finely mani-cured slopes are the product of one of the largest snowmaking systems in North America and a fleet of snowcats that work from closing to opening every single night. The manmade snow, which is almost as good as the natural stuff, acts as a solid base and covers up the rocks. Once new snow falls, the cats come out and produce sweet, sweet corduroy. A few years ago, the Valley installed a snowmaking system that covers over 600 acres of the area. In addition, area management has invested over a mil-lion bucks in 10 new Bombardier Plus M.P.s. The new snowcats are equipped with the most sophisticated grooming gear available.

There is nothing quite like carving high-speed turns down a perfectly manicured slope for 3,400 feet. About the only time snowriders will find poor ski conditions is when it's raining. But as the name might suggest, this doesn't happen too often in Sun Valley. Guests will find great snow no matter what Mother Nature dishes out.

Photo courtesy Rossignol

On the River Run side, try *The Ridge* from the top. A designated green trail, *The Ridge* is yet another finely man-icured slope with a solid pitch. Novice to expert snowrid-ers can all enjoy this trail. At about 75 yards wide, *The Ridge* is full of smooth turns at any speed. From there, hit *Blue Grouse* to *Roundhouse Lane*. *Blue Grouse* is a short, smooth con-nector run. At the bottom, novices should hang a right onto *Roundhouse Lane* and follow it to *Olympic Lane*, which turns into *Olympic Ridge*. This wide, gentle trail leads all the way to the bottom of *River Run*. Advanced skiers and boarders will want to take *Exhibition* before heading down the Olympic runs. In the 1970s, during the height of freestyle skiing, *Exhibition* attracted skiers from all over the country. Proving one's ability on *Exhibition*, under the chair and in full view of the crowds, was a must for any skier claiming to be a true freestyler. To this day, *Exhibition* is still the best bump run on the hill.

Strong intermediates can try *Holiday* or *Mid River Run* at the bottom of *Blue Grouse*. Each transports snowriders back to the bottom of the Lookout Express. Or keep on going to the bot-tom of the River Run Express. The last choice is to cut across *College* and head back over to the Warm Springs side of the mountain. *Upper* and *Lower College* are accessible from the Lookout Express and Challenger (Warm Springs' high-speed quad). *College* is a specified slow-skiing zone, but advanced skiers often can't help ripping turns down its face. The slope is so smooth and the pitch is just right for big, fast turns. Just remember that control is the key in this area. *College* rides the ridge between the River Run side of the mountain and the Warm Springs side. *College* heads to the bottom of *River Run*. To access the River Run area, as well as the Seattle Ridge area, take *Roundhouse Lane* across the mountain. Another option, leading you into the Warm Springs area, is to take the *Graduate*, *Can-Can*, or *Flying Squirrel*. All three are intermediate blues. On foggy or stormy days, these runs are sheltered from the weather and usually provide better visibility than the rest of the mountain. Taking *College* to the bottom means a ride on the Frenchman's lift, as it is the only way to return to the mountain.

Warm Springs, named for the warm and bubbling water at the base of the lift, is a favorite among intermediates and experts. The top of the area is home to *Warm Springs Face* and the difficult runs *International* and *Limelight*. The interest here, for most, isn't so much negotiating the difficult terrain as it is making it from top to bottom as fast as possible. After a couple thousand feet of warp-speed turns, the thighs will start to burn. Novice snowriders can take the *Greyhawk* chair from the base of the Warm Springs area roughly halfway up Greyhawk and spend all day close to the lodge on blue and green trails like *Hemingway* and *Lower Warm Springs*.

The only types of skiing terrain that Sun Valley lacks are steep chutes and big-air cliffs and drops—though some would argue that catching air isn't really skiing anyway. The name of the game at Sun Valley is speed. Even young kids and mature adults get in on the action during giant slalom races and day-to-day freeskiing. It is not uncommon to see them jamming down the face of *Limelight*, *College*, or *River Run*.

There is one more region on Baldy to explore—and locals won't be thrilled to find their secret has been made public. From the top of Baldy, backcountry bandits can head in the opposite direction of the Mayday lift and be out-of-bounds within 500 feet, carving fresh turns in knee-deep powder. The backcountry skiing is about as good as it gets—even if you had a helicopter at your disposal. For days after big storms there are hundreds of turns in fresh snow to be had. Best of all, snowriding in the Idaho backcountry is legal. As with any type of backcountry adventure, however, tree skiing in unpatrolled, unmarked areas has its dangers. Check ahead for avalanche conditions, look out for fallen trees covered in snow, and travel in groups to prevent getting lost in the forest. It's always a smart move to hook up with someone familiar with the terrain, who knows the way in and the way out. Finding a willing local may prove as difficult as getting it to snow in the desert, but it's well worth a try in order to experience some of Idaho's best turns.

The resort did make venturing into the backcountry much easier in 1998 when a mountain bike trail was constructed up the mountain's backside. Now snowriders can hook into this trail and follow it back to the Warm Springs area. If you drop below the mountain bike trail, however, be aware and considerate of the fact that you'll be trekking through someone's backyard in order to exit. There are many houses and cabins butted up to the edge of the forest and the backside of Bald Mountain. It's also a good idea to arrange for a ride rather than trying to hitchhike back to the lodge, as traffic in this area is unreliable.

Dollar Mountain

Dollar Mountain, located just a few miles east of Bald Mountain, is the area's designated learning center. Dollar dedicates its 13 runs and 628 feet of vertical entirely to novice skiers and snowboarders. At most resorts, beginner areas lie at the foot of the mountain, leaving the possibility open for more advanced skiers to whip by at breakneck speeds. Dollar provides beginners with safe haven, sheltering them from advanced skiers and helping them along with a dedicated staff. On Dollar Mountain, the novices are welcomed with treeless terrain and patient and dedicated instructors who specialize in making the first steps on skis or snowboards a breeze. For information and reservations, call 1–800–786–8259.

Snowboarding **Highlights**

Sun Valley is one of the few areas in the Northwest that doesn't cater to snow-boarders. Currently there is no terrain park or halfpipe on Baldy and plans to build them are suspect at best. Instead, Sun Valley caters to the rich and famous, and these folks tend to be skiers. Snowboarders are welcome on all areas of Baldy with the following exceptions: No riding is permitted on *Christin's Silver* or *Southern Comfort* in the Seattle Ridge area. Riders may use Seattle Ridge to access *Gretchen's Gold*, *Broadway*, and *Fire Trail*. Snowboarders are definitely second-class citizens at Sun Valley, which is why many of the snowriders out in the backcountry are snowboarders. The backcountry offers excellent freeriding.

More Fun in the Flakes

Cross-country skiing. The Sun Valley Nordic Center sits in the backyard of the world-famous Sun Valley Lodge. Cross country skiers here have all the amenities of America's first year-round destination resort surrounding their Nordic ski experience. Two heated outdoor pools, **ice skating**, elegant dining, exclusive shopping, and village ambiance complement some of the most heralded Nordic skiing in the Rocky Mountains. Roughly 25 miles (40 k) of manicured and marked trails begin at the Nordic Center. Gentle terrain at the trailhead progresses to challenging hills. Gliding over glistening meadows at an elevation of 6,000 feet is a unique experience for cross-country skiers seeking a wide variety of classical, skate-skiing, and ski touring.

The largest Nordic ski school in the Sun Valley-Sawtooth National Recreation Area is under the direction of Hans Meuhlegger and comprised of PSIA-certified instructors. The very latest teaching techniques are incorporated into all levels of instruction. (Clinics require a minimum number of students.)

Cozy and warm, Trail Creek Cabin is by far one of the most popular Sun Valley experiences, and is just a short 1.3 miles (2 km) from the Sun Valley Nordic Center. Tours to this famous spot lead skiers along a designated trail that passes gentle terrain and the Hemingway Memorial, offering spectacular views of open meadows along picturesque Trail Creek. A roaring fire warms the rustic cabin and greets skiers. Built in the 1930s, Trail Creek Cabin is a favorite New Year's Eve hideaway for Sun Valley celebrities and also serves as a popular destination for lunch and memorable dining.

Snowshoe trails. The Sun Valley Nordic Center offers 3.7 miles (6 km) of groomed and ungroomed trails for snowshoeing (rentals available). The Nordic Center is open daily from 9 A.M. to 5 P.M. Call for more information: (208) 622–2251.

Skier Services

🟦 Lift Tickets

Bald Mountain

Adults: $59/full-day, $43/half-day • Children: $33/full-day and $26/half-day • *Prices based on the 2000–2001 ski season.*

Dollar Mountain

Adults: $22/full-day, $16/half-day • Children: $16/full-day, $10/half-day • *Prices based on the 2000–2001 ski season.*

📼 Rentals

Sun Valley resort has two rental shops, plus there are six or seven rental shops in Ketchum. **Ski Rentals:** $20/adults for full-day; $15/kids for full-day; 800 sets. Type of Gear: Rossignol and Salomon • **Snowboard Rentals:** $30/adults for full-day; $15/kids for full-day; 115 sets. Type of Gear: Rossignol • *Prices based on the 2000–2001 ski season.*

🎒 Services

Ski & Snowboard School: 220 ski instructors; 35 snowboard instructors; Private lessons $90/hour and $170/two hours; Group lessons $40/ two and a half hours; For ski and snowboard school reservations call 1–800–622–2248 • **Childcare:** For children 6 months or older. Call (208) 622–2248 • *Prices based on the 2000–2001 ski season.*

Room & Board

Sun Valley has developed beautiful lodging accommodations and serves delicious dishes at its restaurants. The skiing combined with the glamour of the resort make the stay a memorable experience for those who want to spend the big bucks. For more thrifty skiers, nearby Ketchum offers more affordable accommodations and restaurants.

🛏 Lodging

On-site

Sun Valley Resort is a full-service walking village with 520 rooms and condos on the slopes and near other winter sports activities; rates $99–$400/night; 1–800–786–8259 or (208) 622–4111 or *www.sunvalley.com* • **Elkhorn Resort and Golf Club** is home of the "skiers country club," with a 132 room lodge and village, oversized guest rooms, king and queen beds, suites with fireplace, separate bedroom, Jacuzzi, and kitchenette, studios, and condos with luxurious accommodations for families and groups; rates $94–$125/night; 1–800–355–4676 or (208) 622–4511 or *www.elkhornresort.com*.

Ketchum–1.5 miles (2.5 km) away

Knob Hill Inn is an Austrian-style chalet with 24 comfortable rooms and suites in the mountains with a pool, spa, sauna, workout room, and two restaurants; rates

$175–$450/night; 1–800–526–8010 or (208) 726–8010 or *www.integra.fr/relaischateaux/ knobhill* • **Best Western Kentwood Lodge** offers rooms and suites with balconies, covered parking, and mountain view; rates $109–$149/night; 1–800–805–1001 or (208) 726–4114.

Stanley–75 miles *(121 km)* away

Stanley Outpost offers rustic lodging with nearby hiking, fishing and whitewater rafting; rates $65/night; 1–888–774–3640 or (208) 774–3646 • **Mountain Village Lodge** offers rooms and suites with beautiful views; rates $60–$120/night; 1–800–843–5475 or (208) 774–3661 or *www.mountainvillage.com*.

⑪ Dining

On-site

Sun Valley Lodge Dining Room serves cocktails and continental cuisine; (208) 622–2150.

Ketchum–1.5 miles *(2.5 km)* away

Felix at Knob Hill serves a delicious menu of continental cuisine; (208) 726–1166 • **A Winter's Feast** offers gourmet dining in a pleasant atmosphere; (208) 788–7665.

Fred Lindholm/Sun Valley Resort

Bogus Basin
Ski Resort

Bogus Basin Ski Resort
2405 Bogus Basin Road
Boise, ID 83702

Ski Report: (208) 342–2100
Information: 1–800–367–4397
E-mail: *info@bogusbasin.com*
Website: *www.bogusbasin.com*
Credit Cards: Visa, MasterCard, & Discover

Operating Hours: 10 A.M.–10 P.M. weekdays;
9 A.M.–10 P.M. weekends and holidays

Season: Late November to mid April

Background

With a name like Bogus Basin, skiers unfamiliar to the resort might expect the snowriding to be…well…bogus. Not so. Bogus is Idaho's largest ski and snowboard area—that's right, even bigger than celebrated Sun Valley, with 500 acres more skiable terrain. Just 16 miles from Boise, Bogus Basin earned its curious moniker over a century ago when excited settlers struck pyrite in the area—that is, "fool's gold." The only thing being mined at Bogus these days are turns of all shapes and sizes, and grins from ear to ear.

Bogus offers up a menu of over 50 runs, 1,800 feet of vertical, 250 inches of annual snowfall, and night skiing on two-thirds of the mountain. Throw in the resort's fairly cheap lift ticket, and it's no wonder many area locals prefer to stay close to home rather than drive the two-plus hours to Sun Valley. True, Sun Valley is one of the America's premier ski resorts, and Bogus' skiing and amenities can not compare. But the lower costs and quality snowriding make Bogus a great alternative that is much easier on the wallet.

Bogus is also home to the only earthen-formed freestyle aerial site in the Western United States, the Meredy Davidson Memorial Aerial Facility. The resort hopes to attract teams that want to train for the 2002 Winter Olympics in Salt Lake City, Utah. In the meantime, catch one of the major events at the area. It's amazing to see professional freestylers twisting, turning, and spinning through the air.

Mountain Stats

Base Elevation: 5,800 feet *(1,769 m)*
Summit Elevation: 7,600 feet *(2,318 m)*
Vertical Drop: 1,800 feet *(549 m)*
Primary Slope Direction: Primarily north
Annual Snowfall: 250 inches *(635 cm)*
Skiable Days: 140
Skiable Terrain: 2,600 acres *(1,053 ha)*
Runs: 51
Longest Run: 1.5 miles *(3 km)*

Lifts: 2 high-speed quads, 4 doubles, triple, 1 paddle tow
Lift Capacity: 8,200 skiers per hour
Terrain Classification: 20% novice; 44% intermediate; 36% advanced
Night Skiing: 66% allowance
Snowmaking: 21%
Annual Visits: 300,000

Getting There

- **From Ontario, OR, and Twin Falls, ID**: Take I-84 west to I-184 (Exit 49). Follow I-184 into Boise. Take Exit 4 off of I-184 on to Fairview Avenue. *[Follow Boise directions below.]*
- **From Boise, ID:** Take Fairview Avenue to Main Street. Briefly take Main Street to North 16th Street. Head north on North 16th Street to West Hays Street. Take a left on West Hays Street and then turn right on to Harrison Boulevard. Follow Harrison Boulevard north. Bogus Basin Road splits off of Harrison Boulevard. Take Bogus Basin Road to the ski area.

Airport Services: Guests can fly into the Boise Airport (BOI), which is serviced by Delta, Northwest, United, Horizon, and Skywest. Should you rent a car, the drive to the resort is 20 miles (32 km).

Shuttle Services: The Bogus Basin Ski bus departs from several locations in Boise—unfortunately the airport is not one of them. For schedules and locations call Caldwell Transportation at (208) 459-6612.

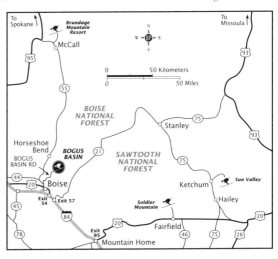

Trail Profiles

Bogus Basin covers both sides of Shafer Butte (7,590 feet) and Deer Point (7,070 feet). They are actually back-to-back basins, with the Butte and the Point forming a ridge between the two areas. Novice snowriders spend most of their time on the front side riding the Morning Star chairlift, which cuts across the basin. Visitors can park in Bogus Creek Lodge's parking lot (at 6,100 feet) or continue up Bogus Basin Road to the Pioneer Lodge lot (at 6,800 feet). Whether novice skiers and boarders start from the top or the bottom the terrain serviced by Morning Star is first-time-skier-friendly. From *Silver Queen* to *LuLu* to the *Sunshine Cat Track*, novices will enjoy riding the wide, gentle slopes.

Intermediate snowriders often head to Deer Point Express—the resort's first high-speed quad—which provides access to the front and back side. The front-side intermediate runs are short, with just under 1,000 feet of vertical. But with the high-speed quad servicing the terrain here, racking up tons of vertical is easy. *Ridge*, *North Slope*, and *Mambo Meadows* are all groomed daily and place skiers and snowboarders near the pickup at Deer Point Express.

Advanced snowriders will find *Suicide* and *Widow Maker*—both serviced by the Deer Point Express—to be challenging runs. Both are often left au-natural for those skiers and riders who like the bumps. During big snow years, snowcats groom out both runs after all the powder shots are spent.

There are five expert-only runs from the top of Shafer Butte as well. *Injun Joe*, *Inspiration*, *Last Chance*, *Liberty*, and *Tiger* are perennial favorites of longtime Bogus Basin skiers. *Injun Joe*, though it's a short run, has some of the best scenery on the mountain. When the grooming fleet hits *Tiger*, late in the season, it can be one of the fastest, steepest runs on the mountain. It rocks on a warm spring day! The only way to access these runs is to take the Deer Point Express to the top and ride down the backside. Then take the Pine Creek Express, installed in 1999, to the top of the Butte. Drop back into the front side and hold on for a great ride.

Novice snowriders can explore only a couple of trails on the backside. *Smuggler* and *Snoozer* will deposit them at the bottom of the Superior or Bitterroot chairlifts. Before venturing over the backside, beginners should know exactly where they're going. It doesn't take much to get off the green trails and into trouble.

Intermediate snowriders have several choices on the backside: *Upper Nugget*, *Paradise*, *Bonanza*, and *Good Enough*. *Upper Nugget* holds the snow and is a real favorite of Bogus guests. *Paradise* is the resort's longest run. It rolls 1.5 miles down the backside for some excellent skiing and riding. Advanced snowriders spend most of their time on the backside riding the Superior chair because it provides access to more expert terrain like *Night Hawk*, *Triumph*, and *Tempest*. These runs hold the best powder skiing on snowy days—and they're lighted at night!

Unfortunately it is a real pain in the neck to predict the ski season at Bogus, as the area only catches the corners of the storms that blow through Idaho. Though the amount of snow can be inconsistent, the quality is always dusty dry.

More Fun in the Flakes

Bogus Basin offers 20 miles (32 km) of **cross-country skiing** trails. Located a half-mile past the Bogus Creek Lodge at Bogus Basin Ski Resort is the Nordic Center. Open seven days a week—10 A.M. to 5 P.M. weekdays and 9 A.M. to 5 P.M. weekends and holidays—the center operates from late November through March. Call (208) 332-5389 for information on trails and lessons.

Sleigh rides are available through Bogus Creek Outfitters by calling (208) 336-3130.

Snowboarding Highlights

Over the last couple of years Bogus has made a big effort to attract snowboarders by building a halfpipe and a terrain park. To access *Playboy Pipe & Park* ride the Deer Point Express to the top and hang a left. The pipe is built and maintained by area crewmembers with input from local riders. The eight- to 10-foot verts are smooth as the pipe is constructed with a Pipe Dragon. By competition standards the pipe is relatively short, at only 120 feet; however, this doesn't stop riders and skiers from showing off in the pipe and making laps all day long on the Deer Point Express.

The Playboy Park is located directly under the top of the Deer Point lift in the *Playboy Meadows*. Though the park is relatively small—there have been only five manmade features over the last couple of years—it is growing. Each year Bogus adds more features, including tabletops, spines, and big-air launching pads and landing zones. Despite its size, the park is fun for riders and entertaining for spectators on the chairlift.

Skier Services

🟥 Lift Tickets

Ages 12–69: $35/full-day, $20–$27/half-day, $20/night • **Ages 7–11:** $8/all times • **Ages 6 & younger and 70+:** Free • *Prices based on the 2000–2001 ski season.*

🎿 Rentals

Ski Rentals: Ages 12+: $18/full-day, $16/half-day, $14/night; Ages 11 & younger: $14/full-day, $12/half-day, $10/night; 800 sets. Type of Gear: Rossignol shaped skis • **Snowboard Rentals:** Ages 12+: $30/full-day, $26/half-day, $22/night; Ages 11 & younger: $26/full-day, $22/half-day, $18/night; 300 sets. Type of Gear: Rossignol and K2 • *Prices based on the 2000–2001 ski season.*

🏨 Services

Ski & Snowboard School: 150 ski instructors and 60 snowboard instructors; Private lessons $40/hour; Group lessons $19/hour. Call (208) 332-5340 for information on times and availability • **Nordic Ski School:** Private and group lessons are available at the cross-country facility. Call (208) 332-5389 for information on times, rates, and availability • **Childcare:** Fully licensed and open Monday–Sunday, 9 A.M.–4:30 P.M.; Friday and Saturday nights 4:30 P.M.–10:00 P.M. Ages six months to six years. Full Day: $30 (diapers) $25 (out of diapers). Half Day: $20 (diapers) $18 (out of diapers). Reservations are required, so call (208) 332-5558 for more information • *Prices based on the 2000–2001 ski season.*

Room & Board

■ Lodging

On site

Pioneer Condominiums offers guests condominiums with a fireplace and balcony, within close proximity to the slopes and the mid-mountain Pioneer Lodge; rates $130–200. 1–800–367–4397 or (208) 332–5224 or *www.pioneercondos.com.*

Boise–16 miles *(26 km)* away

Boise Park Suite Hotel offers free airport shuttle, holiday and weekend rates, and is 10 minutes from Bogus Basin; rates vary. 1–800–342–1044 or (208) 342–1044 • **Idaho Heritage Inn** offers a cozy Victorian environment just 19 miles from Bogus Basin, with private baths, queen beds, and free breakfast; rates $65–$90/night. (208) 342–8066 • **J.J. Shaw House** offers rooms with complimentary breakfast and a separate guest cottage with kitchenette; rates $79–$119/night. 1–877–344–8899 or (208) 344–8899 or *www.jjshaw.com* • **Shilo Inn Riverside** offers rooms with private baths, double beds, indoor pool, sauna, spa, and fitness room; rates $65–$79/night. 1–800–222–2244 or (208) 344–3521 • **Statehouse Inn** offers free breakfast, VCR, and TV; rates $100–$195/night. 1–800–243–4622 or (208) 342–4622.

⏻ Dining

On site

Bogus Creek Lodge (located at the base area) offers tasty cafeteria style menus as well as a pizzeria with fresh baked pizza on the second level • **Pioneer Lodge** (located at mid-mountain) boasts spectacular views and three restaurants: **Bogus Bob's Burgers**, which offers appetizers and a wide array of spirits; **Dirty Bob's Saloon**, a full-service bar; and **Paradise Pizzeria**, which offers fresh baked pizza.

Boise–16 miles *(26 km)* away

Lock, Stock & Barrel serves hand carved steaks, fresh grilled fish, prime rib, all-you-can-eat salad bar, and nightly drink specials and entertainment. (208) 336–4266 • **Milford's Fish House and Oyster Bar** serves fresh seafood and Pacific Northwest spirits. (208) 342–8382 • **Sandpiper Restaurant** serves legendary prime rib, great steaks, fresh seafood, chicken, salads, pasta, and wines with live entertainment. (208) 344–8911.

Brundage Mtn Resort

Photo courtesy Brundage Mountain Resort

Brundage Mountain Resort

P.O. Box 1062
McCall, ID 83638

Ski Report: 1–888–255–7669
Information: 1–800–888–7544;
  (208) 634–7462
E-mail:
  brundage@cyberhighway.net
  Info@brundage.com
Website: *www.brundage.com*
Credit Cards: Visa, MasterCard, & American
Express

Operating Hours: 9:30 A.M.–4:30 P.M. daily

Season: Mid November to mid April

Background

Located in the Central Mountains of Idaho, 100 miles north of Boise, Brundage Mountain Resort is uncrowded and unspoiled. This medium-sized resort offers both reasonable prices and friendly terrain, as well as an abundance of high quality powder, blue bird skies, and awe-inspiring scenery. Brundage is surrounded by over two million acres of wilderness. This spectacular forest is bordered by two of the deepest canyons in North America—the Salmon River Canyon on the north and Hell's Canyon on the Snake River to the west. From the top of Brundage, snowriders can take in the beautiful Payette Lake, Oregon's Eagle Cap Wilderness, and the famed Seven Devils towering over Hell's Canyon. The Seven Devils are seven jagged peaks, all above 7,000 feet. The glacially carved Payette Lake is more than 10,000 years old. McCall is located on the shores of the south side of the clear cold body of water.

Notwithstanding McCall's imbedded roots in timber, mining, and cattle ranching, the community has definitely earned its nickname Ski Town USA. Several Olympic athletes grew up in the area and all but one now make their home in McCall. Patty Boydstun, Jean Saubert, Corey Engen, Dave Engen, Frank Brown, Mack Miller, Tuck Miller, and Lyle Nelson all competed as members of the U.S. Ski Team.

Mountain Stats

Base Elevation: 5,840 feet *(1,781 m)*
Summit Elevation: 7,640 feet *(2,330 m)*
Vertical Drop: 1,800 feet *(549 m)*
Primary Slope Direction: West
Annual Snowfall: 300 inches *(762 cm)*
Skiable Days: 140
Skiable Terrain: 1,300 acres *(527 ha)*
Runs: 38
Longest Run: 2-plus miles *(3.2 km)*

Lifts: 1 high-speed quad, 2 triples, 1 platter tow, 1 handle tow
Lift Capacity: 5,135 skiers per hour
Terrain Classification: 20% novice; 55% intermediate; 25% advanced
Night Skiing: None
Snowmaking: Less than 1% *(4 acres)*
Annual Visits: 108,000

Photo courtesy Brundage Mountain Resort

Trail Profiles

The terrain at Brundage is similar to other modestly sized Pacific Northwest mountains—intermediate friendly and relatively gentle. But it's the 300 inches of light, dry powder that falls each year that distinguishes Brundage from similar areas. And even when Mother Nature isn't cooperating, Brundage's weather conditions tend to be favorable. Often the resort is operating when other resorts in the region don't have enough snow to open. Nearly all of Brundage's 1,300 acres of skiable terrain and 38 trails are below treeline. Not only does this protect snowriders from harsh Idaho winters, it prolongs the life of the snow. The dry climate and tree-provided shelter keep snow fresh long after snowfall deposits.

Novice snowriders delight in the opportunity to explore over two miles of lullaby gentle terrain on *Temptation*, which starts at the top of the mountain and winds its way down the south end of the area. *Temptation* is accessible on the Blue Bird Express quad, which was installed just three years ago.

Terribly nervous novices will find the ballroom dance floor flats of *Easy Street* to be perfect for learning the basics. *Easy Street* is right at the base and is accessible from the Easy Street triple.

Intermediate skiers and boarders typically start the day with Brundage's classic cruiser *Main Street*. The double-wide run starts at the top of the Blue Bird Express and descends a gentle ridgeline. On each side lies ungroomed snow on which intermediates can test their skill—and return to the groomed slope quickly if trouble pops up. Farther to the skier's right of the Blue Bird Express is the *North* trail. It's been given black-diamond status, but most intermediates should fare well. *North* opens with a short, somewhat steep section before transitioning into a lazy-afternoon pitch the rest of the way down the mountain. *North's* strong point is that its snow remains more consistent and softer than anywhere else on the mountain, thanks to the trees that protect the snow from sunlight and wind.

Advanced snowriders spend hours exploring *Hidden Valley*, which is the most northern trail at Brundage. From the top of the Blue Bird Express, hang a left and head out to the edge of the area. The entrance is often littered with rocks and can be exposed to a few cliffs. The best plan is to have a local lead the way as *Hidden Valley* is riddled with cliffs, steep lines, trees, and surprising terrain. Once in the gut of the Valley the trees thin out and it feels like turning through a Christmas tree plantation.

The most intimidating trail at Brundage is the *Northwest Passage*, also accessible off of the Blue Bird Express. From the top it appears to fall away into oblivion. While the *Passage* is fantastic on big powder days, it is brutal when full of bumps—roughly 1,000 feet of mogul-mashing madness.

Snowboarding Highlights

Currently, there is no halfpipe or terrain park at Brundage. However, the area is snowboard-friendly and plans are being made to build a terrain park. In the meantime, boarders freeride in areas like *Hidden Valley* and the lightly gladed lines between *Sidewinder* and *Ranger Trail*. The medium pitched slope here is never groomed, making for ideal turns in soft powder or forgiving crud. More tree skiing can be enjoyed anywhere along the ride by dropping in and heading down the mountain.

Getting There

• **From Ontario, OR, and Twin Falls, ID:** Take I-84 west to I-184 (Exit 49). Follow I-184 into Boise. Take Exit 4 off of I-184 on to Fairview Avenue. *[Follow Boise directions below.]*

• **From Boise, ID:** Take Fairview Avenue to Main Street. Briefly take Main Street to North 16th Street. Head north on North 16th Street to West Hays Street. Take a left on West Hays Street and then turn right on to Harrison Boulevard. Follow Harrison Boulevard north. Bogus Basin Road splits off of Harrison Boulevard. Take Bogus Basin Road to the ski area.

Airport Services: Guests can fly into the Boise Airport (BOI), which is serviced by Delta, Northwest, United, Horizon, and Skywest. Should you rent a car, the drive to the resort is 20 miles (32 km).

Shuttle Services: The Bogus Basin Ski bus departs from several locations in Boise—unfortunately the airport is not one of them. For schedules and locations call Caldwell Transportation at (208) 459-6612.

More Fun in the Flakes

Brundage has recently made **snowcat-skiing** a permanent part of their activities. Experienced backcountry guides show skiers and snowboarders around their personal playground of open bowls, gladed trees, steep chutes, and untracked pow pow. The cats will take snowriders almost anywhere on four mountains providing 19,000 acres of terrain and as much as 2,500 feet of vertical per run. Half-day trips run $125, full-day trips are $200, and two-day trips are available for $495. Be sure to call ahead for reservations. The number is (208) 634–4151.

Sledding, tubing and **ice-skating** are available in McCall. Call 1–800–260–5130 for more information.

Skier Services

💲 Lift Tickets

Ages 19–64: $32 • Ages 13–18 and 65+: $25 • Ages 7–12: $18 • Ages 6 & younger: Free • *Prices based on the 2000–2001 ski season.*

📆 Rentals

Ski Rentals: $15–$28/adults; $12–$28/kids; 375 sets. Type of Gear: Rossignol and K2. Call the Brundage Mountain Rental Shop at (208) 634–7462 to reserve equipment in advance • **Snowboard Rentals:** $24/all ages; 75 sets. Type of Gear: Rossignol, K2, Van's, Hobie. Call the Brundage Mountain Rental Shop at (208) 634–7462 to reserve equipment in advance • *Prices based on the 2000–2001 ski season.*

🎟 Services

Ski School: 30 ski instructors; Private lessons $44–$150; Group lesson $23/1.5 hours; Beginner's Special $29–$36 (includes beginner lift, lesson, and rentals) • **Snowboard School:** 20 instructors; Private lessons $44–$150; Group lesson $22/1.5 hours; Beginner's Special $36–$43 (includes beginner lift, lesson, and rentals) • **Childcare:** State-licensed professional care for children six weeks to 10 years old. Children six weeks in diapers: $30/day and $18/half-day; Children out of diapers up to 8 years old: $25/day and $16/half-day; Hourly Rate $6. For information or reservations call: (208) 634–7462 ext. 128 • *Prices based on the 2000–2001 ski season.*

Photo courtesy Brundage Mountain Resort

Room & Board

Brundage has no on-site lodging, but there are many choices in the town of McCall. In-Idaho Vacation Services runs the lodging information and reservations service for Brundage. For more information on reservations, call 1–888–844–3246 or visit their website at *www.inidaho.com*. McCall also offers many delicious choices for restaurants.

Lodging

McCall–8 miles *(13 km)* away

Scandia Inn offers close proximity to Brundage Mountain, single rooms, and one furnished three-bedroom cabin; rates $40–$50/night, cabin $125/night. 1–888–MCCALL4 • **Brundage Bungalows** features private cabins with kitchenettes; rates $44–$160/night. 1–888–844–3246 • **Woodsman** offers an economy motel with a café; rates $42–$58/night. 1–888–844–3246 • **Silver Fox Tail** is a B&B with a large suite that sleeps up to six people; rates $70–$105/ night. 1–888–844–3246 • **Lodge at Riggins Hot Springs** offers luxurious rooms near Brundage Mountain and hot springs, with all meals and beverages included in room price; rates $125–$320/night. 1–888–844–3246 • **Bear Creek Lodge** offers beautiful and comfortable lodges, cabins, and suites with queen and king beds, fireplaces, and whirljet tubs; rates $99–$175/night. (208) 634–3551.

Dining

On-site

Brundage Mountain Resort offers guests a large menu of food and beverage selections at a reasonable price, so reasonable that even locals recommend it.

McCall–8 miles *(13 km)* away

Bear Creek Lodge offers some of the best dining in town, and serves excellent gourmet Northwestern cuisine with friendly service. (208) 634–3551 • **Bev's Cafe-Bakery** serves a full breakfast and sandwiches for lunch with dinner fare of burgers, steak, and roast on Friday and Saturday. (208) 634–3737 • **McCall Brewing Company** offers a variety of dinner entrees and pastas along with sandwiches, burgers, salads, and has microbrews on tap. (208) 634–2333 • **My Fathers Place** features a traditional menu of burgers, shakes, salads, and a variety of dinner entrees served in a family atmosphere. (208) 634–4401 • **Sharlie's Hideaway** features burgers, wrap sandwiches, and seafood salad and is open for lunch and dinner. (208) 634–1411.

Kelly Canyon Ski Resort

Kelly Canyon Ski Resort
400 Market Street
Ririe, ID 83443

Ski Report: (208) 538–6251
Information: (208) 538–6751
E-mail: *kelly_canyon@hotmail.com*
Website: *www.kellycanyon.homepage.com*
Credit Cards: Visa & MasterCard

Operating Hours: 9:30 A.M.–4:30 P.M.
Tuesday–Sunday (open on Mondays during holidays)
Night Skiing: 6 P.M.–10 P.M. Tuesday–Saturday
Season: Early December to early April

Background

D espite just 1,100 feet of vertical, Kelly Canyon is a well-rounded ski area with a charming, laid-back feel. A lack of lift lines, cheap lift tickets, dry and light snow, varied terrain, and a friendly staff make Kelly Canyon one of those little areas that must be skied. Guests enjoy both the snowriding and the picturesque surroundings of Southeast Idaho. Kelly Canyon Peak rises sharply from sparkling Kelly Creek to reach an elevation of 6,700 feet. Visitors travel from all over the Northwest to witness Targhee National Forest and the Grand Tetons to the east, the Snake River to the southwest, and the towns of Rexburg, Ririe, Idaho Falls, and Rigby to the west. The views get even better after sunset when the small communities come alive and all but the very top of the mountain is lit for night skiing.

With only 120 inches of annual snowfall and only 20 percent snowmaking, you might think that only the lower-mountain beginner runs are open in dry times. Not so. Most of the Idaho mountains are shale, and shale tends to lay flat rather then stick up. Add to that a dry climate and not much vegetation to cover up, and there isn't really a need for a deep snow base.

Mountain Stats

Base Elevation: 5,600 feet *(1,708 m)*
Summit Elevation: 6,600 feet *(2,013 m)*
Vertical Drop: 1,000 feet *(305 m)*
Primary Slope Direction: North
Annual Snowfall: 120 inches *(305 cm)*
Skiable Days: 120
Skiable Terrain: 740 acres *(300 cm)*
Runs: 26

Longest Run: 6,900 feet *(2,105 m)*
Lifts: 4 doubles, 1 rope tow
Lift Capacity: 3,750 skiers per hour
Terrain Classification: 35% novice; 45% intermediate; 20% advanced
Night Skiing: 85% allowance
Snowmaking: 20%
Annual Visits: 50,000

Getting There

- **From Pocatello, ID:** Take I-15 north to Idaho Falls. *[Follow Idaho Falls directions below.]*

- **From Idaho Falls, ID:** Take U.S. 26 east to 160th East. Go north on 160th East to Lyon Creek Road. Turn right on Lyon Creek Road and follow it to Kelly Creek Road. Take a left on to Kelly Creek Road and follow it to ski area.

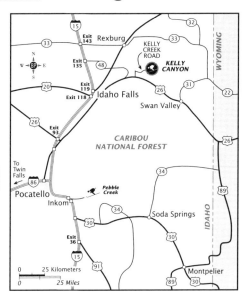

Trail Profiles

Kelly Canyon's 26 trails are cut through a forest of pine, juniper, and aspen trees. A good chunk of the terrain suits the novice skier and snowboarder. One of the most popular beginner trails is *Skier's Lane*—a relatively flat slope on a very slight pitch. With ample width and baby-gentle rolls, even the completely inexperienced can handle this run. To access *Skier's Lane*, take the rope tow up the *Bunny Hill* and ride Chair Three. *Skier's Lane* is clearly marked and clearly visible under the lift.

There is no shortage of blue runs at Kelly. One of the favorite intermediates is *Ernie's*, which meanders down 650 vertical feet of long, rolling terrain through the trees. A few challenging sections keep things interesting, but each levels out innocently enough. The trail takes skiers and boarders to the top of *Skier's Lane* and back to the base area. The fastest way to reach *Ernie's* is to take the Summit chair to the mountaintop and hang a left on the cat track.

Another solid intermediate is *Crystal Cruise* off Chair Four. The aptly named run features gentle, rolling terrain that's groomed daily. Manicured grooming and soft, dry Idaho powder make for an easy-on-the-legs run that winds peacefully around the mountain.

Advanced snowriders have several choices as well. *Dropout* is loaded with 750 feet of piston-pumping moguls on a steep fall line. *Whoa Joe* and *Black Powder* are both steep, ungroomed trails that drop 900 vertical feet from the top of Chair Four. *Dropout* is also accessible from the top of Chair Four.

Snowboarding **Highlights**

The snowboarding train has yet to hit full steam at Kelly. There's no designated terrain park, but boarders do have a small halfpipe on which to cop some air and bust a few moves. Area crewmembers sculpt out the basic shape of the pipe—which runs about 50 feet long with 15-foot walls—with a regular snowcat groomer, then use shovels and other handtools to put on the finishing touches. The halfpipe can't compare with those found at resorts with enough capital to invest in a Pipe Dragon, but that doesn't stop boarders from having fun. The mountain is filled with cruising trails that are ripe for carving and shredding. Located between the runs *Skier's Lane* and *Pinto-Buffalo*, the snowboard pipe is lit for night riding and accessed from Chair Three.

Skier Services

Lift Tickets

Ages 12–59: $25/full-day, $18/half-day and night • **Ages 5–11:** $17/full-day, $13/night • **Ages 60–64:** $17/full-day, $13/half-day and night • **Ages 4 & younger and 65+:** Free • *Prices based on the 2000–2001 ski season.*

Rentals

Ski Rentals: $12/adults; $9/kids; 500 sets. Type of Gear: Rossignol and Solomon • **Snowboard Rentals:** $25/all ages; 30 sets. Type of Gear: various • *Prices based on the 2000–2001 ski season.*

Services

Ski & Snowboard School: 15 ski instructors and 10 snowboard instructors; Private lessons $27/hour; Group lessons $17/hour • *Prices based on the 2000–2001 ski season.*

Room & Board

Kelly Canyon offers a full range of food in their kitchen/cafeteria/restaurant. No alcohol is served on the hill though. Daily specials include barbecue ribs, Dutch-oven potatoes, scones, and drinks. While the resort has no on-mountain lodging, skiers can choose from a slew of hotels/motels within a short drive. Rexburg, Ririe, Idaho Falls, and Rigby are all within 45 minutes of Kelly Canyon and lodging can be found in each.

Lodging

Rexburg–27 miles *(44 km)* away
> **Cottontree Inn** offers queen beds, fitness center, indoor pool, hot tub, and laundry; rates $61–$75/night. (208) 356–4646 • **Days Inn** offers queen and king beds, continental breakfast, and outdoor heated pool; rates $45–$57/night. (208) 356–9222.

Dining

On-site
> There is a cafeteria and lunch counter on the mountain open from 10 A.M. to 9 P.M. daily.

Rigby–20 miles *(32 km)* away
> **Sugar Factory Smoke House** serves a large variety of delicious smoked meats, salads, and Dutch oven stew. (208) 745–7070

Rexburg–27 miles *(44 km)* away
> **Arctic Circle** serves burgers, halibut, ice cream, lots of good salads, and fast food. (208) 356–3640 • **Gringos Mexican Restaurant** serves a variety of authentic Mexican and Tex-Mex dishes. (208) 356–9400

Lookout Pass

Lookout Pass Ski & Recreation Area

P.O. Box 108
Wallace, ID 83873

Ski Report: (208) 744–1301
Information: (208) 744–1392
E-mail: *info@skilookout.com*
Website: *www.skilookout.com*
Credit Cards: Visa, MasterCard, & Discover

Operating Hours: 9 A.M.–4 P.M.
Thursday–Saturday

Season: Late November to early April

Photo courtesy Lookout Pass

Background

L ocated just off of I-90 along the Idaho/Montana border, midway between Spokane, Washington, and Missoula, Montana, Lookout Pass Ski Area often serves as a fun rest stop for through-traffic. Travelers can grab a cup of coffee or lunch in the day lodge and stretch their legs on the slopes before climbing behind the wheel again. Halfpipe enthusiasts might book a more lengthy stay, seeing as the area boasts one of North America's longest pipes. At just over 1,100 feet, it's a wild change of pace for both skiers and snowboarders.

One of the Northwest's oldest yet smallest ski areas, Lookout Pass' location and lack of on-site accommodations make it a non-destination area—especially with the bigger and more developed Silver Mountain just down the freeway. Local residents in nearby Wallace don't mind this a bit. Lookout remains an exceptional value. Where else can skiers spend $20 to carve turns all day? Crowds are unheard of and the snow is excellent. Lookout's 350 inches of annual snowfall are typically of the light, dry, and fluffy variety. And to top it off, the ski area offers a free, 10-week ski and snowboard school for kids ages five to 18 on Saturday mornings throughout winter. Lessons run about 1.5 hours. Call (208) 744–1301 for more information.

Mountain Stats

Base Elevation: 4,800 feet *(1,464 m)*
Summit Elevation: 5,650 feet *(1,723 m)*
Vertical Drop: 850 feet *(259 m)*
Primary Slope Direction: North
Annual Snowfall: 350 inches *(889 cm)*
Skiable Days: 80
Skiable Terrain: 140 acres *(57 ha)*
Runs: 14

Longest Run: 1.6 miles *(2.6 km)*
Lifts: 1 double, 1 surface lift
Lift Capacity: 1,150 skiers per hour
Terrain Classification: 25% novice; 50% intermediate; 25% advanced
Night Skiing: None
Snowmaking: None
Annual Visits: 25,000

Getting There

- **From Seattle and Spokane, WA:** Take I-90 east through Wallace, ID. Take Exit 0 and follow signs to the ski area.
- **From Boise, ID:** Take ID 55 north to U.S. 95. Continue north on U.S. 95 to I-90. Follow I-90 east through Wallace, ID. Take Exit 0 and follow signs to the ski area.
- **From Missoula, MT:** Take I-90 west. Take Exit 0 and follow signs to the ski area.

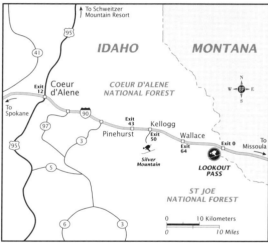

Trail Profiles

Only one chair serves Lookout's 14 trails, but guests can look forward to nonexistent lift lines and crowds. The double chair accesses one small bowl of terrain with 850 feet of vertical. Novices can glide down mile-long *Fitzgerald's Ridge*—to the skier's left of the chair—which skirts the area's boundary over mild, gradual terrain.

Intermediates might take a shot at *Gold, Peretti's Highway*, and *Walt & Merle*. The latter two are wide-open, groomed cruisers that make up most of the Montana side of the mountain. *Gold Run* is accessible from *Fitzgerald's*, on the opposite side of the chairlift and snakes through the trees and back to the lodge. *Gold* is a good choice for beginner skiers who want to take the next step.

Lookout isn't regarded for its expert trails but powder is plentiful. Stashes of snow can be found on either side of the chair near the top of the hill. Skiers can also lay tracks through the trees below *Hank's Haunt*—the second run from the top to the skier's left. As snowriders chew up what little vertical is available, the trees transition from lightly gladed to tightly packed. On opposite sides of the chair, *Idaho Face* and *Montana Face* serve up the area's most challenging terrain. More experienced downhillers often head straight to these two runs on powder days. Understandably, the trails get cut up quickly because of the area's size and lack of additional advanced terrain. To hit the moguls, look no farther than *Silver* and its thigh-burning bumps. *Silver* is a short, steep cut though the trees from *Fitzgerald's* back to the main mountain.

Snowboarding Highlights

In 1998, Lookout opened up *Buzzard's Valley*—an area dedicated to expression sessions for skiers and snowboarders. The *Valley* is actually part of a 1950s mining camp, and the center of it is an old exploration ditch dug by miners in search of minerals. Little did they know that their hard work would result in a winter playground for snowriders. Today, it's a 6-foot-deep ditch that runs 1,800 feet long and about 10 feet wide, and features 10 high mounds of earth along the sides. Lookout removed the trees from both sides of the ditch and built a trail that returns riders back to the base of the ski area. Currently, guests have access to just over 1,100 feet of the ditch. Once the snow falls, the ditch forms the base of the pipe, and the mounds become huge monster hits. Riders can catch major air time and pull freestyle maneuvers from top to bottom. The area is three times the length of regulation halfpipes. The pipe and the rest of the terrain park are maintained by volunteers from a local snowboard academy and area crewmembers. Every Saturday, Lookout runs free time trials as well as several skier and boardercross events.

More Fun in the Flakes

Lookout offers 15.5 miles (25 km) of marked and groomed **cross-country skiing** trails. A one-time $3 lift ticket provides access to the trail system. For **snowmobiling** opportunities call (208) 744-1301. To enjoy **dogsled rides**, call (208) 744-1392.

Skier Services

🅢 Lift Tickets

Ages 19–59: $20/full-day, $15/half-day • **College Students:** $17/full-day, $13/half-day • Ages 7–18 and 60+: $15/full-day, $11/half-day • **Ages 6 & younger:** Free • *Prices based on the 2000–2001 ski season.*

🅐 Nordic Trail Passes

A one-time $3 lift ticket provides access to the trail system • *Prices based on the 2000–2001 ski season.*

🄰 Rentals

Ski Rentals: $18–$15/adults; $11/kids; 300 sets. Type of Gear: Rossignol, Dynastar, and Olin • **Snowboard Rentals:** $24; 65 sets. Type of Gear: Original Sin and Burton • **Nordic Ski Rentals:** $10/all ages • *Prices based on the 2000–2001 ski season.*

🎿 Services

Ski School: 35 instructors; Private lessons $25/hour; Group lessons $15/hour; Beginner's package $32 (includes rental, lesson, and lift ticket) • **Snowboard School:** 10 instructors; Private lesson $25/hour; Group lessons $15/hour; Beginner's package $39 (includes rental, lesson, and lift ticket) • **Nordic Ski School:** $25/hour private lessons only • *Prices based on the 2000–2001 ski season.*

Room & Board

There is no on-site lodging at Lookout Pass, but there are a number of lodging and dining options in nearby Mullan and Wallace. Lookout Pass is close enough to Silver Mountain that a stay in the area would give you easy access to both ski areas in a weekend. For additional lodging and dining options in Kellogg see the Silver Mountain chapter. *(See page 263).*

🛏 Lodging

Mullan–5 miles *(13 km)* away
The **Lookout Motel** is the closest lodging to Lookout Pass available; rates $25–$32/night. 1–800–685–7240 ext. 1670.

Wallace–12 miles *(20 km)* away
Beale House Bed & Breakfast is a turn-of-the-century inn with unique features and architecture and beautiful views, offering a variety of rooms, each distinctively charming, with full breakfast served in elegant dining room and nearby activities such as horseback riding, hiking, and biking; rates $75–$95/night. 1–888–752–7151 or (208) 752–7151 • **The Best Western /Wallace Inn** features regular rooms and suites and has an indoor pool, sauna, hot tub, exercise room, restaurant, and lounge; rates $80–$150/night. 1–800–N–IDA–FUN or (208) 752–1252 • **The Brooks Hotel** offers single and double rooms with a restaurant, lounge, and gift shop; rates $40–$65. (208) 556–1571 • **Down by the Depot RV Park**; rates $33/night. (208) 753–7121.

🍴 Dining

On-site
Lookout Pass Lodge offers a bar and a grill with bar food, hamburgers, chicken, chili, soups and sandwiches.

Mullan–5 miles *(13 km)* away
The **Silver Dollar** restaurant/bar has a great "Big Daddy" sandwich, and spicy fries that are out of this world. (208) 744–1786.

Wallace–12 miles *(20 km)* away
The **Jameson Restaurant** serves steaks, seafood, pasta, deli sandwiches, and Cajun entrees. (208) 556–6000 • **Pizza Factory** serves a variety of pasta dishes, sandwiches, and specialty pizzas. (208) 753–9003 • **Silver Lantern Drive-in** serves diner-style food. (208) 753–8471 • **Sweets Café** offers a full menu for breakfast, lunch, and dinner with homemade pies and puddings. (208) 556–4661.

Magic Mountain

Magic Mountain
3367 N. 3600 E.
Kimberly, ID 83341

Ski & Information Report: (208) 423–6221
Credit Cards: Visa & MasterCard

Operating Hours: 9:30 A.M.–4 P.M.
Friday–Sunday
Season: Mid December to early April

Background

Situated in the rustic outback of South Central Idaho's Sawtooth National Forest, Magic Mountain has the rugged feel of a ski area founded by an Idaho mountaineer. The lodge is reflective of that environment, yet it does get the job done. The food is simple, but satisfying. As for the mountain, it appeals to a freerider's spirit by peacefully co-existing with the surrounding terrain. Eleven runs, steep and challenging, are built around their natural setting, as opposed to plowing directly over it. And so the mountain's raw character is left intact. Ample steeps, jumps, and cliffs allow true snowriders to test their muscle against the might of the mountain.

The real downside to Magic Mountain is obviously the lack of on-site accommodation and guest services. It's always a trade off, but the lack of attention to "resort" services keeps the prices in check, the visitor numbers down, and the lines short. It's enough to say that Magic's loyal locals are not complaining.

Mountain Stats

Base Elevation: 6,410 feet *(1,955 m)*
Summit Elevation: 7,200 feet *(2,196 m)*
Vertical Drop: 790 feet *(241 m)*
Primary Slope Direction: East
Annual Snowfall: 160 inches *(305 cm)*
Skiable Days: 64
Skiable Terrain: 330 acres *(153 ha)*
Runs: 11

Longest Run: 1 mile *(1.6 km)*
Lifts: 1 double, 2 surface lifts
Lift Capacity: 5,000 skiers per hour
Terrain Classification: 30% novice; 35% intermediate; 35% advanced
Night Skiing: None
Snowmaking: None
Annual visits: 6,000

Getting There

- **From Boise, ID:** Take I-84 southeast to U.S. 93. Take U.S. 93 south to county trunk road G-3. Take G-3 east to Magic Mountain.
- **From Pocatello, ID:** Take I-86 west to I-84. Continue west to U.S. 93. Take U.S. 93 south to county trunk road G-3. Take G-3 east to Magic Mountain.

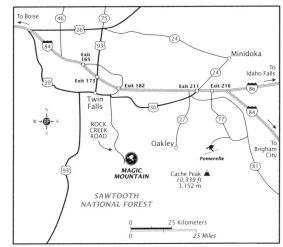

Skier Services

Lift Tickets
All ages: $20/day • Ages 7 & younger and 70+: Free

Rentals
Ski Rentals: $15/all ages; 125 sets. Type of gear: Rossignol

Services
Ski School: Private lessons $28/hour; Semi-private lessons $35/hour; Group lessons $15/hour

Snowboarding Highlights

Snowboarding was first allowed here in 1988. There are 11 trails total. The park has one halfpipe. Clinics are available three days a week, twice daily.

More Fun in the Flakes

Magic has 30 miles (48 km) of **cross-country skiing** trails—15 miles (24 km) of which are groomed. Overnight on-trail lodging is available.

Room & Board

Since there's no on-site lodging, the best bet is to drive the 37 miles (60 km) north to the town of Twin Falls. Carved out of the rugged sagebrush-covered desert along the edge of the picturesque Snake River Canyon, Twin Falls is Idaho's fourth largest city and well suited to providing food and lodging for slope-worn skiers. There are several decent restaurants along Twin Fall's Blue Lakes Boulevard.

Soldier Mountain

Soldier Mountain Ski Area

P.O. Box 539
Fairfield, ID 83327

Ski Report & Information:
(208) 764–2526 or (208) 764–2506

Operating Hours:
9:30 A.M.–4 P.M. Wednesday–Sunday

Season: Early December to early April

Background

Visiting Soldier Mountain is like going back in time to a simpler—and far less expensive—way of life. Owned in part by movie star Bruce Willis, Soldier Mountain is one of Idaho's hidden jewels. Located in the Camas Valley, halfway between Boise and Sun Valley, Soldier overlooks the serene Camas Prairie and provides a perfect vantage from which to see seven different mountain ranges.

In the last few years, Soldier has installed a new handle-tow above the day lodge to enhance the existing beginner area. Beginners can now practice carving turns on a steeper, longer slope before boarding the chairlift and the main mountain. More advanced skiers and snowboarders will rejoice in the recent addition of cat-transport. Snowriders looking for a piece of the outstanding backcountry action used to have to walk or skate it out. Now the treasured powder is accessible by snowcats.

Mountain Stats

Base Elevation: 6,970 feet *(2,126 m)*
Summit Elevation: 9,570 feet *(2,919 m)*
Vertical Drop: 2,600 feet *(793 m)*
Annual Snowfall: 160 inches
Skiable Terrain: 2,300 acres *(932 ha)*
Runs: 36
Longest Run: 6,600 feet *(2,013 m)*

Lifts: 2 doubles, 1 handle tow, 1 rope tow
Lift Capacity: 3,080 skiers per hour
Terrain Classification: 25% novice; 60% intermediate; 15% advanced
Night Skiing: None
Snowmaking: 40%

Getting There

- **From Boise, ID:** Take I-84 south to U.S. 20. Go east on U.S. 20 and then head north at the sign to Fairfield and Soldier Mountain.
- **From Idaho Falls, ID:** Take I-15 south to I-84. Take I-84 west to U.S. 20. Follow U.S. 20 east and then head north at the sign to Fairfield and Soldier Mountain.

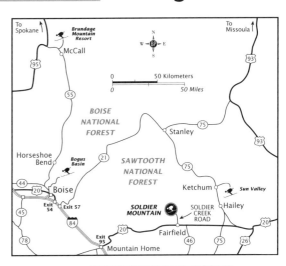

Skier Services

$ Lift Tickets

Adults: $25/day; **Youth:** $19/day; **Ages 6 & younger:** Free • *Prices are based on the 2000–2001 ski season.*

More Fun in the Flakes

Soldier has 1.25 miles (2 km) of **cross-country skiing** trails. **Cat-skiing** is available for $149/day.

Room & Board

Lodging

Fairfield
Elkridge Mountain Inn. (208) 764–2247
Soldier Mountain Country Club & Resort. 208) 764–2506

Bellevue
High Country Motel. (208) 788–2050

Dining

The base lodge serves breakfast, lunch, and dinner with a large fireplace for atmosphere. The nearby town of Fairfield offers numerous restaurant choices as well.

Pebble Creek Ski Area

Pebble Creek Ski Area

P.O. Box 370
3340 E. Green Canyon Road
Inkom, ID 83245

Ski Report:
1–877–524–7669; (208) 775–4451
Information: (208) 775–4452
E-mail: *pebblecr@cyberhighway.net*
Website: *www.pebblecreekskiarea.com*
Credit Cards: Visa, MasterCard, & Discover

Operating Hours: 9:30 A.M.–4 P.M. daily
(closed Christmas day)
Night Skiing: 4 P.M.–9:30 P.M. Friday &
Saturday (January through mid March)

Season: Mid December to early April

Background

L ocated in the southeast corner of Idaho in the Caribou National Forest, Pebble Creek is a wonderful undiscovered ski area with plenty of light snow and virtually non-existent lift lines. The 1,100 skiable acres provides enough playful terrain for all skill levels. Affectionately known as "The Rock" by locals, many under-capitalized plans to develop Pebble Creek have fallen through over the years. As such, the current lift circuit and day lodge are adequate, for now. With an infusion of capital, Pebble Creek would draw more snowriders from all over the western United States. Until then, however, Pebble Creek will continue to be a local's playground with outstanding snow, low prices, and small crowds.

Trail Profiles

Weekends can be crowded with Pocatello Powder Pigs converging on the place and only three slow moving chairs to distribute snowriders across the hill. During the week, however, Pebble Creek is like a ghost town. Visitors share the area with 50 to 100 folks. After big dumps of snow midweek trips guarantee awesome powder skiing and snowboarding.

The current lift-serviced area is limited to a west and northwest lower flank on the 9,300-foot Mount Bonneville. Three old but well-kept lifts (two doubles and a triple) provide access to 45 runs. But the pounding dished out by 1,600 feet of steep challenging terrain makes the 12 creaking minutes on the lift a nice break. However, if the double chair lift is closed for maintenance, as it often is, advanced skiers and snowboarders will get bored.

Novice skiers and boarders will enjoy the terrain that's specifically set aside for them off of the Aspen Lift, a double chair. Tucked away from the more aggressive snowriders, the novice terrain is a combination of several wide runs that overlap each other to form a big rolling playground. But novice skiers and boarders are not stuck with the terrain accessible from only one lift. They can explore the top of the mountain by taking the Skyline lift and

Mountain Stats

Base Elevation: 6,300 feet *(1,920 m)*
Summit Elevation: 8,300 feet *(2,530 m)*
Vertical Drop: 2,000 feet *(610 m)*
Primary Slope Direction: Northwest
Annual Snowfall: 250 inches *(635 cm)*
Skiable Days: 120
Skiable Terrain: 650 acres *(263 ha)* lift-served; 1,100 acres *(446 h)* in-bounds
Runs: 45

Longest Run: 6,000 feet *(1,829 m)*
Lifts: 2 doubles, 1 triple
Lift Capacity: 3,300 skiers per hour
Terrain Classification: 12% novice; 35% intermediate; 53% advanced
Night Skiing: Aspen lift only
Snowmaking: 15%
Annual Visits: 45,000

Getting There

• **From Twin Falls, ID:** Head south on I-84 to I-86. Take I-86 east to I-15. Take I-15 south to the Inkom, ID, exit. From Inkom, take the Green Canyon Road. It's only five miles (8 km) up a newly paved road to the ski area parking lot.

Airport Services: The nearest airport to Pebble Creek is Pocatello Municipal Airport (PIH), which is serviced by Horizon Air and Skywest (a Delta connection). Salt Lake City International Airport (SLC) is the nearest international airport to Pebble Creek (2.5 hours away). Rental cars are available at both airports.

working their way through the kinky *Pebble Lane*. Groomed to perfection every day, *Pebble Lane* twists and turns back and forth across the mountain at least 10 times. Novice riders and skiers love the long trail and all its turns.

Intermediate skiers have their choice of cool cruising and easy powder skiing. From the top *Stacy's* starts off with a steep groomed fall line trail and then heads into *Lower Green Canyon* for a fast trip to the bottom. Strong intermediates and advanced skiers rip turns down the face of *Green Canyon*.

Powder pups will enjoy the ungroomed but gentle terrain in *Evan's Glade* and *Sun Bowl*. The super light Idaho snow makes it easy for intermediate snowriders to have fun off-piste. The only problem with these runs is the long traverse back to the base area.

Advanced/expert skiers and snowboarders relish the fact that Pebble Creek offers so much backcountry skiing. From the top of the Skyline double it's a 45-minute skin up and over. The so-called Backside offers 2,000 plus acres, somewhat gentler than the frontside. Long runs of powder wait for snowriders who are willing to work for their turns. A long run out makes vehicle spotting on the backside tough. The best plan is to leave the car in the Pebble Creek parking lot and go back up and over into the sun at the end of the day. Be sure to carry avalanche transceivers, shovels, other appropriate gear, and DO NOT travel alone. Connecting with an experienced local is the best idea. Pebble Creek provides $5 one-time lift tickets for those who want a backcountry adventure. Keep in mind, the mountain does not patrol the area and snowriders who require rescue are responsible for any associated costs.

A somewhat easier touring adventure can be had by exploring the out-of-bounds terrain on *Bonneville Ridge* and the *Glades*, which are to the skier's far left. Both area's are labeled on the map and can be accessed by traversing high above the Skyline lift. Once snowboarders and skiers begin nearing the bottom of these backcountry areas they can traverse back to the lifts, or certainly the access road.

Snowboarding Highlights

Pebble Creek builds a halfpipe near the base of the Aspen Lift every year.

Skier Services

🆂 Lift Tickets

Ages 13–69: $25/full-day, $20/half-day; **Ages 70+:** $15/full-day, $10/half-day; **Ages 6–12:** $15/full-day, $10/half-day; **Ages 5 & younger:** $5/all times • *Prices based on the 2000–2001 ski season.*

🅱 Backcountry Lift Pass

$5/one-time only • *Prices based on the 2000–2001 ski season.*

🎿 Rentals

Ski Rentals: Adults: $15–$20/full-day, $11–$17/half-day, $7/night; Kids: $10/full-day,

$7/other times; 250 sets. Type of Gear: mostly Rosi, Performance skis (Olin, Rosi, and Salomon) • **Snowboard Rentals:** $22/all ages; 150 sets. Type of Gear: Limited and Rossignol • **Snow Skate Rentals:** $7/day • *Prices based on the 2000–2001 ski season.*

Services

Ski School: 40 ski instructors; Private lessons $40/hour; Group lessons $25/three hours. Call (208) 775–4452 to make reservations (suggested) • **Snowboard School:** 20 snowboard instructors; Private lessons $40/hour; Group lessons $35/three hours. Call (208) 775–4452 to make reservations (suggested) • **Telemark School:** Lessons are available by appointment only. Call (208) 775–4452 to inquire about reservations • *Prices based on the 2000–2001 ski season.*

Room & Board

There is no on-site lodging at Pebble Creek, but the nearby towns of Pocatello and Lava Hot Springs offer a number of hotels and restaurants to satisfy skiers.

Lodging

Pocatello–20 miles *(32 km)* away
A number of chain hotels like **Holiday Inn** (208) 237–1400; **Econolodge** (208) 233–0451; **Comfort Inn** (208) 237–8155; **Best Western** (208) 233–5530; **Day's Inn** (203) 237–0020; and **Super 8 Motel** (208) 234–0888 • **Back O'Beyond Bed & Breakfast** is a turn-of-the-century Victorian home; three rooms; rates $70. 1–888–232–3820 or (208) 232–3820.

Lava Hot Spring–20 miles *(32 km)* away
Riverside Inn is a WWI-era mansion with private, adjoining, and multiple-bed rooms; rates $65–$105. 1–800–733–5504 or (208) 776–5504 or *www.riversideinnhotspring.com.*

Dining

On-site
The lodge offers cafeteria-style dining and fresh home-baked treats.

Pocatello–20 miles *(32 km)* away
Dudley's Sports Bar & Grill offers great food (ribs and specials) and beer (home brew Portneuf Ale). (208) 232–3541 • **Remo's Restaurant** serves a menu of steak, seafood, pasta, and salads. (208) 233–1710 • Visit *www.pocatelloidaho.com* for more information on the area.

Lava Hot Springs–20 miles *(32 km)* away
Duke's Fine Dining and Lounge offers an elegant dining experience; pasta, poultry, beef, veal, lamb, and seafood; full breakfast and lunch menus. (208) 776–5600 or *www.riversideinnhotspring.com/dining.htm.*

Pomerelle

Pomerelle Mountain Resort
P.O. Box 158
Albion, ID 83311

Ski Report: (208) 673–5555
Information: (208) 678–5599
E-mail: *info@pomerelle-mtn.com*
Website: *www.pomerelle-mtn.com*
Credit Cards: Visa & MasterCard

Operating Hours: 9:30 A.M.–4 P.M. daily.
  Night Skiing: 4 P.M.–10 P.M.
Tuesday–Saturday (December 26 through mid March)

Season: Mid November to late April

Background

I f snow quality were all that mattered, Pomerelle Mountain Resort would rank near the top with such holy shrines as Alta, Utah, and Grand Targhee, Wyoming. Nestled inside the Sawtooth National Forest, this vintage "mom & pop" resort receives 500 inches of dusty, dry, light powder annually—more than any other resort in Idaho. The staggering snowfall is due to the high base elevation of 8,000 feet and the resorts location in arid South-central Idaho. Unfortunately, Pomerelle will probably remain in relative obscurity since its most difficult runs would be considered intermediate anywhere else. Still, for Southeast Idaho residents and visitors and beginner-to-mid-level skiers who dismiss the three-hour drive to Utah or Sun Valley, Pomerelle is a fantastic place to lay tracks.

Trail Profiles

Pomerelle operates three well-maintained lifts that rarely fill to capacity: a triple, a double, and a short rope tow. Skiers never wait more than five minutes in line. This has a lot to do with the resort's remote location and the number of other ski areas in the state's lower half.

Pomerelle is a cruising paradise because of the excellent snow conditions and the overwhelming majority of intermediate terrain. Over half of the area's 24 trails are designated blue runs. And nearly all of this terrain can be handled by novice skiers and boarders. *Bull* and *Steer*, accessible from the triple chair, are blue runs, just wide and gradual enough for all

Mountain Stats

Base Elevation: 8,000 feet *(2,440 m)*
Summit Elevation: 9,000 feet *(2,745 m)*
Vertical Drop: 1,000 feet *(305 m)*
Primary Slope Direction: North
Annual Snowfall: 500 inches *(1,270 cm)*
Skiable Days: 120
Skiable Terrain: 200 acres *(81 ha)*
Runs: 24

Longest Run: 2 miles *(3.2 km)*
Lifts: 1 triple, 1 double, 1 rope tow
Lift Capacity: 5,500 skiers per hour
Terrain Classification: 43% novice; 33% intermediate; 24% advanced
Night Skiing: 16% allowance
Snowmaking: 1% early fall
Annual Visits: 60,000

but first-time snowriders. The area's two substantial green runs are *Meadow* and *Milk*, pitched nearly as flat as parking lots. Pomerelle's ski instructors spend quite a bit of time on these runs teaching the finer points of wedge turns.

Intermediates who can link parallel turns have several more options. Staple cruising runs include *Colt* and *Spud*. Both are accessible from the top of the double chair and offer twisting fall lines down wide-cut paths through the trees. After sunset the trails operate under lights, as do *Ponderosa*, *Six Shooter*, and *Spring Creek*. The longest continuous run on the mountain is a combination of three trails—*Meadow*, *Twin Lakes*, and *Buttermilk*. The triple combo leads snowriders out to the ski area boundary, through a big powder field, and back to the area after sweeping through the forest.

Make no mistake; there aren't enough challenges at *Pomerelle* to keep advanced skiers content for a full day. Though one-quarter of the runs carry a black-diamond tag, they'd be blue anywhere else in the Northwest. Nevertheless, considering the area's super-light and deep snow conditions, runs like *Punch Bowl* and *Yah Hoo* can be fun. *Punch Bowl* is full of linked face shots, while *Yah Hoo* abounds with natural hits. Best of all, landing zones here are loaded with soft, forgiving snow. Advanced skiers and boarders will also enjoy powder skiing in the trees of *Giddy-Up* and *Burrows Blvd*. Near the top, the trees are lightly gladed, while timber grows thick and tight near the bottom.

Getting There

- **From Twin Falls, ID:** Head east on I-84 to ID 77 (Exit 216). Go south on ID 77 to Howell Canyon Road and follow to resort.
- **From Pocatello, ID:** Take I-86 west to ID 77 (Exit 216). Go south on ID 77 to Howell Canyon Road and follow to resort.
- **From Northern UT:** Take I-15 to I-84. Continue I-84 to ID 77 (Exit 216). Go south on ID 77 to Howell Canyon Road and follow to resort.

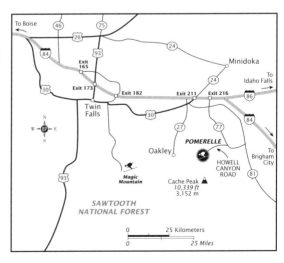

Snowboarding Highlights

Pomerelle carries the distinction of being one of the country's first mountains to open its terrain to snowboarders. Back in the early 1980s, snowboarders spent their time exploring trails like *Yah Hoo* and *Punch Bowl*, mostly for the powder and natural hits. These days, riders earn their wings in a halfpipe and terrain park that Pomerelle has constructed each of the last few years. Located at the mountain's peak on *Milk Run*, the halfpipe runs 200 feet and features seven-foot-high walls. Pomerelle uses a Bombardier Snowcat once the snow falls, but the foundation of the pipe is already laid directly in the ground. Once the snowcat has pushed the snow in place, the pipe is refined by the hands of staff and local boarders.

The adjoining snowboard park covers 1,000 feet of terrain and drops 350 vertical feet on *Buttermilk*. From top to bottom, riders will find eight to 12 features such as tabletops, rollerz, spines, and banked turns. Additionally, Pomerelle builds hits on the *Milk* and *Bull* trails. Neither the pipe nor the park is equipped for night riding.

More Fun in the Flakes

There's free **cross-country skiing** on nine miles (14.5 km) of ungroomed Forest Service trails.

Skier Services

$ Lift Tickets

All ages: $22/weekends and holidays; $17/half-day; $15/mid-week discount; $10/night skiing • *Prices based on the 2000–2001 ski season.*

Rentals

Ski Rentals: $17–$20; 400 sets. Type of Gear: Rossignol • **Snowboard Rentals:** $30; 50 sets. Type of Gear: Burton • *Prices based on the 2000–2001 ski season.*

Services

Ski & Snowboard School: 60 instructors; Private lessons $30/hour; Group lessons $17/hour; Real Deal Class Lesson and rentals $22 (skiers only) • *Prices based on the 2000–2001 ski season.*

Room & Board

There is no lodging at Pomerelle because it primarily serves local skiers. However, guests have numerous lodging, dinning, and après-ski options in the towns of Albion, Burley, Rupert, and Twin Falls. Call the Mini-Cassia Chamber of Commerce at 1–800–333–3408 for more information.

Ski the Sawtooth—Nordic Style

Within the vast, rugged 2,100,000 acres of Sawtooth National Forest are seemingly endless stretches of cross-country track. The 758,000-acre Sawtooth National Recreation Area offers over 70 miles (113 km) of groomed ski trails and additional backcountry terrain. Peaks 10,000 feet, broad valleys, meadows, grasslands, lakes, and forests of pine, fur, and spruce are just some of the features skiers can expect to see. Wildlife includes moose, elk, bighorn sheep, mountain goat, mountain lion, wolf, and wolverine. Also available for Nordic skiers are three designated trails in the Burley Ranger District's Howell Canyon Area, five trails in the Twin Falls Ranger District, and 28 miles (45 km) of track in the Ketchum Ranger District. For information, contact Sawtooth National Forest at 2647 Kimberly Road East, Twin Falls, ID 83301, or call (208) 737–3200.

Lodging

Albion–13 miles *(21 km)* away
   Marsh Creek Inn offers a hot tub; rates $39–$52/night. (208) 673–6259.

Burley–30 miles *(48 km)* away
   Best Western Burley Inn & Convention Center offers a pool, hot tub, playgrounds, and twenty four hour coffee and tea; rates $50–$62/night. 1–800–401–MEET or 1–800–599–1849 or (208) 678–3501 • **Budget Motel** offers a pool and hot tub; rates begin at $56/night. 1–800–632–4952 or (208) 678–2200.

Twin Falls–75 miles *(121 km)* away
   Comfort Inn offers free continental breakfast, indoor pool, whirlpool, and hot tub; rates $60–$130/night. 1–800–228–5150 or (208) 734–7493.

Dining

On-site
   C.J.'s Burger and Brew Eatery serves good food and drinks for a day on the slopes • Day Lodge Cafeteria serves soups, chili, burgers, and more.

Burley–30 miles *(48 km)* away
   J.B.'s Restaurant is open for all meals, serves classic American cuisine with all you can eat salad bar. (208) 678–0803 • **Perkins Family Restaurant & Bakery** serves classic American cuisine, such as sandwiches and salads. (208) 678–1304.

Twin Falls–75 miles *(121 km)* away
   Rock Creek is a delicious steakhouse serving prime rib and seafood as well, dinner only. (208) 734–4154.

Heli-skiing Operations
1. TLH Heli-skiing
2. Last Frontier Heli-skiing
3. Whistler Heli-Skiing
4. North Cascade Heli-Skiing
5. R.K. Heli-Ski Panorama
6. Crescent Spur Heli-Skiing
7. Great Canadian Heli-Skiing
8. Mike Wiegele Helicopter Skiing
9. Purcell Helicopter Skiing
10. Robson Helimagic
11. Selkirk Tangiers Helicopter Skiing
12. Canadian Mountain Holidays Heli-Skiing
13. Sun Valley Heli-Ski

HELI-SKIING & CAT-SKIING:

Cat-Skiing Operations
14. Great Northern Snowcat-Skiing
15. Island Lake Lodge
16. Mount Bailey Snowcat-Skiing
17. Snowcat-Skiing at Brundage
18. Selkirk Wilderness Skiing
19. White Grizzly Adventures

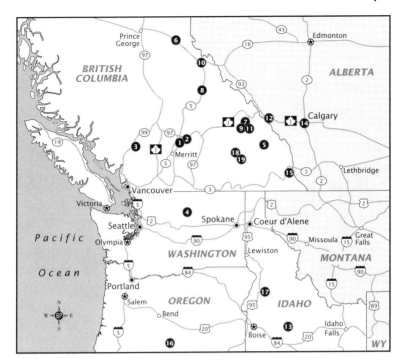

Over the years hundreds of writers and thousands of skiers and snowboarders have tried to describe the essence of heli-skiing. The thrill of being transported by helicopter and the serenity of descending down a long glacier arm covered with cold-smoke, feather-light, dusty-dry, pick-a-cliché powder is a magical experience. It's a soul soothing, spiritual communion, a nuclear sized adrenaline charge, a collage of white satin tapestries, and a rhythmic dance through the forest. It is, perhaps, best summed up by an old heli-guide who said, "If God decided to go skiing, do you think for one second he would do it from a chairlift?"

Heli-skiing is the ultimate snowriding dream. And the Northwest is home to the heli-ski capital of the world. No where else on the planet are there as many heli operations as there are in Canada's British Columbia. Add in a few more operations in Washington, Oregon, and Idaho, and there are over 30 different choices for skiers and boarders to choose from. Snowriders in search of the perfect powder fantasy spend thousands of dollars to trek from all over the globe. And why not? Imagine: piles of powder, ice blue glaciers, snow capped crags, and the peaceful silence of snowriding in relative isolation. There is simply nothing quite like it.

Cat-skiing is yet another grand adventure, but there are several differences between it and heli-skiing. A day of cat-skiing usually runs under $200, and a day trip of heli-skiing (out of areas like Whistler Resort or Panorama) is a minimum of $400. Expect to pay as much as $600 per day if flying with larger, better-known operations like Canadian Mountain Holidays. The rush of riding in a big metal bird, diving into the canyons, and hovering above snow-capped crags makes the price worth it. More advantages: a helicopter can access almost any slope so long as there is a landing zone, and, from bottom to top, a helicopter ride is usually less than 20 minutes. In comparison,

Snowcats are slow and ponderous. Each ascent takes at least 40 minutes and sometimes longer, depending on the altitude the guides are trying to reach. In addition snowcats usually cannot access extremely steep inclines. On the other hand, a snowcat can handle any type of weather. Fog, gray skies, snowstorms, and severe winds won't deter a snowcat from its destination. A helicopter would be grounded in bad weather. In fact, many operations won't fly unless it's a blue-bird day.

Despite assertions that some operations are better than others, the truth of the matter is that most are remarkably similar. Both heli-ski and snowcat-skiing companies usually charge by the day and number of runs while guaranteeing a minimum amount of vertical feet. A typical heli-ski day operation offers three runs and 8,000 to 10,000 feet of vertical drop. Additional runs are extra, and lodging is separate. Multi-day operations also make similar guarantees and often maintain their own private lodges in remote areas. These companies are more expensive, but staying in the heart of the wilderness only a few yards from the heli-port definitely adds to the adventure.

The best time of the season to heli-ski in the Northwest and British Columbia is February through April. In addition to deeper snow depths, the weather is more consistent and the days are longer. There is more sunshine toward the back half of the season than in December and January. The last thing any self-respecting snowrider wants to do is pay a fist full of dollars to be stuck in a remote lodge with nothing else to do. For budget conscious snowriders, though, December is probably the least expensive time to heli-ski. Bear in mind that weather and snow conditions during this time can be inconsistent, and the days are certainly shorter, which means less time to enjoy the powder. The same goes for cat-skiing, but the weather is less critical. Late March and early April are less expensive, but the snow tends to be corn snow rather than powder. Spring skiing from a helicopter or cat in corn snow is a blast in its own right, but it's not the same as the deep, light powder, typically found from February to March.

Are You Ready?

Ask the following questions when considering a heli-ski or cat-ski vacation. If you answer yes to most of them, you can probably handle it. Just be sure to be honest with your guides and yourself about your ability.

- Do you ski black-diamond runs at major resorts without hesitation?
- Have you felt marked improvement in your abilities over the last few years?
- Have you made several multi-day trips to go skiing or snowboarding?
- Can you keep up with most snowriders, even if you may not have the style of more experienced skiers or boarders?
- Are you comfortable snowriding off of groomed trails?
- Do you have experience with tree skiing?
- Can you make confident parallel turns in a wide variety of conditions?
- Can you side slip, step up sideways, traverse, and make kick turns (changing your direction while standing in one spot)?
- Do you have any experience in the backcountry or on glaciers?

Another important consideration is the number of skiers per group and the number of groups per helicopter. Large numbers of skiers and groups means more time spent waiting than riding. Even though most operations claim brief delays, it's a good idea to ask how many people they're expecting. Fewer snowriders per group means more runs per day. Simply look for operations that host fewer and smaller groups in order to avoid crowds.

Riding in a loud helicopter almost necessitates wearing earplugs. As for clothing, skiers are transported by heated choppers, and as a result need less clothing than is necessary on a routine day of lift-serviced skiing. A warm helicopter beats a cold chairlift any day. Wearing too much while heli-skiing causes many snowriders to overheat and sweat profusely. And once back out on to the slopes, they may end up colder than they would have been if they had dressed with one less layer, or thinner layers.

Heli-Skiing Is *Not* for Novice Snowriders

Terrain can range from Alaskan-sized glaciers with gentle pitches to steep, narrow chutes and tight tree skiing. Snow conditions are just as variable. In one run, snowriders might lay tracks in wind-packed crust; light, feathery kneecap powder; heavy crud; ice; and everything in between.

In addition, skiing and boarding in uncontrolled areas requires more awareness of your surroundings than on a patrolled and controlled ski area.

The guides will do their best to find the lightest, softest snow. But due to avalanche conditions and weather, as well as time constraints, terrain can become more limited. Snowriders therefore must be experienced and capable of skiing different types of snow and terrain. Even though the newer, shaped skis have made heli-skiing more accessible to some intermediate skiers, they are not a substitute for solid skills and expert ability.

Courtesy TLH Heli-Skiing LTD.

Skiing Powder

Powder snowriding is not much different from other types of snowriding once your fundamentals are solid. Most virgin powder snowriders are apprehensive about their ability. This fear of the unknown usually disappears soon after that first face-shot or turn in cold-smoke powder. For novice snowriders who are unable to keep up, the experience is frustrating and overwhelming.

A wise bet is to take a class in powder skiing before your trip. Try to spend as much time on snow as possible, and challenge yourself by skiing steeper runs and riding away from the groomed slopes whenever you can. Ask for an honest assessment of your ability. Start a fitness program that will improve your strength and endurance. The stronger you are, the more fun you will have.

Many intermediate snowriders are intimidated by powder. It's unfortunate because carving turns in a deep bowl of fresh frosted flakes is as close to nirvana as many snowriders ever get. Stay positive and have fun with it. Once you get the hang of it you'll be hooked. And the latest generation of powder skis makes it easier than ever before.

It's smart for first-time powder pups to focus on the skiing basics. Proper body position is key. Your skis should be shoulder-width apart, knees and ankles slightly flexed, head up, and hands in the correct position—which is, even with your elbow and at a 90 degree angle. Keep your weight balanced over both skis.

Turning in light powder is easy. Simply roll your knees down the fall line while turning your hips into the turn. Rolling your knees will engage your edges. And, with the aggressive side cuts and wide profiles of today's skis, turning is nearly effortless. Think of your skis as a single platform as you roll your knees from one turn to the next.

Heavy snow takes a little more work. More speed helps as well. In addition to rolling your knees you'll need to un-weight your boards. At the beginning of your turn, bring your knees toward your chest while rolling your knees. This will bring the skis out of the snow slightly and make them lighter, allowing you to turn them into the fall line. As your skis enter the fall line extend your legs into the middle of the turn. At this point they will be on their edges, causing

them to turn. As you enter the end of the turn, suck your knees up again and flow into the next turn by rolling your knees toward the fall line.

This progression is not a step-by-step maneuver. Your turns should have rhythm and flow between each point of the turn. The best way to master skiing in powder is to just do it. Don't be discouraged. The more mileage you get, the more efficient you'll be at carving freshies—which will open up an entire new world of skiing.

Don't forget to touch your poles to the snow to initiate your turns. Keep your upper body quiet and reach into the turn or down the fall line. It's a gentle motion that is more of a wrist extension than anything. Touch the pole to the snow, turn, and start again with the opposite hand. A quiet upper body means no jerky movements with hands and arms. It's about turning your hips rather than your shoulders.

Pole touching will help you establish a rhythm to your turns. Strive for smooth, flowing turns that are linked together with a consistent length and speed. All it takes is one look at your guide to see the rhythm of his turns. The guide will make it look easy. Each turn is identical to the last one. This is rhythm.

Skiing the Steep and Deep

All of the above applies here. In fact, the steeper the pitch, to a point, the easier it is to ski deep snow. Don't let the steepness intimidate you. Gravity in this case is your friend. The increased speed will help you move through the snow with less effort. Stay relaxed and shorten your turns. If your turns are too short, you won't carry enough momentum into the next turn, and you'll slow to a stop or be constantly fighting the snow. Stay in the fall line a little longer and you'll have no problem initiating the next turn, particularly on today's shaped skis. Each time you un-weight the skis, they rebound into the next turn. This is a result of the camber (the bow in your skis) that is built into each ski. When you turn or put pressure on the skis, they decamber. When you release the pressure, they rebound or snap back. This rebound helps you move your boards into the next turn.

If the snow is really deep and light, you will have to time your breathing. Otherwise you'll be choking on the snow that is flying over your head. Hence, the term "face shot," which means the skiing is exquisite Also, be sure to take a good look at your line. With each turn you'll lose sight for a split second. Don't panic. Ride it out and your vision will come back on the next turn. Once you have a taste of linked face shots, you might find yourself addicted to powder skiing, spending the rest of your well-earned free time chasing big snowstorms.

Snowboarding the Steep and Deep

Snowboarders love riding powder just as much as skiers do. It is one of the reasons why people take up riding in the first place. And if you can link turns on groomed runs, then the steep and deep is not off limits. With the size and widths of today's boards, riding through powder is easier than ever.

First, don't be intimidated. The deep snow will help control your speed. Keep this in mind and fight the tendency to overturn in order to control your speed. Overturning will only make riding the powder more difficult.

Do not rush your turns either. If you try to force your turns by pivoting the tail of the snowboard around your front foot, the powder will pack and block your efforts. You'll feel out of control not to mention you will burn up energy with the unnecessary movement. Instead, focus on smooth round turns. Let your board do the work. Roll from edge to edge and the camber and sidecut of today's boards will do the work for you.

Keep your upper body calm. Stay centered over the board and make movements with your ankles, knees, and hips. This applies to all types of snow and terrain conditions. In heavy and/or wind-packed snow, don't put too much weight on your front foot. This will cause the tip of the board to sink and catch in the snow. You'll end up planting your face and somersaulting. In lighter snow, this is less of a problem, but the best plan is to stay centered over your board.

HELI-SKIING OPERATIONS

The number of skiers per group and number of groups per helicopter are based on non-private excursions. Private excursions are available with most operations, but keep in mind that costs are considerably higher.

TLH Heli-Skiing

TLH Heli-Skiing
P.O. Box 1118
Vernon, BC V1T 6N4
Canada

Information: (250) 558–5379
1–800–667–4854 (U.S. & Canada)
E-mail: *info@tlhheliskiing.com*
Website: *www.tlhheliskiing.com*

Helicopter: Bell 205 or 212
Number of snowriders per group: 11 skiers per group with 2 groups per helicopter.
Rentals: Atomic Powder Cruise, Powder Plus and Heli-Guide, Volant Chubbs, and Evolution Wide Glide
Cost: Packages range from $1,400–$5,600

TLH offers multi-day packages in the heavily glaciated Chilcotin Mountains. Packages include lodging, skiing, equipment rental, and all meals. An average day of skiing consists of 40 skiers exploring over 800,000 acres of terrain.

The Tyax Mountain Lake Resort is located on the shores of Tyaughton Lake and is the third-largest log structure in Canada. The heli-pads are conveniently located right at the lodge, allowing snowriders easy and speedy access to the extensive ski area within the Southern Chilcotin Mountains of BC. Other activities include ice fishing, snowmobiling, snowshoeing, and sleigh rides.

Jocelyn Lang

Greg Eymundson

Last Frontier Heli-Skiing

Last Frontier Heli-Skiing

P.O. Box 1118
Vernon, BC V1T 6N4
Canada

Information: (250) 558–7980;
 1–800–665–556
E-mail: *lfh@tlhheliskiing.com*
Website: *www.tlhheliskiing.com/lfh*

Helicopter: A Star
Number of snowriders per group: 5 skiers
per group and 3 groups per helicopter
Rentals: Volant Chubbs
Cost: Packages range from $5,300–$5,500

Last Fontier Heli-skiing is the sister operation to TLH heli-skiing. The Last Frontier Lodge is located in Northern BC, near the Alaskan Pan Handle. The lodge offers rustic, cozy cabins with a communal cook-house for a real backcountry experience. Snowriding in the Skeena Mountains provides some of the most remote heli-skiing in North America, though not for the first-time heli-skier. The area is full of vast glaciers, huge powder bowls, and tight tree runs. The operation is relatively young, which means the area is somewhat unexplored. This gives snowriders the opportunity to ski runs that have never before been skied, plus the opportunity to name them. Seven-day packages include meals, accommodations, and transfers from Smithers to the Bell II Lodge.

3

Whistler Heli-Skiing

Whistler Heli-Skiing
Crystal Lodge
4241 Village Stroll #3
Whistler, BC V0N 1B0
Canada

Information: (604) 932–4105
E-mail: *heliski@direct.ca*
Website: *www.heliskiwhistler.com*

Helicopter: Bell 212
Number of snowriders per group: 11 skiers per group with 3 groups to a helicopter.
Rentals: Rossignol
Cost: One day of skiing starts at $430.

Whistler Heli-skiing is headquartered at Whistler-Blackcomb Resort and recently took over operations from three other heli-ski companies flying out of the Whistler area. The merger benefits skiers and boarders because Whistler was the area's best operation. Snowriders explore the BC Coast Mountains in the area. Heli-skiing out of Whistler is a perfect place for virgin heli-skiers. One-day packages are relatively inex-

pensive, the terrain is mostly intermediate level, and you can usually make the decision to go skiing with very little advance notice. If weather conditions are poor, skiers and boarders can always hit the slopes of Whistler and Blackcomb. One- to three-day packages are available and include lunch, transportation to the heli-port, and skiing. Also offered are semi-private helicopter ski packages. Whistler Heli-skiing does not have a lodge for its guests. However, there are unlimited choices in Whistler Village. See Whistler Resort *on page 61.*

North Cascade Heli-Skiing

North Cascade Heli-Skiing

P.O. Box 367
Winthrop, WA 98862

Information: 1–800–494–HELI
E-mail: *heli-ski@methow.com*
Website: *www.methow.com* (go to Recreation
   link)

Helicopter: Eurocopter A-Star
Number of snowriders per group: Up to 16
   snowriders (4 groups of 4)
Rentals: Rossignol and K2
Cost: Packages range from $550–$2,175

Snowriding in the North Cascades the operation has access to over 300,000 acres of terrain in the Okanogan National Forest. While the Cascades are not known for its light, dry snow, North Cascades Heli-Skiing reaches altitudes high enough to find the goods. Moreover, the Cascades are extremely dependable when it comes to large snow depths. Also, the terrain in the Cascades is some of the steepest anywhere in the U.S. But as with every good heli-skiing operation, North Cascade will find terrain suited to the group's ability. The company offers one- and three-day packages. Guests stay in The Freestone Inn, which acts as a base for the operation. It's a beautiful lodge with a sweeping front porch, soaring ceilings, and grand stone fireplace, and lies on the bank of the Early Winters Creek. There are also private cabins available on the shores of the Freestone Lake complete with fully equipped kitchens.

R.K. Heli-Ski Panorama

R.K. Heli-Ski Panorama

P. O. Box 695
Invermere, BC V0A 1K0
Canada

Information: 1–800–661–6060
E-mail: *info@rkheliski.com*
Website: *www.rkheliski.com*

Helicopter: Bell 212 for groups and A-Stars for
   private smaller groups
Number of snowriders per group: 11 per group
   with as many as 5 groups per helicopter
Rentals: Atomic Powder Plus and Powder
   Cruise
Cost: Package prices range from $516–$5,374

Adjacent to the Panorama Resort in the Purcell Mountains, R.K. specializes in first-time heli-skiing. Terrain includes intermediate snowfields, glaciers, and gladed tree runs. A one-day package includes continental breakfast, lunch, and equipment Rental. Like the Whistler Heli-ski operations, R.K. provides the option of skiing at the local ski resort in the event of poor weather conditions. Five-day packages are available as well, while lodging can be found at the nearby Panorama Ski Resort, offering condominium or hotel accommodations within walking distance of the heli-plex. See Panorama Mountain Village Resort on page 40.

Crescent Spur Heli-Skiing

Crescent Spur Heli-Skiing

Crescent Spur, BC V0J 3E0
Canada

Information: (250) 553–2300
1–800–715–5532
E-mail: *info@crescentspurheliski.com*
Website: *www.crescentspurheliski.com*

Helicopter: Bell 204–10-passenger
Number of snowriders per group: No more than 8 at any one time. No more than 2 groups per helicopter.
Rentals: Atomic Fats and Volkl Explosivs
Cost: Package price is roughly $4,100

Crescent Spur is the most northern heli-ski operation in BC, tucked in a forested valley between the Cariboos and the Rockies, near Prince George, BC. The operation offers over 1,000 square acres of terrain in the Canadian Rockies and Cariboo Mountains. Available packages include meals, lodging, and skiing for multiple days. Lodging is reserved for the 16 guests and staff only, which means the number of snowriders on a run at any one time will never exceed eight. Five- and six-day packages are available.

Great Canadian Heli-Skiing (GCHS)

Great Canadian Heli-Skiing (GCHS)

P.O. Box 175
Golden, BC V0A 1H0
Canada

Information: (250) 344–2326
Email: *heliski@rockies.net*
Website:
www.greatcanadianheliski.com/ski_info.htm

Helicopter: Eurocopter 350BA
Number of snowriders per group: 8 per group, 3 groups to a helicopter. No more than 3 groups in an area at any time
Rentals: Volant Chubbs and Atomic Powder Plus
Cost: Packages range from $4,900–$6,400

Another operation flying out of Golden, BC, GCHS has been snowriding in the Selkirks and the Purcells for over ten years. Only seven-day packages are available. GCHS is exclusive licensee to over 2,000 square kilometers of terrain along the north and east borders of Glacier National Park. Snowriders enjoy open powder bowls, gladed trees, narrow chutes, and big country snowfields. Guests stay at Heather Mountain Lodge, built just a few years ago.

Mike Wiegele Helicopter Skiing

8

Mike Wiegele Helicopter Skiing

P.O. Box 159
Blue River, BC V0E 1J0, Canada

Information: (250) 673–8381
 1–800–661–9170
Email: mail@wiegele.com
Website: www.wiegele.com

Helicopter: Bell 212
Number of snowriders per group: 10 skiers
 per group, 3 groups per helicopter
Rentals: Atomic Fat Boys, Deep Powder, and
 Powder Cruise
Cost: Packages range from $2,975–$5,900

Over 3,000 square miles of terrain, all accessible from Mike's Heli-Ski Village, makes this the largest amount of track from a single point of any North American operation. Snowriding is in the Cariboos and the Monashees. In the early season, there is no charge for extra vertical feet. Three, five, and seven-day packages are available. Lodging is in private chalets or one of two handcrafted wooden lodges.

Purcell Helicopter Skiing

9

Purcell Helicopter Skiing

P.O. Box 1530
Golden, BC V0A 1H0
Canada

Information: (250) 344–5410
E-mail: purcell-heliskiing@rockies.net
Website:
 www.atplay.com/heli/purcell/info.html

Helicopter: Bell 212 for non-private groups,
 The Astar for private groups.
Number of snowriders per group: 11 for non-
 private groups, 4 for private groups.
Rentals: Volkl Explosiv, Snow Ranger, and
 Rossignol Fat Boys
Cost: Packages range from $444–$4,725

A 24-year-old operation, Purcell offers two- to seven-day packages. A five-minute flight takes snowriders to outstanding skiing in the Purcell Mountain Range. The area is well over 2,000 square kilometers, with loads of runs to choose from. Snowriders get to explore the Bobbi Burns, McMurdo, Spillimacheen, Dogtooth, and Battle Range areas. The operation also offers a combo package that includes lodging at the beautiful Emerald Lake Lodge, Deer Lodge, and at Lake Louise in Banff. Located near Golden is the Whitetooth ski area. Families of all abilities will enjoy the skiing. Heli-skiers can spend the day at Purcell, while less-aggressive skiers can hit the local slopes.

319

10

Robson Helimagic

Robson Helimagic

P.O. Box 18
Valemount, BC VOE 2Z0
Canada

Information: (250) 566–4700
E-mail: *info@robsonhelimagic.com*
Website: *www.robsonhelimagic.com*

Helicopter: Bell 206 Jet Ranger, Long Ranger, and the Bell 205
Number of snowriders per group: 4, 6, and 9 per group
Rentals: Atomic Fats
Cost: Packages range from $1,699–$3,899

Robson offers three- five- and seven-day packages. Nestled in the Rocky Mountain Trench, Valemount lies at the junction of three mountain ranges: the Monashees, the Cariboos, and the Rockies. Skiing is in a 1,500-square-kilometer area in the Selwyns and the Monashees. Count on loads of light, dry snow on terrain that includes glaciers, open snowfields, bowls, and gladed forests. Guests stay in Valemount, a short five-minute drive from the heli-port, at the Canoe Mountain Lodge.

11

Selkirk Tangiers Helicopter Skiing

Selkirk Tangiers Helicopter Skiing

P.O. Box 1409
Golden, BC V0A1H0
Canada

Information: 1– 800–663–7080
E-mail: *selkirk@rockies.net*
Website: *www.selkirk-tangiers.com*

Helicopter: Bell 205
Number of snowriders per group: 11 per group and 3 groups per helicopter
Rentals: Volant Chubbs and Atomic Fat
Cost: Packages range from $2,175–$5,100

Selkirk Tangiers skies in two major mountain ranges: the Monashees to the west and the Selkirks to the east of Revelstoke. Both Mountain Ranges are noted for reliable powder snow conditions and great terrain. Snowriders explore over 200 major runs with countless variations, and it is not uncommon to ski new runs. Guests stay in Revelstoke in the new lodge, the Hillcrest Resort Hotel—a 75-room hotel with restaurant, sauna and spa facilities, and exercise room. Staying in town provides many options for dining and entertainment.

Canadian Mtn Holidays (CMH) Heli-Skiing

12

Canadian Mountain Holidays (CMH) Heli-Skiing
Box 1660
Banff, Alberta T0L 0C0
Canada

Information: (403) 762–7100
1–800–661–0252 (North America Only)
E-mail: info@cmhski.com
Website: www.cmhski.com

Helicopter: Bell 212, 206B, 204, 206L3, 209, and 407, and the Areospatiale 350B2
Number of snowriders per group: Most groups are as large as 33 skiers per helicopter.
Rentals: Atomic Powder Cruise, Volkl Explosivs, Olin Outer Limits, and Atomic Beta Cruise
Cost: Packages range from $3,200–$7,000

CMH is the largest heli-ski operator in North America, offering multi-day packages in 11 different locations: The Adamants, Bobbie Burns, The Bugaboos, The Cariboos, Galena, The Gothics, Kootenay, McBride, Monashees, Revelstoke, and Valemount. Most guests fly into the Calgary airport and meet a representative of CMH, who takes them to the lodge. For the Kootenay Lodge, guests can fly into Spokane, Washington as well.

The Adamants

All the great snowriding is in the Selkirk Mountains, well known for its long glaciers, deep valleys, and rugged vistas. The glaciers and granite spires in the Adamant group are as impressive as those found in the Bugaboos. The deep snowpack found in the Adamants throughout winter makes for a long season with superb snowriding.

Bobbie Burns

The Bobbie Burns Lodge is the only area where guests can snowride in both the Purcell and Selkirk Mountains. Bobbie Burns has an abundant selection of runs in the trees and in the high, alpine glaciated terrain. The many valleys of this area have various microclimates that allow for good skiing in virtually all weather conditions.

Gordon Eshom

321

The Bugaboos

Bugaboo Lodge is the only place where guests can snowride in the Bugaboo Mountains. This is where Heli-Skiing began in 1965 among the spectacular granite spires. Snowriding amid these impressive peaks is a remarkable experience. The Bugaboos is Canadian Mountain Heli-skiing's most established area and has several awesome runs below treeline.

The Cariboos

Cariboo Lodge, built in 1974, is the only remote mountain lodge in the entire Cariboo Range. The Cariboos offer skiing on the huge glaciers in the Premier Range. As one of CMH's most developed areas, it also has many options for below treeline skiing on days when the weather is poor.

Galena Lodge

Galena, while not restricted to experienced heli-skiers, is recommended for stronger, more aggressive snowriders who are comfortable in all types of terrain. The lodge is located in a wild and remote setting surrounded by some of the most varied and challenging tree skiing CMH offers. All the skiing takes place in the Badshot range of the Selkirks, known for its abundant snow, rugged beauty, and quality skiing.

The Gothics

Situated in a remote valley in the Northern Selkirks, the Gothics Lodge is named after a group of granite mountains whose steeple-like spires are reminiscent of great Gothic cathedrals. Recent exploration has led to the discovery of many new alpine and glacier runs in the Monashee Mountains, with new terrain being skied every year by guests. The tree skiing is excellent, with many open and well-gladed slopes for everyone's enjoyment on snowy days.

The Kootenay

Kootenay Heli-Skiing was acquired by CMH in 1996, making it the newest addition to the CMH areas. Established in 1982, CMH Kootenay is based in the picturesque town of Nakusp, BC, on the shore of Upper Arrow Lake. The skiing is in two mountain ranges: the Selkirks and the

Monashees. The 2,000-square-kilometer area encompasses over 200 runs and is located south of the Revelstoke area and west of Galena. The skiing terrain features mainly treed runs through old-growth forest, with an abundance of snow.

McBride

Deep in the vast, wild, remote of the Northern Cariboos lies a ski area of impressive contrasts. Rugged, steep terrain; huge glaciated plateaus; and mature, well-spaced forests offer a full range of skiing opportunities, with many first descents yet to be discovered! Unique views of Mount Robson, the Premier Range of the Cariboos, and Sir Alexander in the Rockies contribute to the area's scenic beauty.

The Monashees

There is nothing comparable to heli-skiing in the Monashees. This area offers the most difficult and challenging skiing of any of the CMH areas, and is open only to experienced snowriders who normally ski in the fastest group in the other CMH areas. Known as some of the best tree skiing anywhere, the Monashees are situated in the heart of the interior snowbelt, and features a mature, naturally well-spaced forest that can only develop where the annual precipitation is significant. Between 70 and 90 percent of the skiing is done in the trees. For some people, heli-skiing means "steep and deep," and the Monashees are famous for its long, consistent, steep-pitched runs. The Monashee base is located in Mica Creek, a tiny community along the shores of Revelstoke Lake. It offers a complete recreation facility with a large indoor swimming pool, hot tub, and gymnasium.

Revelstoke

Revelstoke is one of the largest of the CMH Heli-Skiing areas with access to both the Monashee and Selkirk Mountains. The area's vastness, quickly accessed by vans and helicopters, allows snowriders to find good skiing, even in inclement weather. Revelstoke is well known among CMH clients as an area of deep snow, good tree skiing, large glaciers, and a distinctive setting.

Valemount

The vast area of the Cariboo Mountains offers a great variety of skiing, from steep, long, exciting tree runs like the Monashees to spectacular, wide-open glaciers. The entire Valemount area has been set aside to serve only one small, private group. A private group has the ability to select the best snow on any given day in this huge expanse.

Gordon Eshom

13

Sun Valley Heli-Ski

Sun Valley Heli-Ski
P.O. Box 978
Sun Valley, ID 83340

Information: 1–800–872–3108
E-mail: *svheli@sunvalley.net*
Website: *www.svheli-ski.com/whatsup.htm*
Helicopter: Eurocopter A Star and Bell Long
Ranger

Number of snowriders per group: 4
Rentals: Rossignol and Wolfski
Cost: Charges are based on the amount of
vertical feet skied, rounded off to the nearest 100 feet. A variety of packages are
available, including custom tours. Prices
range from around $330 (for about a half
day of skiing) to $760 (for a full day).

Sun Valley Heli-ski has been flying in the mountains that surround Sun Valley resort for over 30 years. The company started in the late 1960s with a Bell 47, the helicopter featured in the TV series M*A*S*H. Today the operation flies over 750 square miles of terrain that includes gladed tree skiing and huge, open bowls of soft, light, dry Idaho pow-der. Lodging is a snap, with hundreds of choices in Sun Valley. Call 1–800–786–8259, or email *ski@sunvalley.com*.

CAT-SKIING OPERATIONS

Great Northern Snowcat-Skiing

14

Great Northern Snowcat-Skiing

P.O. Box 14, Site 13 R.R.4
Calgary, Alberta T2M 4L4
Canada

Information: 1–800–889–0765
E-mail: *info@greatnorthernsnowcat.com*
Website: *www.greatnorthernsnowcat.com*

Snowcats: Kassbohrer Piston Bully Snowcats. The primary snowcat is a PB300 and the backup is a PB260
Number of snowriders: One group of 16 per cat
Rentals: Volkl Explosive, Volkl Snowrangers, and Atomic Powder Plus
Cost: Packages range from $1,680–$3,390

Great Northern operates in 50 square miles of the Selkirk Mountains, roughly 50 miles (80 km) from Revlestoke. The Selkirks are dependable for deep snow and relatively mild weather conditions. Three- and six-day packages are available and include lodging and meals. Great Northern's Lodge is approximately 3 miles (5 km) from Trout Lake at the base of the Thompson Mountains. The lodge itself is 10,000 square feet of rustic comfort. There is a cozy social area with a fireplace, a quiet reading nook, and a spacious game room with a pool and Ping-Pong table, shuffleboard, darts, and a sauna area for relaxation.

Courtesy Great Northern Snowcat-Skiing

15

Island Lake Lodge

Island Lake Lodge

P.O. Box 1229
Fernie, BC V0B 1M0, Canada

Information: (604) 423–3700
1–888–4–CAT–SKI
E-mail: *islandlk@elkvalley.net*
Website: *www.islandlakelodge.com*

Snowcats: Piston Bully
Number of snowriders: 3 groups of 12 per cat, per day
Rentals: K2 Big Kahuna, Explorer, and Volant Chubbs
Cost: Packages range from $1,200–$2,120

Island Lake Lodge offers snowcat-skiing in the heart of Elk Valley at the foot of the Lizard Range mountains, just outside the town of Fernie, BC. Island Lake is co-owned by Scot Schmidt, one of the first big-name professional extreme skiers. The lodge's fleet of snowcats transports intermediate and expert snowriders to over 7,000 acres of powder-filled bowls. The lodge itself is a hand-built tamarack mid-mountain lodge, featuring international cuisine. Three and four-day packages are available.

Mark Gallup

326

Mount Bailey Snowcat-Skiing

Mount Bailey Snowcat-Skiing

218 Aspen Lane
Diamond Lake, OR 97731

Information: 1–800–446–4555
E-mail: *skigus@mountbailey.com*
Website: *www.mountbailey.com*

Snowcats: Piston Bully
Number of snowriders: 12 per group
Rentals: K2, Big Kahuna, X15, and Explorer
Cost: Packages range from $130–$1,750

Snowriders are transported to an altitude of more than 8,000 feet on Mount Bailey in the Southern Cascades. Mount Bailey is conveniently located at Diamond Lake, Oregon, and is easily accessible by road or air. Mount Bailey Snowcat-skiing is based out of Diamond Lake Resort, where lodging, food, and non-snowcat-skiing activities are available for every member of the family. Snowmobile Rentals and tours, cross-country skiing, and lift-accessed tubing are offered for winter fun. Diamond Lake Lodge features cabins near the lake with full kitchens and two bedrooms, and motel rooms ranging from $69-$139 per night. Call 1-800-733-7593 for reservations.

Snowcat-Skiing at Brundage

Snowcat-Skiing at Brundage

Brundage Mountain Company
P.O. Box 1062
McCall, ID 83638

Information: (208) 634–7462
1–800–888–SKII
E-mail: *info@brundage.com*
Website: *www.brundage.com*

Snowcats: Bombardier
Number of snowriders: 10 per group and 1 per snowcat
Rentals: Volant Chubbs
Cost: Half-day: $105 per person. Full-day: $175 per person. Overnight package: $395. (All prices include cost of ski rentals.)

Located at Brundage Mountain Resort, the snowcat service offers full- and half-day packages. Snowriders explore the 19,000 acres on Granite Mountain, Slab Butte, Sargent's Mountain, and Brundage Mountain The combination of snowcat-skiing and the lift-serviced area make this a great destination for families of different abilities. For lodging information, see Brundage Mountain, on page 283.

18   Selkirk Wilderness Skiing

Selkirk Wilderness Skiing
1 Meadow Creek Road
Meadow Creek, BC V0G 1N0, Canada

Information: (604) 366–4424
1–800–799–3499
E-mail: *info@SelkirkWIlderness.com*
Website: *www.selkirkwilderness.com*

Snowcats: Bombardier BR 400+
Number of snowriders: 12, maximum
Cost: Packages range from $2,100–$2,760

Selkirk Wilderness offers snowcat-skiing in the Selkirk Mountains. Five-day ski packages are available and include meals and lodging. The lodge sits high atop the valley floor, which means skiing is just 30 minutes to an hour from the lodge. With other operations, the first run may take up to two hours to reach the top. Plus, snowriders are able to ski right to the door of the lodge at the end of the day. The comfortable lodge accommodates no more than 24 guests at one time. It offers a Jacuzzi, pool, and library, as well as ping pong and billiards.

19   White Grizzly Adventures

White Grizzly Adventures, Ltd.
P.O. Box 129
Meadow Creek, BC V0G1N0
Canada

Information: (250) 366–4306
E-mail: *snowcats@wkpowerlink.com*
Website: *www.whitegrizzly.com*

Snowcats: Bombardier
Number of snowriders: 12, maximum
Rentals: Atomic, Volkl, Salomon, and K2
Cost: Packages range from $375–$1,725
single and multi-day packages available

White Grizzly is another operation that explores the Selkirk Mountains. The base is at Meadow Creek in BC's Kootenay Valley. With five guest rooms, the cozy, round-log, pine lodge houses a maximum of 12 guests and offers hearty homemade meals. Given the small size of the groups, snowriders who ski with White Grizzly can enjoy a practically private excursion. White Grizzly recommends that you be an advanced to expert skier.

Appendix

Glossary of Ski Terms

A

AASI: American Association of Snowboard Instructors.

alpine: the term used to define downhill skiing.

aprés-ski: post-ski entertainment, such as dining, drinking, or dancing.

average annual snowfall: a mountain's average per-season snowfall, based on the last 10 years.

B

backcountry skiing: a term most often used to describe cross-country, or Nordic, skiing on terrain that is often ungroomed and outside a ski area's boundaries.

base elevation: the altitude, in feet, of a ski resort's lowest-lying (base) area.

berm: a bank or wall of snow.

big air: a snowboarding term used by freestylers indicating flight/elevation off a jump or obstacle.

binding: a device used to fasten feet to skis and snowboards.

black diamond: an advanced or expert trail, relative to the ski area's other slopes.

blue-bird days: heli-ski slang for clear, blue skies

blue-level (blue square): reference made to an intermediate run. Intermediate runs are marked with a blue square.

boardercross: a head-to-head snowboard race down an obstacle course that includes banked turns and jumps. Multiple racers on course at once.

boards: skis.

bonking: slang for running out of energy.

bowl: a wide-open, basin-shaped snow field.

bump run: also known as a mogul run, bumps are formed when terrain is left ungroomed, leaving mounds of snow shaped by continuous turning made in the same spot.

bunny slope: a gentle, low-grade slope used by beginner skiers and a resort's ski school.

C

camber: tension built into the ski to facilitate turning. If you place a ski on a flat surface only the tip and tail touches the surface. The ski is flexed much like a bow.

carve: a term used to describe the correct method of making and finishing a turn.

CASI: Canadian Association of Snowboard Instructors.

cat track: a mountain's major thru-way, made by a grooming maching. Often a flat, fairly narrow connector slope (also known as a traverse) between runs. catch lines: a rope line put up by the ski patrol to mark the area boundary and prevent snowriders from skiing out of bounds.

cat-ski: snowriding from a snow cat instead of a chair lift. Often used for out-of-bounds and/or difficult terrain.

cliff bands: a band of cliffs. A cliff line.

cop air: jump.

corduroy: a term used to describe snow wales furnished by fresh grooming of trails.

cornice: an overhanging mass of snow or ice usually found near the top of a mountain ridge.

corn snow (corn flakes): granualar snow formed by alternating thawing and freezing of snow that is produced in the spring.

couloires: a steep mountainside chute or gorge.

crud: cut-up snow that may be heavy, wet, and more than a day old.

cruisers: a long, smooth trail or slope generally groomed by machine.

CSIA: Canadian Ski Instructors Alliance.

decamber: to force the ski flat or even to force the ski to bow in the opposite direction.

diagonal stride: a cross-country skiing term describing the classic kick and glide technique, in which skiers kick with one ski and pole, using the opposite pole for propulsion.

disco sticks: shape skis

double lift: an uphill transport lift that can accommodate up to two persons.

ego snow: soft, light snow that is generally easier to ski than heavy snow or ice, which can reveal weaknesses and can crush egos.

F

face shots: snow that splashes in your face with each turn because it is so light, dry, and deep.

fall line: the natural line of descent between two points on a slope.

freeriders: a term used to describe just going out to have fun. No racing, no competitions of any kind, just out on the hill having fun.

freeskiing: just skiing—no lessons, no racing, no teaching—just fun on the slopes.

freestyle: a term used in both skiing and snowboarding in which anything goes on the mountain.

freshies: fresh tracks in light, deep, fluffy powder.

frosted flakes: fresh snowfall.

fun box: a snowboard obstacle, sometimes known as a mailbox, made of different types of objects. Boarders can jump, stall, or slide on the object.

G

gap jump: a large snowboard obstacle, constructed of snow, with a space in the middle over which boarders can catch varying degrees of air time.

glade skiing: a trail in which skiers can wind through stands of trees, as opposed to a wide-open slope.

ghosts: trees entirely covered in snow, such that they look like "ghosts."

gladed: snowriding through strands of trees, rather than on an open slope.

gondola: an enclosed cabin suspended from an overhead cable. Gondola transports snowriders up and down a slope or over other terrain.

goofy-foot: a snowboarding term indicating a right-foot-forward stance on a snowboard.

granular snow: powder granules identified as hard (near-frozen), loose, or wet.

grooming: a ski area's practice of using equipment—usually snowcats—to smoothen trail surfaces.

GS turns: Giant Slalom turns. Derives from GS course.

H

halfpipe: a concave, cylindrical, snow-filled ditch with hard-packed walls, fashioned like skateboard ramps, that snowboarders use to perform aerial maneuvers. Halfpipes are generally several hundred feet long, over 20 feet wide, and more than 10 feet deep (depending on snowfall).

handle tow: a surface tow lift in which snowriders are transported while grabbing a handle.

heli-ski: snowriding from a helicopter.

hero snow: see "ego snow."

hit: another term for a snowboard obstacle; Any snow mound or object used by boarders to jump, slide, or grind.

hucking: the act of jumping off big cliffs; e.g., "huck yourself over the edge."

I

in-bounds: refers to the designated, marked terrain within a ski area.

K

kicker: a jump that propels snowriders straight up in the air rather than a steady, gradual take-off.

L

lifter: jump.

long boards: long skis. Downhill or giant slalom (GS) skis.

longest run: the longest, continuous trail on a ski area's network, measured in feet or miles.

M

moguls: also known as bumps, moguls are formed when terrain is left ungroomed, leaving mounds of snow shaped by continuous turning made in the same spot.

mono-ski: a single, wide ski featuring two bindings that face forward.

N

NASTAR: short for National Standardized Racing, NASTAR is an event run at ski areas to simulate slalom racing around a series of gates. Skiers and snowboarders use NASTAR to compare their timed runs with a national standard and other downhillers during the day's events.

night skiing: the number or percentage of slopes and trails equipped with lights.

Nordic: a Scandinavian-based term for cross-country skiing or touring.

O

off-piste skiing: snowriding beyond a ski area's marked, designated boundaries on ungroomed, uncut terrain—to be performed by experts only, at their own risk.

one-plankers: snowboarders.

out-of-bounds skiing: see "off-piste skiing."

P

packed snow: loose powder compressed by grooming machines or skier traffic.

parabolic ski: see "shape ski."

Pipe Dragon: a relatively new type of grooming machine designed specifically to till and groom snowboard halfpipes.

poma lift: a surface tow lift that uses a disk attached to a cable, to transport skiers.

pow pow: slang for light, deep, fluffy powder.

primary slope direction: the bearing of a resort's mountain, facing either north, south, east, or west. North-facing slopes hold snowfall longer, while southern-facing mountains leave trails exposed to sunlight.

PSIA: Professional Ski Instructors of America.

Q

quad lift: an uphill transport lift that can accommodate up to four persons.

quarterpipe: one sidewall of a halfpipe.

R

rail slide: a snowboard tabletop with a flat, steel rail on which boarders slide. Rail slides can be found in a variety of places, including snowboard parks, halfpipes, or quarterpipes.

regular-foot: a snowboard term indicating a left-foot-forward stance on a snowboard.

rollerz: a series of small mounds lined up to create undulating terrain. Similar to a roller coaster that rolls up an down quickly.

roll-over pitches: these keep snowriders from seeing the bottom of the run until they commit to going over the top.

rope tow: the first form of uphill transport employed by ski areas, still in use today. Skiers are pulled up the mountain via a continuous loop of moving rope.

runouts: a flat spot at the bottom of a slope that allows skiers and boarders to coast to a stop.

S

serpentine: an adjective used to describe a trail that twists and undulates, shaped somewhat like a snake.

shape ski: a relatively new type of ski that is shaped somewhat like an hourglass. The shape ski is recommended for learning skiers, allowing for easier and more efficient turning.

shred: a snowboarding term equivalent to "carving."

side slip: releasing your edges and sliding downhill without turning into the fall line. You slip down the hill sideways or with your skis perpendicular to the fall line.

skate-skiing: a variation of cross-country in which skiers move by pushing off at an angle; Skating skis are usually shorter than classic Nordic skis.

skiable days: the number of days, per season, open for skiing at a resort.

skiable terrain: the acreage of land available for snowriding.

skier's left: directional reference to any object while the snowrider is looking down the hill, mountain, trail, or run.

skier's right: directional reference to any object while the snowrider is looking down the hill, mountain, trail, or run.

skier visits: the number of lift tickets sold at a ski area during a given year. Some resorts prefer not to divulge their numbers.

skinny skiers/skaters: another term for Nordic skiers, based on cross-country's thin equipment.

ski rags: ski magazines.

ski-in ski-out lodging: lodging featuring instant slope access, from door to snow.

slalom: competitive racing around a series of gates; Giant Slalom requires extreme precision around more narrowly placed gates.

sled dogs: a type of snow skate.

sleds: skis

slopes and trails: a total count of individual runs and skiable areas offered at a resort. Slopes and trails are broken down by the number of beginner, intermediate, and advanced runs available.

snow base: the depth of snow on a ski area's track, not including freshly fallen powder.

snowboard park: also known as a terrain park, a tract of downhill terrain with built-in obstacles or hits (made of either snow or objects) that snowboarders use to catch air, ride, slide, or perform maneuvers.

snowcat: a vehicle used by ski areas to spread and groom manmade snow over slopes and trails.

snow gun: equipment used by ski areas to produce man-made snow. Snow guns spray atomized water that falls and freezes on slopes and trails.

snowmaking: machine-made snow crystals produced by snow guns in the absence of natural snowfall. The percentage of slopes and trails a ski area equips with manmade snow.

snowrider: anyone who rides the snow. Includes skis, snowboard, ski blades, or other devices.

snowshoeing: an on-snow activity. A snowshoe has a webbed, racket-shaped frame that enables the wearer to walk and slide on deep snow.

spine: a terrain park obstacle in which two quarterpipe-like snow mounds meet. Snowboarders grind on the top, middle section or rail—known as the spine.

steeps: steep terrain

sticks: skis

summit elevation: a resort's highest skiable point, in elevation.

surface lift: means of uphill transport in which skiers are pulled on the snow itself. Surface lifts include poma, rope tow, or T-bar.

switchback: terrain that turns at an angle, requiring a quick carve by snowriders.

T

tabletops: a snowboard park obstacle with a launch ramp, a flat area in the middle, and a landing ramp. Boarders work the level middle section.

T-bar: a surface tow lift that uses a pole with a crossbar attached to a moving cable, for uphill transport.

Telemark skiing: an early form of skiing, the Telemark ski has a detachable heel for uphill climbing, while its sturdy frame allows skiers to carve turns downhill.

terrain park: see snowboard park.

tracked-up: snow that is cut up, as opposed to fresh snow with no tracks in it.

trackset: tracks that are groomed into the snow.

trannies: the transition between the floor of the halfpipe and the vert or wall of the halfpipe.

tree skiing: gladed skiing.

treeline: the elevation point on a particular mountain at which trees do not grow above.

triple lift: an uphill transport lift that can accommodate up to three persons.

un-weight: means to un-weight the skis by pulling them toward your body or by raising your body away from the snow.

uphill capacity: the number of skiers a resort's combined lifts can transport per hour.

verts: walls of a halfpipe.

vertical drop: a measure of the drop in feet from a ski area's highest point to its base; summit elevation minus base elevation.

wedge turns: executing turns while your skis are positioned in the shape of a wedge. In other words, your tips are a pole basket width apart and your tails are open just past your shoulders-like a piece of pie.

whoop de do's: undulating terrain. Up and down rollers like on a roller coaster.

Y

yard sale: the unfortunate event of crashing and leaving equipment and clothing littered on the slopes.

Index

Index

S

T

V

W

Y

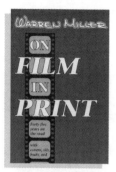
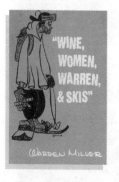

Meet the Author

Santo Criscuolo, a 1990 graduate from the University of Washington, is currently Director of Business Development at Internet start up *Onvia.com*. Prior to joining *Onvia.com* Santo launched *DirtWorld.com*, an online mountain bike resource, worked in TV and radio as a sales representative, and was the editor of *Northwest Skier* magazine in the early 90s. His on-snow experience includes nine years of teaching for Husky Winter Sports as a PSIA level III instructor and 26 years of carving turns all over Western Canada, the U.S., Europe, and South America. If it's snowing, you're sure to find him on a ski slope somewhere in the Northwest.

Author

Conversion Chart

English to Metric	Metric to English
LENGTH	
1 statute mile = 1.609344 km	1 km = 0.6213712 statute mile
1 yd = 0.9144 m	1 m = 1.0936133 yd
1 ft = 0.304799 m	1 m = 3.280851 ft
1 in = 2.5399956 cm	1 cm = 0.39370147 in
1 in = 25.399956 mm	1 mm = 0.03937014 in
AREA	
1 mile^2 = 2.589998 km^2	1 km^2 = 0.3861007 statute mile
1 acre = 0.4046873 ha	1 ha = 2.4710437 acres
1 acre = 4046.873 m^2	1 m^2 = 0.0002471 acres
1 yd^2 = 0.8361274 m^2	1 m^2 = 1.19599 yd^2
1 ft^2 = 0.09290304 m^2	1 m^2 = 10.7639104 ft^2
1 in^2 = 645.16 mm^2	1 mm^2 = 0.0015500 in^2

United States/Canadian Monetary Exchange Rate*

MONEY	
US $1.00 = CAD $1.47	CAD $1.00 = US $0.68

*Please visit **www.x-rates.com/calculator.html** for up-to-the-minute foreign monetary exchange rates.